Praise for *The Devil*

"In this heartbreaking memoir of Forna's quest to find the truth about her father, she outlines the grim prospects of a poor and largely illiterate populace that still suffers the legacies of colonial exploitation, the misguided concept of 'benign dictatorship,' and a brutal civil war."   —Emily Mead, *Entertainment Weekly*

"Reminiscent of Jung Chang's acclaimed *Wild Swans* . . . Forna provides a peek into the black hole of time, giving a view of so much of Africa that is mythical, ephemeral and intangible. . . . Egregious episodes of political genocide and everyday barbarism—all met with a resounding global disregard—are interwoven through Forna's fond childhood memories. . . . [*The Devil That Danced on the Water* is] the story not only of Africa's political turmoil but also of its promise and potential."
            —Charlotte Moore, *Atlanta Journal-Constitution*

"Forna capably fills in the events of Sierra Leone's complex and confusing history. . . . When Forna loses herself in the bittersweet memories of her childhood, her descriptions dance on the page. . . . By sharing the travails of her vivid journey, she casts light into the darkness of Sierra Leone's history."
            —Heather Hewett, *Christian Science Monitor*

"Riveting . . . *Memoir* seems to soft a word for Aminatta Forna's *The Devil That Danced on the Water*. . . . The intimacy of a child's domestic world contrasts acutely with the looming political backdrop . . . Mohamed Sorie Forna was the kind of young man upon whom a society's hopes are built."   —Eve MacSweeney, *Vogue*

"Poignant . . . Stunning . . . Amazing . . . What isn't hard is to feel her deep sense of disappointment about what happened to her father and her country."   —Steve Galpern, *Rocky Mountain News*

"Riveting [and] fascinating . . . As Forna gleans bits of truth from a mass of lies . . . her father gains new definition, and the story gains new power."   —Jay Goldin, *Fort Worth Star-Telegram*

"Forna's stunning memoir is both a tribute to her brave father and an important look at the sad state of politics in Sierra Leone."
                            —Kristine Huntley, *Booklist*

"More gripping than a political thriller . . . *The Devil That Danced on the Water* is Aminatta Forna's attempt to make coherent a personal fate inextricably tied to the fate of a nation."
                            —Julie Brickman, *San Diego Union-Tribune*

"An evocative, disturbing mixture of memoir and investigative reporting . . . [Forna's] re-creation of the country she knew as a child and the father she idolized is deft and moving."
                            —Sarah Goodyear, *Time Out New York*

"[A] moving account . . . A vivid history of [Forna's] years as a child moving back and forth between Africa and the UK, borne on the shifting wind of her father's changing status in Sierra Leone politics."
                            —K. A. Dilday, *New York Sun*

"An exposé as gripping as it is devastating."
                            —Vicki Cameron, *East Bay Express*

"Harrowing . . . Forna writes with a compelling mix of distance and anguish, intent on explaining her father's death and reclaiming his memory. Lush descriptions of her idyllic childhood provide eerie counterpoint to chilling depictions of the hell Sierra Leone had become upon her return in recent years. . . . Reminiscent of Isabel Allende's *House of Spirits*, Forna's work is a powerfully and elegantly written mix of complex history, riveting memoir and damning exposé."   —*Publishers Weekly* (starred review)

"An important work . . . More than a tale of vindication, this book is filled with powerful descriptions and moving details. . . . Highly recommended." —A. O. Edmonds, *Library Journal*

"An extraordinary and gripping story . . . Forna's book glows with compassion. A modern classic, of which her courageous father would have been proud." —Peter Godwin, author of *Mukiwa*

"An engrossing account of pain, love and discovery that had the capacity not only to make me understand but also to move me to tears." —Gillian Slovo, author of *Every Secret Thing*

"A searing indictment of African tyranny mingled with bittersweet childhood memories." —*Kirkus Reviews*

"I had tears in my eyes almost the whole way through, although it is the least sentimental of books. . . . Forna manages, quite brilliantly, to evoke not only all the honor and pity that is in her family's story, but its beauty and tenderness too." —Katie Hickman, author of *Daughters of Britannia*

"This is a book of quite extraordinary power and beauty. Aminatta Forna has excavated not only her memory but the hidden recesses of the heart." —Fergal Keane

"Impossible to forget . . . An obsessive, driven, refreshing book about Africa, despotism and exile. It is also a beautifully drawn portrait of childhood . . . A memorial teeming with life, anger, love." —Christopher Hope, *The Independent*

"Devastating . . . [Forna] writes so well. . . . Her book deserves to go on the shelf next to Malan's [*My Traitor's Heart*]. It is excellent." —Aidan Hartley, *Literary Review*

"Remarkable . . . Extraordinary . . . In writing this book [Forna] has acted her part well. She has lifted out of herself the emotional and cultural world of her childhood and represented it in scenes of startling beauty and tragedy. Few books merit being called courageous; this one does."   —Rachel Cusk, *Evening Standard*

"Gives a more personal framework for understanding the horror of the 1990s in the linked wars of Sierra Leone, Liberia, and Guinea . . . [Forna's] interviews with broken men are extremely moving, and tell everything of the world that vanished with her father."
                    —Victoria Brittain, *The Guardian*

"[A] moving, impressive account . . . [Forna's] harrowing description of her struggle in adulthood to establish the truth of [her father's] death makes enormously compelling and painful reading."
                    —Alex Clark, *Sunday Times* (London)

"[An] engaging memoir . . . It can also be read as a detective story . . . The observations have an appropriate strangeness and wonder, and there are moments of humor. . . . An impressive contribution to the literature of post-colonial Africa."
                    —Jason Cowley, *The Times* (London)

The Devil
That Danced on
the Water

Also by Aminatta Forna

Ancestor Stones
The Memory of Love
The Hired Man
Happiness
The Window Seat

AMINATTA FORNA

The Devil
That Danced on
the Water

A DAUGHTER'S QUEST

GROVE PRESS
New York

Copyright © 2002 by Aminatta Forna
Prologue copyright © 2023 by Aminatta Forna

All rights reserved. No part of this book may be reproduced in any form or
by any electronic or mechanical means, including information storage and
retrieval systems, without permission in writing from the publisher, except by
a reviewer, who may quote brief passages in a review. Scanning, uploading,
and electronic distribution of this book or the facilitation of such without the
permission of the publisher is prohibited. Please purchase only authorized
electronic editions, and do not participate in or encourage electronic piracy
of copyrighted materials. Your support of the author's rights is appreciated.
Any members of educational institutions wishing to photocopy part or
all of the work for classroom use, or publishers who would like to obtain
permission to include the work in an anthology, should send their inquiries
to Grove Atlantic, 154 West 14th Street, New York, NY 10011
or permissions@groveatlantic.com

First published in Great Britain in 2002 by
HarperCollins Publishers, Hammersmith, London, England

This paperback edition: November 2023

Printed in the United States of America

This book is set in 11.5-pt. Minion Text LT Std
by Alpha Design & Composition of Pittsfield, NH.

Library of Congress Cataloging-in-Publication data is available for this title.

ISBN 978-0-8021-6086-7
eISBN 978-0-8021-9195-3

Grove Press
an imprint of Grove Atlantic
154 West 14th Street
New York, NY 10011

Distributed by Publishers Group West

groveatlantic.com

23 24 25 26   10 9 8 7 6 5 4 3 2 1

For My Father

Honour and shame from no condition rise;
Act well your part: there all the honour lies.

From *An Essay on Man*, Alexander Pope (1733)

Prologue to the 20th Anniversary Edition

In 1999, when overnight I quit a good job to write *The Devil That Danced on the Water*, I did so in the grip of a fury. From the United Kingdom I had watched my paternal country of Sierra Leone, finally and after decades of oppression, erupt in a violence that had simmered too long. For months my stepmother had lived with me in my London home as a refugee. Inside Sierra Leone a decade had passed in which no one had made contact with the remainder of my father's family, who were caught behind rebel lines in the north of the country. When the government in Sierra Leone declared it was safe to return, I had put my stepmother on a plane home, a terrible mistake as it turned out. Within weeks the rebel army of the RUF began what was intended as the final onslaught on Freetown. They called it 'Operation No Living Thing'. On the telephone to my stepmother I heard the shells exploding nearby, the gunfire of the advancing rebel soldiers. All of this made me feel desperate and very afraid, but it was not the cause of my fury.

The fury came from listening to and watching the reports of the war by the Western press, who salivated over stories of mutilation, rape, child soldiers, forced marriage, and especially cannibalism, of which there were multiple accounts. What was missing was any apparent effort to understand or to report the causes of the war. There was no context, no history, no politics, just the senseless violence with which Africa had long been associated. I was then a reporter at BBC TV. My beat, though, was British politics and current affairs. The BBC was not the worst offender, by any means. When I let it be known that I was from Sierra Leone, at least one correspondent sought my advice. Once I called in from home and corrected the pronunciation of Magburaka, where my father spent part of his childhood, while the presenter was on air. For another correspondent, I translated interviews with my people caught up in the January 6 invasion of Freetown. Still, even within the most responsible news organisations, there seemed to be little interest in the question of *why* this was happening.

Elsewhere, the world went on with its business. Barely a soul asked after my family, even among those whom I considered my friends. Perhaps Sierra Leone seemed too remote a land to appear as more than an abstraction, or perhaps the absence of peril in the lives of most of my London friends resulted in a failure of imagination. I know now that my experience is shared by many people who endure war remotely, whether those people are returning combatants or refugees.

War in Sierra Leone had been turned into a spectacle without ever becoming a tragedy.

I have often been asked how long it took me to write *The Devil That Danced on the Water* and I have replied that it took me two years and a lifetime. Two years, because that was the duration of time in which I researched and wrote it, as the furies snapped at my heels. A lifetime, because sometimes you have to see enough of the world to begin to understand it. In her Nobel Prize speech, published later as the essay 'Witness: The Inward Testimony', Nadine Gordimer describes the task of the writer as the 'transformation of events, motives, reactions, from the immediacy into the enduring significance that is meaning'. And it was this 'meaning', viewed through the lens of subsequent events and the shock of war, at which it took me twenty-five years to arrive.

Following publication of the book, I returned to Sierra Leone year upon year. I gave talks at the schools and universities. I remember the first young man, a student, who approached me to tell me that he had heard me speak at Fourah Bay College and had then gone to talk to his parents. 'Are these things true?' he had wanted to know. And his parents had replied, 'Yes, they are true.' Then the young man had asked them why they had never told him and his parents had replied, 'Because we were afraid.' This is the silence of oppression. From that time on many young people came up to me in the street, or in a restaurant or store, or else wrote to me. All told the same story as the first young man, a story that they had never known. The silence of a generation had been broken. In time the history books used to teach schoolchildren in Sierra Leone would be rewritten to include the events related in *The Devil That Danced on the Water*.

A 'meaning' I have derived from writing this book is that certain patterns of historical events, sometimes including but not limited to cowing people into silence and terrorised inaction, could be repeated anywhere. What had begun as a quest to discover the truth behind my father's murder would grow into a twenty-year investigation into the causes and effects of civil conflict.

In 2017, by then teaching at Georgetown University in Washington, D.C., I was invited to lunch with Hillary Clinton shortly after she had lost the election to Donald Trump. I was seated next to one of her advisers, who listened with interest as I described my writing and where it had led me. I told her what I had learned of the signs of incipient and growing authoritarianism: control of the press and judiciary, co-option of the loyalty of the police and the army, rise of militias, manipulation of elections. There was one more element, most crucially: a transformational leader, someone both charismatic and deadly. In the case of Sierra Leone this had been Foday Sankoh. In Yugoslavia the ambitions of

Slobodan Milošević had placed the country on the course to war. The woman appeared to be listening with a great deal of interest. So, I concluded, these were the reasons I was worried about the United States of America.

My companion looked at me and frowned, then she swatted the air with the back of her hand and pronounced: 'Not in freedom-loving America!' I wonder what she thinks now. Even then, Donald Trump had begun to discredit the mainstream press and to promote his own 'truth' on social media. He was wooing the military by bringing generals into his administration and was seeking control of the judiciary by appointing federal judges at breakneck speed. Four years after that conversation, on the day before the invasion of the Capitol on (coincidentally also) January 6, I sent a text to an American friend in London: 'Are you ready for the coup?' I was only half joking. He would later ask me how I'd known, and all I could say is that I had spent a long time thinking about the ways in which a country strays from the path of peace.

In Sierra Leone in the 1980s, even as war raged in neighbouring Liberia, people did not believe it could happen to us. We Sierra Leonians saw ourselves as essentially peace-loving, even if our leaders were venal. If anything, our problem was that we were too passive. But when things begin, they must begin somewhere. There is a schema, one that might be traced from the first flap of the butterfly's wings to the hurricane.

On a noticeboard in my office, for a long time, I had taped a handwritten note to myself with the lines 'Nonfiction reveals the lies, but only metaphor can reveal the truth', which is true, I think, of a certain type of story. Two novels set in Sierra Leone followed *The Devil That Danced on the Water*. I continued to explore the themes of civil conflict in fiction. Fiction allowed me to reach for a deeper, less literal kind of truth. *Ancestor Stones* took the reader back to pre-colonial times to examine the century-long antecedents of state collapse. *The Memory of Love* examined the immediate prelude and the aftermath to the war and the silence of censorship, of self-censorship, of trauma, but also of complicity. How did a generation account for their actions, or inaction, to the generation whom they had failed?

The road to conflict may be long or short. Sometimes countries find their way back. Certain events may tip a country finally into war, chief among them an economic crisis. In time, my attention moved out of Africa and turned to the former Yugoslavia for the reason that the war that led to the collapse of that union had been almost exactly contemporaneous with the war in Sierra Leone (Yugoslavia 1991–2001; Sierra Leone 1991–2002). Though just as savage, the Yugoslav conflict had been reported completely differently, with both causes and consequences analysed in forensic detail.

The war in the former Yugoslavia encompassed several nations. I chose to concentrate on Croatia, because there were striking parallels between Croatia and Sierra Leone. The first is size: Sierra Leone is 22,000 square miles, Croatia 28,000. At the start of the wars in 1991, the population of each country was around 4 million. Both are coastal countries of outstanding natural beauty, with a chiefly peasant population and a rural economy supplemented by tourism. Then, of course, there is the key similarity, the one that drew me in the first place—both nations had endured decades of authoritarianism, followed by economic free fall and, finally, civil war.

I have friends from the former Yugoslavia and we talked about our similar experiences. I was interested, too, in the differences. The war in Sierra Leone had never gone down ethnic or nationalist lines, despite the misreporting of the war as 'tribal'. In contrast the war in Yugoslavia had indeed been fought along viciously exploited ethnic divides. The war in Sierra Leone had begun after thirty years of exploitation of people and resources by a corrupt regime; it had been a slow burn. The war in Yugoslavia had been, comparatively, fast burning. A friend who had reported there commented: 'The reason those wars kicked off so fast was because every man had a gun and knew how to use it.' This helped answer my question about speed. Men in Yugoslavia had been obliged to do military service, making for a supply of trained citizens who could be recruited into the militias that characterised that war. A nation in which guns are easily available is a tinderbox relative to one in which people have little access to high-powered weaponry.

My friend's remark led me to understand something else, too. The war in the former Yugoslavia became a sniper's war. Civilians were shot and killed by the thousands in cities under siege by men in the surrounding hills. Yugoslavia was a nation of hunters; Sierra Leone is a nation of farmers. The war in Sierra Leone had been characterised by amputations: the rebel army hacked off people's limbs. When people go to war they pick up the weapon at hand, be it a machete or a rifle.

As time went by I became interested in the ways in which a population survives the aftermath of a civil conflict, when you must continue to live side by side with your enemy (as in the case of Sierra Leone) or with the knowledge of what you have done to them (as in the case of the former Yugoslavia, where communities were 'ethnically cleansed' in the form of mass deportation and murder). In *The Memory of Love*, two of my main characters are trauma specialists, and in the years of writing those books I spent many hundreds of hours talking to victims and those who try to help them. Early in my research, a Sierra Leonian psychiatrist had remarked to me, 'These people will be all right, you know.' He was talking about the mental health of most of the population over the medium to long term. He thought that trauma diagnoses were being applied too widely and too quickly, in particular by Western aid workers. His views echoed those of the French psychologist Boris Cyrulnik. Cyrulnik lost his parents in the Holocaust and worked professionally with many survivors of genocide. He challenged the orthodoxy that pain necessarily equals trauma. Instead, he argued that emotional vulnerability could be transformed into emotional strength. He called this 'resilience'.

In May of 2014, I received an email from a woman asking if she might put me in touch with a former political detainee from Sudan. Sudan was then under the rule of the longtime autocrat Omar al-Bashir. In 2013, Ezekiel (the name he used) and three other men had been arrested and charged with treason. They were held in custody at the National Security Headquarters, where on many days they heard rifles being fired within the compound, which they feared were the sounds of prisoners being executed.

One day a guard gave the prisoners each a copy of *The Devil That Danced on the Water* with the order to read it. The men did as they were instructed, but they also took to discussing the book among themselves. They saw the obvious parallels between their story and that of my father, and they concluded that both the book and the gunfire were part of a process of psychological intimidation. 'They were trying to tell us that the same fate awaited us as had awaited your father.' But far from inviting despair, the book 'had the opposite effect'. It renewed the strength of their convictions. They promised that, when and if they were ever released, they would find the author of this book and tell her about the inspiration they had derived from it. Following the collapse of the government case against them, Ezekiel fled into exile. Soon afterwards he began his search for me. Omar al-Bashir, the dictator, would eventually be unseated in a popular uprising in 2019.

A positive temperament, an inclination to humour, the passage of time, being surrounded by people who care but do not 'catastrophise' and by a society that does not turn every adversity into an existential question (why me?) but accepts that sometimes 'shit happens'—all these factors help. In the end most of us develop the characteristics that help us overcome the bad things that have happened. Thus, my twenty-year enquiry into the causes and effects of civil conflict ended with a novel called *Happiness*.

To write a memoir is to live in the minds of readers as the person you were in the pages of the book, all of which leads me to a question readers often ask me. What happened to the members of my family after the events in the book were over? Here is the answer. In my father's last will, written shortly before he was executed, he stated the wish that we children should be reunited with our mother. An international search for her took place, about which we, the children, were kept mostly in ignorance until one day we were summoned before a lawyer and asked if we remembered anything at all about our grandparents in Aberdeen. Anything at all, he said, perhaps the part of town where they lived? To which we replied: 'Gran and Grandad live at 38 Gairn Terrace.' And so our mother, who was living in Zambia with her husband, the New Zealander, was found. My mother is now in her eighties and retired in New Zealand. My brother and sister both have families of their own. Morlai, along with my husband, Simon, and myself, established a primary school in Rogbonko, a village founded by my grandfather where my father was born. Immediately following the war and the years of missed schooling, not a single child was able to read or write. Today Rogbonko Village School boasts university graduates among its alumni. And as for my stepmother, Yabome, she has lived quietly and contentedly in Sierra Leone ever since.

Aminatta Forna
Georgetown, 2023

Book One

❧ 1 ❧

In the early morning he stands in the doorway of his hut and listens for the distant rumble. The cool air bears the earthy scent of promised rain. From the veranda above I can see the plume of red dust rising in the lorry's wake long before the man with the pickaxe who waits below me hears the engine. I am ten years old. It is 30 July 1974. I am watching a dust devil heading for my home. It writhes as it chases the driver around the rocky lanes, towering above the truck, forcing the vehicle away from the main routes, past the tumble of houses towards the edge of the precipice where we live. Now I can hear its roar begin; at first low and deep it rises to a shrieking cacophony. And suddenly, silence. The driver swings out of the cab down below. Behind him the devil slumps to the ground and waits.

I watch the driver speak briefly to the waiting man, who nods in return. The driver climbs back into his cab. The man with the pickaxe moves to within a few feet of his hut and gestures with his right hand. The driver manoeuvres his vehicle forward and back, until it is almost up against the shack. The massive hulk of the truck might easily crush the flimsy *panbody* of rusting corrugated iron, wooden slats and cardboard. The roof is held down with old tyres. Twelve people live in there, my stepmother tells me. I wonder if they are inside now, while all this is going on. Finally the driver pushes a lever and the load of rocks slides to the ground, freeing a mighty dust devil which spins up above the heads of all of us: the mother devil.

When the truck is gone the man and I contemplate the mountain of rocks. He leans over and picks one up. In his hand it is about the size of a melon; the surface is pitted and full of holes and it looks like a red moon rock. He positions it with care upon the edge of a boulder protruding from the ground. Then he lifts his iron-handled pick and, with the practised grace of a tennis player about to serve an ace, he swings the tool in an arc up behind his back, over his shoulder and down, lunging at the heart of the rock. It shatters, pleasingly, into half a dozen pieces. He glances briefly up at me and nods; I wave back a small acknowledgement. Then he selects another rock and repeats the same, perfect action.

The plateau where he stands is just at the point where the level ground gives way to the steep sides of the valley. There are no more houses, just a dense, green mat of tangled vegetation crossed with narrow paths of bare, red earth leading to and from the stream on the valley bed. I am forbidden by my father to go anywhere near the water. Farther up the valley a slaughterhouse built directly above the narrow channel pours effluent directly into it. The slaughterhouse attracts vultures, who wait out the time between meals on the roof of our house. I often do go down to the stream alone because I can't equate the joys of playing with the glittering, cool water with the invisible danger. Neither can the family in the *panbody*, who carry water from the stream to wash their pots and cook their rice.

On the opposite side of the stream, halfway up the valley, stands a wooden shed. Empty by day, it serves as an illicit drinking den at night where men and women from the low-cost houses gather and drink *omole*, a twice-distilled palm wine so strong, I'd been told, that it could rob a man of his sight. The fermented liquid had to be strained of dead flies and live maggots before it was considered fit to drink. On the weekends the drinkers become revellers and turn up the music until it reverberates across the slopes and drowns the night-time sounds. Every Friday night the clamour of the frog colonies at the water's edge, the nocturnal serenades of stray dogs and the constant clatter of the crickets give way to the rhythms of Carl Douglas singing 'Everybody Was Kung Fu Fighting' again and again, until the early hours of the morning.

In our house, we love it. We learn the words and improvise dance routines. My cousin Morlai scrunches his eyes, spins on his heels, kicks and punches the air. He is in his twenties and wears a slim-fit, patterned purple nylon shirt and matching flares with patch pockets. The girls Esther and Musu, also our cousins, laugh as though they are fit to burst. Afterwards Morlai and Santigi (who is not our cousin but lives with us all the same) leave to go out on the town. As they depart we tease them from the same veranda I watch from now. They take turns at wearing a pair of cheap sunglasses and disappear from view enfolded into the un-blemished blackness of the night. In the morning there will be stories of bars and bravado.

Against the metronome of cracking rocks I can hear car horns and the *poda podas* on Kissy Bypass Road revving their engines as they prepare to take the workers into the city. High above the motors come the sing-song sopranos of the boys who lean out of the back door to call the routes: 'Kiss-ssy, mountain cut, savage street, motor ro'ad.' I can imagine the people pressing forward, cramming their bodies into every available space on board, the fetid odour, the heat. The latecomers climb onto the roof, or hang on the back step.

Poda poda: 'hither and thither' the words mean. Rival teams of minibuses, covered in painted slogans and boasting the names of their owners, flying through town all day long. From here they weave their way through the tight alleys of the East End into the downtown area, where the office workers drop down and disappear into a grid of low-rise office blocks and old colonial government buildings. Some buses go up Circular Road and past the cemetery, beyond whose walls thick tropical climbers coil round the gothic gravestones as though they'd like to drag them back into the very graves they mark.

Other *poda podas* inch their way around the massive trunk and soaring branches of the Cotton Tree, which appears on postcards and in calendars as the symbol of Freetown, home of the freed slaves, once but no more the Athens of Africa. The words are always written with capitals: the Cotton Tree. In between the massive roots the lepers sleep on, undisturbed under their makeshift awnings. The *poda podas* start up Independence Avenue but turn off half-way up, before they reach State House, where the president rests in air-conditioned rooms; across to Pademba Road they go and past the prison. At Savage Street the schoolchildren jump down and separate into shoals: royal blue follows royal blue, brown checks group together, green blazers and boaters drift into one.

On a free run down Savage Street the *poda podas* pass the brightly painted shutters and cottage gardens of the old Krio houses: little enclaves of Louisiana brought home to Africa. At Congo Cross passengers for the fishing villages at Juba and Goderich or those going out to Lumley Beach and Aberdeen switch to transport headed in their direction. Next the buses ease up the hill to Wilberforce and Hill Station, where the view from the windows opens out onto the curved line of the hills of Freetown. At their base, lying like grounds in a broken coffee bowl, is the city. Beyond that the sea. Up here, above the heat and the constant clamour, is where the British once lived in a line of looming, identical wooden houses built on stilts with covered balconies and latticed stairwells. Here they thought themselves safe above the rank, malarial air of Freetown. When enough of them had died, in revenge they dubbed this whole region of West Africa 'the white man's grave'.

There was a time when we lived up here, too. The roads are lined with fruit trees: avocados, breadfruit, and mangoes hanging on loops like a woman's emerald earrings. We children used to pick the mangoes green and eat them with salt, then roll around with bellyache. We stole the long seed pods from the flamboyant tree and used them as rattles. Weeks later, when every pod had fallen, the tree burst into beautiful, fiery blossoms. There were the tamarind trees, *black tombla*. In the tamarind season all the local children went their way holding on to branches of the tiny, dark fruit and sucking the sweet-sour sticky brown flesh from the smooth seeds. But that was nearly four years ago. Almost half my lifetime away.

Today from west to east above the city clouds slowly mass, crowding in between the hills. They drift above the trees on the slopes below Wilberforce and mingle with the fumes from factories and diesel exhausts above Kissy. They seek one another across the sky. They are waiting. Today rain is certain.

Last night it did not rain. I lay on my bed reading a book and outside the night was still. In the middle of the ceiling a naked sixty-watt bulb glowed. Above me my mosquito net was draped over itself. A few insects were beginning to gather around the light, but it was still early, only a little after seven. Daylight had just departed. It would stay dark another twelve hours. This close to the Equator the days and nights are measured with precision. Long before bed time Morlai would spray the room with repellent and leave a mosquito coil burning under my window.

My rubber flip-flops had fallen off my feet onto the bare, stone floor at the end of the bed. I was lying on my stomach in shorts and T-shirt, lost in the lives of Gerald Durrell's family and their anthropomorphic pets, when my brother's head appeared at the door. His face was riven with the excitement of one who knows and is about to tell: 'Have you seen the man?' was all he asked.

Our house has two verandas. The one at the back, away from
the road, overlooks the crevasse and is next to the kitchen. We
reached it in moments. We ran along the corridor, skidded round
the corner, raced through the living room, past the dining-room
table and out of the kitchen door. There were a number of people
already out there and they were crowded around in a semicircle
facing the other way from me. The span of their backs blocked
my view. People were talking in low voices. I edged around the
outside of the group.

A man sat almost motionless on one of the hard-backed chairs.
His face was damp, great globes of sweat hung on his forehead, his
head and eyes rolled slightly backward. Our father, balanced on
the arm of an old black plastic easy-chair, was bent towards him.

I pushed in past them all and eased myself in next to my father. I smelled stagnant sweat and alcohol rising from the man,
who must have been in his twenties. His skin was dusty grey. It
reminded me of something I once saw on a trip we made up-
country. We were driving back to Freetown, late at night; everyone around me in the car was asleep. Our driver swung the car
around a bend and we came suddenly upon a dark figure walking
at the side of the road, miles from any village, petrol station or
even crossroads. The walker turned abruptly and the headlights
lit up his face. I gasped and so did Sullay, the driver. The man's
black face was smeared with pale ashes. His robes were dark, their
colour obscured by the darkness. He came like an apparition out
of the night. Seconds later the car had left him far behind. That,
and the time a boy I knew was stung by a scorpion, were the only
occasions on which I had ever seen someone turn that colour.

The light was yellow and poor. I peered down until I was able to
see what my father was doing. In the man's lap there lay a blood-
ied object. I thought at first he was holding on to something, a
wounded creature maybe, so badly hurt as to be unrecognisable.

Then I realised it wasn't an animal but a hand—his own hand. Or rather, what remained of his hand. It lay in tatters. There were no fingers, no fingernails, no palm to speak of. The flesh seemed to be everywhere and nowhere at once. It looked just like raw meat. Amid the quantities of blood there was a gleam: a nub of bone, a sliver of white tendon, a glint of grey muscle. I stood mesmerised, as my father set to work removing pieces of dead flesh with a pair of tweezers.

There was no breeze; the air was close. I began to sweat. I wanted to stay and watch but my father ordered me quietly: 'Am, you go and help with the bandages.'

My cousins were sitting at the dining-room table just inside the door. They were tearing a sheet into strips and sewing the pieces end to end. I moved to obey, disappointed at being sent away, placated that I had a task.

My father called for antiseptic and Morlai dashed into the house at once. A moment later he reappeared with a near-empty plastic bottle. 'Uncle, the Dettol is done done.' He gestured with the bottle, half shrug, half question.

A beat passed and then I pitched in: 'I have some.' I saw my opportunity to be of real use and seized it.

I raced to my room, slid to my knees and reached under the bed. One day I wanted to be a vet. In a cardboard box that I kept hidden was my first aid kit for injured animals. Week by week I used my pocket money to add something new: gauze, tape, splints. Everything else I foraged, like the cotton wool, or else was donated: my father had given me a couple of plastic syringes from his own medical bag. So far I had effectively treated only the dogs and, with less success, a lizard that lost its tail.

At Choithrams supermarket a few days before I had bought a tiny glass quarter-bottle of Dettol. It was still new and unopened, easily the most prized piece in the entire collection. I loved the long Excalibur sword on the label and the sharp scent when I unscrewed the top. It was this I returned bearing, primed with self-importance.

'Here's some Dettol. It's mine but you can use it.' I held the little bottle up high. I took up the position next to my father again, and again he sent me away. For the next hour I sat with my cousins and stitched yards of bandages—more, I imagined, than anyone could possibly need.

A long time later, after the wounded man had been taken away and the detritus of soiled dressings cleared, I fell asleep on the same plastic-covered armchair where my father had been sitting. Someone must have carried me to my bed. When I woke up this morning, less than half an hour ago, I was lying under my mosquito net, sheets tangled round my legs. Dawn was barely a memory across the sky. For a little while I stayed there half dreaming until images of the previous evening began to come back to me.

In her bed on the other side of the room my elder sister lay still sleeping: I could hear her breathing. Outside a cock crowed, a tuneless, inarticulate and abrupt cry. It was a young cockerel and it hadn't quite mastered the full-throated song of the rooster. It annoyed me because it often woke me up. One morning I went outside and threw a stone at it.

I lay there listening to the ordinary sounds. I hadn't fallen asleep and been put to bed for years. Had I somehow imagined all of it? I wriggled free of my sheets and yanked up the mosquito net. Pulling it over my head, I leaned out, balancing myself with both hands on the floor. I ducked my head under the bed and slid out my vet's box. The tiny bottle of Dettol was still inside, the top was on. Everything else was in place. I was about to close the lid and push the box back, when I paused and instead I removed the bottle to inspect it. It was my bottle, that was certain, and someone had returned it to the box. But there were no more than a few drops of liquid left inside. And the label was spoiled. It was bloodstained and covered in reddish-brown fingerprints so that you couldn't even read the words any more.

At breakfast our father tells us the man had a car accident. He is wearing a brown suit, ready for the office. I am eating Weetabix, soaking them in milk and mashing the biscuits up. At the weekends my stepmother supervises in the kitchen and we have *akara,* deep-fried balls of banana, rice flour and nutmeg; or else fried plantains with a hot peppery sauce made with fish and black-eyed beans. On weekdays we eat cereal and toast.

'How did he crash?' we ask. I layer sugar thickly over the cereal.

'I don't know,' our father replies.

'What happened to him?'

'He's gone to a hospital.'

We nod. I spoon the soft brown mush into my mouth while I begin to formulate another question, but my father's next statement stops me dead in my tracks.

'Am, I'm seeing someone today. A maths tutor. I want you to have some extra lessons during the holidays.'

My mouth is full of Weetabix and I am left speechless. It's true that my maths is not good. I routinely come midway down my class, unacceptable by my father's standards. Every term he hands out awards for first, second and third place but I rarely manage to make the grade. At the last minute he comes up with a booby prize 'for effort' which somehow always has my name on it. But the holidays have only just begun; we arrived home from our boarding schools in England ten days ago. I cannot decide whether I am affronted or pleased to be singled out for such attention, to have my own maths tutor. While I am considering all this my father finishes his breakfast and borrows my milk glass. He pours himself a glass from one of the bottles of boiled water we keep in the fridge. As the glass fills the water turns cloudy. It doesn't look very appealing.

'Ugh!' I say.

'It all goes to the same place.' My father smiles, amuses us by draining the whole glass with exaggerated delectation. He kisses us and he is gone.

In the afternoon the rain begins. The ground around the house fills up with rust-coloured puddles. Little rivulets of blood join into ever-larger tributaries which weave down the slopes to the slaughterhouse stream. The heat doesn't abate and the smell of steaming dirt is like a wet dog. The drops hurtle onto the corrugated roof of the garage, bouncing obliquely on the curves of tin and crashing like a thousand demented timpanists. Through their discordant rhythm rises the regular beat of the man with the pickaxe, who keeps on splitting stones. He has stripped down to a pair of torn shorts and the water washes away the sweat and shimmers on his torso. The man doesn't pause once. On his right a second mound of small stones has begun to overtake the original pile of rocks.

On the balcony, below the curled iron railings, pools of water form and stretch out over the tiles. I take my book and sit in one of the long line of chairs. I am alone. No one comes to the house today. Ordinarily, by mid-afternoon the people have begun to arrive alone and in pairs, usually on foot from Kissy Bypass Road, more rarely by taxi. Anyone known to the family goes through the house and keeps company on the back veranda. The others sit out front on the roadside. They come from Freetown and from the provinces in need of help.

The chairs are strung with green and yellow plastic cord which is no longer taut and cuts into the flesh. The people sit uncomplaining on the uncomfortable chairs, nursing their requests until my father comes home from work. If he is late or busy, they come back the next day. Some of them are his former patients wanting further treatment but without money to pay another doctor; others bring news of a death or need help to school a child. Sometimes he is asked to intercede in a family dispute or help find someone a job. Most of them just want a little money.

When they start to arrive I usually disappear somewhere else. Once a blind man climbed up the stairs from the road and accidentally sat on top of me. In school we were taught that blind people had super sensory powers and hearing like a bat's radar; we were warned never to treat them as though they're helpless. So I watched as the blind man lowered his bottom, believing, until it was too late, that he must somehow know I was underneath him, my tongue locked with the shame of the moment. As soon as his buttocks touched me the blind man shot up in the air like a jack-in-the-box and groped his way silently into another seat. The blind man isn't here today. There are no visitors at all. Perhaps it is the rain that is keeping them away.

After an hour or so I wander through the house. Inside all are preoccupied with their own business. Santigi is at the back of the house sorting the laundry. Morlai is in the room they both share off the kitchen. I expect he is studying. Santigi wants to go to school too, but he's already over thirty, though he fibs about his age and says he's twenty-one. He was once sent to literacy classes but he struggled to learn to read and write. Still, on occasions he borrows my maths and English schoolbooks and works through the chapters alongside me. 'I want to learn,' he always says. A few months ago Santigi bought a Bible and changed his name. One day he stood before us all at supper and addressed our father directly with a deadpan face: 'Doctor,' he said, in Krio, 'ah wan change me nam. Do ya, oona all for call me Simon Peter.' He has remained resolute since: he withstands our teasing and corrects us every time we call him Santigi.

Santigi arrived at the same time as my stepmother four years before. No one knows who Santigi is, meaning that we don't know his family or to whom he belongs. In a society built, layer upon infinite layer, on the rock of the extended family, Santigi can produce neither mother nor father, aunt nor uncle, sibling nor cousin. All he knows about himself is that he was born in a village called Gbendembu, near Makeni in the Northern Province. After giving birth his mother, who was without a husband, put herself to work digging diamonds in an illegal pit many miles away in Bujubu. She left her baby with neighbours and never returned to claim him. Much later news came that she had died. Once Santigi was of an age the couple who had taken care of him sent him to Magburaka to work for my stepmother's family. He first met my stepmother Yabome off the train when she was a schoolgirl returning home for the holidays and he has been by her side ever since. Santigi often spends time with me, but not right now.

The rain and the day wear on. Sullay drops by at lunch time and stays at the back of the house whispering with Santigi and Morlai. Sullay has a deep, matt-black complexion, a strong jawbone and sharp eyes shaded beneath a rather brooding brow. His whole face is a study in intensity. He rarely smiles, but he is very kind. I stop by to say hello. Sullay doesn't stay long.

Shortly before dusk the sound of the pickaxe stops. There are no more rocks to split. The man stands in his doorway out of the rain, dwarfed by the enormous pile of stones. He is listening and waiting for the truck to come back.

My stepmother drives up in her Volkswagen and goes through to the master bedroom. A little while later our father comes home, running through the rain.

I am restless. I fetch a game of bingo given to me for Christmas. It is an inexpensive set with small wooden discs upon which the characters are stamped, slightly irregularly, in red ink. Once I had unwrapped it I ignored it in favour of grander gifts, but this summer holiday I have rediscovered it and there have been several uproarious games involving the entire household.

We use matchsticks instead of money and today I ask Santigi to let me borrow the big box of Palm Tree matches. On the cover it has a drawing of an inky native stepping between two palm trees that reminds me of the pictures in an old book of Edward Lear poems I used to own. I empty the matches out and count them into neat red-tipped piles, one for each player.

Each card has a row of numbers along the top and another row of letters down the side. The caller must pick from corresponding bags of letters and numbers. As our games draw to a close everyone always starts to call the combinations they need to win. It's the best part of the game. Some of us call our numbers out as loudly as possible; others jig with anticipation; Morlai half closes his eyelids and mutters the figures like an incantation. Whoever is calling blows his fingertips, plunges into the bag and with great theatrics calls the winning sequence. Since I own the set I get more turns to do this than anyone else.

The last time we reached this point our father was sitting in the front on the settee, his card covered with little torn squares of paper. He only needed one more to win but several others were in the same position. The atmosphere was intense, and yet there was one outcome in which we were all united: if you couldn't win yourself the next best result was that our father should win. After a few games I had reached the point where I stopped wanting to win at all. Instead I wanted to protect my father from the disappointment I imagined he would feel if he lost.

I had been calling the numbers. My father needed a B and a five. He said: 'Give me a B five, Am! B, five!'

Everyone was hopping about, waving, calling out. I took my time, drawing the process out for as long as possible. I closed

my eyes. I wished for a B and a five. I put my hands in the bags
simultaneously and pulled out two wooden discs.

'B, five!' I was astonished. I dropped the five back into the bag.
No one believed I had actually drawn it. 'I did, I did!' I shouted
and started to grow upset.

I saw my father watching me. He was not sure what to believe.
He smiled as if to say, 'You don't have to do this, Am.'

Outside the truck has arrived. The two men are shovelling
stones into the back. Afterwards the driver takes some money
out of his pocket, flicks off two notes and hands them to the man
who lives in the *panbody*, who nods in return but doesn't smile.
As the truck departs he leans on his shovel and watches.

On the coffee table I lay the bingo cards alongside the matchsticks. Outside the window a movement makes me look up. Two
men have come up the outside stairs and are standing on the
veranda looking in at me. I go out to see what they want. They
are standing directly beneath the fluorescent strip light with their
backs against the growing darkness; the white light casts down-
wards, bouncing off their cheeks and their foreheads, turning their
eyes into dark orbs. I have never seen either man before but I sense
something indefinably familiar about them. They are both slim,
sinewy with close-cropped hair and they wear short-sleeved safari
suits. One of them has on a pair of fake crocodile-skin shoes, of
a type sold in the market. The shoes are badly scuffed. Who are
these men? Many years later I will discover they are called Prince
Ba and Newlove, names as surreal as stage names—or aliases.
Their faces are impassive; they impart an air of unutterable men-
ace. One of them tells me they are here to speak to the doctor.

My father appears directly and speaks to them for a few moments. My bingo set is beside me on the table ready for our game.
He turns to me, sees that I am there and says: 'I have to go with
these two gentlemen now, Am.'

He walks ahead of the two men through the door and out onto the veranda. I see them pass the window.

'Daddy, when are you coming back?' I am unsettled.

My father half turns from me, seems to pass a hand across his eyes, takes a few more steps. Then he stops and faces me again. The two men wait and so do I. All my life my father has had a habit of chewing the ends of toothpicks. He always keeps a couple in his breast pocket. Now he says to me in a low voice: 'Am, go and get me a couple of toothpicks.'

So I run to the sideboard on the other side of the room and find the little plastic toothpick dispenser. I shake out three or four toothpicks and hurry back to him. My face still holds the question. 'Tell Mum I'll be back later.' These are the last words, the very last words he says to me. And he steps out into the rain.

At the bedroom door I call to my stepmother that my father is gone. A moment later she runs past me with Morlai right behind her. They run silently, eyes fixed ahead, and disappear into the crystal darkness. Through the rain I hear the sound of the car engine starting; the tyres splashing through the puddles.

The next morning we three children have our breakfast together, just the three of us. Outside the truck arrives and deposits another load of rocks. The rain is still coming down: it rains all through the day and the next night. It rains until October.

❧ 2 ❧

'Daddy's back!' It was my brother. I had never seen him so excited, adult poise utterly cast aside. The early morning sun was bright and reflected in his face and eyes; his whole expression was radiant.

Everyone was smiling hard at me, Yabome and my sister. The same excitement glowed in their faces, too. Obviously, I was the last to find out and I stared up at them warily, not wanting to believe.

'It's a dream,' I said at last.

'No, it's not. He's really here.'

'It's a dream,' I insisted. 'I've had them before.'

Yabome put her arms across my shoulder and squeezed me. The others laughed; it was a beautiful, silver sound. 'It's true. He's coming. Sheka and I are going to fetch him.' And before I could shake the feeling of unreality that clung to me, they were gone.

I sat down again. Breakfast was laid at the big, wooden table. Memuna stayed behind with me, but she seemed to be taking events in her stride, as ever. Her calm was a source of envy for me. I, who became so easily heated and could be wound into a frenzy by my family.

When I was ten, after my father was taken away, I began to suffer migraines that remained undiagnosed for years. With the heels of my hands pressed against my temples I would run round the house making desperate circles, as though if I moved fast enough I might succeed in leaving the pain behind. Often there was nobody at home except for us three children, but if my stepmother or Santigi were in the house they'd take me to my bed, fetch me aspirins and try to subdue me, holding me by the shoulders and pushing me down against the pillows. It never worked: when they left I would cry and bang my head hard against the bare walls of the room.

I poured a glass of orange juice and drank half of it. I found myself dithering, unable even to find a place to put the glass. The table was laden with food and with the debris of a half-eaten breakfast. The room was part of a stately home, heavily furnished, oak-panelled and cold. I didn't recognise the house, but it was familiar as the kind of old country house where I had gone to boarding school. Eventually others started to come down to break-fast: friends of mine, who joined us at the table. A red squirrel appeared at the window. It was large and had a strange, pointed face. To me it didn't look much like a squirrel at all: the nose was too long, like a mongoose I once owned as a child.

When I heard my stepmother and brother come back, I started up from the table. The sound of their footsteps was on the stairs.

'July the fourth,' said Sheka. He was still breathless. 'He's going to come on July the fourth now!' What the reason was for the delay nobody suggested. I thought he would be here, with us that very day. But I didn't feel disappointed. Instead I felt this was how it should be: time to prepare after so many years. I left the dining room.

The huge staircase dipped away below me and the carpeted stairs swung round in a lush sweep. I put a hand on the banister, feeling the cool, varnished wood, one foot out onto the first step, and I began to walk down the stairs. My family were crowded around behind me. I could hear the rustling and feel them jogging each other. What on earth were they all doing?

As I turned the arc of the stairs I understood. The bearded fig-ure standing in the hallway at the bottom wore a tan, short-sleeved suit, despite the cold. He had on polished brown shoes and a gold watch and although he was talking on the telephone with his back half turned towards me, I recognised him in that instant. I could still hear their voices behind me as I hurled myself down the stairs. He hadn't seen me yet and I felt like a child again, my legs moving in great, galloping strides as I threw myself towards him. In that moment he turned round, smiling with surprise, and caught me in his one free arm.

'Hey, hey. What's all this?' he said, as though I really was an overexcited ten-year-old. But I didn't care. I put my arms around him and hugged him. I could feel everyone gathered around behind me. My face was against his shoulder and I squeezed my eyes shut.

When I opened them again the pale, grey London dawn had cast a triangle of light on the wooden floor. I could see the shadows of my clothes hanging from the pegs on the back of the half-open door. The blinds were still closed. On the chair by my bedside the faint glow of the alarm clock lit the shapes of a pencil, paper, a lip balm, a book and a wooden box. The sheet below me was wrinkled, cold with sweat.

Once a year, twice at the very most, the dreams had grown fewer as the decades passed. Sometimes I dreamed he came back from living in a faraway country, that he had been looking for us, but couldn't find us. Other times I dreamed that he had been in hiding and everyone around him sworn to secrecy. I'm sorry, Am, he'd say with a smile. We wanted to tell you sooner. Yes, the dreams came less frequently now, but despite the twenty-five years that had passed, they had never ceased entirely.

❧ 3 ❧

All my life I have harboured memories, tried to piece together scraps of truth and make sense of fragmented images. For as long as I can remember my world was one of parallel realities. There were the official truths versus my private memories, the propaganda of history books against untold stories; there were judgements and then there were facts, adult stances and the clarity of the child's vision; their version, my version.

There were times, a summer holiday or a few months, when I lived my childhood as a seamless dream where time ebbed like the tide and there was nothing to break the rhythm. But for the most part that was not so. Over and over the delicate membrane of my sphere would be broken and I tumbled out of my cocoon into the outside world.

Afterwards no one explained. People imagined these were things children shouldn't know, or they did not think we had a right to know. We were encouraged to forget, dissuaded from asking. Gradually I learned to spy: I eavesdropped on adult conversations, rifled hidden papers, devised lines of questioning and I began to build onto my fragments layers of truth. And as I did so I discovered how deep the lies went.

I grew older, became a journalist and made a living using the skills I spent my childhood honing. All the time I hoarded my recollections, guarding them carefully against the lies: lies that hardened, spread and became ever more entrenched.

Yet what use against the deceit of a state are the memories of a child?

In the African oral tradition great events and insignificant moments, the ordinary and the extraordinary, are notches on the same wheel. They exist in relation to each other. The little occurrences are as important as the grand designs: the threads are the texture of truth that separate man-made myth from fact. They are the testimonies; the words of history's eyewitnesses.

I remember cockroaches.

The tiniest of tickles across my toes made me look down. Early morning and I stood alone, chin high to the bathroom sink, both taps running. The cockroach was standing next to me and his sweeping, chestnut antennae brushed my foot in a way that seemed remarkably intimate, as though he imagined we were friends. Glossy wings tucked flat across his back; legs angled outward below the armoured undercarriage; the jaws which dominated his minuscule head worked steadily like a toothless old man. I kept my foot still, one eye on my flat-backed companion, while I reached for the tooth mug. As fast as I could manage I upended the beaker, pulled my foot away and trapped the cockroach under the glass. It sat unperturbed, as at home as a fish in an aquarium.

By the end of the day there were half a dozen inverted objects on the floor around the house: two china cups in the sitting room; a plastic toy cooking pot and a second glass in the hallway; and in the bathroom a toilet roll with a wad of paper wedged into the top. They were put there by the three of us: my sister, my brother and me, and we waited for our father to come in. This was our daily routine. When he arrived he went round the house picking up each object and dispatching the creature beneath, while we followed behind gazing at him with a mixture of disgust and admiration.

You could hear the crack and crunch of the cockroach as its skeleton gave way underfoot, pale innards spurted out. We were in awe at the way this grotesque feature didn't seem to bother our father, who would squash a cockroach with his bare feet. If you caught him at a particular time, when he was still in his pyjamas in the morning, say, and asked him to kill a cockroach for you, he would go right ahead and stamp on it with his naked feet.

My mother had a story about cockroaches that took place in the same house. We'd just moved up-country, where my parents planned to set up a clinic, the only one for hundreds of miles. For several months my father had scouted the regions looking for a suitable spot and finally settled on Koidu, three hundred miles to the east, right on the border with Guinea, in the heart of the diamond-mining region. He rented a rambling bungalow with several wings, set within its own compound, with the idea of turning one wing into a ward for in-patients and living in the others. My mother and we three children left our noisy, downtown flat in Freetown and flew to Koidu in a plane that bounced from town to town across the interior of the country, while my father drove up in our Austin with the dogs and the luggage.

When we arrived it was late into the night. My parents stacked our belongings in the main room and my mother set up cots for us in one of the bedrooms, camp beds for my father and herself in another. In the early hours of the morning, when it was still black, she awoke to the sound of my cries. She rose and came to me, turning on the lights as she passed through the house. She soothed me and returned me to my cot. Just as she was back in her bed and falling asleep again she heard me crying. This happened three times.

The fourth time she didn't bother to turn on the lights. She paused at the door to my room and as she looked around she saw that the walls seemed to be moving. My mother decided that she must be exhausted or else still dreaming and lingered a while in the dark at the bedroom door. Yet beneath her gaze the entire room seemed to have lost density: ceiling, floor, walls, even my cot heaved. Her baby was still shrieking. She flicked the light switch. Nothing. Turned it off and waited. Slowly the walls turned fluid again. She ran to fetch her husband, who was still sleeping deeply on his camp bed. As they stood at the door of my room, she showed him what she had seen, flipping the lights on and off.

He saw it, too. He rubbed his face, yawning widely. 'Cockroaches,' he said, and he turned to go back to bed.

My father's feet had strong, yellowish soles. He told us that he didn't own a pair of shoes until he went away to secondary school, and up until that time he had to walk five miles to classes and back again. This deeply impressed us, at the first telling. I disliked wearing shoes and at first I assumed the story's purpose was to let us know that shoes didn't matter. After all, my father managed without. Both of us had the same broad, long, flat feet: African feet. While I was growing my feet shot out first, ahead of the rest of my body. By the time I was eleven they were size seven and I barely cleared five foot. I was an L-shaped child.

In fact, our father's story was a multipurpose parable with everextending dimensions of meaning. At its very simplest it was a warning against the dangers of catching hookworm by wandering outside without shoes on. I learned that one the hard way. They burrowed through the skin on the soles of my feet and made a home in my bowels.

Then the story was an inducement to be grateful for what you had. My father grew up in the villages, where life was very harsh indeed. There were no hospitals and very few schools. When Ndora, my grandmother, was sick the family had to take her all the way to Rotifunk, on the other side of the country, where there was a mission hospital. In Freetown there were several hospitals to serve the British administrators and their Krio civil servants, but these were not open to people from the country. They walked most of the way, carrying pots of food and sleeping mats on their heads. When they got to the hospital, amenities there were so basic that the doctors could not come up with a diagnosis. So they shrugged and sent her away, telling the relatives to bring her back if she got any worse. As if that were possible.

Five months later she died, leaving a six-month-old baby girl and her two beloved boys. Our father was five years old then. That evening as he was sitting among the men at the back of one of the houses he heard a high-pitched, rhythmic wail coming from the street. It was a Bondu elder, speaker for the secret society of women, and she was holding a broom up to the sky. That was the sign that one of the village women had died. A fragment of her song came across: '. . . the one from Rothomgbai'—my grandmother's village. Then he knew Ndora was gone.

Soon afterwards, our father ended up being the only person in his entire family to go to school just because his mother had died. The missionaries had opened a school nearby in Mamunta. The days passed and nobody came to enrol their children in the new school, so the missionaries approached the chief, who listened to what they had to say and then passed an edict: each household from the villages neighbouring Mamunta would volunteer one child to the new school. None of the women wanted her son to be chosen. People were very suspicious of education back then; they said that people who went to school never came back. With no mother to defend his interests my father was elected to go. Fourteen years later, when he left for Britain to become a doctor, he thanked them and they were pleased they were right. See, they said, he's leaving for ever, as we knew he would. This was the final meaning of my father's story: it was about the value of education and not shoes at all. Do well in school and thank God you had an education, because lots of people don't even know its value.

In fact the new school was closed within the year after the head teacher was caught having an affair with one of the paramount chief's wives. The headmaster was fined, which was the correct punishment. But the cuckolded chief wasn't satisfied and he closed the school down as well, saying that there would be no more white man's education in Mamunta. Privately Chief Masamunta, who was also my father's uncle, arranged for his own two sons and his nephew to be transferred to another mission school in Makeni some miles away.

My mother didn't have African feet like ours. She had European feet. They were similar in the sense that they were quite big, but the arches were high and the soles smooth and thin and pale as paper. I had my father's feet but, on the matter of cockroaches, my mother's western sensibilities.

Gradually the cockroaches moved on as we swept the house out, washed cupboards down and covered the thick green and blue gloss on the walls with white emulsion. We hired a local man to help us with the work, and under our mother's instruction he cut down branches from the trees and pushed them into the earth around the edges of the compound to protect the house from the churning dust of the road. When the rains came the branches flourished miraculously and our house was enclosed in an elegant screen of trees; we were all astonished and delighted, my mother as much as the rest of us.

My father bought iron beds and mattresses for the maternity ward and my mother donated my cot for the newborn babies. Within a very short time word got around that the clinic had opened and new patients began to arrive; every day the line of people trailed out of the waiting area and onto our veranda.

Our father worked ever-longer hours. He ran two clinics in the centre of town—one for prescriptions, the other for minor surgical procedures: cataracts, circumcisions and the like. He tried hard to persuade people to bring their boys to him, instead of cutting the foreskin the traditional way, by a cleric or medicine man who tugged on it three times before slicing the skin off with an unsheathed blade. Certain days were set aside for circumcisions and sometimes fathers arrived from the countryside with six or seven boys of different ages. The obstetrics clinic was at the house, so my father could be on hand for those women whose babies came at night.

There was no nurse, so our mother helped. She held the women's hands while they were in labour, especially the Fulah women, who had to endure childbirth in silence. They were also supposed to give birth alone and by the time their relatives forced themselves to break their own traditions and bring them to the clinic the women often didn't make it. Other times my mother monitored heart and blood pressure when an anaesthetic had to be administered; often my father just wanted my mother to stay in the room for propriety's sake, so few of the women had ever been to a gynaecologist before.

When she wasn't helping out in the clinic, or in her parttime job at the Volkswagen franchise in town, my mother sang: '"Dance, then, wherever you may be, I am the Lord of the Dance," said he.' Her mighty voice was the loudest, purest sound I had ever heard; it ran through my body with a shiver, like a cold drink on a hot day. She sang sitting cross-legged with her guitar balanced on her knee, in a cotton dress she'd made herself, hair hanging loose.

We sang too, after a fashion, like three baby crows gathered around a songbird: 'I danced for the scribe and the far-thest-seas, but they would not dance and they would not follow me.'

She could practically sit on her hair; it was thick, naturally bleached by the Tropics and people in Sierra Leone marvelled at it. One of my aunts thought she must iron it straight and asked to borrow her hot tongs. My father used to have fun taking several strands and tying them into a knot to demonstrate how they unfurled in an instant, sliding like wet ice across glass. The trick was quite a crowd-pleaser among our African relatives, who came forward one at a time and asked to touch it.

Years later, when she no longer lived with us, her hairstyles became the test of memory between us children. 'Can you remember Real Mum when her hair was long?' we asked each other. Around the time she and my father split she cut her hair short. If you remembered her when she pulled it into a doughnut shape on the top of her head, or let it dry in crinkly waves down her back, then you remembered a time when our parents were together.

For me the image of her face and her hairstyles faded and brightened through the years. But her voice: I never, ever forgot the sound of her voice.

✣ 4 ✣

They met at a Christmas dance in 1959. My father was a third-year medical student at Aberdeen University and my mother was in her final sixth-form year at the Aberdeen Academy and a volunteer at the British Council. She wore her hair in a French plait, a tight-waisted skirt that made the best of her voluptuous figure and winkle pickers on her feet.

My father was just five foot eight; one of those people everyone imagines to be a great deal taller. In his student photograph he wears a well-cut suit, narrow in the leg and lapel, in the style of the sixties. His dark skin glows against the starched white cuffs and collar. The expression in his eyes is both amused and utterly self-possessed. Scattered like freckles across his cheeks and nose are dozens of small round scars, remnants of a childhood battle with smallpox. Yet the scars, like his height, were obscured by his own self-confidence. He had an eye for attractive women and he crossed the room to her: 'I'm Mohamed.' He extended his hand. 'And you are . . . ?'

Maureen Margaret Christison was a local girl, raised all of her nineteen years in Aberdeen. Her father was a clerk in a travel agency and a strict Presbyterian; her mother, dark-eyed and anxious, had a job in a milliner's until she began to have babies and slowly developed agoraphobia. Maureen was smart, attractive in the way of a strong, open type that in Scotland they call bonny. The confines of home life were as suffocating to the daughter as they were comforting to her mother. Maureen found herself drawn on many nights to the British Council, to the events held for overseas students which she volunteered to help organise.

For the African students Britain was a new and demanding experience. Many kept to themselves, finding safety in numbers. They were all on government scholarships—men and women chosen to lead their countries one day soon across the post-independence horizon towards a new Africa where they would design bridges, run schools, plan towns, drain swamps, build hospitals or, as likely, become desk-bound bureaucrats.

When he was fourteen my father had won a scholarship to Bo School. The Eton of the protectorate of Sierra Leone was established by the British in order to educate the sons of chiefs to take their place in Britain's empire. He spent seven years there, wearing a white uniform, taught by English masters. In his last year he became head boy and while he was waiting for the results of his scholarship application to read medicine in the UK he taught the junior years. Alongside his formal education the years at Bo gave him an understanding of the men who ruled his country and their values and their history, or at least the version taught in England's public schools.

Before they boarded a cargo ship bound for Liverpool at Freetown's docks, the only understanding of Britain most new pioneers possessed was through their first British Council induction seminar. The arrivals from the provinces were herded into a darkened hall, where they watched reels of black-and-white short films entitled *An Introduction to British Life and Culture.*

In one short film, *Lost in the Countryside,* two young Africans in old-fashioned tweed suits amble through a pastoral scene. Their skin is so dark they almost look like they're white actors in blackface, and their hair is brushed straight upwards. Suddenly they realise they can't find their way back and a crescendo of mishaps parallels their mounting panic. When they emerge from

a haystack pulling strands from their hair an authoritative voice
cuts in: 'If you become lost in the countryside do not panic. Find
a road. Locate a bus stop. Join the queue [and there, in the middle of nowhere was a line of people]. A bus will arrive, board it
and return to the town.' The film ends with the Africans looking
mightily relieved sitting on the bus, surrounded by smiling locals.

They were given a map of the London Underground, a train
timetable, and a talk on expected etiquette, including how to behave in a British home. Visits should be undertaken on invitation
only. Never walk into a British household and sit in the chair belonging to the man of the house. In Britain visitors are expected
to maintain a flow of conversation. It is polite to decline a second
helping of food. And on it went.

So very different from the African household in which I was
raised. On the weekends and even the weekdays my aunts and
uncles appeared at all hours and sat on the veranda for lengthy
periods, just keeping company. They talked for just as long as
someone had something to say and then lapsed into companion-
able silence. Every now and again one of my aunts would break
the silence to begin the routine of greetings all over again. When
they'd finished, people would snort with serene satisfaction; my
aunts would adjust their head-dresses and *lappas*, and settle even
more deeply into themselves. Conversation is a whim, not an art.
Of me no one expected anything except a respectful silence and
the appearance of listening. If I'd begun to try to amuse them with
stories and precocious attempts at conversation, the way children
in England did, they would have exchanged sly glances. 'How dis
pickin dae talk so!'

In time, very often when most people had already been there
for half the morning, the cook would begin to prepare food. I'd
be given a plate with a man-sized helping and if it was a special
occasion we were all expected to go back time and time again to

taste each dish: mounds of jollof rice, cooked in tomatoes so that the rice turned pink, sour sour or stewed sorrel, okra stew, chicken fried with fresh Scotch bonnet peppers, deep-fried plantains. At the end of the day half the visitors left carrying a tin dish wrapped in cloths to take home for the rest of the family.

From Freetown to Liverpool, then by train to Aberdeen, where the green and ochre of Africa was replaced by shades of blue and grey. In winter the sky over northern Scotland turned to black and the granite of the buildings glittered like silver. And the cold, it was alive! It stung legs, bit cheeks, pinched fingers and toes. It was like going for a swim and being caught in a flurry of jellyfish. The newest arrivals were always obvious: they wore old-styled cotton suits made by their provincial tailors, neither customer nor tailor imagining for a moment that they would not be thick enough to stand the coolest weather. By the end of the first week their smart new suits were packed away in tin trunks for good.

No traveller arrived in Britain from Africa without being suitably awed by his first sight of a terraced row. The houses were built in a single row that ran the entire length of the street like a set of dentures. A rich man in Africa builds his house to stand out from every house around it. In Britain people owned their homes, but all the houses looked the same. A story was told of an undergraduate on his first day in Aberdeen who was taken to his friend's student digs in a terraced row. He thought his friend must have made good and exclaimed on the length of the house. When the others laughed and pointed out that the building was in fact many houses, he was crestfallen. Now the house began to look cramped. But once you were inside you saw there were more rooms than you could ever guess at from the narrow frontage.

My father discovered the sin of sweet things for the first time in his life, munching his way through packets of Opal Fruits. Muslim or not, his newly awakened sweet tooth extended to an enthusiasm for sweet alcoholic drinks: sherry or brandy mixed with ginger ale. In Aberdeen he had his first toothache, followed by his first visit to the dentist and his first filling.

The short, round African vowels that fell off the front of his tongue moved further back in his throat and lengthened into local Aberdonian rhythms; he began to draw out his 'e's, to emphasise his 'r's and then to roll them; and finally he adopted the local idiom, talked about patients turning ill and taking scarlet fever, asked them where they stayed. For the rest of his life he spoke with a curious hybrid accent that puzzled some and brought a smile to the lips of others.

In his first year as a student my father spent much of his time on his own, walking up to his chemistry and biology lectures in the Old University buildings in the north of the city. The next year there was a batch of new arrivals from Sierra Leone: Bernard Frazer, a confident Krio, was wealthy enough to fly to Britain when he started at university (generations of his family had been educated in the UK); Dan Sama, a Mende also from Sierra Leone, was dark and serious and had a long-term love affair with a Scottish student. There was Charlie Renner, who sped around Aberdeen in a green Mini; and the Guineans Henry Blankson and David Anamudu. David's square face and glasses earned him the nickname 'Mr TV' and he skated fearlessly over the wet, black cobblestones on a Vespa scooter. They were all studying medicine.

That first winter the wind gusted in from the North Sea, swirled around the harbour like a furious sea god and rushed straight up Union Street in the centre of town. Just when my father thought the weather couldn't possibly get any worse, it snowed until the black city turned white, like a negative of a photograph. The next day the sun shone strongly for the first time in weeks and the sky was like a stretched sheet of sapphire silk, the colour of the Atlantic.

The unpredictable northern European weather systems left the West African students battered and freezing; they felt like pioneers battling up the north face of the city, Michelin men dressed in so many layers of sweaters. At home they spent the best part of their grant money on shillings for the gas and at night they slept with their overcoats over the counterpane.

In Sierra Leone the rains begin on 1 May every year. From then on it rains at eleven o'clock every night, gradually moving forward in the day until the rain falls almost continuously. As the season advances, so the rain recedes at exactly the same pace. Next the sun shines for seven months until the clouds come back again. On 2 May, if for some reason it did not rain the night before, people in the marketplace might remark, 'The rains are late this year, not so?' This, in Sierra Leone, is what passes for a conversation about the weather.

Few of the African students could afford to go home for the holidays. They spent Christmas in each other's company, but New Year was a very different matter. My father and his friends suddenly found themselves on the receiving end of dozens of invitations from their neighbours; they accepted them all and went from house to house downing malt whiskies, enjoying their sudden popularity. The young doctors were already accustomed to locals who crept up to them in the street, reaching out furtively to touch their black skin—for luck, they explained apologetically if they were caught out. Any of the Africans who thought they'd have a quiet night at home spent the early hours of New Year's morning answering the doorbell to revellers hoping to win a little luck in the coming year by catching sight of a black face on Hogmanay.

Mohamed and Maureen were together for two years before her father passed them on the other side of Union Street one afternoon. When she arrived home she found him maroon with rage. He told his daughter that he would not tolerate her seeing or being seen with a black man.

Later, in the little attic flat my father shared with Dan Sama, he listened to an account of the scene from my tearful mother and knew exactly what to do. 'I'll call on your father at home,' he told her, confident he could put things right.

Gairn Terrace is a row of plain semi-detached houses built on the edge of Aberdeen close to the river Dee and the road to Perth. There is nothing to distinguish one house from the other, except the colour of the woodwork that brightens pebbledash facades the colour and texture of porridge. The Christisons' window frames were painted pale yellow and two net-curtained windows faced the street, one above and one below. Curiously, in a world in which appearances mattered, the houses were built with no proper front door, just an entrance reached by a dark side passage.

When my mother was growing up there was an army training ground opposite and, farther on, a crater where a fighter plane had been downed during the war, in which wild blueberries grew. In 1935 Robert Christison bought one of the new houses for four hundred and twenty pounds and from then on he kept three boxes on the dresser. For the next eighteen years he put two and sixpence into each one every Friday to pay for the mortgage, insurance and bills. In all respects life in number 38 was equally regimented.

My grandfather's chair was closest to the fire and faced the bay window onto the street. To the left was the wireless, which replaced the old crystal set after the war. It was a magnificent piece, in two-tone polished mahogany, and stood about three and a half feet tall, occupying the entire corner of the room. From his place my grandfather could reach it comfortably. Its prime location was really the only outstanding feature of my grandfather's chair, which was just one part of a three-piece suite, upholstered in rust and sufficiently yet not excessively comfortable. A lace-edged antimacassar covered the headrest. My father, wearing a suit and tie, took the chair opposite.

My mother and grandmother stayed in the kitchen—Maureen preparing the tea things and Lydia smoking Woodbines—while my father asked Mr Christison's permission to continue seeing his daughter. Mr Christison listened, though not with his lean, sparse body nor with his brisk blue eyes; he sat with his arms crossed and never once looked my father in the eye, but he didn't interrupt either. My father spoke fluidly and directly, describing his many aspirations, including his plans to specialise in obstetrics.

Mr Christison was not impressed by the black man's credentials. Nor did he like his forthright manner. 'Arrogant' is how he would dismiss him later. He stated his position, an entirely simple one: 'I'm not prejudiced. I'm sure you've done well enough. But I won't have Maureen going about town with any man of a different colour. It's my view you stick to your own. There are black women for black men, Chinese women for Chinamen and, for all I care, green women for green men.'

'Forgive me, sir, but if Maureen dated a teddy boy, would that be all right . . . as long as he was white?'

'I wouldn't tolerate that either, as a matter of fact. But that's as much as I have to say to you on the matter.'

Mr Christison stood up, shaking the newspaper from his lap. He was much taller than my father; he once tried out for the Rhodesian police. He said: 'Thank you for stopping by.' Their eyes still did not meet and he excused himself from the room.

While the visitor was still in the house Mr Christison remained outside, standing on the steep slope of his garden digging at his rhubarb. His wife fed the visitor angel cakes and tea and chattered nervously all the while. If her husband was unimpressed, Lydia Christison was secretly delighted by Maureen's African doctor, who in that hour charmed her entirely. For years afterwards she defied her husband, paying visits to her daughter carrying petits fours and children's clothes, and allowing my mother and her little ones back for hot baths in the years we lived without a bathroom.

Afterwards my father told my mother what had transpired in his conversation with my grandfather. And I can imagine exactly how my grandfather behaved during the exchange, because almost forty years later, shortly before he died, he was the same way with me when I asked him about the day he met my father for the first and only time. There we sat in the very same room, the decor barely changed in all that time. A clown doll made by my grandmother after she had her stroke sat on an occasional table. A set of tiny ornamental sabres I used to play with as a child had gone. Those were the only differences I could see. He sat in his chair, and I cross-legged on the floor, my back leaning on the chair where my father had sat. Between us on the leather pouf was a great pile of photographs and a tape recorder.

My grandfather was preparing to die: emptying drawers, sorting through closets; he had even finally given away my grandmother's clothes. The next day the two of us took a trip up the coast towards Inverness. By then he was over ninety, had trouble walking and had been forced to stop driving, but he read the map and worked out different routes there and back that carried us through the finest scenery. On the way up we stopped at a roadside tea room— a lodge, he called it—and told me how he used to bring my grandmother there. Among the trinkets for sale I found a pretty rococo coffee cup and saucer, but when I showed it to him he called it tat and said I was daft to want to buy it.

In the morning I stopped by Gairn Terrace to say goodbye: I was on my way back to London. He called me upstairs, to one of the bedrooms. Inside, piled on the bed were dozens of different household objects: framed pictures, coat hangers, an old heater. He handed me four yellow and black coffee cups and a set of tea

cups in the same florid style as the single coffee cup I had chosen
at the lodge. They were my grandparents' wedding gifts, entirely
unused in almost seventy years.

I smiled and kissed him and he hugged me back. Three months
later I was up in Aberdeen again, in the snow and sleet, this time
for his funeral.

The end of my father's first year in Scotland coincided with the
culmination in Ghana in 1957 of years of brokering between the
Ghanaian leaders and British rulers over a new constitution which
would bring self-government to the colony. After the Second
World War Britain had promised her colonies independence in
return for their military assistance. Hundreds of thousands of
black and brown soldiers died and, though India was granted
independence in 1947, the African nations remained colonies.
Virtually overlooked by the Marshall Plan, which gave millions
to rebuild Europe and the Far East, impoverished by the low,
fixed prices paid for cash crops while European middlemen grew
fat, Africans began to rally their people against the inequity of
colonial rule.

In Ghana the independence movement was led by a charismatic
former teacher called Kwame Nkrumah, a pan-Africanist who had
been imprisoned for several years by the British. Nkrumah was
Scottish-educated, and during the 1940s a leader in the influen-
tial West African Students' Union. It was inside WASU that the
seeds of pan-Africanism and anti-colonial politics germinated,
fuelled by the hostility of British society and the humiliation of
the colour bar. Later these sentiments were re-imported to Africa,
where they ultimately flowered in rebellion.

All the African students watched and waited as one after another the colonies were granted independence. Shortly after
my parents met, Nigeria celebrated its break from the empire,

alongside thirteen French colonies—practically the entire Francophone empire, with the exception of Algeria, which remained sunk in a bitter and frustrating war of liberation. For the West African states autonomy was not so much a question of if as when, and the anticipation ran like a fever through the exiled students.

Gradually the topic began to dominate every gathering; people turned the record player off at parties, the better to be heard, and huddled over the paraffin heaters in each other's apartments late into the frosty night. For Maureen the talk soon palled. Mohamed, on the other hand, was already deeply politically committed, a member of the British Labour Party and president of the local chapter of the West African Students' Union—although in truth Aberdeen was never able to boast more than a handful of members.

In the years before full independence was finally granted Sierra Leone had moved slowly towards self-government, a wind of change that revealed schisms hidden under the sand of white rule. In Freetown the Krios had fought for self-rule since the founding of the colony by the Nova Scotian blacks in 1792. They were former slaves who fought on the side of the British in the American War of Independence. After the American victory they were forced to emigrate to the British settlement of Nova Scotia in Canada and thence given passage to Sierra Leone with the promise of land and freedom. But Britain double-crossed them: Freetown was first given to the profiteering Sierra Leone Company and later turned into a crown colony. A hundred years on, during the Scramble for Africa, the rest of the country was brought under British protection.

Freetown soon flourished. In the fifty years up to 1900 the city, holding on to the south-westerly curve of the continent, became known as the Athens of Africa. The Krio emphasis was on education and professional achievement, their aspirations essentially European. They looked outward, across the sea, rather than inward to the hinterland, sending their children to Britain to be educated. Freetown had a flourishing free press; the first western-style university in Africa was founded at Fourah Bay; and at that time there were more children in school in the colony than in England itself. When Britain became the dominant colonial power they looked to the Krios, in their starched bibs and laced boots, to fill positions in civil service administrations throughout West Africa.

On the whole the Krios did not view themselves as Africans. They opposed the creation of a single state of Sierra Leone and objected to the right of people from the protectorate to sit on a new postwar legislative council in Freetown. The Krios already enjoyed separate status as British subjects and they wanted this fact to be acknowledged in any new constitution, a wish that was ignored by Britain. In 1957 Sir Milton Margai, an elderly doctor from the provinces, successfully led a broad-based coalition to become the country's first prime minister; a year later all British officials relinquished their government posts.

During the university vacations most of the African students took the train to Norfolk and worked in the Smedley pea factory, filling and labelling cans. At night they slept together in long dormitories of bunk beds, up to a hundred young men side by side, above and below. The factory was some way out of town, and evenings were quiet. Among the gathered students from universities all over the country and as many different nations, talk turned frequently to the question of independence.

At that time most of the African students studying in Britain were still young men from privileged families, town dwellers. Mohamed Forna was the first Sierra Leonean from the provinces to be admitted to Aberdeen University. Sitting on a suitcase at the end of his bed, Mohamed described existence in rural Africa, the total absence of basic life-giving amenities, the yawning disparity between the city and the people of the provinces. He was convinced that Africa's poorest were already being cut out of the future.

When the Congolese nationalist Patrice Lumumba was murdered, my father cried. At the time the popular leader's death was blamed on Katangan secessionists led by Moïse Tshombe; not until decades later was it actually revealed to be the work of the CIA and the Belgian government, who had a deal with Tshombe to exploit the vast mineral resources of Katanga. It was the only time anyone heard my father swear. 'Moïse Tshombe is a fucker!' He shook his head in despair.

He joined the British Labour Party and began to attend student meetings regularly. Even among his peers he had a reputation as a firebrand. One evening Bernard Frazer, who took a more languid view, challenged Mohamed. If he thought all the politicians back home were doing such a poor job, why didn't he run the country himself? I will if I have to, replied his friend, rising to the provocation.

In 1960 a series of meetings began to be held in London to agree on a new fully independent constitution for Sierra Leone. As a representative of one of the student unions, my father was invited to meet the Sierra Leonean delegates. They gathered in the tense and heady atmosphere of Lancaster House to weave a constitutional framework for the future.

'Uncle Sam' was a one-time church minister in Freetown who arrived in Britain in the 1930s to train as a doctor. He flunked and switched to law; flunked that too. With the last of his savings he managed to buy a four-storey house in Paddington and he set about restoring it in a haphazard manner. In the meantime he lived quite well renting out rooms to a tidal population of students. Uncle Sam's house was where most young men from

Sierra Leone who were short of cash but wanted to see the big city ended up staying.

What Sam made on the house he regularly lost on the horses and at those times he would go round the house emptying gas and electricity meters of shillings, and shrug soulfully at the bitter complaints of his young tenants.

Some years back Sam won the love of Dora Fossey, an English hospital matron who lived several doors down and regularly bailed him out of his financial straits. Dora and Sam never dared to marry or even to go out in public more than once in a while. Instead, when her shift at St Mary's ended Dora spent every evening at Sam's, watching television and cooking him English meals. Anyone who knew no better would imagine they had been married for years, but their relationship was conducted entirely within the narrow world of the crumbling West London terrace.

One afternoon Mohamed came back to Uncle Sam's to find one of his many cousins standing in the kitchen. Brima Sesay, nephew of Chief Masamunta, was a nursing student making a tour of the country. Neither could believe the luck of the coincidence and they crossed the floor to embrace. Afterwards Brima took Mohamed to Shepherd's Bush market, where they bought slippery okra, palm oil, tiny stinging scarlet peppers and blackened, smoked grouper. That night they stayed in with Uncle Sam and feasted on rice and *plassas*. They hadn't seen each other since they used to play on the Fornas' farm during the school holidays. They had lost touch when my father was eleven, at which point one of his teachers had asked the family permission to take him away to the south as a ward in order to complete his education. Soon afterwards Brima had been adopted into a group of missionaries who brought him to England.

Brima called my father Moses, explaining to a mystified Dora how the mission teachers went round the class on the first day of school changing the names of the children for their own convenience. Around the same time my father chose his birthday: November, which coincided with *tarokans*. The date, the 25th, he decided on himself. A name the bureaucrats could spell and a date of birth: these were the first essentials on the path to westernisation. My father dropped Moses the day he left the primary school; but Brima used both his names: Alfred Brima.

Days later my father caught the train from King's Cross back north and Brima went on to Birmingham. When Alfred Brima was back at college in Portsmouth, a letter arrived. It was from Mohamed and contained bad news. 'Remember Maureen, the girl I told you about?' Mohamed wrote. 'A terrible thing has happened. She is pregnant.'

Mohamed wanted advice from his cousin, someone who knew the family. He had thoughts of marriage but worried about Maureen's father who, he supposed, would detest this solution as much as any other. His greatest fear was that Mr Christison would report him to the university authorities and try to have his scholarship revoked. Then there was the matter of the Fornas. He remembered the Conteh cousins who returned from Britain, one after the other, each with a white wife, and the indignation and upset that the women managed to provoke within the family.

Brima didn't hesitate. Marry her, he said. The older members of the family aren't going to live for ever. But, he warned, you must make sure the family never have reason to resent her. And if you take her from her own country, to a place where she is a stranger, you will have to be utterly loyal to her, too.

Maureen and Mohamed married at the register office in Union Street on 28 March 1961. She was nineteen years old and he was twenty-five. Charlie Renner acted as a witness and Dan Sama was my father's best man. Dan's Scottish girlfriend had given birth the month before, but she had disappeared back to her family and given the child up. She dropped her classes; no one had laid eyes on her since. Bernard Frazer came along and proposed several toasts in the Union building after the ceremony.

On her wedding day my mother, dressed in a pale-blue suit, left Gairn Terrace with a packed suitcase in her hand. She didn't tell her parents she was getting married, though she found out many years later that they already knew because someone had seen the banns up on the board in town. But within the house no one spoke of it.

One month later, in April, the British flag was lowered in Sierra Leone and replaced by the green, white and blue tricolour. My father organised a sherry party in the beautiful stone British Council building in the harbour at Aberdeen. At the end of the evening, flamboyantly drunk, he staggered away under the weight of several crates, declaring there was far too much sherry to leave behind. On the top floor of the bus he lit six cigarettes and smoked them all, three in each hand. Someone teased that he wasn't even a smoker. 'I'm smoking the smoke of freedom, man.' He blew out great gusts of smoke. 'I'm smoking the smoke of freedom.'

At the end of the evening my mother, pregnant and sober, pushed him up the stairs while he leaned back so far he was almost horizontal. Then she put him to bed with a bucket by his side.

❧ 5 ❧

My mother was one of the only white people in Koidu. The only other one I ever saw was her boss at the Volkswagen franchise, Franz Stein from Bischofstauberville in Germany. One day, soon after we arrived to live in the town, my mother appeared in his showroom to buy her first car, a sky-blue Beetle. Franz Stein was just about to lose the bank manager's wife, who did the accounts for him, and so he asked my mother if she wanted a job. Our clinic had barely opened and we could do with the money, so she agreed.

In the mornings, after we dropped Sheka and Memuna at school at the Catholic Mission, my mother left me at home in the care of my cousin and namesake Big Aminatta while she worked at the garage calculating the repair bills. The mechanics told her how many men had worked on a car and for how long. Then she added up the cost of the parts and computed the tax; when the bills were paid she totted the figures up exactly in a big accounts book.

In addition to Volkswagens the showroom also sold Porsches—at least in theory. The same car was on display the entire time we lived in Koidu. Every day people came inside to look at it, but no one ever wanted to buy it. There was barely a few inches' clearance beneath the low-slung undercarriage, little use in a town which could not boast a single tarmacked road. But Franz Stein said he kept it there, buffed and polished and looking about as improbable as a pair of stilettos on a nomad, because it attracted so many people into the showroom.

In the afternoon my mother drove around town in her car asking people to pay their invoices for the clinic and sometimes

I was allowed to accompany her. We drove from house to house, along the corrugated roads, rocking up and down on the car's springy suspension.

In the 1920s Koidu was a rural village of no more than a hundred or so people, built around an intersection of roads heading east and south, in the cup between the Nimini and Gori hills. The people who lived there were mostly farmers, descendants of the same clan, who had lived identical lives for generations.

Almost overnight during the 1950s the population of the tiny hamlet flashed to twelve thousand as people converged from all over the country, drawn by a silent siren's call. Government clerks left their desks in Freetown and took to the road; teachers walked out of the classrooms to dig in the mud of river beds; so many farmers abandoned the fields that the price of rice rocketed. Within months there were nationwide riots.

Diamonds. They washed up in the water of streams, hid in the soft silt beds, even glinted underfoot on the roads and pathways. It was said that in Koidu people didn't look where they were going but walked everywhere with their heads bent down, gaze permanently trawling the ground for stones; people called it the 'Koidu crouch'. Eventually, the government was forced to declare an emergency and even offer to raise salaries to woo their civil servants back.

In many ways Koidu was like a town in the old Wild West. The cinema even had a bullet hole in the middle of the screen where someone in the audience lost patience and shot the baddie. There was only one road that constituted the town; it had a single mosque; next door to this was the nightclub—really just a bar selling beer and spirits—and farther on a few Lebanese-owned shops.

The Lebanese merchants were very sociable and always gave a tiny cup of coffee with cardamom and a piece of baklava to my mother, and a Fanta to me, while they went over the doctor's bill. When time came to pay, my mother told me, they always asked for ten per cent off, sometimes twenty. In the beginning she felt obliged to agree because they had been so hospitable, but after a short while she got into the practice of adding ten per cent before she presented the bill. The whole transaction was executed with displays of excellent humour, smiles, more sweet, black coffee and, for me, another fizzy drink.

My mother told me a story about her visits to our Lebanese clients. They always pressed her to accept a drink, but my mother rarely touched alcohol. One day she laughed and declared: 'I only drink champagne.' They took her at her word and the very next time she visited a bottle of champagne was brought from the fridge and opened. Of course, she had to accept. Gradually the word that the doctor's wife only drank champagne spread and everyone began to keep some in the fridge just for her.

They liked to spoil her. When she shook hands to go the men would hold on to hers, patting it, and look directly into her face; they smiled, showing gold teeth. The women complimented her clothes. They treated her as though she were special, as though she were one of them.

The autumn after my parents were married in Scotland, my brother was born. My father delivered his first son himself. He graduated soon after and almost exactly a year later my sister came along. Then the family moved to Glasgow, where my father pursued an extra qualification in obstetrics.

All this time my mother had been turning slowly from white to black. At the university in Aberdeen the African students were considered exotic. People knew they had gilded careers waiting for them; they were the chosen ones—at least where they came from. Out in the city there were few enough blacks for them to be considered rare birds and accorded a measure of tolerance.

But with each child my mother found her skin darkened, almost as though it were a side effect of pregnancy. By the time we moved to Glasgow she was virtually transformed into a full-blooded Negress. People began to treat her the way they sometimes treated my father. They stared at her as she walked with me in the pram, my sister perched on the back and my brother following behind; and they cast remarks under their breath, barbed like a fisherman's fly, deftly designed to land just within earshot.

When my father was with us men would yell, 'Look at the darkie!' and spit the word 'whore' with guttural emphasis. If we were alone then quite often old ladies would come up to say how cute we children looked, and stroke our heads.

Bellshill Maternity Hospital, where I was born, served the working-class outlying Lanarkshire suburbs. It was a massive concrete edifice, entirely surrounded by council houses, like a factory producing baby Glaswegians by the score. I went back only once in my life on my way through from Aberdeen to London, when I looped round the country via Glasgow to see my first home. As I walked into the maternity hospital I was forced to squeeze past a group of heavily pregnant women, dressed only in pastel dressing gowns and slippers to guard against the damp October air, chain-smoking outside the front entrance.

Outside our bungalow in Ardgay Street I sat in my car, waiting, trying to make up my mind whether or not to knock on the door and explain to the inhabitants that I had once lived in their house. My drive through the neighbourhood had told me it was poor, but beyond that I hadn't much idea of what sort of people lived here. I had seen no black or brown faces, but then again there had been few people on the freezing streets. I dithered, folded and refolded my map. I reached for the door handle. At that instant the door of 19 Ardgay Street flew open: a man with a shaved head, holding a piece of wood, stood there and seemed to stare straight at me. A Rhodesian ridgeback bounded past him and up to the front gate. My nerve failed. I started the ignition and drove away.

Back then we were broke and we were black. We survived on my father's grant, stretched to meet the demands of each new baby. It was tough to find anyone who wanted to rent us a place to live. Lots of the advertisements specified 'no blacks'; sometimes it said 'no foreigners', which was another way of saying the same thing.

Searching for a house could be so difficult that one medical student put a large advertisement in the local newspaper in capitals: BLACK DOCTOR SEEKS ACCOMMODATION. He said it cut short the process of going to see apartments which were always gone the moment you showed your face. My father went to Bellshill Maternity Hospital, where he was taking up his internship, found another black doctor who was leaving to go home, and asked him if he could rent his apartment.

The five of us lived in two rooms in Ardgay Street. The Shettleston house was owned by a couple who ran a driving school and lived in the other wing. Above the door was an inscription to 'Our Lady of Fatima'. There were times on a Saturday night when a brick would crash through the two windows facing the street; but my mother said it was because they were Protestants and thought we were Catholics, not because we were black.

The hospital where my father did his rounds and delivered babies was a different world; he was treated with great respect and his patients adored him. People talked about his wonderful 'bedside manner'. It was years before I understood what they meant. I imagined my father sitting next to his patients, eating from a table elaborately laid with every kind of silverware, de-boning a sole or delicately peeling a peach with a knife.

When I was six months old a letter came from the family in Sierra Leone. It was from our father's father. Ibrahim, one of my father's elder brothers, had died; our grandfather begged Mohamed to come home at the earliest and help take care of the family.

We sailed on the passenger ship the *Aureol*. It docked in the Canaries, where the crew filled the pool on the deck with sea water; then we set sail for Freetown. The other passengers were mostly returning former colonials, who played cards, organised a fancy dress party and sat at each other's tables in the evening without ever inviting us to join them.

When the ship docked alongside the massive warehouses of the Queen Elizabeth II quay, the first thing my mother saw was the fedora belonging to my father's friend Dr Panda bobbing in the surging crowds. She stepped off the boat and into the throng of Africans and she was transformed, once again, into a white woman.

In Freetown people stared at her wherever she went, especially when she rode by on her bicycle. 'Look! White woman dae ride bicycle!'

White again, my mother was accepted, on certain conditions, into the ex-pat community in Freetown. She joined a Scottish dancing group that met at the Railway Club and at the exclusively white Hill Station Club. Before independence black people were not even allowed up to Hill Station unless they worked in one of the big houses. A special train was sent down every day to bring the workers up to the hills. Certainly, there were no African members of the Hill Station Club. My mother was popular there: she had grown up performing songs and dances and she entranced everyone with her outgoing personality. Her only disappointment was that at the end of the evening the other members never invited her to their houses for drinks or supper, and she made her way home alone.

Marriage to my father turned my mother into a multi-hued chameleon. He, by contrast, had been a black man in Scotland and was a black man in Africa. Once I asked my mother how my father regarded her patronage of the Hill Station Club. She said she didn't know.

'What if he'd wanted to come too?' I pressed.

'Well, he wouldn't,' she replied. 'He didn't know the Scottish dances.' That was the way she thought about these matters. It was as simple as that.

My father's visiting brothers were kind to her, especially Uncle Momodu. He had an appetite for all things western and always wore western clothes. He came down to Freetown 'on business', he stated enigmatically, and, when he wasn't at one of his assignations, he flicked through the magazines my mother brought with her from Britain, questioning her about life 'over there'. Momodu wandered in and out of the house, played with the babies and loved to tease his serious younger brother's wife. But Maureen felt frozen out by the wives of my father's friends who, she thought, disregarded her, though she could never quite put her finger on the problem because it lay in what was missing from their welcome rather than what was present.

Soon after we arrived Pa Roke, my grandfather, came to visit, bringing with him several live chickens, some sacks of rice and one of his junior wives. He cast an eye over my mother: 'So you went to the sea and turned into a fish,' he said to my father in Temne. He'd warned his son not to come back with a white wife. There were a lot of local families who would have liked to make a match. 'How much did you pay?' He meant how much was the dowry. She was young; her breasts hadn't fallen yet.

'Ten shillings,' my father replied, straight-faced. That was what he'd been charged at the register office on the morning of the wedding. Pa Roke smiled: he was pleased. His son's wife might be white, but she had come at a good price.

In Koidu as we passed people waved and called out to my mother and me. Young men offered to carry her packages; shopkeepers ushered her over to look at the latest imported fabrics. Everyone recognised her. She was the doctor's white wife. And there was only one white woman in Koidu. And only one doctor.

❦ 6 ❦

A few months after our clinic opened a battered bush taxi drew up in front of the house. There were quite a few people crammed inside; at first it was difficult to see exactly how many. They struggled out, among them a woman so emaciated and feeble that she couldn't walk, as well as a boy of around eight or nine who looked as if he were unconscious.

Our father came out and helped carry them into the surgery; it was obvious he was upset and angry: 'Why do you bring them to me when it's too late?' No one replied. And he knew the answer: they had nothing, there was no way to pay a doctor.

The woman was close to death. The boy, who was perhaps her son, had died in the back of the car a short while before: his body was still limp, no signs yet of rigor mortis. My father asked the family about the woman's and the boy's symptoms. Were there others? They nodded. Yes, they replied, there were many others in the village, too ill to make the journey.

My father didn't have a laboratory but it took him less than a minute to reach his diagnosis: what the people described was a cholera epidemic. He took his bag, swept up armfuls of drugs, threw them all onto the front seat of our Austin and left. The family sat in the back giving him directions to their village, cradling the body of the small boy wrapped in a sheet.

My father didn't come back until much later that night, until after he had traced the source of the contamination and persuaded the village headman to stop people using the water. It was never easy; there was often only one well or stream; people didn't understand the basic principles of infection, spread and cure. Outbreaks of disease were almost always blamed on witchcraft. He taught them how, at the first sign of diarrhoea they should shake the gas out of a bottle of Fanta or Coca-Cola and drink it at room temperature. It was a simple trick: the equivalent of sugar and salts. But it was a lifesaver.

When my mother was alone in the city and our father was in the regions planning the clinic, a measles epidemic gripped Freetown. In Britain measles was a childhood illness; in Africa the same virus killed and continues to kill as recklessly and easily as a child tumbling a tower of wooden blocks. That year hundreds of children died. At Connaught Hospital they didn't have space to admit any new cases. All three of us children were infected; spots even erupted down the inside of my brother's throat. My father wasn't due back for many days and there were no telephones up-country, no way to reach him. So my mother nursed us at home, letting us sip flat Fanta when we were too weak to eat anything else.

Eventually a colleague of our father's was reached and he drove over to see us. He put my brother on a drip and told my mother she had done just the right thing. She was so relieved when we began to improve after ten days that she ran across the road to Patterson Zochonis, the expensive and only department store in Freetown, where she bought us absurdly expensive Swiss maraschino cherry ice cream, and spooned it down our tender throats one by one.

In Koidu there was so much to do and no other doctors with whom to share the load. The building of this clinic was the realisation of a simple dream for our father. Many of the western-trained doctors preferred to stay in Freetown and work in the larger hospitals. With a modest private practice on the side within a few years they could own a Mercedes and be waited upon by servants wearing white gloves, like Dr Panda and his wife. But our father had a vision that one day there would be a network of cottage clinics across the country. The success of our clinic was important to him and his motives were plain.

When our father was a child during the war, a vaccination programme was announced. Scores of families left their villages to make the trip to the mission hospital. They settled on the rows of long wooden benches under the sun in the courtyard, alongside patients who arrived with other complaints. When the benches were full, the line continued along the walls and encircled the building. My father sat for hours on the ground, his back against the wall, listening for his name to be called. In front of him in the queue was an old man. When the Fornas appeared, the old man asked for help going to the toilet and he gave my father some cola nuts in thanks afterwards.

The hours passed and when at last his name was called the old Pa seemed to have fallen asleep, so my father leaned over and shook him lightly. The man slumped over sideways and lay face up, blue cataract-filled eyes reflecting the sky. A few minutes later the orderlies pulled him up by the arms and carted him away. They were used to it: the old ones who died before they made it to see the doctor.

Following Ndora's death our father left the village to live with Teacher Trye. Soon after he left, a second tragedy struck his tiny family. A letter arrived in Bo, written by a hired letter-writer, informing Mohamed that his elder brother Morlai had died 'of a headache'. He lay down one afternoon saying his head hurt and simply never got to his feet again.

We never, ever turned a patient away. And if someone couldn't pay, we treated them for free. It was hard to imagine, given the principles that governed our father, that the clinic was making money but remarkably it was.

In the town there were a small number of extremely wealthy diamond dealers. They operated cheek by jowl with the Sierra Leone Selection Trust, who paid the government millions to exploit the country's reserves, as well as the Diamond Corporation, a holding of the De Beers empire, who held the rights to buy the lion's share of gems. Some independent dealers bought government permits allowing them to mine restricted quantities of gems. Others dispensed with the law and sent teams of their own men to dig illicitly in the restricted area. Many did both.

After dark on most nights just outside Koidu hordes of young men and some women scaled the fences, easily avoiding the single SLST helicopter that patrolled the area with searchlights. In the early morning they wriggled back under the wire, gritty brown diamonds wrapped in small pieces of cloth tied round their necks. The dealers paid their illegal diggers a retainer to bring the gems, which they then sold on through the official government offices or shifted illegally on the black market. The world of the dealers was a closed one, a tightly run business controlled by a few men who maintained a private code of honour designed to hold on to their monopoly and increase the sum of their wealth.

The men who risked their health and liberty to dive hundreds of times to the bottom of the river and bring up pans of silt had no option but to sell the gems they found to their patron at the price he chose to give them. There were frequent accidents: several times we were all roused in the middle of the night or early morning because there had been a drowning. Sometimes the illegal diggers were caught and prosecuted—they were the only people who ever were. If their patrons couldn't bribe the judge to let their man off, well, he'd be well compensated for doing time on behalf of the boss. In Koidu everyone knew their place.

Regularly men would arrive at the clinic bearing notes which simply stated to whom the final bill should be sent—inevitably one of several Lebanese dealers. After my father had treated their ailments and given them drugs, he sent the bill through to my mother to prepare and he instructed her to charge the dealers at the highest rate. At least eight out of every ten people who passed through our clinic paid nothing, even for their medicines, which my father fetched from the dispensary in the house and handed to them; people who could afford it were charged at the regular rate; and between them the diamond dealers paid for the healthcare of the rest of Koidu and the surrounding villages.

Almost always people who had not been charged came back on another day with something in return: a pair of live chickens, a sack of oranges or a basket of yams.

Late one night we were all woken up by a frenzied rapping on the door of the house, so loud it sounded as though they were trying to hammer their way in. When our father undid the bolts, there on the step was a young man, sweating and teetering on the edge of hysteria: 'Oh, Doctor, I say do ya help me. I get syphilis.' He babbled in Krio, fidgeting and jumping, utterly unable to contain himself. 'I able feel am crawling pan me skin.' He shuddered at that. We all did. 'I need *tchuk*.' He made the motion of giving himself an imaginary injection in the left arm. Our father, still half asleep, led him through to his surgery and treated him then and there. When the young man confessed he had no way of paying, our father waved him away.

A few weeks later my mother was out at night. She had been to a dance at the Diamond Corporation, alone because my father was working. On the way home she drove over a pothole and burst a tyre. The road was dark and empty as the DiaCorp compound was some way out of town; dense elephant grass grew up on either side to well over seven foot. She couldn't see a single light and within a few moments she began to consider her predicament: a woman, in an evening gown and high heels, without a torch on an empty road in the African bush. She had been there some time when she saw a car's headlights in the distance. Conflicting thoughts occupied her mind and she prayed that this was someone who would help her, perhaps someone else on their way back from the party.

As the car came closer she saw that it was dented and old, obviously belonging to a local because no European would drive a car in such a state. It drew alongside, slowed and stopped next to her. My mother could see that there were several young men inside.

'Na de doctor een wife,' someone announced. It was 'Tchuk'. He jumped out grinning and proud, evidently in the best of health. Within a few moments Tchuk and his companions changed the punctured tyre and saw her away.

By the time we had been in Koidu a year our father's name and reputation had spread for miles. As with my mother, everywhere he went people greeted us, yelled and waved at the passing car. Yet to me at that time he was a distant figure.

My days were spent in the house, playing with our dogs Jack and Jim, and being guarded by Big Aminatta. I say 'guarded' because that is just about what she did: she pursued her many chores around the house, of which I was just one. Her task was to make sure I didn't escape or run into trouble. She kept me within the confines of the compound by telling me of the devils lurking in the elephant grass beyond the screen of trees that marked the compound boundary. Devils with faces like gargoyles just waiting for the opportunity to feed on a child like me. At night she got me to clean my teeth with stories of cockroaches that crawled onto pillows and feasted on the crumbs left at the side of a sleeper's mouth.

At that time we had two Old English Sheepdogs. With their heavy coats they were hopelessly unsuited to both the humidity and the ticks that burrowed into their flesh, but they seemed to manage all the same. Given to us as puppies in Freetown, they were at first presumed to be mongrels until they grew into apparently full-blooded Old English Sheepdogs. My mother called them Jack and Jim and they were the only pedigree dogs I ever saw or have ever seen since in Sierra Leone. I spent my days tumbling with Jack and Jim in the yard and kissing them on the nose, playing in the dirt until I contracted enormous tropical boils, which my father lanced for me from time to time, and generally ingesting enough germs to give me a lifelong immunity to hepatitis. In the evening our father came back long after we were all in bed. He literally worked every hour of the day.

Morning, when our father went to the bathroom for his early constitutional, was our quality time together. The three of us followed him to the bathroom, carrying our colouring books, toys and stories. We sat on the floor around him, chatted, finished our drawings, showed him the work we had done the day before or persuaded him to read aloud to us. At some point I suppose he sent us on our way. I don't remember that, only lying on the lino colouring a picture of a princess for him.

From my three-foot-high perspective, my strongest memory of my father is from the waist down: mid-grey slacks, open sandals. I remember the exact shape and hue of his toenails, his strong, muscular thighs and rounded bottom, but the face on the top remains a blur on top of a vaguely light-coloured, short-sleeved shirt and stethoscope. He had a beard at that time, but my memory of him only truly begins when he shaved it off a few months before we left Koidu for good. Most of the time our worlds barely collided, and those moments when they did were the most memorable.

A deranged woman was brought to the clinic. I guess she must have been in her forties, although she looked much older. She snatched at the *lappa* she was wearing and at her blouse, screamed and started like a mare, and behaved as though unseen hands were pinching her or, I thought, tickling her armpits and squeezing her sides like my uncles did to me in a way that both hurt and made me howl at the same time. The more I shrieked the more they thought I was enjoying it and continued. The family said she was bewitched and they couldn't look after her any more, so our father put her in one of the rooms in our house, I think with the intention of sending her or driving her himself down to a mental hospital in Freetown. Later the same day I wandered past the window of the room where she was being held and saw her face staring at me behind the mesh of the fly screen. She shouted and her eyeballs reeled. I fled back to Big Aminatta.

Some time later in the afternoon she escaped. Nobody in the house knew how or when, but she couldn't have been gone long. My father raced to the car and the three of us leapt in behind him, standing on the plastic seats and blaring at the top of our voices that we were off to look for the madwoman. My father drove at speed telling us to keep a lookout; he seemed to be enjoying the adventure as much as we were. Everyone was making a riotous amount of noise and we felt no fear.

We hadn't been gone long when we saw her. She was standing at the side of the road, on the balls of her feet with her back pushed hard against a tree. Her shoulders were drawn up high and she was shrieking. Above her the tree was in flower, decorated with splendid, fleshy coral heads framed by thick petals that grew upright, like hands reaching to the sky. The orange and pink colours made the flamboyant tree look as if it were alight with burning candles. From a distance I could see the woman was staring at a branch from the tree that was lying in the middle of the road. She seemed to be fixated on it, as though it were alive. When we drew nearer I saw the branch wasn't what I thought at all, but a snake.

The car went straight over it, I felt the bump under my bottom and thighs. A moment later we were in reverse. My father kept going, changing gears backwards and forwards, until after a while

I couldn't feel the point where the snake's corpse lay on the road any longer. When we were certain it was dead we felt like heroes who had vanquished a dragon.

In my mind's eye the snake had been enormous, stretching the entire width of the road. As I grew older I thought perhaps I imagined it: no ordinary snake could really be that long. Now, I realise it was almost certainly a twig snake—six foot long, yes, but absolutely harmless. It wouldn't have wanted anything to do with the madwoman except perhaps to get past her up the tree to lie in peace on its favourite branch.

We drove home with the mad lady now sitting quite calmly between us in the back. The next day she went off to Freetown. I wasn't there when she was taken away, and when I discovered she was gone, I missed her.

7

My mud pies were too dry and the sides were crumbling. I'd sloshed water into the mess and begun to swill it all with a stick when Pa Roke showed up. He was my grandfather. Everything about him—the way he dressed in long embroidered gowns with a matching fez or skull cap, his solemn bearing and formal manners—came from a different age of Africa, one that still existed among the rural people for whom life hadn't changed in centuries, but was disappearing everywhere else.

Whenever my grandfather arrived he seemed to materialise out of nowhere. Although I'm sure he must have carried his clothes in a bundle, he never appeared to have anything resembling luggage. And when he walked into the compound there was no evidence of the means of transportation he had taken, no bush taxi disappearing in a whirl of dust, no car or bus. Not even a bicycle. He looked as though he had just come from the end of the road instead of Magburaka, where he lived, a whole day's travel away. By necessity, since there were no telephones and no mail service to speak of, he arrived unannounced and would stay for a few days or sometimes a few weeks.

Because I was the only one at home and he seemed to have little to do during those visits except wait for my father, Pa Roke and I spent our days in each other's company—although it's true to say that there was very little contact between the two of us. Pa Roke sat around the house, calling occasionally to Big Aminatta to fetch and carry for him, and for the most part ignored me,

though it gave me some small pleasure to see Big Aminatta, my
own constant nemesis, being ordered around.

Big Aminatta was in awe of Pa Roke, an awe which struck so
deep into her core it even altered the way she walked. Usually
she swayed her bottom and slid her flip-flopped feet across the
floor so that they made an insolent sort of sound, like a market
woman hissing through her teeth. In front of our grandfather she
took short, fast steps and moved around at quite a clip. She was
permanently bent at the waist, as though stuck in a half-curtsy,
and she never spoke to him, except to say, 'Yes, Pa,' keeping her
eyes lowered all the while.

I suspect Pa Roke had little time for me. By my age most children were beginning to learn how to be useful. They were started
on the smallest of errands, fetching and carrying glasses of water
and passing items to their mother. European child that I was,
at least in part, I did nothing all day except make mud pies and
attempt to divert adult attention. Every now and again I felt Pa
Roke watching me, but when I looked at him appealingly I never
elicited much by way of response.

In the afternoon Pa Roke accompanied my mother and me
on our rounds, taking my place in the front of the car while I
was relegated to the back seat. My mother communicated to him
using improvised sign language and practising the Temne she
had picked up. Her Krio by that time was quite good too, and
Pa Roke understood her a little. When all else failed she spoke
loudly in English, affecting an African accent, smiling brilliantly.
Pa Roke said little but nodded agreeably and smiled back at her,
showing the gaps in his teeth, or rather, since he had so few, it
would be more accurate to say he displayed the teeth in the gap
of his mouth.

He and my mother rubbed along, watching each other through
the veils of age, race, gender, language and culture. They seemed

fond of each other in the way visitors like the locals in a new place, where everyone welcomes them and people are reduced to cartoons of themselves without nuance, detail or subtlety: a superficial world where everyone laughs and exchanges are full of feigned bonhomie.

When my father arrived home later in the day a transformation came over Pa Roke. He filled out into a real person, talking and laughing, suffering the occasional coughing fit. He even seemed to notice I was in the room and he asked my father about us, pointing in our direction every now and again.

Pa Roke wore *mukay,* pointed leather shoes, that men used as slippers with the back trodden down. He would slip them off and cross his bare feet at the ankle. Likewise my father took off his sandals. This signalled the beginning of their sessions. They talked for hours together in Temne, who knows what about, since I couldn't understand a word they said. Perhaps they discussed the cases Pa Roke judged in the villages. My father once took my mother to Magburaka to watch Pa Roke sitting in the *barrie* and listening to the people's grievances. One particular case involved a woman and three men. My father explained to my mother that they were watching a paternity suit. My mother tried to follow the proceedings for a while. Then she nudged my father and asked him whether the woman had been asked to name one of these men as the father. My father shook his head. No, he had explained, each of these men wishes to claim the child as his own. No man would ever give up a child that might be his.

A few days into his visit Pa Roke and I had lunch alone together. Everyone else was out: Sheka and Memuna at school; my father had a meal sent to him at the downtown surgery and my mother had plenty of other things to do. Before the meal my grandfather pulled out a small straw prayer mat with a picture of a mosque on it in black and red and laid it down on the ground. His *mukay* were left discarded on the tiled floor as he stepped onto the mat. He stood still with his hands at his side, his head bent, then he knelt, hands resting on his thighs, palms to the heavens in a gesture of supplication. It was beautiful to watch him kneeling and stretching his body out to touch the floor with his forehead with the grace of a water bird stretching its neck out across the surface of a lake.

A time would come when I would be made uncomfortable if I was caught in a room with someone who was praying, never knowing whether to go about my business and pretend I hadn't noticed them or keep still out of reverence. My father was a Muslim, yet we had not been brought up in any particular faith. I had a Muslim name and all my relatives regarded me as a Muslim, but I had never been into a mosque or held a Koran.

It happened once that I came across Pa Roke at his midday prayers and the idea lodged in my head that I should be praying, too. So I knelt behind him, copying all his movements with no earthly idea what it all meant. Halfway through I began to feel foolish and decided to extricate myself, but that posed a new difficulty: to sidle away midway through prayers seemed sinful; at the same time I worried my grandfather might think I was making fun of him. I couldn't make the decision, so I went on, standing, kneeling and bowing for what seemed like eternity. When he finished, he stood up, rolled his mat and walked away without looking back or acknowledging that I was there. I didn't get the impression he was angry. Rather that he understood, better than I, the struggle that had played out in my young mind.

Pa Roke was used to eating with his hands, although sometimes he used just a spoon. Before his prayers and again afterwards he called for Big Aminatta to bring a basin of water and she held it, bracing under the weight, while he washed his hands elaborately and shook the water from his long fingers. We had a bathroom with running water, but it didn't seem to occur to him to get up and go and use it. He was just used to a different life, one in which one of the young girls in the family fetched him water from the stream every morning.

Lunch that day was groundnut stew and rice, made with plenty of hot cayenne pepper, chicken and beef stewed for hours in a stock thickened with finely ground peanuts, which Big Aminatta roasted and crushed using an empty bottle as a rolling pin. The local chickens were so tough she had to boil them up for ages with onions and tomatoes. But once cooked they were tender and full of flavour. She added small pieces of hairy, cured fish which gave off a strong, smoky taste. Groundnut stew was one of my favourite dishes.

Pa Roke worked his way through the food on his plate until there was nothing left but a small pile of chicken bones. These he picked up one by one, and devoured them methodically. First he bit off the soft tissue and cartilage. Then he slowly chewed the knuckles at either end. Finally, he cracked the fragile, splintering bone with his back teeth and licked out the dark marrow. When he had finished there was nothing, but nothing, left of the fowl to speak of. I had never seen anything like it.

I was brought up to chew my bones; they were good for my teeth and the marrow full of vitamins. But I was sickened by the rubbery, slippery texture of the cartilage in my mouth and I left those pieces discarded on my plate. The grainy, soft ends of the bones I liked, but though I usually chewed them I stopped short of attacking the shaft of the bone with its sharp, jagged slivers.

I always called my grandfather Pa Roke. All my uncles, aunts and cousins did the same and even those people who were not related to us. It never occurred to me that this was not his name and I was well into adulthood when I made the discovery that Pa Roke wasn't a name, it was a title: Pa Roke, Regent Chief of Kholifa Mamunta.

* * *

In the 1880s the chiefs of Temneland double-crossed a fearless young warrior by the name of Gbanka, whom they had hired to fight the Mende people and force open the trade routes to the Bumpe and Ribi rivers. Gbanka was born of a Mende mother and a Temne father. When he realised he had been cheated he went to his mother's people, whom he had just defeated, and allied himself to them. There he swore a bloody revenge upon the Temne people and over the coming years he captured town after town in Temneland.

My great-grandfather Pa Morlai was a Loko and a warrior from Bombali. At the time Loko fighters were amongst the most skilled in the land. They had long-standing connections to the Mende people and an interest in the lucrative trade with the Europeans who sailed their ships far up the rivers into the interior looking for gold and ivory. When the Temnes fought back against Gbanka's war boys, the Loko were drawn into battle on the side of the Mendes.

Pa Morlai captured and became commander in charge of the town of Mamunta, in Tonkolili, deep inside Temneland. When finally Gbanka was captured and imprisoned by the British, who soon tired when the fighting began to disrupt trading, Pa Morlai left Mamunta to return to his village. Matoko was on the other side of the Katabai Hills and when Pa Morlai entered the home of his birth he was a wealthy man, bearing the spoils of his war, including a sizeable retinue of slaves.

Among those wearing the round wooden collar of the enslaved was a young girl of twelve or thirteen called Beyas. Pa Morlai presented Beyas as a gift to his mother Ya Yalie to raise—a companion who would help her around the house and in the fields.

Beyas was the daughter of Masamunta Akaik, literally Chief Big Beard, of the Kamaras, one of the ruling families of Mamunta. As a slave with an aristocratic bloodline she was a trophy. And as she went about her tasks she impressed Ya Yalie with the delicacy of her demeanour: one day, when Beyas was about fifteen and was maturing into womanhood, the older woman went to her son and suggested that he take Beyas as one of his wives.

Beyas and Pa Morlai had four children together: three sons and one daughter. The years passed but Beyas, now called Ya Beyas by everyone in recognition of her status as a mother, never grew accustomed to her life. For all that she was married to a big man, she was still a slave.

One day, more than twenty years after Ya Beyas arrived in Matoko, a trader appeared at the marketplace selling round baskets of different sizes. They were woven out of coloured raffia and known as *shuku*, which people used to store clothes or pack their belongings for journeys. At the sight of him Ya Beyas became distraught and none of her children, who had accompanied her that day, could fathom what had upset her so much. Ya Beyas waved them away; refused their solicitations. She wanted to talk to the basket weaver alone. For a few minutes the two conferred, then Ya Beyas, seemingly much recovered, returned home and did not speak of the matter again. In time the incident was completely forgotten—by everyone, that is, except Ya Beyas.

The weavers of Mamunta are renowned for their basketry. Ya Beyas recognised the intricate weave, the bands of turquoise and mauve that made up the design, which came from her home. Secretly she had sent a message with the trader to take to her brothers (she was certain that by now Masamunta Akaik was dead), telling them she was enslaved in Matoko. She begged them to find her and redeem her.

It took a whole year for the basket seller to complete his travels and return to Matoko. When she began to expect him back Ya Beyas invented every kind of excuse to go to the market by herself. Eventually one morning she saw the man sitting behind his huge pile of *shuku* and her heart lifted. But the trader had failed in his task. He had nothing to say for himself except that he had somehow forgotten.

Not one of my elderly aunts, who recounted the story of Ya Beyas to me, could tell me how or why he should do so. But they were clear: he had forgotten. He had not been waylaid or confused, found her family had disappeared or never returned to Mamunta. He forgot. Perhaps, I thought to myself as I listened, he drank too much *omole*.

Again Ya Beyas begged him to take a message and the trader promised that this time it would get there. In the meantime she resigned herself to twelve more months in Matoko.

The trader was true to his word. Some months later two of Ya Beyas's brothers, Pa Santigi Kamara and Pa Yambas Sana, arrived in Mamunta, splendidly attired in gold-embroidered robes as befitted their status, followed by retainers carrying everything required formally to redeem their stolen sister: a barrel of palm oil, a sack of rice, a cow, a sack of pure salt, a tie of tobacco leaves, one woven country cloth and four silver shillings. These gifts they presented in the *barrie* before the paramount chief, the elders and Pa Morlai. When the ceremony was over Ya Beyas was a free woman.

Ya Beyas wanted nothing more than to go back to Mamunta to see her family, but Pa Morlai was loath to allow her to leave. She might no longer be a slave, but as his wife she had to obey her husband. A sore on her foot had turned septic, and Pa Morlai insisted that she stay under the care of his healer until she could walk properly.

The seasons had run through twice more by the time Ya Beyas wore her husband down. He seemed to find an unlimited number of new reasons why she should stay in Bombali and he obliged her to do his bidding. At last he relented and agreed to the journey. Ya Beyas wanted her daughter Hawa to accompany her, but Pa Morlai imposed his will one last time and refused to allow it, for the young woman was betrothed to a youth in Matoko. He suggested she travel with their second son Saidu instead.

Pa Morlai waited in his house in Matoko for Ya Beyas to return, but the rains came and went and there was no sign of her. Unlike his wife, who had learned patience, Pa Morlai was not born with a great deal and his small store soon ran out. One morning he rose, walked to the door of his house, snapped his fingers to summon his retainers and ordered them to begin preparations for a journey. Within a short time he and his entourage were ready and they set out, back across the Katabai Hills to Temneland, carrying with them a large calabash.

In Mamunta Pa Morlai stood before Pa Santigi's house, knocked and waited. After a few moments he knocked again. The third time the door was answered and he entered.

In front of him walked a delicate girl, his youngest niece, who carried the tremendous calabash on her head. Under the weight of it her neck swayed like a pawpaw tree overburdened by fruit. The room within was full of people. Trembling, the girl laid the calabash at the feet of Pa Santigi, who sat cross-legged on a low stool. He looked inside and helped himself to a few of the cola nuts before passing the rest around the assembled company. After a few moments he looked expectantly at Pa Morlai, the conqueror now turned supplicant, who cleared his throat and announced his business.

'I have seen a flower,' he said, using the customary words of a prospective bridegroom in the house of his beloved. 'And that flower is growing here, in the house of the Kamaras.'

Pa Santigi gave a signal and three girls were brought forth. The first one advanced and stood before Pa Morlai. Her face was covered by a cloth and he carefully raised it. No—he shook his head. Each woman was presented and each time, even though they were fresh and lovely, he looked at the woman he had been offered, declined and waited.

The three young women left through the door and stood outside, where their muffled giggles could be heard in the stately silence of the room. A fourth figure appeared at the door: rings of age thickened her waist and her neck; as she moved she dragged her foot slightly. Pa Morlai had no need to raise the cloth that covered her face. He nodded. 'Here is my flower.'

In front of her gathered family—elders, brothers, uncles, aunts, cousins, nephews and nieces—Ya Beyas paused; then she bent and picked up the calabash. With that gesture she accepted Pa Morlai as her husband, not as a slave, but as a free woman. She sat on the floor next to her elder brother with the calabash containing her bride gift on her lap.

Inside Ya Beyas's wedding calabash were cola nuts, a symbol of friendship; bitter cola nuts to represent hardship; a prayer mat; a head of tobacco for the elders who would counsel the couple through the highs and lows of married life; *atara* alligator pepper which, if the seeds were kept in the pod, would for ever bring peace to a union; and a needle and thread, to remind the bride of her wifely duty. And finally, at the bottom of the pot, in gold, silver and precious stones was the measure of her worth as a woman.

A few days after the ceremony Pa Morlai prepared to leave Mamunta for Matoko. He went to Ya Beyas and told her he planned to leave. He assumed she would accompany him, but he was careful to couch his command as a request. 'So, Beyas, it's time for you to say goodbye to your family. We should leave for Matoko in a few days.'

Ya Beyas looked at her husband. Pa Morlai was nearly seventy, an old man, and she was already middle-aged. She let her eyes linger on his face, his eyes, his mouth. He was her captor, her owner, her husband and the father of her children. She looked down and replied slowly, barely audibly: 'No, my husband. I will not.' This was Ya Beyas's sole act of defiance in her entire life: a life lived as a daughter, sister, slave and junior wife.

And so Pa Morlai returned alone to Matoko, where he died some years later. Ya Beyas stayed in Mamunta, with her son Saidu. And no one knows, to this day, whether Pa Morlai and Ya Beyas ever laid eyes on each other again after their wedding day.

8

Once Pa Roke noticed me. I was following a line of ants across the ground to the entrance into their nest, a hole by the roots of the mango tree. Above me the trunk of the tree seethed with ants. I was placing obstacles in the path of the column to see whether the ants would break formation. When Pa Roke's shadow fell across me, I had just laid a long stick on the ground in front of them.

I fancied I knew how the ants communicated with each other. When the giant obstacle suddenly appeared across their path, a couple of ants raced each way some distance down the length of the stick. They were the scouts. The others, the bearers, waited patiently with their loads. The scout ants came back and reported that there was no way of going round the object, it would take too long. They would have to climb over. The other ants waved their antennae in agreement, or so I imagined. And without delay an advance party set out up and over the stick.

The lives of ants could hold me spellbound for hours. There were the regular black ones that everyone knew. Then there were the tiny red ones—they were the ones that gave you stinging bites. If you stood near their nest they swarmed up your leg and sank thousands of tiny teeth into you, leaving painful red marks. Several times the size of the ordinary ants were the giant ones, which could be either red or black. They were harmless, but discouragingly large. Overall the black ants were by far and away the friendlier of the species.

There were ant hills all over the surrounding country. Acre upon acre turned to moonscape by the giant moguls, often interspersed

with termite hills that towered over the ant hills like giant stalag-
mite fortresses. War raged constantly between the armies of the
termites, the red ants and the black ants. They killed, captured
and enslaved each other.

I once saw red ants swarming over one of the big black ants; it
staggered like a bull brought down by a pack of wild dogs, helpless
as the red ants began to eat it alive. When it stopped struggling
they carried it away, still twitching, even though it was several
times bigger than each of them. Much later, someone told me
that the only two species who wage war against their own kind
are ants and men.

Pa Roke watched me for a short while and then he beckoned
to me to follow him. We went a little way to the edge of the compound where the earth was soft and sandy. There were several
funnel-shaped holes, each barely an inch across. Pa Roke waved,
indicating to me to crouch down and watch. He picked up a dried
leaf and broke off a fraction of the tip and dropped it over the
rim of the tiny crater.

'What is it?' I asked. Pa Roke put his finger to his lips.

For a few seconds nothing happened. We waited. I began to
think there was something wrong with Pa Roke. But when I
glanced up at him to check, he pointed impatiently back at the
ground. I looked back and the piece of leaf was gone. A second
later it came flying out of the hole and landed on the ground by
my feet. I started. Pa Roke laughed, a short, hoarse sound. He
looked genuinely amused.

A small, black ant wandered by. Pa Roke used the edge of the
leaf still in his hand to ease it over the edge of the hole. As the
ant slid down the sandy incline, it began to scrabble desperately,
raking the smooth sides as it failed to find a grip. When it reached
the bottom it waved its antennae around, apparently trying to get
its bearings. I knew now what was going to happen. There was a

tiny flurry. The ant reared up and then disappeared beneath the sand, its angular legs the last to go under.

'Ant lion,' said Pa Roke. And he got up and nimbly stepped back up to the house, his robes flapping behind him like a great bird.

I fetched a stick and poked around the sand in the hole. I wanted to save the ant. I unearthed an insect the shape of a miniature armadillo; it was still holding on to the ant, which had accepted its fate and stopped kicking. But freed from the earth the ant seemed to fight with renewed vigour. The ant lion gave up, retreating back under the sand while the ant hobbled away: a crumpled body on broken legs.

In Mamunta, Pa Santigi, brother to Ya Beyas, decided to run for the forthcoming chieftaincy elections. The chieftaincy rotated between the three ruling families and the last ruler had died some months before. Now the elders were busy organising elections for a new king, though since the arrival of the British there were officially no more kings, only paramount chiefs. When the protectorate was brought under British colonial rule the newly installed governor declared the only recognised sovereign from that day on was Victoria, Queen of England.

Ya Beyas's son Saidu helped in the elections, canvassing votes for his uncle among the people of the outlying villages. Now a grown man with two wives, he had moved away from Mamunta and farmed at a small settlement called Rogbonko. He spent many days and weeks on the campaign trail, sometimes taking his two children to accompany him.

Nearing the crucial run-up to the election, Pa Santigi's campaign began to run out of funds. The uncles needed to raise cash in the fastest way possible and they decided to sell their nephew Saidu into bondage to a wealthy farmer in Mayoso. There he worked long days and slept in the fields at night alongside other indentured men and prayed that his uncle would win the election and redeem him as soon as possible.

A year later Saidu found himself living in the forest, taking part in the *kantha* of his uncle, now Chief Masamunta Kanakoton of Kholifa Mamunta. Though he was still young his political skills and commitment were evident and Saidu was to be honoured with the title Pa Mas'm, chief minister and principal adviser to the new king. For months the king and his ministers stayed hidden beyond the darkness of the trees in the sacred bush, where they learned the principles of governance from the elders and took part in induction rituals carried out by the secret society, the Poro.

At the end of this came the three-day *kathora*, the ceremony to install the new ruler. On Chief Masamunta's head sat the stiff, embroidered head-dress; on his chest lay a heavy necklace of amulets and animals' teeth and he carried a long, forked staff covered with leather and adorned with fragments of leopard skin. He led his cabinet forward into the village to the *barrie* and they circled it thrice before they entered and took up their places.

Weeks later the new Pa Mas'm returned to Rogbonko only to find that in his absence his two wives had quarrelled badly. Ya Monday G'bai, a mature widow inherited by Saidu from an uncle on his passing, had departed. According to custom she left her son, and also the message that she had gone back to live in peace with her own family. Now Yima, Saidu's spirited and mischievous younger wife, claimed for herself the role of first wife to the Pa Mas'm.

It was Ya Yima who, passing through Rothomgbai one day on her way back from Mamunta (where her husband now kept a second home in order to attend to his court duties), noticed a girl standing by the side of the path carrying a water jug. There were four miles more to Rogbonko and Ya Yima asked the child for a drink. As she watched the girl quickly pour the water she was impressed by the girl's demure manner. Yima made enquiries. She found out the child's name was Ndora; she was the daughter of Yamba Soko Serry and Digba Kamara and the great-granddaughter of a chief.

It was at Ya Yima's instigation that Ndora became Saidu's sixth wife and went to live in Rogbonko. Ya Yima herself made all the arrangements. For the first few years Ndora helped the older wives around the house. She fetched water for her husband in the mornings. Late in the day she joined the other young girls down by the stream in the deep channel that ran behind the clay-brick houses; they scrubbed clothes, pounding them against the rocks, creating a froth of suds, while cascades of water drops made rainbows above their heads, flashing the same vibrant colours of the kingfishers on the opposite bank.

Some time after her first blood showed, Ndora went to her husband's room. On the first occasion she was carried, according to custom, on the back of one of the senior wives. From then on she spent three nights with Saidu in turn with each of her co-wives. Ndora named her first son Morlai and suckled him for two years. The second child, another son called Mohamed, was born after the harvest in the month of *tarokans,* a year after Morlai began to eat his first mouthfuls of pap.

Ya Yima was entranced by Ndora's fat, bright new son. After Mohamed was weaned she insisted on taking over care of the baby herself and, ignoring Ndora's protests, she brought the child into the big house she shared with Saidu. Ndora was left outside. Yima passed her time playing with the little boy, while Ndora worked long days in the fields side by side with the other junior wives and the indentured men. Sometimes on her way home, she would go by and take little treats to her son: a catapult she made herself or a little piece of canya made of rice flour, sugar and peanuts.

Months passed and still Ya Yima kept little Mohamed by her side. She brushed aside all Ndora's entreaties. Didn't she take good care of him? Besides Ndora was so busy. And the little boy was happy, said Ya Yima.

When all else failed Ndora determined to bypass her senior wife's authority and beg her husband in order to have her child returned to her. Saidu, by now, was used to Ya Yima's wilfulness. It came as no surprise she had upset a co-wife; nevertheless he did not expect to have to intervene in their concerns. He told Ndora he would handle the matter himself, to be patient and not to worry. But when Ya Yima refused to listen to even his efforts to persuade her, he lost his temper and ordered her to return the boy to Ndora.

Ndora sent her son to join his brother Morlai at the home of an aunt in Rothomgbai. One night a snake crept into the hut where several children lay sleeping side by side on a mat. A few minutes later Mohamed woke screaming, with two small puncture wounds on his foot. The poison lodged in his foot: he survived, though nearly lost the foot. Not one of the other children was harmed. A diviner was brought in and an investigation mounted. There was only one explanation: witchcraft. Suspicion fell on many and rumours rustled through the villages: Who had seen a soul stir? What old grudges were borne? Who else might fall ill? Nothing was ever proved.

Realising the folly of his actions had put his own son in danger, Saidu immediately brought the child back to Rogbonko into his own home, and returned him to the arms of Ya Yima.

Two years later war broke out in Europe. Up in Rogbonko at first it had little impact. But after the British lost control of the Mediterranean and were forced to route their supplies bound for the east through Africa, they were attracted for the same reasons as the slaving ships two hundred years before to Freetown's deep natural harbour. Men from the protectorate were recruited to fill the demand for cheap labour, including many from Mamunta and the surrounding villages. Thousands more were drafted to fight the Japanese in the jungles of Burma. There was an even greater demand for produce for export and yet the prices offered by the colonial rulers never improved. With the extra hands gone from the fields, life grew hard for everyone in the villages.

Ndora began to lose weight. The white doctors at the hospital failed to heal her, so the family turned to their own medicine. The day came when Ndora couldn't climb up off her sleeping mat. Fearing the worst the family sent for the healer, Pa Yamba Mela, at the house Pa Mas'm provided for him in the Fornas' compound.

Pa Yamba Mela arrived at Ndora's bedside carrying his divining thunder box. He was as handsome as he was terrible; it was he who smelled the odour of magic behind the snakebite on Mohamed's foot and again when the boy was struck with smallpox some years later. People for miles around claimed Pa Yamba Mela could even draw thunder out of the sky to strike wrongdoers down. Indeed, it had been known to happen to some errant souls who had committed God knows what crime. They were found lying in the fields or under a tree during the rains. Some died; the others were never the same again.

The medicine man knew immediately he had found the culprit. Only by confessing to dabbling in witchcraft could Ndora save her own life; she had become ensnared in the power of the rites she had tried to use for her own purposes and now she was being consumed from within. All day Pa Yamba Mela stayed with her mouthing incantations and exhorting the dying woman to admit her guilt, even as the delirium overwhelmed her. Finally, just before her last breath slipped over her lips and mingled with the air, Ndora confessed.

Shortly afterwards Chief Masamunta passed away and his spirit
flew home to Futa Jallon, the home of the Temne kings. Before he
was interred his head was removed, to be preserved and buried
alongside the next king, whose own head would be buried with
the next and so on in perpetuity. Chief Masamunta's Pa Mas'm,
Saidu Forna, presided over the burial rituals and was afterwards
elected to take the place of the dead ruler: he was anointed Pa
Roke, Regent Chief of Kholifa Mamunta.

While the other children were raised by their mothers, my
father grew up in my grandfather's house. And so, even though
Mohamed was only the younger son of a junior wife, Pa Roke
came to favour our father above his other children.

It may have been the weekend. At any rate, unusually for the time
of day, my father was in the house. The sun was high, so it must
have been early afternoon, at the time when everyone had just
eaten lunch. At the back of the house Big Aminatta filled the dogs'
bowls with scraps from the table and put them out in the yard.

'Daddy?' A moment later I trotted to my father, who was sitting
on the veranda with my mother. I scarcely allowed a moment to
slip past before I began again: 'Daddy?'

'Yes, Am.'

'Jack's making a funny noise.'

Everyone followed me round the side of the house. I was right.
There was Jack, the Old English Sheepdog, standing with his head
low, his stomach in spasms, heaving violently. With each painful
contraction he gave a wheezing noise and a sort of hacking bark.
He looked like dogs do when they are trying to be sick, but I'd
never heard one make that noise before.

Jack had a chicken bone stuck in his throat. The walls of his
oesophagus were torn and with each effort he made to dislodge

it the sharp fragment of bone tore deeper into the wall of muscle. The pain must have been terrible. My father grasped the dog
and, gripping Jack between his legs, bent over and prised his jaws
open. Then he plunged his hand deep into the dog's throat. You
could see him feeling down inside the dog's gullet. He pulled his
arm out and tried again, over and over. And Jack just let him. He
didn't snap or wriggle; he submitted as though he already knew
this was his only chance at life.

Minutes seemed to pass. The whole family watched and waited.
There was nothing anyone else could do.

When my father realised the bone was too deeply embedded
and it would take an operation to free it, he went to fetch his medical kit. There was no vet in Koidu. By this time Jack was feeble
and had begun to whimper. My father took out a needle and sy-
ringe and gave Jack a dose of the anaesthetic normally reserved
for humans. The hacking and whimpering stopped. Jack's body
relaxed and he stopped breathing.

For most of my life that image was all I could summon of my
earliest years. I was very young the day Jack died but I remember vividly the sight of my father standing over him with his arm
down the dog's throat.

Afterwards my parents explained to me what had happened,
although I wasn't overly distraught because I didn't have any understanding of what death meant. Gradually as the days went on I
watched Jim prowl the yard looking for his brother and playmate,
or lie listless in the shade and howl at night.

The next time Pa Roke visited and I saw him demolishing a
chicken bone I thought: How come Jack dies and Pa Roke doesn't?

Soon after that Pa Roke left us and returned home, departing
as he came. He walked to the end of the road and vanished into
the wind.

9

Our house and compound were my entire world and together they created a dizzying universe. Two mango trees stood like sentries in front of the veranda of our house, overshadowing the corrugated iron roof. Despite the fact we had no air-conditioning and perhaps because of the trees, the house stayed reasonably cool even on those days when the temperature outside reached forty degrees. Koidu was far inland, lying in the sweaty pit between three bodies of mountains and there was rarely even a light breeze to break the torpor.

Our part of the building, the front wing of the house, was modest and consisted of no more than a couple of bedrooms and an open living area. Farther back the rest of the space was given over to my father's surgery and the drug store. There was a spare bedroom next to the store, where the mad lady stayed for a day and a night. A narrow walkway joined the living quarters to the obstetrics ward behind and there were toilets and showers on the left: one for the family and the other for the patients.

The door of our house was always open and people wandered in and out of my world. From the moment they crossed the threshold they were given flesh and blood, voices, laughter and life: humans and animals, chickens, even the slow-moving chameleon I followed as it made its way across the dirt. I was a child, I lived my life in the moment. For me people existed only when I could see them. When they left, as far as I was concerned their flesh turned into air and they ceased to be.

The appearance of visitors at all times of day and night annoyed my mother. She didn't like strangers coming into the house, especially when they expected to wait there for my father. Often men arrived claiming to be brothers all the way from Magburaka. By then my father was practically supporting his whole family, paying school fees for children and helping out in dozens of different ways; the list of requests was never-ending and the appearance of a visitor certainly meant someone in need. My uncles had been educated by the Imam according to Islamic custom, and in virtually every way they still lived the existence of their forefathers in the villages. By pure chance my father alone had acquired the skills to survive in a modern world.

When the brothers arrived my mother asked them to come back another time. She complained to my father about the constant visitors, but when he heard she had turned his brothers away without offering them a drink or anything to eat he was incensed. Her behaviour offended his family greatly. In return my mother demanded hotly to know what she was supposed to do—she couldn't remember them all: my father had twenty-eight brothers and nineteen sisters. Fortunately for my mother, his sisters rarely, if ever, managed to make the journey.

Besides the patients and the trail of uncles, another group of people became regular visitors at the house. They were young men, most of whom didn't ask to come in but sat on the veranda, and the murmuring sounds of their conversation drifted through the house. Other times they simply sat in silence. When I skipped past with my hand in my mother's they always greeted her most respectfully.

One or two men would go straight into my father's surgery. After a couple of hours they would come out and the waiting men would jump up. Everyone would mill about, exchanging greetings. They'd all take turns shaking my father's hand, nodding when he said a few words to them: 'Yes, doctor, yes, doctor.' The men who'd been in his office would clap him on the shoulder, with ca- maraderie. Then they'd all leave together, squeezing into a couple of old cars, and my father would turn to go back to his surgery.

All the time we had been living in Sierra Leone talk was grow- ing of a one-party state there. The ruling SLPP (Sierra Leone Peo- ple's Party) had come under the leadership of Albert Margai, the younger brother of Sir Milton Margai, who had passed away. Al- though the prime minister was known to be gravely ill, a troubling rumour persisted that Albert had dispatched him early in order to avoid allowing Sir Milton to hand over to his protégé, John Karefa- Smart. Everyone in the country assumed Karefa-Smart, who was also a doctor and Sir Milton's confidant and evident favourite, would be the next leader of the country. But instead a series of po- litical manoeuvres ousted him from the cabinet. Accompanied by his American-born wife and children he fled the country, claiming he had become the target of a campaign of harassment.

Once in power, Albert, a British-trained lawyer, tabled propos- als to change the constitution with the aim of introducing a one- party state. In Ghana, Nkrumah was the first African leader to take his country down the path to becoming a single-party state. He claimed multi-party democracy encouraged ethnic divisions and drew too much energy from the real business of social and economic development. Soon African leaders by the score were following Nkrumah's lead; they too insisted that only this way could their emergent nations acquire the stability they needed. Kenyatta in Kenya, Nyerere in Tanzania, Kaunda in Zambia, and Banda in Malawi all moved towards a unitary system of govern- ment. And this they did with the tacit blessing of their former colonial rulers who, in the climate of the Cold War, preferred to back dictators they knew rather than leave the door open to new leaders with different, possibly left-wing, sympathies.

In Sierra Leone, especially in Freetown with its entrenched, well-educated Krio population, Albert Margai's proposals were seen as a transparent attempt to hold on to power by the SLPP. Besides, Margai was accused of introducing precisely the kind of Mende tribal hegemony he now argued could only be redressed by changing the constitution. The press was busy unmasking incidences of ministerial corruption, and every day stories and rumours appeared in the notorious 'Titbits' column of the opposition *We Yone* newspaper. The country was in serious financial straits, already mortgaged to the IMF and defaulting on foreign loans.

My father's reputation, boosted in Koidu by his work as a doctor, had in fact begun to grow much earlier. When my parents first returned from Scotland he went to work for the government medical services at Princess Christian and Connaught hospitals. There he and the other young doctors, who had been trained in a National Health Service less than ten years old in Britain, were appalled by the standards in force in Freetown. Nurses frequently disobeyed the doctors' orders; equipment wasn't properly sterilised; supplies were pilfered. One day my father lost his temper at the discovery of stillborn babies left stacked on shelves in the maternity delivery room, where other women came to give birth.

The young doctors organised protests to the minister of health, with my father acting as one of the leaders. But despite the assurances they received, change if it came at all was slow. When our father's frustrations reached a zenith he found himself summoned to the minister's office. Eventually, a solution was agreed. He was given his own hospital to run: the military hospital at Wilberforce barracks with his old comrade Dr Panda; the two men determined to run it as a model hospital.

There's a picture of us together at the time. Me, wearing a pale dress with white ribbons in my hair, in the arms of this army officer, my father, who is so smart and proud of himself. I was only two years old then, but I fancy I can really remember the touch of that rough serge and the feel of his newly shaved chin. At the time we hadn't yet moved into the barracks at Wilberforce, but were still living in the government bungalow given to us when my father worked in the hospitals. It was opposite Graham Greene's famous City Hotel, and at night you could hear the prostitutes hurling personal insults at each other as they vied for clients. On that first morning a friend of my father's, an army major, came round early to dress him. He demonstrated the correct way to knot his tie, the proper angle for his cap, the way to wear each and every item of his uniform. Afterwards my father and I posed for our photograph.

The army had recently come under the authority of Brigadier David Lansana. He was the first native-born force commander, a Mende, and popularly seen as a Margai stooge. A few months after my father arrived a young woman appeared at the military hospital. She was pregnant and wanted an abortion. Abortion was illegal in Sierra Leone and my father declined her request. Some time later the force commander called the new doctor and, as his superior officer, commanded him to perform the operation. Both my father and Dr Panda resisted. They resigned their commissions in protest, but this only enraged Lansana more. He wanted them court-martialled for disobedience—my father especially, for his insolence. When the brigadier was advised his authority did not extend to medical personnel he tried to have him dispatched to Kabala, the most remote outpost imaginable.

For a short while the case became something of a *cause célèbre* in Freetown. My father's self-assurance had always bordered on arrogance and he refused to budge an inch. I believe he probably enjoyed the stand-off. The privates, who already respected him for his dedication as a medical officer, loved him even more for standing up to Lansana and they were vocal in their support. Lansana was forced to back down. Our father left to set up his own practice. He had worn his olive green uniform for less than six months.

All the time Lansana was persecuting him, my father never revealed the incident which was the cause of their argument. He could easily have done so. It would have publicly humiliated Lansana and brought a halt to the whole debacle, but it would have meant breaking his doctor's oath of confidence to the young woman. The issue, as far as he and Dr Panda were concerned, remained their authority as doctors to determine the use of the hospital facilities.

The story quickly reached members of the opposition party, the All People's Congress, who searched our father out and asked him to join in their struggle. Two of his close friends were already APC activists: Ibrahim and Mohammed Bash Taqi, Temnes like us, who even came from Tonkolili, the same district as the Fornas. Ibrahim was the man behind the 'Titbits' column, a dedicated journalist obsessed with amassing evidence of SLPP corruption. He had once been a laboratory assistant while my father was head boy at Bo School; they next met when Ibrahim covered the independence negotiations in London, dashing between Lancaster House and the telex office to brief his newspaper. He was an ebullient and tireless man. Taqi in Temne means 'troublemaker', and as far as the SLPP was concerned the Taqis lived up to their name. Mohammed, a chain-smoker who wore a toothbrush moustache and had bright, melancholy eyes and hunched shoulders, was the quieter of the two. To the world he was known as M.O.; I called him Uncle Bash.

In Freetown my father resisted joining the APC. He had long opposed the activities of the SLPP, but at the time he was still convinced his calling lay as a doctor. In Koidu he spent every day working with people who died of easily preventable diseases, whose life expectancy was well below forty and whose children's stomachs were bloated with malnutrition. It didn't matter that he worked all day and most of the night, drove himself to the point of exhaustion, the cure for the malaise lay beyond the talents of any doctor.

Every day for over forty years the Sierra Leone Selection Trust had wrenched minerals by the ton from the river beds, leaving red earth exposed like suppurating sores across the landscape. Every week the De Beers plane flew another consignment of diamonds out of the country. Before independence, diamonds were merely the spoils of conquest; of the money the company now paid to the government in Freetown as taxes in return for the diamond concession there was no evidence in Koidu, which remained as backward as ever. Inside the company compound was another world: paved roads, street lights, telephone lines, a school—for the children of employees only—tennis courts, flower beds and lawns.

The environs of Koidu were littered with the rusting frames of expensive cars, abandoned by dealers who found it easier to replace a Mercedes than go to the bother of repairing it. The diamond merchants' wives flew back and forth to Lebanon on extended shopping trips. Every day illegal digging became more and more blatant, and yet the government did little to curb it.

As opposition to Margai grew, the APC swelled in popularity. Their leader, an ex–trade unionist by the name of Siaka Stevens, was amassing a huge amount of grassroots support, particularly among the Temnes and other protectorate people who saw no future under the Mende-dominated SLPP. But Stevens was convinced the party lacked the one element it most needed to seriously challenge Margai, and that was intellectual credibility: the kind of brain power required to create policies and a manifesto capable of winning the Krio vote in Freetown. Teams of young APC activists went out scouring the country. Their brief was to search out young, western-educated professional men and win them over to the cause.

During the day I rarely played inside. If I wasn't doing the rounds with my mother I stayed in the yard where I could, if I cared to, see everything that went on in my world.

One day there was even more toing and froing than usual; it began in the morning and went on all day. In the afternoon a man arrived, older than the usual visitors. Uncle Bash was with him, and he and the other young men darted like egrets around a buffalo.

The man moved slowly, with the authority of age, as though he'd never been young, in fact. He had a stout build and a large square head on a muscular neck. Fleshy lids sloped down at the far corners of his eyes. His lower lip was thick, protruding and dark, and when he spoke he revealed his lower teeth. The curious feature was his hairline: a perfect semicircle above a high forehead; the hair at the sides was cropped so close there was barely any at all. The whole effect was of a small cap, like a judge's black cap, on the top of his head.

This was Siaka Stevens, who at this time was effectively in hiding and moving from safe house to safe house. He was undertaking an extremely risky tour of the constituencies in an attempt to garner support. In order to change the constitution and introduce a republic with himself as president with sweeping new powers, Albert Margai needed the approval of two sessions of parliament with a general election in between. He'd won the first vote by a two-thirds majority. Now he had called the elections and these he was determined to win at any cost. Four APC MPs had already been arrested and held without charge, then deprived of their seats for absenteeism. Stevens was choosing to keep a very low profile.

When he reached me he paused for a moment and looked down. The whole entourage came to a halt and they gazed upon me too. Then Stevens said something to them and they all laughed. I didn't understand. They passed on. At that moment my father came out into the living room, drying his hands on a cloth. My mother was there and she went to fetch cold drinks. Obviously this man, although I didn't know then who he was, wasn't one of my father's brothers. He sat comfortably in one of the low wooden chairs we bought from the Forestry Commission shop and they spoke for a while. My father was very polite to him and acted in the way he usually reserved for Pa Roke. After a few moments my mother left them and the two men sat talking a while.

Uncle Bash sat outside on the veranda, with the other men. It was January and the temperatures were beginning to rise. The young men waited, beginning to sweat in the heat. They seemed very tense and excited. When Siaka Stevens reappeared they all sprang up and flew around him again. A few seconds later the cars were reversing, one after another, turning tightly in the restricted space of the compound until they drove off together, creating a great huff of dust that engulfed me.

Much later, when the day was old, Uncle Bash came back and hurried in. When he left my father was with him. They climbed into the Austin and drove away. My father didn't come back that night, or the next. When he returned several days later he was dishevelled, unshaven and on foot.

10

One night I heard my mother's voice—distorted by the dark, muffled through the walls of my room, disfigured by anger and tears. The three of us, my brother and sister and I, crept out of bed and opened the door. In the light of the corridor our mother and father faced each other and shouted. My mother's hair tumbled around her shoulders in disarray, sticking to her face where the tears glistened. She was wearing her night clothes. My father's anger was dark and rumbling. I had never seen him this way.

We stood there for a moment watching in silence. Big Aminatta had clearly made a decision to stay in her room. I have no idea now what the argument was about. I could not hear the words, but I could sense the emotions as painfully as boiling water poured onto my skin. Sheka and Memuna felt it too and, like frogs disturbed in their pool at night, we opened our mouths and lungs together and began to wail. I stood, in my patterned pyjamas, watching my parents fight and I screamed louder and louder.

The hot tears clouded my eyes and the scene in front of me blurred and faded. I felt as disorientated as I had once when I thought we were lost in the car during a thunderstorm; rain poured onto the windscreen, lightning shattered the sky and thunder crashed all around us. Now, completely lost in my own sorrow and fear, I threw back my head and howled. Snot welled in my nose, blocking my air passages and making it hard to breathe. I began to feel nauseous. In the farthest fields of my vision I could just about make out my brother and sister crying too. I took choppy, shallow breaths and pushed the sobs up through my chest and out of my gulping mouth.

Our mother's voice briefly cut through the clouds. 'You must be joking if you think I'm staying here. I'd rather sleep in the car.' She was holding on to a sheet and a pillow. Maybe she had them before. She may have even been on her way there already. I don't know. Whatever, she still didn't move. Her eyes locked onto my father's.

In that second Memuna broke ranks, ran forward and put her arms round my mother's thighs. Our mother hugged my sister to her and they stood defiant. Our father looked exasperated but no less angry as he stared at them both.

I'm going with you, Mummy,' said my sister, a cub facing off the leader of the pride.

For a moment I had no idea what was going to happen. We were all suspended in the moment, afraid to breathe or move. My father shrugged. 'Fine, fine.' He turned away. Suddenly he swung around and his gaze dropped down on my brother and me, hard like a pebble. The sob in my throat hung suspended, bobbing and trembling, too terrified to come out, but incapable of returning. My chest quaked.

'And you two? Do you want to go with your mother as well?'

Us, us? What did this have to do with us? Up until then I had thought I was just watching, as I did everything else that went on in the house. I couldn't even begin to imagine why my father was suddenly questioning us. I automatically thought I must have done something wrong. I certainly didn't want to sleep in the car.

'No, Daddy,' we said.

My sister and my mother went out to the car and stayed the night there. Sheka and I crept back to our beds.

By the time of their fifth wedding anniversary our parents' marriage was falling apart. The only time I remember them together, actually physically together in the same space, was the night their raging broke into my dreams. My father, obsessed only with his patients and politics, had withdrawn almost totally from his wife. He was away for days at a time; when he returned he was wearing the same clothes he left in; he was unwashed and the skin round his eyes sagged with exhaustion.

The young activists were travelling huge distances, moving from village to village around the country canvassing and holding meetings, many of them clandestine. They were forced to stay out of the way of the authorities, especially the police, who were breaking up APC gatherings and arresting the leaders. At night they slept rough or on floors and ate whatever their supporters, who were mainly poor villagers with little to eat themselves, were able to spare.

My father went round his Lebanese diamond-dealer clients, soliciting funds and persuading them to back the APC. Most of them traditionally supported the SLPP but they were alert to the mood of the country and anything that might influence their chances of making money. They donated generously to the new party and, to cover themselves, funnelled a bit more cash in the direction of the SLPP as well.

At home my mother was left holding the fort. She spent her days with no idea where her husband was or when he was coming back. There was nothing to tell the sick people who came to the clinic, except that the doctor wasn't in. When my father did eventually come home, usually after two or three days, it was late in the evening. He showered quickly and changed his clothes, but instead of going to bed he would unlock the surgery and usher any waiting patients inside.

One evening a young woman arrived at the house in time for evening surgery. She was haemorrhaging badly: the back of her *lappa* was stained dark red and blood streaked her legs. She was weak and stumbled as she tried to walk, supported on her husband's arm. My mother let them wait on the veranda. By now my father's appearances and disappearances had a sort of rhythm: he tended to be gone for two nights, three at the most, return for one night and depart again early in the morning of the next day. He was never at home for more than a day at a time. The woman settled to wait. On our veranda her husband spread out cloths to lie on and mixed a little of the rice and sauce they had brought.

In the early hours of the morning the headlights of a car lit up the front of the house. My father was home. As soon as he saw the bleeding woman he admitted her straight into the ward. After she was comfortable he lay down and slept for a few hours. In the morning he called my mother and she helped while he rapidly performed a D&C. When the patient had recovered sufficiently, he was gone.

By now our income was dwindling fast. My mother still worked at the Volkswagen garage and gradually her earnings alone supported the family. The clinic was no longer bringing in money and our father had contributed the family's savings to the political fight. Added to that, the Austin was gone—given to the party to help ferry activists around the country. Fortunately, my mother still held on to her Beetle.

In February 1967 a date for the elections was announced. They were to be held in March, just one month away. Everyone in the country had been waiting and preparing for this moment. The APC planned to challenge virtually every seat, with the exception of some of those in the southern Mende heartlands, where they reckoned they could not possibly win. They mobilised a formidable campaign. At its heart was the message to the people that the APC intended to stop Albert Margai's republican constitution from advancing any further.

One night we children were already in bed; my mother was sitting up talking with Foday, the man who owned the bookshop in town and who occasionally stopped by for a visit. We were good customers; my sister and brother were avid readers, my sister especially: a precociously early learner, she earned her place in family lore by finishing *Lorna Doone* when she was four. I hadn't conquered reading or discovered the world of books; my pleasures were as yet confined to ants, dogs and mud. Foday had brought my mother a gift: a copy of the newly published Encyclopaedia of Cooking.

They had been keeping company a while when my father stepped through the door. He was as unkempt as usual, but beneath the tiredness he was restless and evidently excited. He kissed his wife, sat down next to her and waited. Foday sensed his company had become superfluous and stood up to go. When the door closed behind the bookseller my father pulled a folded piece of paper out of his pocket and passed it to my mother. He gave no explanation, just watched her closely. He looked pretty pleased with himself, my mother said later, puffed up from inside with pride.

In her hand was a flyer, no more than about eighteen inches in size. At the top of the sheet was the red rising star, the symbol of the APC; in the centre a picture of my father. He had recently shaved off his beard, and in the photograph his chin was clean. The printer had touched up the white shirt he was wearing and also the whites of his eyes, ever so slightly, in order to give some definition to what was a rather poor-quality image. The whole effect was to make my father, who already looked startlingly young, even more wholesome. His name was printed in capitals, below that his qualifications—MB, ChB, DRCOG—and then the words:

'This is Your APC Candidate.
He is your Karefa-Smart's Choice
Vote APC all the way.'

Siaka Stevens had personally asked him to take on John Karefa-Smart's former seat of Tonkolili West and our father had agreed. It was his home constituency. My father was the obvious—indeed, the perfect—choice.

As the election date drew closer, my father was absent round the clock. His constituency was a whole day's journey away. By now the small, discreet meetings had burgeoned into rallies attracting huge crowds, but in order to hold a political meeting of any kind the candidates needed the approval of the paramount chiefs, most of whom were loyal to the government. It became routine for permission to be refused. Under these circumstances any meeting that went ahead, impromptu or otherwise, was likely to be heavy-handedly broken up by the police. Across the country there were frequent, sporadic clashes between government and opposition supporters.

Koidu, in Kono, lay on the axis between the SLPP Mende strongholds of the eastern provinces and the Temne north, which was mobilising behind the APC. One afternoon, on the way back to our house from school, with us three children in the car, my mother turned a corner and drove into a pitched battle between several hundred APC and SLPP supporters on the main street in town. Some people were waving guns, others hitting each other with their fists, sticks—anything they could lay their hands on. My mother pulled up, intending to reverse out. But the people nearby, who were as much engaged in the fighting as anyone else, recognised our car and started to shout for people to clear the road. There was a pause in the battle, like a black-and-white slapstick movie when the music stops, and we drove through the crowd. When we emerged on the other side and looked out of the rear window, the music and the fighting had started up again.

Some evenings later my mother was at the 'nightclub' having a drink with her Lebanese friends. It was a favourite haunt of the

Lebanese merchants and other well-to-do folk and she often went
to sit and chat in the evening air. The bar was next to the mosque,
a typical provincial prayer house built in concrete with four squat,
plain minarets, one of which housed the muezzin. These were the
days before it became standard practice to rig up an automated
loudspeaker system, and in Koidu the muezzin still climbed the
stairs of the tower and called the faithful to prayer five times a day.

That night my mother's attention was caught by the familiar
sound of the prayer call starting up. It was well after midnight—
nowhere near time for prayers. Gradually it became apparent to
everyone this was no muezzin, but an audacious protester who
had seized the mosque's loudhailer. For a time everyone was still
as the words ricocheted off the tin roofs, fluttered like feathers
down into the streets, whizzed around the heads of the people as
they sat on the steps of their houses.

'No more Albert, no more Margai, no more Albert over me,'
he sang.

Within minutes a crowd of supporters and detractors gathered in the street below the mosque, shouting encouragement or
insults accordingly. Soon enough they started to scuffle between
themselves. The man in the minaret sang on: 'And before I'll be
a slave, I'll be buried in my grave.'

Thirty minutes later the police arrived. They dragged the protester down from the tower and took him away, but not before they
had given him a hearty beating in front of the crowd of onlookers.

By now SLPP support in Kono was wavering badly. Determined
to win at all costs, some in the government were beginning to
resort to extreme tactics. My father was campaigning in other
parts of the country, supporting candidates in more marginal
seats, as well as canvassing for votes in his own district. Driving
home from the south, he stopped one night for petrol at Panguma
Junction, by coincidence encountering a local APC candidate on

the run from the police. A warrant had been issued for the arrest of all four opposition candidates in the region: the plan was to stop them registering themselves as candidates by using the law to hold them for forty-eight hours over the crucial registration period. My father gathered the four together and urged them to stay. He found a good lawyer, who also happened to be the cousin of the attorney-general, and they all went to the police station and challenged the local police chief. By the end of the afternoon the warrants were withdrawn.

There were only four weeks between the date parliament was dissolved and polling day. With my father away for the whole period, life in our house moved quietly from day to day. My mother followed her usual routine of work, friends and family life. Ade Benjamin, an old friend from Freetown, turned up unexpectedly to stay and the two of them went out dancing together, lifting her spirits considerably. Meanwhile, she waited to hear from my father.

Even during this intense period my mother remained detached from the swirl of political activity around her, despite the fact that the election outcome and our own lives were now completely intertwined. Although she chose not to say so to my father, she was frustrated to see the success of the clinic faltering. My mother was as pragmatic as my father was idealistic; she saw herself first and foremost as a doctor's wife, and it had been her plan to remain one.

Polling day, when it came, created a storm of speculation and excitement in the rest of the country. This was the second democratic election in our fledgling state, and a great deal hinged on it, including, as far as many saw it, the future of democracy itself. People were beginning to anticipate a victory by the opposition APC and an end to the Margai government. The anticipation and even trepidation as people queued to cast their votes was intense. Yet the tempest passed over our small house, leaving the domestic scene inside untouched.

The news took a while to reach us that my father had won his seat. He not only took Tonkolili West for the opposition but by the greatest margin and the greatest number of votes cast in favour of any one candidate during the entire election: close to eighteen thousand. The ruling party candidate had not even managed to secure five hundred.

In Kono the APC took two of the four seats. In Freetown every single seat went to the APC. The party's triumphs were sweeping the country as opposition candidates toppled government incumbents in constituency after constituency. Victory began to look inevitable.

Four days later, in the early morning, a car arrived at the house. It was a long, low Mercedes, one my mother recognised as belonging to one of the wealthiest of the Koidu diamond merchants. Inside were two young APC party workers, smartly turned out in clean white shirts, unrecognisable from the sweat-stained young activists we were used to seeing. They told my mother they were to take us down to Freetown to attend the swearing-in ceremony for the new prime minister and cabinet.

The inside of the car was air-conditioned and smelled of leather. Under my bare legs the seats were cool and smooth. We took the new road to Freetown; it was still being built and hadn't been tarred but it surpassed the old, rocky road. Our route that day took us through Magburaka, in Tonkolili district, and it was strange to see posters and flyers of our father's face pasted everywhere: on shop fronts, on the sides of market stalls, rows and rows of them. People cheered as we drove in; young men ran alongside the car to catch our companions' outstretched hands; little boys dressed only in shorts danced barefoot in the dust, sticking out their bottoms and stamping their feet, and the driver sounded the horn at pedestrians who waved back at us.

We pulled up outside a house in the middle of the town and within moments the car was surrounded by people. There was a lot of backslapping and clapping as our companions climbed out. We were all led inside and my mother and we three waited while the clatter of excited voices speaking in Temne flew around our ears.

Presently, a woman came forward bearing an enormous dish piled with rice and cassava leaves, stewed with meat and peppers. Everyone ate from the same dish. Cold, sweet drinks were pressed into our hands. All the time an unending stream of people arrived and the clamour of laughter and congratulations swelled until it could scarcely be contained by the walls of the room and burst out of the windows, trickled through the cracks in the floors and flew into the street, where other people heard it and came to join the throng. It was like a wedding party and we were unexpectedly the bride and groom.

Makeni, Lunsar, Port Loko, Waterloo—everywhere we passed the electorate had just voted to overturn their government and on the roads the people were in celebratory mood, heady with the first sweet success of what democracy could do. Young men in freshly pressed trousers and open shirts wandered about in groups; at the roadside bars the owners strung up rows of coloured bulbs; in village after village people gathered on their verandas overlooking the street. On the roads crowded *poda podas* raced along, full of supporters travelling to the capital to take part in the festivities. The Mercedes swept on towards Freetown.

We had been travelling all day and now the shadows were just beginning to chase away the remaining sunlight. Our plan was to go to a friend's house so that we could shower and change into the clean outfits our mother had packed. After that no one really knew, but we had all the confidence in the world that once we reached our destination our father would have taken care of everything.

In the back of the car our mother entertained us with games of I Spy and songs. My favourite at the time was 'Soldier, soldier'. We took turns at the verses while my mother sang the lead:

'Oh, soldier, soldier, won't you marry me, with your musket, fife and drum?'

'Oh, no, sweet maid, I cannot marry you, for I have no shirt to put on,' sang the next person.

Everyone joined in—eventually I think even the APC boys learned the words:

'So off she went to her grandfather's chest and brought him a shirt of the very, very best and the soldier put it on . . .'

I hadn't yet assigned myself a gender and I liked the idea of having a musketfife'n'drum, whatever that was, as well as all the rest of the fancy regalia that the young woman kept in her grandfather's chest. My mother must have shown me a picture because I had a very strong image of the gold-braided coat and tall, peaked cap I would wear one day.

It was dusk as we passed through the outskirts of Freetown an hour or so later. Strangely the long road into town was almost empty of people, even the tradesmen who normally sat at the roadside in huddles around their lamps seemed to be few and far between. In the front of the car the two party workers exchanged a few words in Temne. I suppose they were wondering whether we were late and all the people had already made their way to State House to greet Siaka Stevens, the new prime minister. What if we'd missed the ceremony?

Some distance ahead something had fallen across the road and two men were standing by it. As we drew closer we saw there was a long pole balanced on two oil drums; large stones had been placed across the road in front. It was a road block and the two men were soldiers. When they saw the Mercedes they began to move towards us, waving the car to a halt. Inside everyone was silent as we watched the uniformed men approach us, one on either side of the car. Tucked in under my mother's arm, I could feel the beating of her heart.

The men were in full battle kit and carried automatic weapons slung across their shoulders; their faces were sullen and dark. Nothing about them brought to mind the brave redcoats of my imagination with their long, shiny black boots. They indicated we should all get out of the car. 'Commot!'

The grown-ups climbed out. We three stayed sitting in the back seat. Still no one spoke. The soldier who had given the command sauntered round to the back of the car. He asked where we were going, but didn't seem very interested in the reply. He took the driver's licence and studied it at length before handing it back.

The other soldier now put his head through the open door on the passenger side and looked around the car. His glance passed over us as though we were invisible.

'What's in here?' The first soldier tapped the boot.

'Nothing, there's nothing there. Bags, that's all.' It was our driver: he ran round holding up the key.

'Open!' The monosyllabic soldier gave a slack wave of his hand. Inside were our bags, full of children's clothes and my mother's personal effects. Our mother walked over and, at his instruction, opened each one. He leaned in and watched her. When she had finished he nodded and stepped away, while she pushed everything back into the bags and closed them.

She ventured a question for the first time: 'What's going on?'

The soldier looked at her. 'They've taken over State House,' he said. 'Everybody is under martial law. The army's in charge now.'

The empty streets, the silent suburbs all began to make sense. People were retreating to their houses, waiting for trouble. The soldiers let us go and told us to hurry.

Back in the car the APC men began to talk rapidly between themselves in Temne. Their faces had tightened into frowns of concentration. The driver gripped the steering wheel tightly. They seemed to have completely forgotten we were still sitting in the car behind them. Once we were out of sight of the soldiers the Mercedes began to accelerate.

The soldier hadn't asked us who we were and all we'd told him was that we were visiting friends in the city. My mother asked only as many questions as she dared and all we knew was that someone, just one person—presumably Siaka Stevens—was under house arrest in State House.

My mother hadn't said anything for a few minutes, but now she asked: 'Where are we going?' The car was moving at speed.

'We have to go to State House and find out what has happened to our brothers. Once we get there we'll know what to do.' The young man in the passenger seat looked round and into her face. 'Don't worry.'

He didn't smile.

11

Rumour of an army takeover had been rife in Freetown for several days.

Forty-eight hours after the closing of the polls the Sierra Leone Broadcasting Service announced the election results—SLPP: 31 and APC: 28. Five results were still outstanding. Two independent candidates had yet to declare their support for either party. The five awaited results were popularly assumed to be certain APC wins, but the two independent candidates were former SLPP loyalists who had fallen out with Albert Margai and been refused the party symbol at the elections. Now the race was on between both sides to secure their allegiance.

That night Sir Albert flew south in a private plane to meet the two candidates on their home turf in Bo and Kenema in order to try to persuade them to rejoin the ruling party. But although the prime minister didn't know it, he had already been beaten to it. Our father and the Taqi brothers proved themselves to be the sharper political strategists, though they were half the veteran politician's age. The very night the votes began to be counted my father left Uncle Bash to supervise in his constituency while he and Ibrahim drove hell for leather down the length of the country, first to Bo and then to Kenema, where they held private meetings with each of the candidates. The two would not support the APC, but they agreed to withhold their support from the SLPP if Sir Albert remained leader.

The APC celebrated their triumph, but in Freetown the confusion was mounting. Sir Albert tried to buy time by insisting the independent candidates couldn't formally declare for one side or the other until parliament opened. The five awaited results were delayed, prompting accusations of government gerrymandering; all the time newly elected MPs and convoys of their supporters trucked into Freetown and paraded the streets in support of Siaka Stevens.

Media reports added to the chaos. A local newspaper published a new set of figures giving the APC a clear win; next the BBC World Service declared a dead heat. A telegram was dispatched from the high commissioner in Freetown instructing the World Service to broadcast an immediate correction. Still no official statement was made. Bursts of violence erupted. In Kroo Town pro-APC protesters torched Fulah shops in revenge for Fulah support of the government. The tribesmen replied by firing upon their tormentors.

In the avenue outside the governor-general's office the chanting crowds massed; inside his red and gilt chambers the governor floundered. Then, not a moment too soon, a messenger brought him the final count. The SLPP and the APC had 32 seats each, not including the two independents. Four other independents had already been claimed by Sir Albert and added into the SLPP total. The governor-general summoned the two leaders and asked them to form a coalition government. They refused. The pressure on the governor-general to bring a swift end to the impending crisis was immense. He decided to appoint Siaka Stevens prime minister of Sierra Leone, believing that he alone could command a majority in parliament. No sooner had he done so than rumours that David Lansana would lead the army in a takeover to reinstate Sir Albert quickened into life.

From his office the British high commissioner issued hourly reports back to his superiors at the Africa Department of the Foreign and Commonwealth Office in London. The next morning he received a call from one Dr Forna and Ibrahim Taqi; the latter he knew as the editor of *We Yone* newspaper. They were concerned about the country's stability and asked if Britain might intervene to prevent an army takeover in Sierra Leone. The high commissioner declined, but was sufficiently impressed with the foresight of the idea to request London to position a naval ship secretly along the Guinea coast, just in case he needed it himself. His next caller was the force commander. David Lansana warned the high commissioner that the appointment of Siaka Stevens as prime minister would be considered unconstitutional. The army commander confided that he had taken the precaution of moving some of his units and had already taken over the Sierra Leone Broadcasting Service building. The queen's representative, Governor-General Henry Lightfoot Boston, was the next through the door. He arrived after lunch looking 'shaky and uncertain', reported the high commissioner to his superiors later. Sir Henry repeated his decision to appoint an APC government with every possible haste.

From early morning a euphoric crowd had begun to gather outside State House for the swearing-in of the new prime minister. The throng swelled through Independence Avenue and flowed down the hill and around the roots of the Cotton Tree. Students from Fourah Bay College, supporters from the provinces, locals, old, young, men, women and children turned out in their thousands. Music was playing on transistor radios tuned to pick up the next official announcement; some people began to dance. Young men climbed the Cotton Tree and lay like lizards along the branches; others perched on the walls of surrounding buildings; in the street everyone waited.

At about three o'clock a motorcade arrived and eased through the crowd. The applause rippled through the people and then rose up into a great roar as the heavy gates of State House swung open and the motorcade passed through. In the first car was the familiar profile of Siaka Stevens. In the next car were the four new APC MPs who were to be sworn in alongside him as members of the new government. They were the Taqi brothers and, sitting next to them, our father.

March is the hottest month of the year—in Temne *Gbapron* means 'walk on the side', in the shade of the trees because the sun is too high to walk down the middle of the road. Many in the crowd had been there all day, as the temperature nudged up to forty degrees. There was little to eat or drink, but the people ignored the heat and discomfort; they waited patiently for the country's new leaders to emerge and greet them from the circular balcony overlooking the avenue on the top floor of State House. An hour passed.

At first it felt like a low rumble reverberating through the masses like distant thunder. The sensation shuddered through calves, thighs and chests, growing ever more distinct. It seemed to emanate from the road beneath them. The new sound replaced the chatter of the crowd as a hush fell. People began to look around.

The military convoy appeared at the top of Independence Avenue, where it turned and began its descent: truck after truck. The drivers didn't slow as they neared the densely packed avenue: people were forced to scramble to one side. Armed soldiers were moving in on State House. At the gates they stopped. There was silence.

One, two, three, four, the soldiers jumped from the back— dozens of men. They ran, guns at the ready, until they had surrounded the entire building. Once in their positions the soldiers turned as one and slowly levelled their guns at the crowd.

Nobody moved. The heat shimmered across the white painted facade of State House and glinted on the metal balustrades. Sweat dripped from under the helmets of the soldiers, slipped down their faces and stung their eyes; it ran down the backs of the legs of the people as they stood; it trickled under the dresses and between the breasts of women; it bubbled on the backs of men and streamed down their spines. It bloomed darkly under thousands of arms, and prickled the soldiers' palms wrapped around their gun barrels. Salt drops hung on the upper lip of the commander in charge.

All was still.

Inside State House Siaka Stevens had just taken the oath of office when the governor-general's Mende aide-de-camp Hinga Norman stepped in and placed the governor, and the four men with him, under arrest. Briefly the governor-general continued, swearing in Ibrahim Taqi as minister of information. When he had finished Sir Henry turned and walked slowly past his disloyal lieutenant. He left the room and took the stairs up to his private quarters. No one stood in his way. The five remaining men sat down to wait in the company of their captor, while guards were posted outside every door of the building.

At 5.55 p.m. David Lansana's voice came on the radio to tell the people of Sierra Leone that the country was under martial law.

At 6 p.m. the crowd of people outside State House were ordered to disperse.

Somebody began to chant: 'No more Albert, no more Margai.' In ones and twos, finally by the score, other voices joined the chorus. Some people sat down in an act of defiance, to show that they had no intention of ever leaving.

At 6.03 p.m. the order to disperse was repeated.

At 6.05 p.m. the soldiers raised their weapons and fired in the air above the heads of the crowd. The crowd fell silent, muscles tightened as fear spread from body to body, through bellies and bowels, but everyone clung to their positions.

'They're only blanks,' a man swivelled around and called out to his comrades. 'Blanks. That's all.' People nodded to each other. Just blanks, to scare them. They held their ground.

The soldiers lowered their weapons. The people sighed, in one great exhalation of air. One or two even laughed. Of course, these boys were their sons, their brothers, their cousins. Someone began to clap the soldiers, but then stopped.

The commander in charge wiped his upper lip. A minute had passed, according to the watch on his wrist. He gave the next order, as he had been told to do. The soldiers raised their guns and lowered the barrels in the direction of the crowd.

The commander gave his men the order to fire.

Among the first to fall was a teenage boy wearing a red T-shirt and green shorts. He went down face first under the Cotton Tree; his jaw hit the dirt with a crack, arms wrapped around his stomach, his legs began to perform a grim little jig as he lay in the dust. Someone close by bent down to help, saw the blood spreading like a shadow across the earth, red on red, and screamed.

The soldiers began to shoot indiscriminately. The crowd split apart as people scattered in every direction, pushing and grabbing each other, slipping in the blood of the fallen, silent, flailing, stumbling. From their bodies rose the thick odour of fear; it drifted up above the trees and the houses, where it hung in a cloud over the city for days.

❧ 12 ❧

By the time we reached the Cotton Tree the crowds were gone and the wounded dragged away. A knot of press men converged on the gates of State House, like a crowd gathered below a man threatening to throw himself from a rooftop. By now the world was alert to the possibility that one of the last democracies in Africa might be about to fall. All around the building soldiers remained in position, guns at the ready. We drove up Independence Avenue almost to the gates of State House before we were ordered to halt. Our two companions climbed down and we watched from the back seat while they argued and pleaded with some of the soldiers. Finally, they walked back to the car and started the engine. The gates of State House swung open and we drove inside.

Neither my mother nor our two companions had any idea of what had just occurred on the same spot or what would happen next; but whatever confusion our party felt was matched by that of the soldiers. They were under orders to stay at their posts and to hold the men inside until Brigadier Lansana and Albert Margai arrived at State House, but although the two men were expected imminently, hours had passed and yet there was no sign of them. The soldiers stayed on, with no idea what to do next.

My father appeared, walking easily and wearing a white shirt and grey trousers; he looked just as he did every day at home. He was alone and we stood in the courtyard of the prime minister's offices while he kissed us and we gripped his knees. I held on to my mother's hand. He told our mother he was fine; she should take us to our friends the Benjamins, where we would all be taken care of and perfectly safe in their house overlooking the city. 'Don't worry, my brothers and I will be OK.'

'Won't you come with us now?'

He refused: 'I need to be with the others, with my colleagues. Ibrahim is here and so is Mohammed, we should stay together. You go on. I'll see you all later. Ade and Bianca are there. You can send my regards.' He smiled and kissed us all again; his mood seemed light.

My mother allowed herself to be reassured by our father's words but, she discovered many years later when I was able to tell her otherwise, his easy manner was deceptive. He wasn't free to leave, although in front of us he acted as though he remained of his own volition. The men had been warned that if they tried to leave the confines of State House they would be shot. The governor-general, the Queen of England's representative, had relinquished responsibility and remained in self-imposed solitary confinement in his chambers. The radio played nothing but monotonous military music. The city was alive with armed soldiers and protesters had begun to take to the streets once more, as whispers carried the news through the city that once darkness fell Siaka Stevens and the other men held in State House would be taken away to an unknown fate. The country was in free fall.

Outside State House my mother waylaid a British journalist. He turned out to be the correspondent from Reuters. She tried to explain to him that Siaka Stevens wasn't alone; there were others with him, including her own husband, but he brushed her aside.

That night our mother sat by the window of the Benjamins' house on Old Railway Line Road watching the military head-quarters at Wilberforce on the opposite hill. Truck after truck passed through the gates and down Motor Road into Freetown. Some hours earlier the Mercedes and our two friends from the APC had driven away, leaving us at the Benjamins' comfortable home; they promised they'd be back with any news. After a meal and showers the three of us were put to bed in a room with the Benjamins' own children.

Two old friends arrived: Donald Macaulay, the lawyer who helped my father free the APC candidates in Kono, and Susan Toft, a teacher of anthropology at Fourah Bay college, an old friend of my mother's from her days in Freetown. Moments after they arrived they found themselves trapped for the night when a brief announcement interrupted the music on the radio with news that the city was under curfew with immediate effect. Together with Ade and his Maltese wife Bianca, they tried to pass the time and, with less success, to distract my mother with continuous games of cards.

Inside State House food and water had run out and as the night deepened our father resigned himself to sleeping in his luxurious prison. The men were moved up to a drawing room on one of the upper floors and told to make themselves comfortable. When the doors closed they moved around the room, swiftly checking out their new surroundings, and discovered to their amazement that the soldiers had failed to disconnect the telephones. Within moments they were making calls. Ibrahim Taqi, the brand-new information minister, called his contacts in the foreign press and for the rest of the evening Siaka Stevens sat in the carpeted suite that ought to have been his own office, and gave interviews to western reporters, including those from the British *Times* and Reuters.

This was how the prisoners came to hear the rumour spreading through the town that they were to be smuggled out of the city later in the night, possibly to be shot. There was substance to the fear; a dark night, a cold bullet and an unmarked grave had already become the fate of several African opposition leaders. My father would have recalled how, in the Congo, the newly elected prime minister Patrice Lumumba was flown away in full view of the world, to be tortured and killed.

In the streets leading away from State House the protesters who had fled several hours before were re-forming into human barricades with the single idea of sealing all the exit routes and preventing the transportation of the prisoners. They tore up paving stones, knocked down roadside bollards and pushed cars into the street to create impromptu barricades. At the same time soldiers formed lines across the roads, effectively closing off the centre of town, and moved in on the protesters. The crowd was caught in a closing net. Hundreds of people took to the alleyways, trying to escape the military by running through the back streets where the trucks couldn't pass. But there they found themselves confronted, not by soldiers, but by armed youths who wore bandannas and white vests bearing the palm tree symbol of the SLPP.

Our mother and her friends heard the gunfire up in Tengbe Town and they exchanged glances at each other round the table; our father and his colleagues heard it in State House, where they waited for dawn. The smell of cordite and tear gas swirled upwards on the currents of air.

By nine o'clock in Connaught Hospital the waiting room and beds were full; people lay bleeding in the corridors in rows all the way from the out-patients department to the operating theatre. The few doctors on duty set to work in the theatres, amputating limbs shattered by bullets. Even the plaster room was turned into a makeshift operating room. In the early hours of the morning a gang of SLPP youths, brandishing automatic weapons, ran through the hospital and burst into the theatres, intending to finish off their APC victims as they lay under the surgeon's knife. The doctor in charge, unarmed and wearing bloodstained greens, confronted the ringleader with such ferocity that the attackers turned tail and slunk back into the night.

The official figures from that night stated that fifty-four people were shot and injured. Nine more were killed.

The next day Bianca and Susan found my mother sweating in her bed, reeling from nausea. Since arriving in Africa she had been given to bouts of malaria. Bianca took away the thick blanket my mother had wrapped herself in and directed the electric fan onto her. My mother was shivering uncontrollably and she felt chilled to the bone, but her temperature was spiralling upwards of one hundred degrees.

Outside the city was silent. No activity could be seen beyond the windows of State House; no more announcements were broadcast on the radio. We spent the whole day indoors. Donald and Susan went home and came by later in the afternoon. There was no more news: no newspapers; even the telephone lines were out.

In the evening the music on the radio stopped abruptly and the radio fizzed and sputtered for a moment. Finally a crackling voice became audible. Bianca crossed the room and turned the volume up. It was David Lansana. His voice, ponderous and heavy, filled the air. He declared the appointment of Siaka Stevens unconstitutional.

'In order to prevent further acts of violence . . . civil war in our country, I have carried out my duty as first commander of the army of Sierra Leone and taken charge of the situation. The army is in control and you have my promise that I will do all in my power to see that justice is done.' Here the broadcast ended. He had added nothing more than everyone already knew.

In the early hours of the following morning David Lansana was arrested by four of his own men.

A few hours later, when it was light, we heard the familiar growl of the Mercedes. The two APC men were back as they had promised. There was no news of my father who, as far as anyone knew, was still being held in State House. But the two men had an idea.

'Dr Forna was once in the army, yes?' one of them asked.

'Yes.' By now my mother was more or less recovered from her malarial fever.

'Where do you keep his uniform?'

'It's up in Koidu at the house. But he hasn't worn it for ages, at least two years. He left the army. Why?'

'We must go and bring it down. Can you come with us?'

Our mother caught their drift. The men who had arrested Lansana were majors. As one of the medical personnel my father had been a major in the army, too. He was their equal plus; he outranked the men who were holding him at State House. Challenging Lansana had brought him enormous popularity among the ranks, which was still well remembered. Perhaps, in his uniform, he would be able to command loyalty from enough of them to secure his release and that of his colleagues.

It was a long shot and more than a little dangerous. Our mother would have to travel up to Koidu and back, and then, God only knew how, smuggle the uniform to him in State House. But to my mother, in the light of her current predicament, any plan seemed like a good one.

They left immediately. Susan accompanied her, lending moral support, and they bluffed their way through the road blocks by pretending to be missionaries on their way up-country. Outside Freetown the checkpoints ended and they drove at speed, stopping only once to buy drinks at the roadside. At the house they slept briefly and set out again while the sky was still flushed with pink; under the front seat of the car, folded and ironed, was the uniform. The atmosphere in the car on that journey along the roads and in villages could not have been more different, said our mother, from our triumphant passage to Freetown, just two days before.

The next time my mother saw my father's uniform he was wearing it—or assorted parts of it, at any rate. We were back at home in Koidu; back into our old life—as far as that was possible. In our father's absence family life became one-dimensional: we had routine without substance, days with form but no purpose, like a water pot with a broken base. One afternoon he strolled back through the front door wearing khaki shorts beneath a plain cotton shirt and long military socks incongruously worn with his sandals. His beard had grown back and he was looking altogether leaner. He went straight into the bathroom, shaved his face clean, changed his clothes and opened the surgery.

Early in the evening of the third day of their incarceration soldiers had arrived at State House; they had seized Siaka Stevens and taken him to Pademba Road Prison. There, he was joined shortly afterwards by Albert Margai and Brigadier Lansana. My father and the Taqi brothers remained imprisoned along with the governor-general at State House for two more days before they were all released without ceremony. He had searched us out at Bianca and Ade's house; once he was reassured we were fine, he departed with his colleagues. Who knows whether he had the chance to put the uniform to the test? I never found out. My father barely spoke of his experiences and my mother did not ask.

Back together my parents concentrated on the functions of living: the clinic, the patients, their children. My father strode through life making his own decisions; he didn't know what it meant to feel afraid; he saw no reason to explain his actions to anyone but himself. His autonomy and unswerving confidence was matched only by my mother's detachment; but whether with hindsight this was symptomatic of the deterioration of their marriage or the very source of their growing distance from each other, I have never known. Nothing in her upbringing had prepared my mother for the reality of the Africa with which she was now faced; these were not her people and she did not share our father's passion or the political conviction that might otherwise have carried her through.

Instead she hoped for the best. My father immersed himself once again in his work as a doctor, and my mother prayed that life would continue that way. The military junta had banned all political activity and closed down the newspapers. The country was still under martial law; the House of Representatives had been dissolved and the new government had given itself extensive powers. The governor-general had been released, persuaded to go on extended leave, sparing the British the effort and inconvenience of having to intervene on his behalf. He was, after all, officially the representative of the Crown and until further notice the queen was still head of state of Sierra Leone.

The first twenty-four hours of the new regime were marked by numerous switches in the leadership within the group of young majors calling themselves the National Reformation Council. Colonel Genda, an old friend of ours, had been flown back from America to take command at the request of the coup leaders. My mother had been friends with Ruth, his British wife, and we used to play with their children when we lived at Wilberforce barracks. But Colonel Genda had made the mistake of confiding to an army colleague, Major Juxon-Smith, who was on the same flight, that he intended to reinstate a civilian regime as soon as possible. While the plane refuelled at Lanzarote, Major Juxon-Smith slipped away and used the interval to telephone his contacts in the NRC. In a single call he alerted them to the colonel's democratic inclinations; he then usurped Genda and took the leadership for himself.

From the moment Juxon-Smith turned up at his first press conference wearing an outlandish Russian fox fur hat in the stewing heat of Freetown, it was evident that in him our country had a ruler with all the hallmarks of a true African dictator. Within a matter of weeks he wanted the name of the country changed to the more African-sounding Songhay, the national anthem rewritten, and cars to drive on the opposite side of the road. He shared a birthday with Winston Churchill, whom he greatly admired, and he proposed a plan to the British government to fly the great man's widow out for a state visit.

Juxon-Smith liked to turn up early in the morning at government offices and fire anyone who wasn't at their desk on time. He forced car drivers who failed to stop for his cavalcade to appear at State House and apologise to him in person. His habit of waving his arms and legs around when he spoke earned him the nickname Juxon Fits. Juxon-Smith was soon extremely unpopular among his own aides; he telephoned them with orders to report to his office in the middle of the night only to take every decision himself anyway.

Yet despite all his eccentricities, Juxon-Smith would find history and her bedfellow hindsight fair judges of his brief period of rule. Only a personality so extreme could tackle government corruption in the way he did, or force an unpopular but essential austerity budget onto our unruly populace. He was in many ways a true visionary. He would stand trial for treason, survive and reputedly end his days as a preacher roaming the southern states of America.

In Koidu, three weeks after he returned home our father began to disappear again, slipping away with his colleagues for an hour or two, then a day and a night. In no time at all we were back living in the uncertainty that had prevailed before the elections. The rules shifted, the security and substance vanished from our lives, as though the walls of our house had turned from concrete into paper, likely to fly away at any time if someone outside blew hard enough. And beyond the walls there were indeed those watching and listening, beginning to huff and to puff.

In Sierra Leone at that time the milk came in triangular cartons. They stacked up, top to toe, alternately in the fridge so they formed a block. It was really quite a clever design. To open them you snipped one of the ends off—of course, it didn't matter which one. In my opinion that was the beauty of them. The milk came in regular and chocolate flavour. The chocolate was the best: velvet smooth, not at all grainy like the sort made with powder. Ours tasted as though it came straight from chocolate cows. We had ordinary milk at home, but the chocolate was special. I have a memory from that time, a memory of chocolate milk and subterfuge.

One day, for what reason I have no idea, my mother took us to a café where she ordered each of us a triangular carton of chocolate milk as a treat. I can't remember where we were, whether it was in Koidu or in Freetown at some earlier juncture. I do remember the café had booths, a little like an American diner, with red plastic seats. There was a counter by the door and a big freezer behind the till. The room was air-conditioned, with the quality of airtight quiet you only get from artificially cooled spaces. We didn't have air-conditioning at home and I imagined this was what it would be like to crawl into the fridge and close the door. I was sitting in a booth opposite my mother, my arms resting on the cool metal edges of the table, sucking my drink through a paper straw, when my father came in.

We were surprised and pleased to see him. 'Hello, Daddy,' we greeted him in unison.

He slid in beside my mother and ordered a drink. 'What are you having?' His question was directed at me.

'Chocolate milk—want some, Daddy?' I stopped sucking for a moment, enough to speak. I pulled the straw out of my mouth and offered it to him. He took a sip and sat with us a while, talking in a low voice to our mother. After a few minutes he slipped out of the booth. He kissed us quickly and said goodbye, then he set off in the direction of the kitchens. He seemed to be in a hurry.

'Daddy, you're going the wrong way. There's the door.' We pointed past the counter and the till at the glass door. Everyone knew you left a restaurant the way you came in.

'Yes, I know. But it's easier for me to go out this way. No one will mind. I need to go to a shop just here. And you don't want me to have to walk all the way around, do you?' He smiled, shrugged, pulled a pleading sort of face, pretending we had the authority to insist he left through the front entrance.

We giggled. We were children. We thought it was hilarious to see our father come in one door and leave through another. We let him. No one said anything, not even the big Lebanese shop owner. We thought our father was funny and we loved to see an adult break the rules.

My father was being followed. He had already warned my mother and it wasn't long before she had a tail of her own.

Our mother ran our household with Presbyterian efficiency; it was her habit to go to the butcher twice a week: Saturday and Wednesday. As early as five o'clock in the morning she would rise and drive out to the other side of the town to the halal butcher. She timed her arrival to the moment the butcher finished slaughtering the animals and she selected the prime pieces of fresh meat.

This particular Saturday she noticed a car behind her on the road. With the curfew still in force until six, the streets were empty: no early risers, insomniacs or all-night revellers. As a doctor our father was permitted to break the curfew, ostensibly just for emergencies, though in practice many of the local police afforded both my parents the same degree of laxity. At road blocks, as soon as the local police recognised either of their cars, they waved them through. It was still dark and as she drove through downtown Koidu on that morning, the sight of another car behind her struck our mother as curious.

In the driver and passenger seats were two men. Whoever they were, they were not at pains to conceal themselves. They pulled up behind her outside the butcher's; when she came out ten minutes later they turned the car and followed her back to the house. For the rest of the day the two men lounged in the shade of the trees opposite and whenever our mother left the house, within moments, in her rear-view mirror, she would see their car swing out on the road behind her.

The men following my parents took a very matter-of-fact view of their jobs. They never bothered to disguise themselves, didn't seem to care that they were about as unobtrusive as a pair of ostriches in a chicken coop as they sat opposite our lone house, under a solitary tree, on a road headed nowhere.

One morning my mother opened the door to a loud knock. A clean-cut young man stood on the step. He was wearing a white shirt, slacks, and shoes—which was unusual for these parts. Most ordinary people could not afford shoes. My mother didn't recognise him.

'The doctor isn't here . . .' she began.

'No, missus.' He smiled, shook his head. 'It isn't the doctor I am looking for. I have come to follow *you*.' And he jabbed his forefinger at her chest.

My mother shaded her surprise, said hello and even offered him a soft drink. The young man declined. Then she led him through the compound and showed him the spot where the tails usually sat.

'No problem, missus. See you.' He bounded off to take his place.

Sadly, the polite young man didn't last long in the job. Our mother found it too easy to give him the slip. She would leave her car in the cinema car park and go into the film. The cinema was owned by Emil Massey, a diamond dealer who, like every-one else, was one of our father's patients, and he let her in free of charge. She would sit in the darkness for a few minutes, then walk out the back, going about her business in town on foot while the new tail sat in the car park watching the abandoned car. At other times our parents went to a friend's house, parked their cars at the front and drove away later in a borrowed car. They laughed about it when they could.

My parents did not know whether the men were stooges of Margai and their old adversaries the SLPP, or acting on the or-ders of the military regime. My mother told me she had always assumed it was Margai, gathering intelligence, trying to find ways to regain his hold on power.

One cool, silver January afternoon in the Public Record Of-fice in Kew I came across the answer in a thirty-year-old British government manila folder marked TOP SECRET. The man who had given the order to have our parents followed was William Leigh, the commissioner of police. He had previously answered to Albert Margai and now served the junta. Sometime before the elections he had put Special Branch agents onto several of the country's opposition politicians as well as placing his own spies in the army. Now he did the same again, without sharing the in-formation with his colleagues or with Juxon-Smith. The British high commissioner he kept informed during their private chats.

Under our first dictatorship paranoia flourished and the nerves of the nation were stretched taut as a dancer's hamstring. All that bound the men ruling our country together was a fondness for power and an eye for an opportunity. The army was in charge, trusted no one and ruled by force. The police spied on the army, at the same time as they kept an eye on the former rulers and opposition politicians. Members of the APC and SLPP met in secret, trying to second-guess the army and each other. The world was watching surreptitiously, their representatives in Freetown affected lofty impartiality, all the while exchanging whisky and sodas for secrets and tattle.

The British and Americans were alert to any hint of communist sympathies in the political landscape of the country. Next door Sékou Touré ruled Guinea with his own unique brand of communism. On the other side of us was Liberia: a satellite of US interests in Africa where the people spoke with American accents, the flag was a wan copy of the Stars and Stripes and you could buy hamburgers. Our tiny nation found itself in a strategically important position at a time when two world powers were concerned lest the Reds gain another foothold in West Africa. Official documents from that time are full of whispered suspicions; many fell upon the APC for its left-wing ideologies and Stevens as a former trade unionist. Visits or periods of study in the People's Republic of China or Cuba on the part of party officials were noted and included in the risk calculations, like a red mark in the margin of an exercise book. Both communist regimes openly wooed the newly independent African states— especially the People's Republic of China, desperate then to accumulate vital votes at the United Nations and recognition for Mao's post-revolution regime.

At Kew I leafed through thousands of documents. After the 1967 elections my father's name began to appear in the records for the first time. At first no one on the circuit of cocktail parties and diplomatic dinners in Freetown was at all sure who he was and they mistook him for a run-of-the-mill politician with a similar name. Our father walked out of nowhere, a nobody from the despised provinces with the biggest following in the country, a bigger majority even than Siaka Stevens. He made them jittery because they'd been caught looking the other way. A red-hot APC man, they called him. No wonder the police chief had begun to spy on us.

Farcical as the Special Branch agents' methods were, they brought new strains into our household. And in a short time the behaviour of the police transformed into something altogether more menacing.

Our father was away as usual at one of his meetings. But on this occasion he was gone for several days, much longer than was normal. At home our mother waited with knots coiling like snakes in her stomach as she watched the hours pass. When he finally returned to the house he told her what had happened: the meeting he had attended had been declared illegal under martial law and broken up by the police. Several of them had been arrested, held at the station and only just released.

The police were successfully gathering intelligence and using it to halt all political activity. A Sierra Leonean man, now an academic, who described himself as 'a youthful supporter of the APC', recounted for me what happened at one meeting:

A group of men, including our father, were gathered late at night in a deserted shelter in fields close by a village whose chief was sympathetic to the party. The shelter was made of poles and layered with palm fronds, used by workers to rest and sleep during the harvest but otherwise unoccupied. About twelve men were present. The talk circled around whether the military rulers of the NRC would continue to resist pressure to hand over to a civilian government. In the last few months the election results had been finalised: our father's party the APC had been declared the clear winner. But Juxon-Smith had recently elevated himself to the rank of brigadier; he showed no signs of stepping down from the limelight.

People were talking in low voices; the room was barely lit by a single hurricane lamp; above the motor hum of the crickets, the only sound in the melting night air was the fluttering of a fat-bodied moth, the occasional scratch of an animal in the bushes. Someone excused himself from the discussion to go outside and urinate. The conversation lulled while people waited for him to come back. Minutes passed. He was taking his time. Someone made a joke. Laughter, followed by a gasp as realisation dawned too late. A uniformed figure appeared in the entrance of the hut and ordered them all out. When they stepped out of the shelter they saw they were completely surrounded by police. A Land-Rover stood nearby; the back door was unlocked and everyone pushed inside. There, lying on the floor, was their handcuffed colleague.

Within a matter of weeks the meetings were being broken up regularly. Sometimes the organisers were held for a few hours, at other times overnight. The activists refused to back down. They held 'pocket meetings' in cars: three or four people travelling together. When they were stopped they claimed to be relatives on their way to a wedding, or sometimes a funeral. They came into the house in ones and twos, masquerading as patients, and talked behind the surgery doors. Finally they began to meet under the auspices of the Poro, the Temnes' secret society.

My father's society name was Bomo, Burning Flame, chosen by Pa Roke, who paid a fee to the Poro before he placed his young son in the care of the Poro elders for three days of initiation. The purchase of the name guaranteed the boy a high status within the brotherhood and determined his future role in the Poro. In the final moments of the ceremony the skin of each novitiate was twice pulled taut and sliced through with a sharp blade. On our father's chest, high on the sternum, were double sickle moons, scars of the Poro.

At night in Koidu Poro men came by the house, remaining in the darkness beyond the rectangle of light cast by the windows. We would hear the three-note whistle of the Poro call. Our father rose from whatever he was doing and slipped outside: '*Termoni*.' He gave the Poro greeting.

'*Telka funka kinka*.' They acknowledged him as one of them and they went by foot to the meeting.

They met deep in the sacred bush where nobody, including and especially heavy-booted Mende policemen, dared to go. In Tonkolili, in our father's constituency, a blue-and-white hut stood in every village. This was the Poro hut, really little more than a storage hut for the masks and costumes used by the society members to stage dances at festival time. But it was considered a sacred site, like everything else connected with the Poro, and provided the activists with a safe place to meet.

The true success of the Poro, however, was to dam the trickle of intelligence that had been reaching the authorities. Men who might become loquacious over a beer or for the price of a few leones thought hard before they broke the Poro oath of silence.

Two months after my father's election victory, my parents sat up late into the night talking. Pressure was mounting; my father was locked into a dangerous game. There were reports of scattered violence, even talk of civil war. Our European mother was conspicuous; without family she was alone much of the time. The day had come for us to go.

One minute I was chasing Jim in the dusty confines of our compound; the next I was gazing at green scenery that raced past my window as, for the first time in my life, we drove along smooth roads that didn't cause the car to shake and rattle like a can tied to a stray dog's tail. After our father drove us to Free-town we boarded the ferry across the bay to the airport at Lungi, where we walked up the steps of the plane and left him behind. I remember nothing of leaving Sierra Leone or arriving at Gatwick, nothing of our journey to Scotland to my grandparents' house in Aberdeen. This was the first of a pattern of sudden departures and unheralded arrivals in new countries that would mark my childhood.

❧ 14 ❧

The first time I saw snow I stood, layered in clothing, at the top of the steps of our caravan and surveyed my brilliant world. It was as though the clouds had tumbled out of the sky and covered the earth. I could see across the roofs of all the other caravans in the site at Nigg, across fields—only yesterday thick with heather, broom and gorse—to the rows of houses and blackened buildings of Aberdeen. The view of the city from Nigg was uninterrupted save by a single Norman church. To the right and behind me was yet more heath land; half a mile beyond that the North Sea. On a cloudy day, which this was not, it was hard to tell where the city ended and the sea began, so seamless was the transition from granite cityscape to flinty grey water.

I hadn't seen snow before, but perhaps it was the memory of my mother's retelling of Grimms' fairy tales, bristling with forests and spired castles; or the pictures on cards sent to us in Sierra Leone at Christmas time: of snowmen, of fat-cheeked Dutch children with strange medieval features throwing snowballs and skating on the canal. I knew what to do. I set off down the five metal steps leading from the caravan.

A narrow path to a sloping driveway led sharply off to the right, down from the plinth of rock and stone upon which the caravan squatted. Overnight flurries of snow, glistening like salt pans, had levelled the land and the opaque expanse looked smooth and secure. From my position on the bottom step, without waiting for my mother and without hesitation, I ran straight out onto it where, for an instant, I pedalled rapidly before plunging through the layers of soft, cool crystals until finally the snow closed over my head. Startled, though unafraid, I opened my eyes. The sun was bright, penetrating the snow; I looked into miles of radiant, white wonderland. It was marshmallow quiet. I felt as though I could swim into it and tried to move. Moments later I felt my mother's groping hands latch onto me from behind.

I trudged through the site in the wake of my mother's footsteps. The snow squeaked beneath our feet as we went past the other caravans to the road, where we searched for our Mini under the snowdrifts. From the surface the snow was still glorious, but in my mind the beauty of the world beneath the snow was matchless.

The day after we arrived at Gatwick our mother had bought a yellow Mini and we loaded it onto the train from King's Cross to Perth, where we disembarked and drove the rest of the way to Aberdeen. For the first few weeks of the summer we lived with my grandparents: I shared a bed with my mother in her old bedroom overlooking the stepped gardens behind Gairn Terrace, while my sister bunked with our grandmother and my brother slept on a camp bed.

One morning in the first weeks of August a blue aerogramme arrived. On the front it bore the large diamond-shaped stamps of Sierra Leone; inside our father's sloping hand. He had been arrested on the orders of the junta on 29 July after rumours circulated that he had been raising money to buy arms for the APC. He had not been charged and he didn't know when he would be freed.

As it turned out his spell in detention lasted four months. Years afterwards our father confessed to being baffled by the curious circumstances of his arrest. The envoy sent to Koidu by the NRC to investigate the rumours turned out to be a young man called Colonel Jumu, someone my father had taught at Bo School. Instead of pursuing his inquiries the young colonel tried to persuade our father to give up the APC and join the junta. My father refused. A letter followed reiterating the offer; he ignored it.

Shortly after the encounter with Colonel Jumu our father was arrested and taken to Pademba Road Prison. There a second letter from the NRC hierarchy, which promised him promotion to lieutenant-colonel within a year, was forwarded by some thorough soul to the detainees' wing of the central prison. From his cell our father penned an uncompromising reply refusing to join an illegal regime.

There were cracks in the NRC leadership, rumours that Colonel Jumu and several cohorts planned to topple Juxon-Smith. The British offered to pack Jumu off on a military training course in England, which was soon quietly effected. The commissioner of police, no fan of Juxon-Smith himself, had been encouraging the dissidents whilst making efforts to secure his own position. All the while there was no indication that the NRC had any intention of making way for the rightful winners of the election. A newly appointed council of civilians briefly brought hope that democratic rule was on its way, but time passed and—nothing. William Leigh, who now had a new job on the council, was certain the APC had hidden caches of arms around the country with plans to remove the junta by force if necessary. It could have been either him or Juxon-Smith who gave the order to arrest our father.

My mother showed the letter to her parents and my grandfather absorbed the news in the same detached manner he had greeted her return home six years after he had turned his back on her. About a year after we moved to Koidu a package had arrived. It was unsigned and bore no return address, but inside was a copy of the *Aberdeen Evening Post*. That was the closest my grandfather could bring himself to apologising to his daughter. You'd better get out and find yourself a job then, he observed; his advice was delivered without embroidery, short and to the point, as ever.

Our mother enrolled on a teacher training course at a local college and applied for a grant. With the money left over from our savings she found boarding schools for Sheka and Memuna and paid the first term's fees. One darkening autumn evening our grandfather drove us all out to Drumtochty Castle. The castle was pink, built of rose granite with several impressive turrets and a tower; it lay in a hollow surrounded by thick pine forests. For all the world it looked to me just like the witch's house in Hansel and Gretel.

We led my brother, dry-eyed, innocent of his fate, up to the long attic dormitory with rows of iron beds spread with tartan rugs. A boy whose parents had already driven away sat on the bed next to my brother's own and watched us. My mother asked his name. I stared, fascinated by his dead-straight, pale hair, equally pale skin and confident manner. Our grandfather placed Sheka's tuck box, with his name in stencilled letters, at the end of the bed and we said our farewells. Poor Sheka was to spend the next two years of his life in that bleak hideout. A few days later my mother and I deposited my sister, two weeks short of her fifth birthday, in her school ninety miles to the south-west in Ayr.

My mother and I began to look for a place to live. We drove up and down the hills of Aberdeen looking at likely apartments. My mother was anxious to leave her parents' house as soon as possible but there were few affordable alternatives.

One afternoon we thought we'd struck lucky. The apartment comprised the upper floor of a sturdy, turn-of-the-century semi-detached house belonging to a widow who lived downstairs. She was fragile-boned, grey-haired and her face seemed kind. She showed us the rooms, explaining at the same time that the house was too big for her and she was looking to let part of it. The entrance was shared, but beyond that we would have complete privacy. As we walked from room to room my mother's optimism flourished. The space was clean, airy and decorated in plain Scots style: oatmeal walls, sprigged curtains and a settee covered in hard-wearing bouclé fabric.

As we stood in the hallway preparing to leave my mother told the woman we'd be happy to take the apartment. Is it just the two of you, then? The woman glanced at me. I was holding on to my mother sucking my thumb. I've two other children, a boy and a girl—they're away at school. And what about your husband? My mother certainly wasn't going to tell her he was in prison. He's a doctor, she replied. Her voice was deliberately casual as she added, He's in West Africa. Oh, I see, said the lady. She had a voice like a whisper, and the rhythm of her accent made it sound almost as though she were crooning. She paused and gave a troubled smile. The problem is, she said, and I'm sure you'll understand—it's just me on my own here and I don't want any foreigners coming into the place. Even if I didn't mind, it's my sons, you see. They'd worry about me awfully. Knowing, well . . . you know.

After that my mother gave up hunting for a flat. An advert for a caravan for sale looked like the solution to our problems. My mother put a deposit on it immediately. It was parked on a site just south of Aberdeen on the other side of the Dee, but still close to her parents, and we moved in. At one end there was a separate bedroom complete with double bed; at the other end the caravan narrowed into a bay window with a pair of benches along either wall. Between them was a Formica table that folded down at night and the benches converted into bunk beds.

My mother painted out the interior, sewed orange covers for the seats and hung a ribboned divider between the kitchenette and the sitting room. There was no bathroom, just a toilet in a concrete shelter shared with the caravan next door and a shower block in the middle of the camp. Near the entrance was the office, run by a woman who wore her peroxide hair teased into a high beehive, and the man who owned our site, Mr Gordon. He was middle-aged and had black hair, side parted and slicked down with oil. He wore square, black-framed glasses and a sheepskin driving coat with big leather buttons. Most days we went into the office to collect our post or buy milk and bread. When we passed I would see Mr Gordon looking out of the window by his desk and whenever he saw us he would slip out from his seat and come over to talk to my mother.

In autumn the long grasses turned golden and the heather browned. A crisp wind blew straight in from the North Sea, and the site up on the crest of the hill caught the worst of it. My mother needed help to pay the hire purchase loan and the bills, so Sonia and Brian, a brother and sister who were also students—Sonia was at the same college as my mother—moved into the tiny space with us. I slept with my mother in the big bed; Sonia and Brian on the bunks. When Memuna and Sheka came home for weekends and holidays there was barely enough room for us all even after everyone doubled up.

Sonia wore a sixties bob with wings of dark hair that framed her face. We three children referred to her between ourselves as 'the lady whose hair was longer at the front than at the back'. We didn't do this to distinguish her from all the hundreds of other Sonias we knew, but rather because we remained deeply awed by her avant-garde hairstyle, the memory of which remained after her name faded.

Brian was Sonia's younger brother and a student of architecture at Gray's. Brian and I got on well; we spent a lot of our time together. Early on weekday mornings, often before dawn, he dropped me at Gairn Terrace on his way into classes. Every day Gran opened the door, nodded briefly at Brian, and pulled me inside. At other times, if there was no one else who could look after me, if my mother was still in classes and Gran was busy,

Brian took me to his lectures at the School of Architecture, where I waited for him in the common room in the company and under the care of a dozen male students.

We had arrived in Britain from rural Africa in the middle of the Summer of Love of 1967. London and San Francisco throbbed to the beat of the sixties. The same could not quite be said of Aberdeen, but there was a vibrant student life and my mother's sense of fun, suffocated under layers of tension in Africa, resurfaced. There were parties in our tiny caravan late into the night, snapshots in my memory: sleeping next to my sister in the big bed, beneath a pile of heavy coats left by guests; the melody of 'Daydream Believer' plucked on a guitar; the collection of nylon-haired gonks I kept on the shelf above my bed.

The Summer of Love, or at any rate the autumn, brought Alistair into all our lives. He was tall, bearded and flame haired: a movie director's idea of a Scots nobleman whose family were gentry from somewhere around Perth. Alistair came with us on trips, crossing fords and hills out towards Deeside and north in the direction of Inverness. We took turns to ride on his shoulders through the prickly gorse and he skimmed stones for us over the translucent water of the lochs. My mother had met him through the folk music group at the college and together they went out night after night, singing songs and recording old tunes in pubs and community centres in the outlying villages.

Our mother transformed into a different woman; she cut her hair into a smooth pageboy that curved under her ears; she was no longer Maureen. Her new friends all called her Chris.

Winter arrived. On a dark, icy morning I woke up and slid my feet into my slippers to go to the toilet. I tried to take a step. My slippers resisted. They refused to part company with the lino. Overnight the temperature had plummeted below freezing and all our shoes had stuck fast to the floor. It was almost as though

they were more afraid to go outside into the cold than their owners. We won a goldfish once at a fair, where I tasted the melting
sweetness of candyfloss for the first time. The ill-fated creature
survived the confines of life in a plastic bag, overfeeding by three
small children, only to perish when we went away one weekend
and came back to find the pipes frozen and the goldfish entombed
in ice. Our mother thawed the ice, thinking that the fish might be
held in suspended animation, but the corpse disintegrated and
then she couldn't even flush the pieces down the loo, because that
was frozen too.

These are the memories that are left behind from our lives in
that caravan. I didn't question my life: I hadn't learned to. Nor had
I yet learned not to. I don't think I asked about Big Aminatta, or
Jim or even my father. I had no yesterdays and no tomorrows. My
days were routine, punctuated by small deeds, minor happenings;
I was roused by the occasional petty excitement and endured a
series of childhood mishaps.

I was hospitalised by a Highland terrier called Paddington
whose teeth tore through the flesh of my lower lip and slashed
my nostril. On the way to the hospital I sat between my mother's
legs; she had a flannel held to my mouth. By the time we reached
the children's wing of the Aberdeen Royal Infirmary, the cloth was
so drenched in red the pattern had been obscured.

I spent an eternity in the hospital in a bed opposite two American boys. I recollect nothing of the pain. Or the hours of stitching
to reconstruct my lower lip. Or being unable to eat because of my
ruined mouth. I only know that I was angry because the nurse
who made the rounds of the children's ward with a potty made
me pee in the pot on the top of my bed. The American boys, being
several years older, she allowed to take the pot under the covers.

The scars were eventually entered into my passport: 'scars on left
lower lip' in mauve ink next to the heading 'Special peculiarities/

Signes particuliers. That meant I would always be identified in the event of an accident. I was the only person I ever knew who had a special peculiarity listed in their passport. Eventually the lopsided slant to my mouth evened and the scars faded, almost.

The teacher training course had given our mother an enthusiasm for organising educational trips. Somewhere along the way she met an architect who worked on the design of the Forth Road Bridge. At his invitation we all drove down the coast road to the crossing over the Firth, where her friend led us on a tour of the bridge. Thirty minutes later, at the halfway point, we stopped to look at the view. And what a mighty scene it was, truly. There we were, hanging perilously over miles and miles of uninterrupted sea. I clung to the steel railings and looked through the bars at the white-peaked waves and the seagulls gliding past at eye level.

Above my head I could hear the architect's voice. My mother asked questions. Their conversation bubbled on. I wasn't tall enough to see above the railings and the heavy top bar blocked the view, so I slipped my head between the bars, where the murmur of adult voices was carried away by the buffeting bluster.

Minutes passed; our guide decided we should press on to the other side, where coffee, juice and biscuits were waiting for us. Everyone moved away. I tried to follow them, but I couldn't seem to withdraw my head. Each time I tried to pull it out, my ears caught against the bars.

There was no choice but to stare at the view for another hour. Help and emergency equipment were summoned; two men worked around me. In time the bars were forced open. I was out.

Back home in Sierra Leone my father was released from prison. Two months later he left the country to join the APC government-in-exile in neighbouring Guinea, where they were indeed amassing arms and men, bankrolled by the diamond millions of Henneh Shamal, a Koidu-based Lebanese diamond dealer. Siaka Stevens and Henneh had known each other for many years, from the time when Stevens served as a minister of mines under the pre-colonial native administration. Shamal, previously an SLPP supporter, was ready to switch allegiances and ally himself openly with the prospective new power.

They planned to invade Sierra Leone and topple the military junta by force, if necessary. Colonel John Bangura, a pro-APC military man who had been sent into comfortable exile to Sierra Leone's embassy in Washington, returned to train the troops. Our father's job was to act as medical officer to the men and he joined them in their bush retreat, where they lived and were drilled. He left everything behind; even the clinic he handed over to an old schoolfriend, Dr Turay, without expecting anything in return. He wrote to my mother and asked her to send him a portable medical kit, which he packed, alongside a copy of the speeches of Che Guevara, and departed for the bush.

Meanwhile my mother spent more and more of her time with Alistair. One chilly evening Brian came home from a trip to London to find me asleep alone in the caravan. On the table was a note from my mother: 'Please look after Aminatta. We've gone to a concert.' Brian was due to attend an event himself that night, at one of the architects' professional associations. Seeing no alternative, he fetched me from my bed, dressed me in mismatching clothes and carried me with him. At the entrance to the cocktail party, in one of Aberdeen's smart hotels, the doorman refused to let me into the room, which was full of men in dinner jackets. We stood at the door not knowing what to do next.

'Come on, then. Bring the bairn here. Come on.' It was the receptionist who had overheard everything from her place at the front desk. For the next four hours I slept on the floor under her desk until past midnight, when Brian came to fetch me, and we walked the three miles home, me riding high on his shoulders.

Brian and Sonia left the caravan soon afterwards, and I had completely forgotten Brian until he wrote to me after I began to present a series of programmes for the BBC in the early 1990s. I have the letter still, asking if I was the same little girl from Sierra Leone who lived in a caravan up at Nigg. A dark photocopy of an old photograph was contained in the brown envelope. It was taken one Christmas spent at the ski slopes at Aviemore. He thought the date was 1969 or 1970 but I knew it must be perhaps two years earlier. Our mother is on the right of the picture, next to an unknown man, and Brian is on the left. Between them is my sister. Sheka alone is forward of the group, peering into the camera lens. For some reason, I am not in the picture.

Yet I remember the day well. We had been ice skating for the first time and everyone had eventually conquered it except me. I wobbled and slid until my mother persuaded me off the ice. I sat in the empty stands and watched. Someone brought me a cup of hot orange juice, so hot I scalded my tongue. I remember the strange rough feeling, like licking rubber, that lasted the whole of the next day.

There was a telephone number at the top of the page; Brian still lived in Scotland—in Elgin on the coast north of Aberdeen. In his letter he wrote how he often wondered what had become of all of us; he had tried to trace my mother several times without success.

My mood was light as I dialled the telephone number. I thought it was fun: here we were after all these years. Yet as soon as he answered I realised the mistake I had made in telephoning without warning. I announced my name and the man's voice that answered trembled with emotion.

I feigned confidence, but I was experiencing the sensation of walking back into my dark past, the geography of which was both familiar and confused. A feeling of dread; too late to turn back. So much of the past was covered in veils. Whatever was coming, he would expect me to provide the answer and as likely I would not be able to do so.

Brian's enquiries among my mother's friends and acquaintances in the early 1970s had met with a series of blanks. Finally he came across a woman who told him, apparently on good authority, that Maureen was living overseas. He asked about the children, the girl he used to babysit. He was told I was dead, slaughtered as a child along with my brother and sister somewhere in West Africa. Until he saw my photograph in a newspaper twenty years on Brian had no idea I was alive.

15

'Stand here, dearie. And if you see anyone, you let me know.' Gran
leaned over and straightened my anorak on my shoulders. She
smelled of cigarettes and Parma Violets. Then she walked away as
I stood still and watched her: blue cloth coat, fur hat, brown zip
booties. Today she had a large handbag slung over her forearm.

Gran and I came together to Duthie Park—for years I called it
Dusty Park—almost every afternoon in the days before I started
school at St Margaret's. The park was a short walk from the house,
just the right distance for a small child and a woman in late middle
age who was finding it ever more difficult to leave the confines of
her own home. Above us the sky was open and cloudlessly blue,
and the park was in full bloom. On either side of me banks of
flower beds displayed clashing blooms: grape hyacinths, heavy-
headed yellow crocuses, rubbery scarlet tulips. Unseen hands had
arranged them into a cacophony of colour—the first I had seen
since we arrived in Scotland—and their brilliant attire brought
back hazy memories of the women in the markets at home.

Opposite the gates of the park flowed the river Dee. Where the
river entered the city of Aberdeen swans glided on placid waters
that widened and stretched until they slipped into the sea. But
only a few miles farther west the same water crashed dangerously and dramatically down a narrow channel over rocks and
boulders. There, on a crag opposite the bridge at Peterculter, a
brightly painted statue of Rob Roy stood poised on the banks, in
perpetual readiness to escape his English captors. In my eyes he
looked magnificent: dressed in a kilt painted red and black with

shiny waterproof paint, matching gaiters, a round shield in one hand and a long, broad sword in the other, framed by a forest of Scots pines.

Gran's father, my long-dead great-grandfather, was crippled in the exact same spot, so the story went, when he tried to save a drowning man from the water below. He leapt in only to find that the water was only a few feet deep and he compressed several vertebrae, confining himself ever after to a life spent living off his wife's earnings. When I was a child I failed to spot the question begged by the story: If the water was so shallow, how then could a man possibly be drowning in it? My grandfather told the story quite differently. He claimed his father-in-law wrecked his legs one night performing a leap of drunken bravado in imitation of Scotland's hero.

On the other side of the park from where I was standing was a concrete boating pond, a good one hundred yards long. On the weekends we came to the park with my mother and watched the boats skate across the surface like beautiful winged insects. To the side of the pond, facing the river, were the swings: six box swings—the sort with bars on each side to hold you in so that you felt as though you were in a flying orange crate. Next to those were three of the regular swings. I wasn't allowed on them after Memuna fell off backwards once while my mother was pushing her. Memuna didn't complain but walked stiffly back to the Mini and stayed silent on the trip home. At bed time Memuna's shirt was stuck fast to her body, dried onto her back with the blood from her skinned back.

In between the swings and where my grandmother and I had entered the park was the bandstand, ringed by oak trees and copper beeches. To the right was a memorial to Elizabeth Crombie Duthie: a girl in a toga with a snake wrapped around her upper torso standing on a tall granite column overlooking the Granite

City. She was surrounded by roses contained within a perfect semicircle of privet.

Beyond the trees were the glasshouses, where thousands of bright buds were raised to be planted out each season. Old ladies in beaver coats walked in pairs in the sun. Below them, masked by trees, was the pond—the focal point of my outings with my grandmother. In her handbag were half a dozen slices of stale bread from yesterday's tea and in a short while we would go together to feed the ducks.

In the meantime I waited, concealed behind a wall of rhododendrons, in a netherworld of understanding. I wasn't exactly sure what we were doing, but I understood my instructions as far as they went. Wait here until I saw someone. Then what?

My hands felt hot, restricted in my mittens as I stood in position. The top of my head tickled under my hat. I tried hopelessly to scratch it with my floppy woollen paws. Beyond the curve I could see my grandmother bend over one of the flower beds. As I watched she took a paper bag from the large handbag she was holding and placed it on the path next to her. Next she produced a small garden trowel and began to dig around the bedding plants.

The itch under my hat was getting worse. I tried to pull my hands out of my mittens. They were tied on tight with a bow of wool at my wrists. I curled my right hand into a fist and pulled clumsily at the end of one mitten with the other hand. Finally, by sheer force of will, I freed my fingers. I let the discarded mitten fall and reached under the warm, tight bonnet to the crown of my head. My grandmother was easing marigolds out of the soil and putting them one by one into the bag.

I scratched my head with my nails and calming relief chased the frustration away. I glanced back at my grandmother; she was still busy. I reached down to one of my wool-encased calves and gave it a hearty scratch, too. It felt good. I began on the other one.

'Are you lost?'

A man stood directly in front of me, about eight foot tall, clad in a greenish-brown uniform.

'Well, Button? Are you all by yourself? Where's your muther?'

I stood still. I had instructions, but they had not prepared me for this eventuality. I tried to think but I hadn't learned how yet. I stayed quiet and looked at the man. Also, I was not supposed to talk to strangers. I stood still. I said nothing.

'You are lost, aren't you? Come on. She can't be far. Let's see what we can do, shall we?' He held out his hand.

Taking it was simply out of the question. My mind was numb. The world around me moved at thrice the pace of my brain. I was terrified of being led away, but I didn't know how to resist. And I had my instructions. Able to go neither forward nor back, I stuck to my position and felt the first surge of alarm in my bladder and my belly.

His tone changed into something brisker. 'Yours, is she? Cute as a button.' He looked from my gran to me and back again curiously, smiling and frowning at once.

'Oh yes, she's mine all right. Come on, Pudding. Where are your gloves?' My grandmother was next to me and all around me, fitting mittens back onto reluctant fingers, straightening my bobble hat and retying the bow under my chin.

The warden watched her. 'Well, no harm done,' he said. 'It's a lovely day for a walk, a lovely day.'

'Ay, well, it is that. Quite lovely.'

I put up my hand to be taken. Gran and I walked away from the park warden, who stood in the same spot, watching us go. At the corner my grandmother turned and waved, as best she could, her right arm hampered by the heavy bag that hung at her elbow.

My grandmother's parents, the Bruce Duncans, had been successful leather merchants—some of the first in Aberdeen. But by the time Lydia, my grandmother, was born just a few streets away from Gairn Terrace, their fortunes were already waning. As soon as she was of age Lydia went to Canada in search of work and a decent standard of living. It was the 1930s. Recession and a pattern of emigration set in place by the land clearances prompted thousands to leave Scotland in answer to advertisements placed by the Canadian and Australian governments. But it was said a bout of meningitis shortly after she arrived put paid to Lydia's dreams. She was repatriated to her family. Soon after that she met Robert Christison and never returned to Canada.

Our grandfather amused himself by saying he had received two warnings not to marry her. After they met at a dance in King's Wells she called out to him from a passing bus as he walked home. He ran and jumped on at the lights. On the day of their wedding the taxi he had hired to drive him to the manse took him to the wrong address. That was the first warning. When he arrived at the right house he found his bride waiting, but no minister. The minister had gone out, forgetting a wedding was booked for that morning. That was the second warning. Eventually the minister was tracked down and hurried back to do his job. Mr and Mrs Christison spent their honeymoon weekend at Arbroath, and on Monday Lydia moved her possessions into her husband's bachelor digs in Crown Street.

Back at Gairn Terrace Gran stripped me of my layers, removed her own coat and slipped a housecoat over her twin set before she went to the kitchen to start the tea. She had a pale yellow and white checked housecoat, and another in lilac. She wore them all the time except when she was going out of the house, when she put on her blue coat or, on certain occasions, a brown wool one with an astrakhan collar.

In the days before she married our gran worked in a milliner's on Rose Street. With her curled hair, pert nose and soft eyes she was often called upon to model hats for well-heeled customers. Years of working in shops among expensive items had given her a taste for fine clothes. She dressed meticulously in skirts, stockings and pastel sweaters, a copy of a style favoured by the women she used to serve. But unlike those women, my gran had to cover her carefully coordinated outfit with an ordinary housecoat to carry out her chores.

I had my bath in the pink-tiled bathroom next to the kitchen. My grandmother ran the water hot and deep, and scrubbed me with Lifebuoy. I had never had a bath tub before. In Koidu we had showers, without even hot water—although in truth the sun on the tank meant the water was always tepid. At the caravan site there was only the shower block. Gran moved between the two rooms keeping an eye on me and laying the tea table at the same time. Left alone for a few minutes I would try to swim up and down in the water.

At six sharp my grandfather came home from the travel agency for tea. There were slices of bread and margarine and hot, sweet tea in yellow Melaware cups, home-made Scotch broth with bloated grains of barley, mince and boiled potatoes or poached haddock followed by glasses of butterscotch Angel Delight. My grandmother did all the cooking, apart from my grandfather's morning porridge; he insisted on making that himself, putting the oats on to soak at night before he went to bed.

Around tea time my mother's car pulled up outside. Once her teaching assignments were over for the day she came to collect me and joined us at the table. We ate, more or less, in silence. My grandfather did not approve of talk at the meal table. My grandmother stepped back and forth between the sink under the window and the table, clearing dishes.

'What'll you take, Am, brown bread or white bread?' Every day the same question. Every day the same answer.

'I'll have white bread please, Gran.'

In my book of poems, alongside the tale of Shock-Headed Peter and the tailor with the enormous scissors who snipped off the thumbs of children who sucked them, was a ballad about three wicked boys who teased a blackamoor. On the opposite page was a sketch of a savage, a little golliwog figure with a faint look of bemusement etched upon his not-quite-human features. The boys were sketched in quite a sophisticated manner, but the little black boy was like a child's drawing: a perfectly circular head, big round eyes and a striped outfit. In punishment for their cruelty a magician took the white boys and dipped them into a giant pot of ink, turning them all into blackamoors themselves.

My grandmother liked to call me 'her little savage', but I didn't want to be like the little inky man in my book. I refused to eat brown bread. I would not eat my boiled egg if the shell was brown. I wanted nothing but white meat, carved from the breast of the chicken. 'Brown bread makes you brown and white bread makes you white,' I recited my own mantra. Did I come up with it myself?

My grandmother took a slice of Mothers Pride from the wrapper, spread it with margarine and cut it into pieces for me.

When we were through eating, my grandfather went back to his chair in the sitting room to finish reading the *Express*. Gran washed the plates while my mother dried, and as soon as the kitchen was set back to rights the two of us drove home in the dark, across the bridge to our caravan site.

16

Spring in my grandfather's garden brought rows of daffodils shuddering in the breeze like a brass band marching to a silent tune. We had been in Scotland for nearly a year. As the evenings lengthened he spent hours in his garden, where he grew rhubarb, raspberries, blackcurrants and vegetables. Late in the summer he collected the fruit and spent a whole day in the kitchen, behind closed doors like a scientist surrounded by bubbling pans and glass jars.

My grandfather had tiny, birdy blue eyes and long dry fingers with which he pinched my cheeks. He dressed in the colours of the hills: tweed jackets flecked with tiny yellow threads like the gorse-covered slopes and sharp creased trousers the same shade as the grey-green heather. When we came to visit he would kiss me sloppily on the lips and never noticed me wipe my mouth with the back of my hand afterwards. At tea he let me share his kippers, carefully stripping a portion of dozens of feathery bones to put on my plate.

Grandad was the first person to tell me I was a changeling. Afterwards I asked my mother what he meant.

'A changeling? That's what the faeries leave behind in the crib when they steal human babies and take them back to their secret world.' She told me about faeries—how they lived in caves in the hills, deep in the forests and glens, and very few people ever saw them. At night faeries came to the homes of overburdened housewives. They cleaned the entire house from top to bottom in exchange for a glass of milk left out for them the night before. When the woman came down the next morning the pots were gleaming and the little people were gone, no trace of them left behind.

My grandmother often referred to the faeries. 'Ay, well. The faeries will do it,' she would say, if the washing up lay in the sink and she was busy with other things. The next morning the washing up would indeed be done. Or if I didn't eat my fish or mince, she'd threaten to let the faeries have my pudding.

I was a faerie, from a hidden world. I liked that idea, so much so I began to tell people I was a changeling.

Months later, on my first day at school I stood up and introduced myself to my teacher and my new classmates as a changeling. Inspired by this information the teacher went out of the room and brought back a book of Scottish myths to read to the class. She showed us a picture of the creature found by an unsuspecting mother in her child's cot. We gazed at the illustration. I was as horrified as the rest of the class by what I saw there: a cringing long-snouted beast wrapped in soft baby blankets fixed the woman with a dreadful, vicious look.

'Are you really a changeling?' asked the boy next to me; he had a pudding-bowl haircut and a mole on his cheek. I didn't answer, I wasn't sure any more. At the end of the day while we were waiting at the bay window for our mothers to come and collect us, the boy with the pudding-bowl hair crept up behind me and pulled up my skirt.

Faeries were not like fairies. I had heard fairy stories. Faeries cleaned the housewife's house in exchange for milk, but if the unfortunate woman forgot to leave a glass of milk out on her kitchen table or started to take the little people for granted they threw tantrums, dropped newly baked pies, overturned butter churns, terrified the cat and played in the flour bins. Faeries stole farmers' horses at night and rode them deep into their enchanted kingdoms, returning the animals to their stables before light, so that in the morning the farmer found his horse too exhausted to pull the plough. Faeries cast spells on men and women, luring them to places from which they never returned; if they managed to escape from the faeries' lair they were rendered deaf and dumb by their experience and could never tell what they knew about the faeries' world.

When he suffered toothache our grandfather removed his own teeth with a pair of pliers. He never visited the dentist or the doctor. One weekend Sheka, home from school, showed me how he could wiggle his bottom tooth by poking it with his tongue. After tea our grandfather fetched a piece of string and called Sheka into the sitting room. He tightened the string around the wobbly tooth and then looped it over the handle of the sitting-room door. Under Grandad's instruction Sheka stood still with his mouth open in the middle of the room, frozen in an expression of surprise. Grandad warned Sheka to brace himself, then he stepped forward and gave the door an almighty heave.

The door banged shut and the tooth flew across the room after it, trailing the string like a kite. We raced forward to pick it up, engaged in a macabre inspection and felt especially rewarded to see a little bit of tattered gum left clinging to it. Sheka was sent to the kitchen to rinse his mouth and have his wound staunched with a wad of damp cotton wool. One by one our baby teeth were dispatched in this way. When my turn came I sat in Grandad's chair afterwards working the tip of my tongue into the soft, metallic-tasting hole in my gum. Gran gave me my tooth, wrapped in a piece of toilet paper. Later that night the Tooth Fairy switched it for a tiny, warm silver sixpence.

As I was growing up I was only remotely aware of the rift between my grandfather and my mother. In each other's presence they behaved with reserved indifference. When my mother came to collect us she always kept her visits to Gairn Terrace brief. She had inherited from her father a distaste for discussion of the emotional or personal kind. They both acted as though they were unaccountable to the other, glided over the pain and let their eyes slide past each other's gaze. They used my grandmother as a medium, deflecting conversation through her, and Gran allowed them to: she soaked up the anger, sifted the rage, allowed her soul be choked with the briny silt of past hurt. Anything to keep the peace in the family.

When my mother had announced she was pregnant my grand-father refused to speak to her or allow her under his roof. She had made her bed and must lie in it, he said. Three years later, a few days after I was born, my mother had contracted appendicitis; our grandfather drove his wife down to Bellshill to the hospital, but would only wait in the car park while she went up to the ward. Until he sent our mother the newspaper while we were in Koidu, they had not exchanged so much as a word.

Back then our mother had left Aberdeen without regret. She had dreams of the life that awaited her and had never intended to live it out in Aberdeen. Her friends worried she might be dis-appointed. Now she was back in Aberdeen, with three brown children; her husband had only just been released from jail, six thousand miles away. A truce between my mother and my grand-father had been achieved, but there was a dark space at the centre of their relationship.

In Guinea our father was still in the bush preparing for armed insurgence. Letters continued to arrive along with money for our school fees. All the while my mother thought he was back in Koidu running the clinic. In the meantime their relationship was apparently on hold. My mother carried on with her degree and her own interests. She had a large circle of friends; her life was reasonably well organised and she seemed happy.

At Easter my brother and sister came home for the holidays. Behind our caravan, travellers arrived and camped in the outlying fields. And in the long grass pitched battles were fought between the kids of the poor whites and the swarthy travellers. No one questioned that we would fight on the side of the home team against the travellers. Stones and insults flew across the divide as Sheka, Memuna and I fought side by side. In a lull between exchanges of fire we whispered and waited, lying hidden from our enemies under cover of the grass. The seconds ticked past. Perhaps the gypsies had retreated. Sheka put his head up above the tall stalks and caught a flying rock in the centre of his forehead. Blood spurted from his wound. We retired from the field.

On 17 April in Daru, a border outpost a long way from Freetown, a group of young soldiers arrested their senior officers, locked them up and took control of the radio. The rebellion spread to Freetown, to the barracks at Murraytown, Wilberforce and Juba, where men broke into the stores and stole arms and ammunition. By evening the privates had locked the entire officer corps in Pademba Road, including Juxon-Smith and Police Commissioner William Leigh, both badly beaten and lying on the floor, alone in their cells. The leaders of the Privates' Revolt, as it came to be known, celebrated and told the press that they had mutinied over pay and conditions, accusing their officers of driving around in smart new cars while the men received nothing. They called themselves the ACRM, the Anti-Corruption Revolutionary Movement.

Our father left Guinea for Freetown as Siaka Stevens's envoy. The takeover had pre-empted the APC's plans and the leadership needed to act fast. He had covered no more than twenty-five miles when he met Mohammed Bash Taqi on his way from Freetown to Conakry: he was in the company of two of the soldiers of the ACRM. The privates in charge of the army had insisted that Colonel John Bangura be asked back from Guinea to lead the movement, with Colonel Genda as his deputy. For the APC it was a good sign.

Later the same night in Freetown our father and Colonel Bangura met the youthful ACRM leaders, alongside a man called Lami Sidique; he had been secretary-general of the NRC's civilian committee. Our father had first met him aboard the *Aureol* when we were all on our way home for the first time. Sidique was an experienced civil servant, a decent man, and he led the negotiations in tandem with the new acting governor-general, Banja Tejan-Sie. The young privates, who had absolutely no agenda beyond exacting their revenge on their officers and commandeering expensive cars, had at least the sense to realise they were in over their heads. They agreed with the proposal to a return to civilian rule. In the last year, though, the political landscape of the country had shifted. Albert Margai was no longer leader of the SLPP. The party was now headed by Salia Jusu-Sherriff, who had been minister of health during my father's brief stay at Connaught Hospital. No one was certain exactly what model of civilian leadership there should be. After countless late-night discussions all the successful candidates from the previous year's elections were called to State House to decide.

Nine days after the Privates' Revolt Siaka Stevens was named prime minister of Sierra Leone for the second time. Everyone waited for the announcement of the next most senior post, that of minister of finance.

Two days later, on 28 April, Mohamed Sorie Forna, our father, was sworn in as minister of finance. He had been with the party only a year and few people had ever heard of him outside the tightest political circles. The rumour mill crackled with whispers. He was described as brilliant, ambitious, ruthless. There was astonishment at his age—thirty-two—followed by a surge of indignation among those party stalwarts who had been bypassed. The opposition had hoped Stevens would give the portfolio to their leader, as a gesture of unity. The Krios for the most part pretended to be above it all. The new minister retired to his new, empty house, with just two months to produce his first budget.

I would have given a lot to be at Gairn Terrace when the cable arrived bringing the news; to know what passed through my grandfather's mind. Here was the black man whom he had snubbed, husband to his daughter despite my grandfather's best efforts, father to the dark-skinned grandchildren who ran in and out of his home, now a cabinet minister. It should have been his worst nightmare, but perhaps it made no difference. Would he, could he now forgive his daughter for defying him? Would it have occurred to him to do so?

Prejudice, though, doesn't depend on logic. It distorts images; it is like viewing a pebble through the waters of a stream. And like water it slips through your fingers: there is nothing to grasp hold of, wrestle with. It can always find another opening. It leaks into everything and in the end, if it drains away, it leaves everything damp. Still the same, but slightly stained, with a tide mark around the edges.

I was too young to ask those questions and my mother would not. I didn't see my grandfather or my grandmother again until I was twelve and by then I was coming to terms with something altogether more momentous. Much later, I came round to asking Grandad, but although he spoke to me of many things he would not speak to me of that.

17

We returned to a new house and a city I could barely remember.
I was only a year and a half old when we left Freetown for Koidu.
The only reminders of our lives up-country were Big Aminatta,
who was even bigger now, and Jim, the Old English Sheepdog.
Poor Jim. Twelve months of neglect had exacted their toll upon
him. I caught sight of him wandering the grounds a day after we
arrived, confused and listless, looking like he had a bad case of
mange. It was only when I saw Jim I remembered that he had once
been our dog. A memory bubbled up, but never quite surfaced.
Gazing at Jim, my dog, who looked at once familiar and strange,
produced a swimming sensation, of lives leaking one into the
other. As for Jim, he didn't remember me at all.

The ministerial residence in Wilberforce was grand, certainly
by African standards. In contrast to the pitched roofs and layered
rooms of the colonial homes, the concrete house was built in the
shape of a letter P, flat planes at one end, curved walls and balconies at the other. It was painted bright white, except for under the
eaves and the pillars supporting the roof over the veranda, which
had been daubed with turquoise.

At the front a sloping garden overlooked a view of the hills and
the sea. At the back, the direction from which the house was approached, there was an expanse of empty land bordered by a row
of concrete cabins that served as the boys' quarters and several
piles of gravel. The gravel had probably been there since independence; it gave the whole place an unfinished look, as though the
money for the job had run out or the last occupants had left in a

hurry. Given the sorry state of our government, either, or both, were entirely possible.

The rains were just beginning. The city looked burned out and exhausted, as if it needed a grand soaking to reach the depths of the earth, bring back the greenery and live again. The brief night-time showers did little more than leave streaks on the cars, on the painted facades of houses and down window panes. A year had passed and the populace had endured a lot; the jubilation had ebbed away a long time ago. People were becoming too accustomed to the lingering sourness of disappointment.

At the end of June our father presented his budget speech to parliament. He wore traditional robes: pure white with curls of gold embroidery cascading down the front and at the cuffs and hem, and a matching round cap. He had worked on his presentation round the clock.

In the Margai era the government misspent so flagrantly that suppliers refused their worthless IOUs and began to demand cash on delivery. Juxon-Smith, with his customary zeal, had investigated the wealth of ministers and where he found evidence of corruption he forced the miscreant to repay the money. People relished the sight of big men cut down to size, but little cash was actually recouped. Juxon-Smith raised taxes and went begging to the International Monetary Fund for the second time. We were nine million leones in debt.

New countries like ours were easy prey for western lenders, who persuaded leaders to finance new projects on credit. In the five years following independence, factories, roads and hotels flourished, springing up across the landscape. They were popular, too, yielding jobs and manufactured goods; they made people feel that our country was developing—never mind that they were bought at an inflated price or that repayments swelled each year, leaving every man, woman and child bound and the country in hock for years. Ministers, contractors and suppliers were satisfied. They built new houses and bought gleaming, growling cars with their cut of the deal. But greedy hands had strangled the golden goose. When the cars broke down there were no parts or trained mechanics to fix them. Houses begun were never finished. They turned into ruined building sites, bristling with steel girders, lacking outside walls so that rooms were exposed to view, like a doll's house. Homeless people moved into them, living their lives in front of an audience like actors on a stage, with velvet drapes of moss hanging down and hordes of African pied crows screaming in the wings.

There was no more chocolate milk in triangular cartons. The milk-processing factory was closed; the company had gone bust, leaving the government with outstanding loans. Along the beach at Lumley, in the curve of the bay where I spent days of that holiday rolling in the surf, the Cape Sierra Hotel stood on the tip of the peninsula. The modern building was equipped with a swimming pool, luxury reception rooms and an outside dance floor, but the bedrooms were unoccupied half the year.

Our father called the Cape Sierra Hotel a folly, 'mocking us all from Aberdeen Point'. He said so in his speech to the House of Representatives. The next day's newspapers wore his words across their front pages like a bandanna, alongside a picture of him sweeping into the house, confident and smiling. His first priority was to end the cycle of borrowing and bankruptcy. There were to be no tax rises. Ending diamond smuggling was the next priority, and in exchange for the assured security of their mines the diamond companies would pay an extra tax, a hypothecated tax to be used purely for development projects. It was a cautious budget, but an optimistic one. It reassured genuine international investors and won the confidence of local people.

Our father had a brilliant mind, combined with unshakable self-belief. He had set about mastering his new job in a matter of months. Brian Quinn, the IMF's representative, who used to teach at an American university, lent him Samuelson's *Principles of Economics*. Our father spent his days at the ministry and his evenings with his team of advisers, cramming his head with information just as he had during late nights in the front room of my parents' tenement flat when he was a medical student. For a man of his ability it wasn't an impossible job: ours was a tiny country with a rudimentary economy. And besides, what alternative was there? This was government in the newborn states of Africa. Lines of graduates, trained specialists: these did not exist. Africa had to make do with what she had. In many countries it proved disastrous, but it could also be exhilarating. Within the struggle there were moments like these when suddenly everything seemed possible.

At home, though, the ephemeral hopefulness that follows a reunion had already drifted away. By 1968 our parents' marriage was a bowl patterned by a thousand hairline fractures; it was not to survive the holiday.

They had been apart for more than a year. They had both had other relationships. My mother arrived from Aberdeen to find a pair of hair combs and a jar of skin-lightener in the bedroom.

Over those hot, wet months, while mildew grew on our new suitcases in the cupboard, we watched as our parents acted out the inevitable denouement of their marriage. Their war was conducted with the weapons of silence and withdrawal. There was not even the comfort of an angry confrontation, no vivid scenes to focus our floundering emotions or anchor the insecurity in something solid.

One morning we all had breakfast together. Our father took his coffee heavily sugared, and he asked my mother to pass the sugar bowl. She carried on, blandly eating her breakfast as though she hadn't heard. He repeated himself in a clear, even voice. We all looked up—everyone, that is, except my mother, who had suddenly turned stone deaf. Her eyes were fixed somewhere on the centre of the tablecloth, as though she were examining a stain. I slipped out of my seat and with one foot on the floor I stretched out towards the sugar bowl. It was just out of reach. My fingers fumbled on the rim as I tried to drag it closer. The bowl toppled and fell. Crystals scattered on the white tablecloth. *Now look,* my mother exhaled in exasperation. I climbed back into my seat as she began to scoop the sugar up; then she replaced the bowl—exactly where it had been before, next to her elbow.

Our mother was the first person in her family to marry a foreigner. Our father was the first person in his to marry for love. When the passion leached out of their union and left a colourless husk, he offered her something else. An African marriage, my mother pronounced with scorn, where the men and women do their own thing. She could not accept such a compromise, for she was a European woman who deserved nothing less than to be loved and cherished.

Our mother always denied what others talked about openly: that she was pregnant when she married my father. Times changed and women married or lived alone, kept their maiden names, worked at their own careers, had babies out of wedlock—still our mother clung to her position, which became less tenable as the years mounted. I always thought she was protecting her reputation, in an old-fashioned sort of way. But in time I began to see her motivations might be different: she wanted people, us especially, to see her marriage as an act of daring, precipitated by true love.

It should have been a brave, compelling love, the love of myths. And yet the prosaic truth hinted at a different reality. It had been an inauspicious union, sadly flawed at its inception.

That holiday our mother spent her days with friends, old and new. Somehow in that fractured atmosphere she blossomed nevertheless. She loved the sun and soon her skin flushed pink and gold, streaks of nacre shone in her hair. When she was around our father her mouth hardened into a straight line and she stared into the corner of the room, but when she was with her friends she seemed radiant.

Our father focused on his official engagements. He flew to Israel with his economic adviser to persuade the Israeli government to buy back the oil refinery they had built. It was overpriced and, since Sierra Leone had no oil to speak of, useless. He rose early and spent long hours at the ministry. In the evenings he played tennis at the Hill Station Club and often we joined him, fetching the balls that rolled into the corner of the courts, or were pitched over into the hedges on the other side of the fence. Weekends we all went to the beach as a family, to Cape Club, where we spent our afternoons playing on an old wreck. The boat was washed up on the sand, beached so that it was beyond rescue and would never sail again. But for that one holiday it was still a boat and we played in the cabin, spinning the wheel this way and that. Gradually, the gentle waves tore into the hull, pulling it apart until eventually, years later, I could only find a snag of rusty metal in the sand.

Much of that holiday is lost to me now, although curiously I recollect with great clarity events leading up to it as well as those that took place shortly afterwards. Perhaps the atmosphere at home discouraged me from forming memories. I have seen the photographs: me at the beach, hand in hand with Big Aminatta, my hair a mass of dense ringlets, crystals of salt sparkling like precious stones on my darkened skin. In another shot I am leaning over the balcony overlooking the garden at Minister's Quarters, my feet on the lowest rung, laughing wildly at who knows what, and that wild hair again, blowing across my face. They are happy images, there's no doubt. Yet they exist in a vacuum with barely a corresponding memory alongside.

18

Milik was the steward in the house on Spur Loop and he was there when we arrived. He doesn't appear in any of the photographs, nor was Milik his real name.

In the mornings he laid the table and served breakfast. The milk, mixed from powder and water the day before, was kept chilled in the fridge. The cold masked the chalky flavour, made it seem almost like real milk. In the mornings, after I poured my Rice Krispies into the bowl, Milik would ask: 'Milik?'

'Milk,' one or other of the three of us corrected. 'Milk. It's milk. Say "milk".' We pressed our lips together—'mmm'—and to enunciate the final syllable we stuck our tongues out to touch our upper teeth in an exaggerated manner: 'Mmm-ilk. Mmm-ilk.'

'Mi-lik,' he repeated carefully. 'Milik.' No matter how he tried, or how much we teased him, he couldn't form the word without slipping in the extra vowel. In time we gave up, but we called him Milik between ourselves and sometimes as a nickname. He took our teasing as it was meant, as a sign of our affection. Gradually we stopped using his real name altogether and now I can't even remember what it was.

During the days Milik worked in the kitchen, carrying out his chores alongside our two cooks, Amara and Amadu. He sorted the laundry and washed it by hand in a big zinc basin under the tap at the back of the house; at other times he sat on the step by the back door and plucked chickens with Big Aminatta. Above them the vultures circled and landed, one by one, until there was a queue on the roof's edge waiting for the scraps. In the evening, just before the official Mercedes appeared in the drive, Milik changed into a clean white shirt and as soon as our father called he carried through a glass and a bottle of cold beer on a tray. The rest of the time he sat on a stool in the corner of the kitchen, polishing our father's shoes, rubbing with tight circles over the same spot until the shoes shone like a stag beetle's back.

I loved Milik. He was never impatient with me, the way Big Aminatta and even Amadu and Amara could be. We three children spent most of our time in the kitchen and out the back, climbing the mango tree that crowded over the kitchen door, collecting the taut, green fruits and eating them sprinkled with salt. He warned us we would get stomach ache. 'Why?' I asked—the question I asked after every adult statement.

Milik simply shrugged: 'There are things you know, but you don't understand,' he replied, and there was nothing I could say.

Sometimes Milik would oblige my continued presence with a story. Some were the tales of Mr Spider. In America, where the fables were carried by enslaved Africans two centuries before, the foolish character whose deeds and misdemeanours are driven by greed and self-interest became known as Br'er Rabbit. In Ghana he is Ananse, the Spider. Other stories, the ones I really preferred, were the rambling accounts without an obvious meaning that featured devils or bush spirits and their encounters with men.

'There was a man with a lump on his back,' started Milik one day. He was sitting on the kitchen step with a chicken, its throat freshly slit, in his hands.

'A hump?' I checked.

'Yes, a hump. There was a man with a hump on his back.'

I interrupted a second time, just to revise my correction: 'A hunchback.'

'Yes.' Milik, like most people I knew in Sierra Leone, didn't take umbrage when you corrected his English. He plunged the chicken into scalding water and went smoothly on: 'Everyone in the village knew the hunchback because of his hump. One day this man was walking back from the fields when he stepped off the path to piss and while he was standing there some devils saw him and they said to each other: "If a thing is on a thing, let us take it off. Or if it is not on, let us put it back on!"

'They led the man into the middle of their dancing ring under the hump tree, where humps were hanging. They danced around him and sang their song:'

> Round and round,
> If you meet a person in the dance, they will beat you,
> Round and round,
> Let us hang it there, they will beat you.

'What does that mean? Who will beat you?' I asked.

'It's the devils' own song. It doesn't mean anything.'

'It must mean something.' Although I enjoyed Milik's stories, I'd become used to the sort of tales, like 'Snow White' or 'Cinderella', in which every detail has its place and purpose, driving listener and storyteller to an inevitable moral conclusion. It didn't occur to me that something of the song might have got lost in the translation.

'It's just a song these devils sang among themselves. Listen. You don't worry about it. They said: "If a thing is on a thing, let us take it off. If it is not on, let us put it on." And whoop, they lifted off his hump and hung it on the hump tree. The man went back to the village, where the people were amazed to see him with a straight back.'

Milik paused, tearing a handful of feathers off the bird. I hated the smell of wet chicken feathers and scalded skin, but not enough to leave.

'Now, the chief in that village had a son who was also a hunch-back. When he saw the man around the village, he ran to him and asked how he rid himself of his hump.' Milik paused and leaned closer. 'Well, what passes between a devil and a man is supposed to be kept secret, but anyway the man told the chief's son.'

'Just because he was the chief's son?'

'Yes, because he was the chief's son and because the man for-got he should have kept the secret. So the chief's son went to the same place and stepped off the path, and the devils saw him, and they put him in the ring and sang their song.' Milik skipped sing-ing the song again. Probably he didn't want to answer any more questions about it.

'Then they chanted, "If a thing is on a thing, let's take it off. And if it is not on, let us put it on," and they ran up and snatched the hump off his back and threw it up on the hump tree.

'The chief's son was very, very pleased indeed and he rushed back to the village to show his father how straight he had be-come. He decided he wanted to thank the devils for their deed. The first man had not done so—he was poor. But the chief's son was rich. He did not know that you shouldn't thank a devil, that they do what they do. If you want to go saying thank you, you will offend them.

'The chief's son bought a fine country cloth and took it to the devils' place. He called them: "You took a hump off the back of a man who is poor," he explained, "and he did not give you any-thing. But my father is rich and so I am bringing you this fine country cloth."

'The devils listened in silence. They were annoyed, you see. Nobody should thank a devil. So they took the chief's son and put him in the middle of the dancing ring and sang their devils' song. Then they cried: "If a thing is on a thing, take it off. And if it is not on, let us put it on." And they grabbed a hump from the hump tree and put it on his chest. *Whump!* And they told the man that if a devil does something for you, you should go quietly. You shouldn't go back with gifts and say thank you to them. This is not why they do it. They sent him away.'

I waited. Milik was silent, using his fingernails to extract from the skin of the fowl the tips of a few feathers that had broken off.

'What happened next?' I asked.

'Nothing. It's the end of the story.'

'Well, it's not fair!' I became indignant. 'The man who said thank you got punished. What happened to the other man? The one who broke the devils' secret?'

'Nothing.' Milik was unperturbed. 'He went on with his life.'

'But it must mean something.'

'It means when you see someone with a lump on their chest, they bought it with a country cloth.' Milik laughed. He picked up the bowl of greasy water and threw it out into the yard. Several vultures dropped down, hitting the ground soundlessly, the span of their great wings billowing like parachutes. 'You wouldn't go back to find a devil. Just like you wouldn't buy a dead chicken,' he finished and ducked back through the dark mouth of the kitchen door.

I remembered Milik's story months later in Aberdeen. We returned in October, back to our caravan since the value of the leone against sterling made moving unaffordable. One of the local newspapers even did a story about us: the African minister's wife and children who lived in a caravan. Our mother came back to finish her course; Memuna stopped boarding and joined me at St Margaret's. It was cold and raining, the wind danced and kicked the leaves high up so that they swirled around in front of the bay window as we waited for our parents to collect us.

Our school days finished with a story from the teacher. We were allowed to bring books to class with stories for her to read, and it

occurred to me, as we sat in a circle around her, that the faeries
in Scotland were just like the contrary devils in Sierra Leone. So
I asked her to tell the story about the man with the hump on his
back. She thought I meant *The Hunchback of Notre Dame*. No, I
said, the story with the devil in it. The teacher looked at me frowning and told me to shush. We would not talk about the devil or
tell stories about him. She would hear no more about it.

The next time the butcher's van stopped outside 38 Gairn Terrace to deliver Gran's messages, I looked through the back door
and saw headless chickens, lying on their backs, stumpy legs in
the air. At the kitchen counter Gran prepared the chicken for high
tea, cutting off flaps of skin with a pair of kitchen scissors. I told
her she shouldn't buy dead chickens.

'Whatever makes you say that, dearie?' She looked down at me
in surprise. 'You don't think I'm going to kill it myself, do you?'

Milik's soft, moulded features rose in my mind and I heard
his voice. For a moment I smelled the pungent scents of Africa. I
couldn't begin to explain to Gran. *There are things you know, but
you don't understand.*

We were in our yellow Mini, sliding sideways down a hill at
Nigg. My sister and I were in the back seat, my brother and our
mother in the front. I saw a red car gliding uphill towards us.
Winter had glazed the roads with ice as dark and clear as sugar
on a toffee apple. After a slow motion slide the two cars met with
a crunch. Nobody was hurt. Two milk bottles on the back seat
shattered, bathing our school uniforms, skirts and knickers.

On bonfire night, on the beach with my mother and her student
friends, I gasped and held my breath as a rocket exploded and lit
up the black sky. Burning embers fell earthward and landed on
my foot. A weal appeared on my red Wellington boot; it bubbled
and the bubble burst, a hole appeared and my nylon sock began
to melt. When the fire touched my skin I screamed. My mother

flew towards me across the hard pebbles, pulled my foot free and plunged it into the freezing sea.

Two months later in Freetown, at five o'clock in the morning, my father overslept by a few minutes and was late for his morning shower. Moments later a blast tore through the empty bathroom, gouging a great hole in the exterior wall and sending a jagged crack from floor to ceiling across the adjacent bedroom wall. He went into the bathroom to find the air opaque with smoke; on the other side of the room he could just make out the remains of the air-conditioning unit lying on the floor. When daylight came the police arrived and said there was evidence of foul play. The following day the newspapers reported an attempt on the life of the finance minister.

In public our father made light of it, saying it was nothing more than a faulty unit. The police wanted to fly in a special investigator, but our father wouldn't hear of it. He said it would cost too much in public money, but privately he confided to friends that he doubted the culprit could ever be touched by the law.

Siaka Stevens, who had recently appointed him to act as premier while he was out of the country on official business, joked in Krio: 'Na dis job I don gi you make dem wan kill you?' Has the job I've given you made someone want to kill you? Our father took to wearing a gun at his hip, for the first time since he came back from Guinea.

In Scotland the nights were stretching out and the darkness dragged away the few hours of daylight ever earlier. Every morning as soon as I woke up I ran to the window to see what patterns Jack Frost had left for me on the panes of glass. A few weeks later our shoes began to stick to the floor again.

19

Our mother showed us her wedding ring: a yellow, flickering band. Memuna tried it on. It hung loosely on her finger, but she held out her hand like an adult woman checking her manicure. Our mother laughed at her eldest daughter's poise.

When we three were alone, I asked: 'Isn't Mummy married to Daddy?'

'Not any more, I don't think,' Sheka replied. 'Now she's married to Uncle Win.'

'What about Daddy, then?' I asked.

'I don't know,' he said. He stood up and walked away.

Our mother was back from Mexico, where rock stars and actresses went to shed their partners, like old skins, before they wed new ones. Our mother married Winston Prattley, a United Nations official who came from New Zealand and was sixteen years her senior. She had met him in Freetown during our holiday; they had sat next to each other at a dinner at the British high commission while my father was abroad and their relationship started shortly afterwards. Winston Prattley followed us back to Aberdeen and proposed to our mother, promising her that with him she would never need to work again. His offer met with satisfaction: from both the romantic and the pragmatic side of our mother's nature.

It was the summer of 1969. Britain was in the middle of a heat-wave. The world watched Neil Armstrong walk on the moon in fuzzy black and white. In Mexico our mother's wedding plans were delayed by twenty-four hours while the public officials took a break from conjoining foreign couples with careworn faces and stayed at home instead to drink tequila with their families. In America anti-war protesters claimed the walk was phoney, staged in a TV studio to divert attention from the killing in Vietnam.

Back in Scotland we three children spent the week in a farm-house with a lady called Tessa and no television. Instead Tessa, who was a friend of my mother's from college, had a splendid cottage garden, full of strawberries that were just beginning to ripen. We picked all the red ones, swallowing them with illicit pleasure, licking the transparent pink juice from our fingers. Then, unable to resist, we pulled off the ones that were still pale and ate them, too.

Afterwards our mother and Uncle Win collected us from Scotland and he treated us all to a holiday in Yugoslavia. The first night we slept in a castle in Dubrovnik, where the air drifting through the open window was like warm breath flavoured with herbs, scents of wild rosemary, oregano, thyme and bay. I had never been in a country that smelled as sweet as Yugoslavia.

Mornings we spent wandering through the cobbled streets of the old town, where cars were forbidden and old ladies in shiny, black clothes pushed mules along in the aching bright sunlight. A stand sold strawberry and vanilla ice cream, more delicious than any I had ever tasted. Uncle Win treated us all to one almost every day. Afternoons we went for a drive or swam in the sea, where I learned to hold my breath and open my eyes underwater and once watched in wonder as a turquoise sea horse bobbed in front of my nose.

One afternoon we rented a motor boat. My mother stood at the end with a fishing rod in her hands wearing a crochet bikini. The nylon line winged through the water after the boat. In a while it snagged, loosened and pulled taut again. She gave a small 'ooh' of excitement and began to reel her catch in slowly while we all crowded at the end of the boat. Everyone, including the boat's driver, who switched off the engine and threw his cigarette into the water, waited to see what she had caught. The whining pitch of the reel slowed; the water bubbled and the surface split. I saw vivid shades of purple, blue and green, like an oil spill, shimmering strands that trailed off into the wake of the drifting boat. There was silence.

'Medusa,' the driver pronounced. 'Jellyfish. Very dangerous.' He drew his hand across his throat. I thought he meant we were going to kill it and I wondered how. My mother held on to the rod while we drove the boat out to sea, far away from the shore and the swimmers, and there the boatman cut the line.

On the way back to the beach my mother explained that the Portuguese man-of-war was the most dangerous jellyfish in the sea: its tentacles grew to seventy foot and the sting from them could kill a man. Why was it all different colours? Had anyone ever been stung? Why was it Portuguese? We mouthed questions at her, while Uncle Win gazed at his new wife with pride and slowly stroked the copious hairs of his black walrus moustache.

Our mother's new husband was based in Nigeria; when they met he had been in Freetown on a visit to oversee the local office. From Yugoslavia we went back to Scotland, where my mother packed up the caravan for the last time and sold her yellow Mini. She was leaving Aberdeen for the second time, and once again she said few goodbyes. We flew to Lagos and the four of us moved into Uncle Win's spacious home in a neighbourhood colonised by embassy workers and oil company staff. Far away from the seething, sweating swarm of Lagos, the white-painted wooden house was surrounded by a beautifully tended garden with lawns like green felt and borders full of flowers. There were uniformed staff: a cook, a gardener, a driver and a houseboy. Inside the house were rugs, polished wooden floors, even a separate dining room and a wide staircase leading to the upper floors.

Even though the house seemed to be so big, there wasn't room enough for all of us. So while my mother moved into the master bedroom, the three of us shared a room on the other side of the landing. It contained only two beds, and so a sofa was brought up the stairs and put at the foot of the other two beds. That was where I slept.

A few days after we arrived my mother called us to her. We gathered around her in the sitting room. She had something important to talk to us about, she said. 'Uncle Win is your father now. So what do you think you would like to call him? You can carry on calling him Uncle Win, or just Win if you like. But if you want to, it might be nice if you called him Daddy.' She looked at each of us in turn.

I thought for a moment. I liked Uncle Win, I remembered the ice creams. And the thought of calling someone 'Daddy' felt good.

'Sheka?'

'I'm going to call him Win, Mummy.' I was surprised at my brother's choice. I thought he was brave to call an adult by his first name, bare and unadorned. To my ear it sounded impertinent without some sort of prefix or another. Like going into a church without a hat. I could never do that.

'That's fine. What about you, Memuna?'

My sister plumped for 'Uncle Win'. It was my turn, the youngest.

'Am?'

I said I would call him Daddy. My mother was pleased. She smiled her special smile for me, a sudden brilliant flash, and hugged me, pressing my nose against her soft breast. 'Good girl!' she said, rolling her 'r's in the way she did: 'Good gurrl!'

I tried, I really did. But it didn't stick. I would forget, and when I remembered I couldn't quite form my lips round the word and push it out. Instead I dropped my voice and whispered, tagging it onto the rest of the words at the end of a sentence—'Daddy?' The word hung suspended in the air as if I might open my mouth and let it slip back into the warmth. No one else seemed to notice. Not even Uncle Win, who didn't react one way or the other to whatever he was called. So I stopped. I went right back to calling him Uncle Win, which probably was no more appropriate than calling him Daddy, but it would do.

Can-can in combat boots. Past our house the soldiers strode, ten abreast across the width of the avenue, legs flung high as chorus girls, blank eyed as paid performers: young men who had sold their bodies for an infantryman's wage. They wore fatigues and heavy black boots drawn tightly at the ankle with laces woven in and out of dozens of eyelets. I, who had recently learned to tie my laces, found them compelling.

In Nigeria the war in Biafra was reaching its terrible zenith. Two years earlier the Christian Igbo people, who lived east of the delta of the Niger river, declared their independence from the rest of the state, threatening to spark the break-up of the Nigerian Federation. Many African states supported General Gowon's military government in Lagos and Britain supplied him with military hardware. Tanzania and the Ivory Coast recognised Biafra's claims and France shipped arms to the secessionists.

The military might of the government in Lagos dealt the Igbos a series of swift and successful blows, but the Biafrans clung on for two years, refusing to surrender their dreams of a homeland. The war had disrupted food production and gradually the stores ran out. General Ojukwu, the Biafran leader, refused to allow aid supplies into Biafra if they had been shipped through federal Nigeria. The war officially ended after the New Year. Ojukwu fled to the Ivory Coast. By then more than one million Igbo people had slowly starved to death.

In Lagos we were far from the fighting, yet the signs of war were there. The secret police dumped bodies in the sea which sometimes washed back up onto the beaches or floated into the harbour, arms bound at the elbow, the marks left by their final torture still evident upon the bloated bodies. My stepfather was a keen sailor and a member of the Lagos Yacht Club, a popular meeting place for ex-patriates. On the weekends the sailors raced each other round orange buoys in the harbour and drank Heineken on the terraces. During those competitions yachtsmen sometimes sailed past the nameless victims of tribal persecution with whom the police had finished.

Our mother told me how, hanging out on the trapeze of Uncle Win's Flying Dutchman, she had hit a corpse. One minute she was skidding over the waves like a flying fish, the next she felt a bump. The corpse and she came back to back, like two people on a dance floor, just for a fraction of a second—and then the motion of the boat swept her away.

At first we watched the soldiers march past from the upstairs balcony. One day we crept down and crawled through the hedge and stood in the street. The next day we moved closer. And the day after that. We edged in until, at some point, our passive curiosity transmogrified into a game of chicken with the stamping feet of the soldiers. We crouched in the street until we could feel the first vibrations thudding through us. At that moment my stomach tightened. Then I saw the dust swirling at the end of the road. The soldiers were on their way. We held our positions right in the path of the approaching juggernaut. Our bodies were coiled tight as cobras. At the final moment, just when I thought I was about to feel the heel of a boot on my back, we hurled ourselves out of the way and scrambled through the hedge back into the safety of the house.

*   *   *

Our mother stitched brown and white checked dresses for my sister and me, and bought brown shorts and a white shirt for Sheka. We stood for our fittings on the landing at the top of the stairs, where my mother kept her desk, papers and her sewing machine.

Every Sunday we lined up in the same place, dressed only in our knickers, one behind the other. Sheka, Memuna, then me. Our mother checked us front and back for small red pimples and when she saw one she put a dab of Vaseline petroleum jelly on it from the family-sized pot on her knee. A few minutes later a pinprick of white appeared and when my mother squeezed a creamy, fat maggot, no more than a few millimetres long, slid out. We called them *tumbu* boils. The insects laid their eggs in the fibres of clothes as they dried on the washing line and even though the servants ironed every piece carefully, right down to the last sock, sometimes eggs survived the hot iron and hatched in our skin. The glutinous Vaseline cut off the oxygen, forcing the larva out for air. Afterwards our mother gave us our pocket money, a thrupenny bit, with a picture of the queen on it, just like we used to get in Scotland.

In September we started at Corona School, and on the first day it was evident to me our dresses were all wrong. They were the same colour as the other girls' dresses, granted. But while everyone else wore a broad gingham check, our checks were narrow. Not only were we new, with no friends, but our dresses were different. The other pupils glanced at us from the safety of rings of their friends. We lined up on the playing fields next to the long row of classrooms; no one spoke to us, so we in turn pretended to ignore them.

The pupils at Corona were a mixed group; the mass of black faces was speckled with white ones. Most of the boys and girls were Nigerian, but the school's good reputation made it the first choice among the overseas business community.

Mrs Sami, my teacher, however, looked as if she came from somewhere in the South Seas. She had glossy black hair swept upwards so that it framed her broad forehead and high cheekbones; at the back of her head the hair was pulled into a sizeable chignon. Her son Eddie was in my class and I was put into the seat next to him. It was soon evident that he was eager to become my friend. Eddie had skin the colour of butter, a quick grin and a spiky fringe of the same dead-straight black hair as his mother. I never asked myself why he wanted to be friends, or wondered why the desk next to him was empty. That his mother was our class teacher didn't worry me. At that time I had only two ambitions. The first was to catch up with my brother and sister. The second was to become a boy.

At home I made parachutes for Sindy just like the ones Sheka had for his Action Man, only mine were made of handkerchiefs and string. There was a flat roof above the kitchen where we secretly played and melted our wax crayons under the sun, creating giant palettes of psychedelic colours. From the roof's edge I launched Sindy on her missions into enemy territory. Not once did the chute open and Sindy broke both her legs; they dangled at odd angles beneath her well-endowed torso. Later I took to borrowing my brother's shorts, so much better suited to sliding down banisters than my own little skirts. I wanted to be a boy and being best friends with a boy was a fine start, so I smiled right back at Eddie.

Those first few weeks of school we were always engaged in some project or another. We were told to ask our parents for a black-eyed bean. The next day we put it into a jar with blotting paper and water and over the following days we watched our beans germinate, the shoots race up the glass towards the light. Next we were asked to bring an insect into class. All weekend I laid piles of breadcrumbs on the floor and hovered out of sight with a jam jar, but all I did was encourage lines of ants into the house. On Monday morning I sat ready for school, my empty jar in my hand. As I waited for the driver to arrive I noticed on the white wall in front of me a walking twig. I moved closer. It was a creature of brilliant green: perfect oval head, black eyes, long, slender legs, wings like curled new leaves. At school Mrs Sami said my insect was called a praying mantis. She explained how, after mating, the female devoured the male. We stared at her. None of us believed a word of it.

Our mother had dropped her teacher training course when she married our stepfather, but she did not waste all her new skills. Every day after school she gave us additional classes. It was during these extracurricular hours that I learned to write. I joined Sheka and Memuna as they practised their handwriting and while my mother worked with each of them I entertained myself copying out rows of arbitrary letters. One day I lay on my stomach opposite my sister on the floor; her books were fanned out around us. On my blank piece of paper I traced three round, looping letters: C-A-T.

'Look, Mummy,' Memuna exclaimed. 'Am can write. She's written a word. She's written CAT.'

My mother, working at the table with my brother, came over to have a look. 'Clever girl.'

I warmed to her praise like a tomato in the sun, without being at all certain what I had done. The production of this word had been entirely a fluke, but now here I was being told I could write. I didn't say anything. I smiled at her. I thought: she must know. After that my mother began to include me in the writing classes, where from that day on I wrote and wrote and wrote.

A few years along I learned to ride a bicycle in just the same way. Clutching onto a low wall, pulling myself forward at a painful,

wobbling pace, my hand slipped suddenly and the bike spun forward down a small incline. A few seconds passed before I managed to land one of my feet on the ground.

It was Memuna who, for the second time, announced my triumph prematurely. 'Am's riding the bike. She's riding the bike!'
In a moment the whole family had come out to see me do it. And
so I did. I had to. I got on and rode the bicycle up and down for
everyone to see.

During break one day Eddie and I were playing on the scorched
grass of the school fields, in the shade of a large tree. We were
performing rolls, squatting on the grass, tucking our heads in
and rolling over. I could do handstands, too. I flipped my legs up
over my head and stood, ever so briefly, upside down. In time I
noticed I had attracted the attention of a group of the bigger girls,
who were watching us from a distance. Encouraged, I executed
a few more handstands. From my inverted position I saw a few
of the girls smile. They began to walk towards us. I sat down on
the grass with Eddie. I was sure they were coming to ask me to
teach them to do handstands too, and I pretended not to notice.
But inside my head I'd already decided I would agree to show
them. After that Eddie and I would be able to spend break with
their group, playing skip rope and standing around talking the
way they did. I could feel them close behind; I turned expectantly.

'She just wants to show him what colour panties she has on . . .'

And they were gone. The words floated on the air behind them,
like an unpleasant odour, along with the sound of their laughter.
Four of them swept off in the direction of the classrooms. I felt the
heat in my cheeks; shame buzzed in my ears. I glanced at Eddie
and our eyes met for a moment, then slid past each other. We sat
there in silence. The bell went.

'Come on.' Eddie scrambled to his feet. 'Let's go.'

At home I had begun to watch my stepfather with growing interest. He was, in the main, a remote figure who left our day-to-day care to our mother and the servants. In turn I paid him scant attention, until one afternoon. The three of us were playing alone in the garden. A man slipped through the hedge. He wasn't young; he had skinny legs and leathery skin. In his hands he was carrying a large hoop and a gourd. He didn't appear to notice, or perhaps care, that we were watching him as he crossed the garden. At the base of one of a pair of palm trees he opened up his hoop and slipped it around the trunk and around his waist. Then, as we watched with growing wonder, he leaned back, pushed himself off and ran straight up the sloping trunk of the tree like a cat. At the top he took out a knife and cut a V deep into the bark of the tree, below which he fastened the gourd. He dropped down the tree even faster than he had climbed up. He loosened his hoop and clasped it around the second tree. When he came back down he was carrying a gourd: this one was full of palm sap.

In the evening when our stepfather came home we told him what we had witnessed. Uncle Win said he was a thief. Our eyes danced with the thrill of it. A thief?

'What will *we* do if we see him again?' we asked all together.

'You come and find me, and I'll shoot him.' Upstairs in a drawer on the landing our stepfather kept a pair of muskets. Sheka found them and showed them to us one day. They had curved wooden handles, decorated with brass studs, and long, dark metal barrels. Each one was wrapped in a soft cloth. I picked one up; it was very heavy, a dead weight in my hands. I had a sense that our stepfather was telling the truth. I began to hope I wouldn't see the palm-sap thief again. I didn't want to be responsible for his death.

From then on I watched my stepfather closely whether he was moving about the house or sitting going through papers from his open briefcase and drinking beer. I noticed that when he stood he put his hands on his hips, sometimes both hands, sometimes just one. He walked around like that, too, especially when he was looking for something. I thought it looked impressive, grown-up. I practised walking the same way around the house; eventually I took my walk to school.

At Corona the toilets were at the end of the walkway that ran alongside the classrooms. One afternoon I excused myself from class. As I walked towards the toilets I was practising my new walk, keeping one hand on my hip, when I spotted ahead of me the four big girls who had been so nasty the day in the play-ground. They were standing by the cubicles. Determined not to show I was flustered, but that I meant business, I put my other hand on my hip and advanced. They began to laugh. At first a titter passed from girl to girl, like the crackle of a bush fire sweep-ing through grass, then someone snickered openly. I wanted to run, but I managed to keep moving, forcing myself to place one reluctant foot in front of the other. I kept my hands right where they were on my hips. I dived into the cubicle just as they began to laugh out loud and I sat there in the dark until the bell rang and the girls moved off to their next class.

The next morning, as she rubbed lotion onto my legs, I told my mother what had happened. She picked up a wide-toothed comb and began to do my hair, working carefully through the tangles of my natural corkscrew Afro. Every time the comb snagged, I winced. My mother rubbed palmfuls of Vaseline hair oil into the mass to make it manageable. She reset my parting and combed each side, now shiny and slick, before plaiting it. All the while I described the unkindness I had suffered at the hands of the bul-lies. When I had finished she asked: 'Were they African girls?'

'Yes.' Because they were.

'I don't want you to talk to the African girls any more.' She picked up a ribbon to finish off the plait.

My back was turned to her and I couldn't see her face. I wasn't sure I understood. 'The mean girls?'

'None of the African girls.' She tied the ribbon in a bow.

I couldn't see at all where this was heading. I persisted: 'Not to any of them?'

'No, not to any of them.' My hair was finished now. My mother turned me round to face her, and bent down placing her hands on my shoulders. She looked into my face. 'I want you to remember that you're half white.' She stroked my cheek. 'You're better than those girls. Don't you talk to them or play with them. And don't let them upset you.'

I had forgotten that morning until, years later, I came across a letter buried within a pile of documents in a drawer. The letter was from my mother to my father, written either shortly before or just after their divorce. 'You accuse me of having a colonial mentality,' she wrote, denying it angrily in the sentences that followed. Further down the page she charged my father, in turn, with hating white people. I read through the letter, and as I stood there with it in my hand I glimpsed for the first time the whispering spectres that crowded in from the edges of my parents' marriage.

No more brown bread, white bread. I was five. I was just beginning to understand, or rather to realise, what the difference was between me and the girls at school. And how that same difference separated me from my mother.

In Sierra Leone my mother's white skin earned her deference and contempt in equal measure. The poor people looked up to her, for she was educated and white. But there was no place for a woman like her among her own people: a woman who had chosen a black husband and birthed black babies. Far away from the city, in the simmering tension of Koidu, her skin set her apart, glaring hopelessly, shouting her presence to predators like an albino deer, with none of the camouflage of the herd.

In Nigeria her skin marked her as one of the elite, set her apart from the masses in the right way. It was like a protective barrier which diffused experience, allowed for adventures to be viewed as if from behind glass. She would travel the world by my stepfather's side, but never come close enough again to smell the rank sweat of humanity or suffer, like a contagion, the fear of the ordinary African who lives and dies at the mercy of his rulers and the elements.

I went back to school and ostentatiously turned my nose up at the black girls. I soon got into a fight. In front of Mrs Sami I defended myself: the girls were mean to me, and besides, they were Africans. I uttered the word with contempt: I fully expected her to understand. I couldn't believe it when Mrs Sami sent me to sit on a bench outside the classroom for the rest of the day.

In the months before Christmas rehearsals began at Corona for the end-of-term play. We were to perform *The Pied Piper of Hamelin* and the castings were held in the main hall. Everyone in the school would be given a part. It was to be a musical performance and Memuna and Sheka, who were in the choir, had the honour of being on stage the whole way through.

Eddie and I and the rest of our class went along to see what parts we might be given. There was tremendous excitement, for most of us had never acted in a play before. In the end we were all handed not one but three roles in the play and kitted out with our costumes. We had loose brown tunics which we fitted over our heads and tied at the waist with a piece of string. These were to be worn in the first act, when we played the townspeople as they complained to the mayor about the rats. To identify us by occupation we had props; I was a baker and mine was a loaf of bread. On the night I would have a real loaf, Mrs Sami assured me, but for the rehearsals I carried a couple of books inside a brown paper bag. In the next scene I played a rat, and the piece of string doubled as a tail. Mrs Sami pinned it to the back of my dress and it trailed after me as I followed the piper out of the village, wearing a pair of cardboard ears. In the final scene I was one of the village children who follows the piper's enchanting melody into a faraway cave and disappears for ever.

As Christmas crept closer our mother and Uncle Win were out almost every evening, even more than usual. If they didn't go out they invariably entertained at home. In the evening after the steward gave us our bath and once we were in bed our mother, dressed for dinner or cocktails, came in to say goodnight. She wore dresses in vivid colours—tangerine or lime—and carried tiny, matching handbags. Her tanned skin shone against her neckline and her jewellery sparkled.

'Mummy, you look beautiful,' we cooed.

She kissed Sheka and Memuna first and me last because I was closest to the door, leaving us all with Careless Coral lipstick prints on our lips and noses. She sat on the low edge of my sofa and tucked me in. When the door closed behind her the scent of her perfume hung heavy in the air.

Our mother accompanied our stepfather to luncheons, garden parties, cocktails, dinners. While she was out the servants were supposed to take care of us, but they were no more interested in us than we were in them. They had plenty of chores and when they weren't working they went back to their quarters, leaving us alone in the big house. We played on the kitchen roof and in the street, under the boots of soldiers, and we raided the little pantry off the kitchen on the eve of dinner parties, stealing fancy foods and dainties prepared for VIP guests.

One afternoon Sheka called us out onto the upstairs veranda. On the green painted floor he had assembled a small pile of paper and twigs. In his hand he held a box of matches. Memuna and I knew what was coming; we knelt down, pushing our faces close to the miniature bonfire. He struck the pink tip of the match against the sandpaper and set the flame to the edge of a piece of paper. As it browned, a curl of smoke the shape of a question mark lifted into the air and released the delicious smell of burning. The smell was so good we sometimes lit match after match just to inhale it and my sister even ate the blackened ends afterwards.

We watched in silence as paper and twigs transformed into a leaping crown of orange and yellow before deflating into a pile of black ashes. Afterwards Sheka brushed up the cinders, leaving another star-shaped scorch mark on the floor. My mother saw them, knew what we were up to, but she said nothing.

On the weekend we went to the Yacht Club to visit Santa in his grotto. The temperature in Lapland was upwards of ninety degrees and the humidity caused the fake snow to slip down the window panes. I was wearing a skirt and so Santa gave me a blue plastic doll. Memuna, who happened to be in shorts, got a water pistol and refused to swap with me even when I pleaded. 'But you don't even want to be a boy!' I cried.

On the night of our performance I danced after the piper and hid in the wings during the closing scene. On the stage the people of Hamelin searched for their children, wailed and screamed with despair when they realised they were gone for good. They were doing a good job. I wondered where the children went to after the cave door shut, and the one lame boy was left outside. I imagined they would grow up in some enchanted kingdom deep inside the mountain where they would remain eternally young. I imagined the piper's enchantment would last for ever.

From where I was standing I could see all the parents watching their children. I searched for my mother's face. I wanted to wave to her, but we were supposed to be in the dark cave, the entrance of which had been sealed by a boulder. So I contented myself with watching her until after the curtain calls, when we all climbed down from the stage and ran into the audience to find our parents.

Towards the end of the following term, one day after school, we were playing in our room when we heard a voice coming from downstairs. It was deep, mellifluous and as familiar as my own face. We leaned over the balcony until we could see through the open sitting-room door. I saw a pair of legs outstretched and crossed at the ankle, grey trousers, dark socks and polished laced shoes. Daddy! We ran down the stairs and hurtled into the room, throwing ourselves upon him.

Our father was on his way through Lagos on an official trip. His position took him all over the world. In a year he had transformed himself from a medical doctor to a finance minister fêted as one of Africa's brightest and best. His speeches to the world banking conferences received massive ovations; he had spoken up for poor countries against the cartel of the World Bank, the IMF and the rich nations; he had been profiled in newspapers and *West Africa* magazine as the great black hope of our country and of our continent. We hadn't seen him for over a year.

He had brought us comics—the *Robin* for me, and copies of *Look & Learn*. Afterwards we all went swimming together in the pool at his hotel. Much later, but still too soon, after soft drinks and ice cream, he brought us back to the house and kissed us goodbye, promising to return soon.

My sixth birthday followed soon after. My mother pulled out all the stops and organised a celebration in the garden. It was the sort of thing at which she excelled. For my brother's birthday she had made a whole fire engine out of chocolate rolls. When it was my turn she asked who I wanted to invite and sent a card to every child we knew, including Eddie. She wrapped a parcel in dozens of layers of paper for a game of pass the parcel and hid bright boiled sweets among the colourful tropical flowers in the garden. From the moment I woke up to a pile of presents the day passed in a sugar-fuelled whirl until, at the end of the afternoon, for the finale, we were all sent scrambling in search of the sweets hidden in the borders. The next morning I found an orange drop, sticky from the dew, crawling with ants, but I brushed them off and sucked it all the same.

Three days later, in the early afternoon, Mrs Sami called me to one side of the class. I was led out to the front of the building, where our stepfather's driver was waiting; Sheka and Memuna were already there. We drove slowly through the streets and turned into the gate of our house. This was not exactly unusual. Our mother sometimes organised trips for us and collected us from school early. But as soon as I walked through the front door it was apparent that something was terribly wrong. There was our father, standing in the hall. Upstairs in the bedroom our mother was packing three suitcases.

The joy of seeing my father and the sight of my mother's tears overwhelmed me. Moments later she kissed me as she said good-bye. I nuzzled her neck, smelled for the last time the sweet, sugar scent of her skin, of face cream and perfume, tasted the salt of her tears. Then we climbed into the back of a large, open-top Mercedes-Benz and I sat in between my brother and sister, my head tilted back to let the howls escape; tears flooded my eyes.

My mother's lips were moving, but I couldn't hear what she was saying to me. Everybody around me was moving so quickly. Our father climbed into the front and we pulled out of the gate, leaving her standing alone at the porch. I didn't even manage to wave goodbye.

As the car sped down the avenue the warm wind blew into my face. The sensation made me lift my head; briefly it chased away my misery. I stopped crying. Rows of trees, people, houses moved past. I looked around in silence and sat up properly, my tears dried on my face. I could see all around me, above and behind. I turned my head slowly and gazed at the disappearing road, looked up at the sky latticed with branches. All was forgotten for an instant. I was deeply, overwhelmingly impressed by the car.

We stayed overnight in a hotel in Lagos, where we all shared the same room. Our father unpacked our pyjamas and prepared us for bed. In the white, tiled bathroom he wanted to help me clean my teeth, but I showed him I could do it myself now. After we said goodnight I lay quietly between the cotton sheets and watched my father as he rummaged about in his own small suitcase. He had his back to me and thought I was asleep. I could see his hands as he brought out his night things: strong fingers with slightly spatula-shaped ends. My eyes followed him as he carefully closed the suitcase and put it on the floor and then padded across to the bathroom, trying not to make any noise. My mind was free of thoughts. I was fixated, engaged in a simple process: I was committing my father to memory again, in the same way I memorised my letters and numbers at school, by staring at them until they were imprinted on my mind. I watched him as he came back into the room dressed only in his boxer shorts. He didn't see me with my eyes open as he slipped in between the sheets of the bed next to mine and turned out the light.

❧ 20 ❧

The day hovered between light and dark, colour ebbed from the houses and trees. The yard slowly transformed into monochrome tones of grey. The sun's gold had given way to a lesser, silver light. And as daylight dropped away the subtle shift in the hierarchy of the senses began: the sounds of darkness. Somewhere close to me a solitary cricket whirred as loud as a football rattle. The hot air was noisy, turbulent with wings. Birds dropped down onto the branches just as bats rose from the same trees, butterflies sank to the ground and flew up again as moths. It was a humid evening, and the damp coated my bare arms.

The voices of the evening traders drifted across from the streets. The sellers were all children and they walked round the houses at dusk, their bowls and baskets upon their heads, singing in recitative: 'Ah get de fry fry!' 'Ker-o-sine-ay!' 'Mina ya, mina ya, mina ya!'—fried akara, kerosene and minnows. Some of them were my friends, and they had been playing with me up until a few minutes ago, leaping across the piles of gravel. They had raced back home to fetch their wares and join the promenade; they walked slowly under the heavy baskets, kwashiorkor stomachs protruding, like pompous old men carrying their paunches before them.

When he lived with Teacher Trye our father and the other wards used to sell wood in the hours after school. They were supposed to collect the firewood from the forest first, but one day they were too busy playing to be bothered with their chores. In the evening they had no wood to sell, and so they crept out and tried to steal a few bundles from the lorries that travelled down from the forest logging sites and parked up on the main road into town. The boys stripped bare so that they blended into the dark like eels at the bottom of the sea and smeared their bodies in cooking oil so they couldn't be caught. Even so they only narrowly escaped. When he told the story our father laughed out loud at the idea of them, scrambling up the bank, butt naked, chased by the furious driver.

I sat on the still-warm stones of the gravel heap, waiting for my father to come home in his official car. This was where I usually waited for him, and today I was tense with anticipation. I had something very important to say.

Inside the kitchen Amadu and Amara hadn't turned on the strip light yet—it wasn't dark enough for that. Amadu and Amara. I always thought of the two cooks as one person really. People said, Go and ask Amadu and Amara, not Amadu or Amara. Amadu-andamara. Amara was washing the rice for supper. He stepped outside and poured the water, milky with starch, into the yard. Back inside he began sifting through the wet grains for stones.

Santigi was ironing just outside the kitchen door, with one of those big, old-fashioned irons, the type you filled with burning coals. Most people preferred them really, even though you had to stoke them and keep the fire burning under the lid. Few households had electricity and even those that did knew it couldn't be relied upon, especially in the rainy season when the rain dragged down the wires and lightning fenced with the telegraph poles. Santigi Kamara had a high forehead, deep charcoal skin and a set of teeth, with slightly pointed incisors, which his gentle smile was ashamed to reveal—almost as though his teeth belonged to someone else.

With the departure of my mother, the extended family had re-established itself and various cousins and uncles travelled down from Rogbonko and Magburaka to move in, filling up the boys' rooms and the ground floor of the big house. I barely noticed the ebb and flow of relatives and for much of the time they remained shadows at the periphery of my vision.

Albert, one of the younger cousins, came back down the path from the main road carrying his college books, his trademark Afro comb stuck through the front of his hair. He didn't see me and I didn't call to him. I did not want to talk to anyone. Today something happened: my stepmother hit me. No one had ever hit me before.

We had arrived home from Nigeria and, in a matter of weeks, been absorbed seamlessly into the rhythms of the large and busy house. I was a chameleon child, capable of adapting myself quickly to new surroundings. The whirligig of my childhood had made me unquestioning and passive in the face of change: parents, families, houses, countries, schools revolved around me, while I stood still centre stage.

There had been changes at Spur Loop in the last two years: Big Aminatta had gone north to be married and I counted her departure as a piece of good news. Milik still worked in the kitchen and he still couldn't pronounce milk. I was happy to see him—he was an easy place in altered territory. Milik took over some of Aminatta's tasks, supervising us cleaning our teeth at night and switching off the light at bed time.

On the aeroplane our father had told us he had a new wife, a stepmother to help take care of us, and as the car drew into Minister's Quarters she was standing at the front door. Our father introduced her as Auntie Yabome and as I said hello I barely bothered to form an impression. I had assimilated my stepfather into my life with scarcely a ripple, hardly noticing him most of the time, and I assumed the same would be true of this Auntie Yabome. But though I couldn't know it yet, I had never been more mistaken.

Santigi removed the layers of blankets and folded down the ironing board. Apollo, Jim's replacement, lay like an apostrophe in the dirt at his feet. When Santigi moved the dog stretched with liquid languor, curled up into a full stop and went back to sleep. Santigi went inside and the fly screen banged behind him. The iron was left on the step with the lid open, resting on its hinges; the glowing coals made it look like an enormous, stranded firefly. I once caught a firefly: it lay pulsating light in the cavern of my cupped hands while I inspected it—a plain, tan insect with transparent wings. I let it go and it flew off, leaving scribbles of light, like the patterns that children make in the air with sparklers on bonfire night.

The start of the trouble with my stepmother had come a few mornings before, when I couldn't find Milik. I swung open the door of the kitchen to ask Amaduandamara. 'Where's Milik?'

The cooks were working on opposite sides of the kitchen, making okra stew for supper; neither of them looked around. 'Milik is not here,' replied Amara. He was chopping okra with a sharp knife, top and tailing each pod and slicing it into pieces. A thread of slime hung from the knife blade.

'Well, I'm looking for him,' I repeated, waiting for them to tell me where he was.

'Milik is gone,' Amadu spoke. He didn't look at me; he kept his head down and his eyes fixed on his work.

Milik didn't normally go anywhere—he had a room in the boys' quarters. I thought Amara might mean Milik was on an errand, but equally I could sense something wasn't quite right. 'Where's he gone?' There was no answer. 'Well, when's he coming back?' Impatience sent the pitch of my voice soaring.

Amara set down his knife and turned to look at me squarely. He spoke slowly as though I was stupid: 'Milik is gone. He is gone from here. He is gone back to his family.'

'Why? Why, when he lives here with us?' My voice was still too loud by far, but I introduced a plaintive note—I didn't want to annoy them too much. Glances had been exchanged then, crossing in the air above my head, an adult alliance was forming and they weren't going to say any more. 'Is he coming back tomorrow?' I asked hopefully.

Amadu shook his head: 'Milik no dae cam back.'

From then on I could persuade no one to tell me what had become of Milik. At breakfast one day I asked Auntie Yabome. She sat at the head of the table giving rapid orders to the servants, snapping her beringed fingers. She didn't even acknowledge my question before she stood up to go to her bedroom, dress and leave the house. The days eased one into the next and Milik still didn't come home.

We started school. We were given new blue and white uniforms, pristine exercise books of rough, grey paper: one lined, the other printed with squares for maths with a set of times tables printed on the back in purple ink, and a slate to use in the classroom. I had never owned a slate before, and I felt proud and sophisticated to possess such a thing.

Uncle Ismail drove us to school in an old Land-Rover. He was our father's brother by another mother. Uncle Momodu too still came and went on business. But where the other brothers, Momodu included, were dark with the same distinctively handsome Forna features, Ismail was lanky with freckled, ginger-brown skin, an uneven beard and a laugh that erupted from his chest like an old man's cough. My father paid for Uncle Ismail to go to college; he had been sent to us by Pa Roke, who hoped our father's influence would calm Ismail.

In Uncle Ismail's hands the ageing Land-Rover flew along the steep-sided roads and spun round hairpin bends, while every bolt and shaft of the vehicle groaned like a pig in pain. In the back we toppled off the narrow side benches. We thought it was hilarious and that we were immortal. There was only one place where I felt a jolt of fear in my stomach: on the descent into the city, where a flimsy bridge balanced over a deep crevasse. There I looked down and I could see the rusting anatomy of a *poda poda,* lying in the rocks. I wondered about the fate of the people and I imagined the rust on the doors and the window frames was dried blood.

One afternoon, home from school, I jumped down from the Land-Rover and ran towards the kitchen door. Behind me, under Auntie Yabome's instruction, Santigi, Morlai and some others were unloading bags of rice from the Land-Rover. Amara was sitting on the step; he put out his hand and caught me by the arm: 'We have a surprise for you.' He cocked his head towards the kitchen door.

Milik was sitting inside at the kitchen table, dressed in long trousers and a shirt, instead of his usual shorts, but otherwise just the same. He had brought sweets: little brown cough drops, wrapped in transparent orange paper, tasting of camphor and mo-lasses. I hugged him and danced around, showing off the contents of my satchel. From outside came the crunch of heels on gravel, the Land-Rover doors slammed. Milik got up to go. He had stayed only moments. By the time I realised I had a dozen questions still to ask him, Milik had slipped away.

The next morning at breakfast I told Auntie Yabome Milik had been to visit. When I had finished she put down her teacup and marched into the kitchen, where she announced to the staff assembled there that if Milik came back he was not to be allowed in the house. If he showed his face they were to tell her immedi-ately. I ran after her and stood at the door listening. I was worried I might have got Amadu and Amara into trouble. I still couldn't understand why Milik wasn't allowed back. But now I knew it was my stepmother who had banished Milik, and a clot of dislike began to form in my heart.

Eventually we had a confrontation. I can't remember exactly what it was over, but it wasn't Milik. I had amassed so many grievances. There was the way she combed my hair, dragging through it with a plastic comb until my eyes watered, tugging so hard at the knots she all but lifted me off my feet, stretching every strand into tight cornrows that lasted upwards of a week. Afterwards my scalp was singing and the hair around my hairline was pulled so tight I had slanted eyes.

My stepmother sent me on endless errands: to fetch a glass of water, then go back for some ice, take a message to the kitchen, find her handbag; she insisted on going over my homework when I knew it was right; believed passionately in the qualities of Seven Seas cod liver oil on Sunday mornings—for everyone in the house. She'd only just joined our family and she ordered us all around.

Who knows how the altercation began the morning of the day I sat outside waiting for my father to come home, but it came to an end when I called my stepmother an African.

'Get outside and cut a switch.' Her eyes were round with anger and her mouth was smaller than I had ever seen it. 'And when you find one, you bring it back here!' She was going to hit me! Neither my mother nor my father ever struck me. My father was away at the office and Auntie Yabome bore down on me with such seriousness of purpose I ran outside to get away from her. I could hear her high heels clattering across the floor behind me.

Among the long grass beyond the mango tree I found a sapling and pulled down a switch. I chose the smallest, narrowest one I could find because it seemed to me to be the safest bet. I carried it back to my stepmother, who stripped off the leaves and told me to put out my hand.

The switch cut through the air with a hum like a mosquito. Afterwards, Auntie Yabome told me to wipe my face and stop crying, but it was more than I could do. The more I gulped and heaved, tried to arrest the compulsive rise and fall of my shoulders, the more exasperated she became. In the end she had stamped off and left me alone.

My father was later than usual. I could hear the rustle of the plants going to sleep, closing their leaves against the coming dew. During the day the tiny ferns shut like butterfly wings the moment you touched them. In Krio they were called *Close you lappa, man dae cam*—Tie your *lappa*, a man is coming. They grew all round the house, producing their tiny violet blooms like shredded crêpe paper. I liked to tickle the leaves at the edge and watch the entire patch close up in a wave; the plants showed their greyish undersides and the whole effect was as if a cloud had cast its shadow on the earth.

Hazy wood smoke blended with evening scents of night blossoms. Violet funnels of morning glory, their petals twisted like paper, dropped down one by one; the flowers were prettier when they were dead than alive. A gecko flicked its head to catch a mosquito then lay still, lowering translucent lids over black irises.

I had spent the whole day outside, roaming around by myself. I crept into the long grass behind the mango tree, wading deeper and deeper into it, farther than I had ever been before. At some point I must have stretched out my hand to push aside the grass. A coil of abandoned barbed wire lay hidden in the grass like a snake. I looked at my hand and saw a pale slice across my dusty palm. The blood and pain came later.

I can feel it now: a thick keloid scar cutting right across my lifeline. It was a deep gash at the time, and after a few moments dark blood oozed slowly out underneath a flap of skin. But my anger also ran dark and deep and I refused to go inside and ask my stepmother to bandage it for me.

It was almost dark by the time the slanting headlights came into view and the car drew up. I ran down the gravel slope towards my father. I wanted to get to him first before anyone else, particularly Auntie Yabome. He was late and he looked tired, his eyelids were creased and shadows circled his eyes. He swung his briefcase loosely in one hand. Usually I liked to carry it in for him but on this occasion I was feeling too sorry for myself. I stood in front of him and stuck my hand, palm uppermost, in front of his face. He took hold of it, peering in the near darkness. 'Ouch. Poor you! We should clean that up. How did you do that?'

'Auntie Yabome did it,' I said as gravely as I could, and as I did so I glanced at him. In the hours I had been waiting for him I had turned the events of the day over and over in my mind, until I persuaded myself of my own truth. The accident to my hand had happened close to the sapling tree. Why not when I went to cut the switch? I would never have been there at all if it weren't for her. Whichever way I looked at it, my stepmother was to blame.

'Really?' He didn't sound convinced, so I elaborated: she had hit me, hit me with a switch. She had cut me, I insisted. My hand was cut and it was all her fault. Outrage, hurt and betrayal made me determined he should believe me.

'I'll talk to her about it,' he promised and we walked slowly together towards the house.

I lay in my bed that night after the lights were switched off. My hand was lying on top of the sheet, clean and dressed, and I was sated on my revenge. I could imagine what my father was saying to Auntie Yabome, how she must be regretting caning me. She would be begging with him to be allowed to stay. By the time I fell asleep I was convinced there was no way Auntie Yabome would still be in the house when I woke up the next morning.

21

I was so preoccupied with my war against my stepmother that it was a while before I realised something was wrong in our country.

It was Saturday and we were at the market. Santigi, Memuna, Sheka and I followed Auntie Yabome through the crowd, like the tail of a giant beast, as she moved from stall to stall, buying huge quantities of food for the household. We walked when she walked; when she stopped we stopped too; she filled our arms with her purchases one by one. Uncle Ismail did not follow but stayed by the Land-Rover, chewing cola nuts and spitting out the masticated pieces, exchanging greetings with the people around him, waiting to load the baskets of mangoes, plantains, yams and chickens and to drive us home.

Vlisco Dutch wax prints, elaborate *garas,* batiks, weaves and block prints switched and swapped places. I walked along with my head down, lifting my gaze just often enough to keep an eye on Auntie Yabome's costume and head-dress. I was still nursing my resentment, keeping it alive and warm, incubating malevolence like a goose on an egg. Why hadn't my father sent her away for what she did to me? I didn't want to be at the market and I couldn't understand why she was still here at all, in charge of everyone.

I could tell we were in front of the chicken stall by the smell. The birds were held in round baskets, six in each one, stacked one on top of the other. Their legs bound, they were forced to lie on their sides. They looked so awkward and uncomfortable, I felt sorry for them. In front of us the stallholder pulled out a cockerel. Auntie Yabome shook her head. He opened the basket and slung the bird back inside. It landed on its companions, which squawked and pecked at it with malicious beaks. At home, Memuna and I had a pair of chicks. One was blind and the other had an ominous growth on one of its scaly legs. We annoyed the cooks by keeping them in the kitchen, where they were always underfoot and the poor blind chick ran around and pecked at passing toes.

Next door was a woman selling yams. On the ground next to her a young child snatched occasionally at her empty breasts as they swayed loosely. She wrapped the yams in a piece of newspaper, an advertisement for beer featuring a white woman with breasts like light bulbs, held up by a strapless evening gown.

The stallholder gave a chicken a couple of shakes to get my attention as he held it upside down in front of me. Small sounds of protest bubbled up from the bird's throat. I forced myself to put out my hand and take hold of the legs. They felt warm, dry; the feet were unexpectedly soft, the claws were like dead men's nails. Santigi had two chickens, one in each hand, and was holding them down at his sides like a couple of shopping bags. Their wings flapped open; they looked like they were already dead. I made a nest of my arms and settled my bird upright in it. As we walked through the crowds I tried to protect her from the bumps and jostles of the people. The chicken seemed much happier and perfectly calm as she rode high in my arms, a princess and her bearer.

We walked along on the edge of the market close to the road, where young men in open shirts patrolled the boundaries selling single Marlboro cigarettes, Bic pens and plastic lighters. I wasn't really looking where I was headed—my attention was absorbed by the chicken. I didn't see the circle of people until I came right up against the solid row of backs.

In the middle a man was on the ground. He had both arms round a telegraph pole and he was scuttling like a crab as he tried to avoid the kicks of another man. His feet were bare; his rubber flip-flops lay in the dust by the feet of the crowd among discarded leafs of paper; his clothes were torn and stained. The man doing the kicking cursed, hissing spittle through his teeth. He wasn't doing a very good job—he kept on missing because his target was moving so quickly and for a moment, at one point, he very nearly unbalanced and fell on the ground himself. Both of them were not much beyond their early twenties. The attacker wore a red shirt.

I'd seen plenty of fights before, but this was different. People in Sierra Leone didn't usually wait for an invitation to intervene in a fracas. Once I had seen a man hit a woman: a tight, hard rap with his knuckles across her face. He was wearing a ring, and a spring of blood welled up below her eye. The market women nearby, who up until then had been resting on their haunches over their baskets, sprang to their feet and began to upbraid him loudly. His wife joined in, telling everyone who would listen why he was no good. He stalked away, swaggering like a cat but retreating all the same, while people queued to inspect the shiny welt across his wife's cheekbone.

This time nobody moved. I could see two uniformed soldiers in the shade of a tree—one of them even had a rifle but neither of them did anything either.

A new man entered the fray. He was dressed exactly the same as the other man, in a red T-shirt and a pair of old shorts. He strode up to the man on the ground, still limbo dancing in the dirt, coming at him from the opposite side so that the man didn't see him. He swung back his foot and gave a terrific kick which landed on the side of the man's face. I heard the crack. The hurt man's scream died abruptly: his jaw must have shattered. He stopped wheeling around and began to whimper, crawling towards the onlookers. For an instant I saw his fear and tears—and his face all skew-whiff and broken. A memory came to me suddenly of the crippled ant trying to escape from the ant lion.

I shoved through the people, shielding the chicken with one arm and pushing with my other outstretched hand. I felt the texture of the crowd: the pliable stomach of a woman with a baby on her back, the slippery hardness of a shirtless labourer, tangles of clothing grabbed at me. Only when I was free did I realise I had lost the others. I was next to the meat section: flies shimmered like blue satin on every surface—piles of pink pigs' ears, mounds of black kidneys, giant blue-green tongues. I ran on. I found myself engulfed by printed pineapples: a wedding party in *ashobi*, all dressed in outfits of identical cloth. I wheeled round the other way. Panic was closing my throat, and the hot wind streaming into my face dried out my eyes; people were bumping past me all the time. I looked around for Santigi or Memuna or Sheka, but I couldn't see anyone or anything that was familiar. Just endless rows of stalls.

Somehow, I was forced back out onto the perimeter road, where the cigarette sellers stood. I slowed my pace and tried to concentrate. I pushed on, walking now, as fast as I could, round to where I reckoned the Land-Rover was parked. I could feel the sweat prickling across my scalp and my forehead. I felt as though I couldn't get enough oxygen, drawing in deep, uneven breaths of air so hot it seemed to burn my windpipe.

Uncle Ismail was still there, lounging on the bonnet, lying back and gazing at the sky. I sat down on the bumper next to him. He heard me, pulled himself up and glanced down at me. I thought he was about to start teasing me, as was our way, but he didn't say a word. He handed me a piece of cola nut. I didn't much like cola nut—the taste was so bitter—but I bit a piece off and nibbled it, handing the rest back to him. We waited in the sun.

The others appeared. They had been looking for me, of course. Auntie Yabome was out in front wearing a look on her face. I braced myself for trouble. Beside me Uncle Ismail stood up and stretched. He walked towards my stepmother. A few words passed between them. He spoke in Temne. Was it about me? Or had she just had enough of me? My stepmother swept past without so much as a glance, as though I didn't even exist.

I made myself useful, taking care to keep some distance between myself and my stepmother. I helped load the Land-Rover. What didn't fit inside in the space between the benches we strapped onto the roof. Afterwards I climbed up and wedged myself into my place on one of the benches. Uncle Ismail walked around to lock the back doors for the drive home. Just before he closed them he leaned through the gap and passed me a bundle. I took hold of the chicken, feeling the silky feathers and pulsing heart, and I tucked her carefully into a space on top of the sacks.

22

The memories are like the discarded, differently coloured squares of mosaic—meaningless fragments. Two words: 'Ginger Hall'—a name like a place in a children's story; a man dressed all in white; magenta scars blooming on another man's forearm; red T-shirts.

I saw what was happening. Not enough to make sense of, really. I wouldn't be able to gather the many missing pieces, create the entire picture until much later, until now. Back then, in 1970, I saw the detail, but not the whole.

People say they didn't notice, never saw what was happening to their neighbours, knew nothing of the arrests, the burning houses, the children shot at dawn, failed to spot the prime minister's growing power, glimpsed nothing of the shadows drawing in around the edges. People were rendered blind, deaf and dumb and they plead ignorance. How could they have stood up against what they didn't even know was happening?

But even I, a child who lived my life vicariously through my parents, my pets, the people who surrounded me, who saw only what was going on in her own world—even behind the protection of those walls I saw enough to sense the coming storm. My father saw it, too, because he was at the very centre of the cyclone.

Burns upon black flesh, bright like florid pink blooms against the dark earth. I waited for my supper and gazed at the elderly man as he sat patiently on one of the chairs in the hall. He had rosy patches up the length of his forearms. Both his hands were bandaged thickly. The thugs had dragged him from his bed into the street and kicked him in the groin as he begged for his life. The more he pleaded, the more they laughed. They were the same age as his sons, these boys; they forced him down onto his knees and made him clasp his hands and pray to them for his salvation. Then they poured kerosene over his hands and threw matches at him until one caught and blazed. I stared at his bandaged hands. I imagined them pink and curled as chicken claws under the wrappings. The old man had come to ask for help; he went into my father's study and the door closed behind them.

By the time Siaka Stevens ascended to the premiership of Sierra Leone he was riven with grudges, scored as deeply into his soul as fresh tribal marks on an infant's face. In the luxury of the Villa André in Conakry, where he stayed as a guest of Sékou Touré, there was plenty of time to brood. His list of enemies was long: his usurper David Lansana, his political opponents in the SLPP, Juxon-Smith, even some in his own camp: Ibrahim Taqi, who had declined to follow the others to Guinea and stayed behind in Freetown, had fallen out of favour.

Once inside State House Stevens set about securing his position: he ordered the arrests of all those, civilians and soldiers alike, who had served under the NRC and, dropping his fleeting pretence at governing as part of a coalition, he set about jailing members of the opposition. Those men who still held seats in parliament found themselves challenged one by one through the courts. Within six months only four SLPP parliamentarians remained in the House of Representatives.

Upon towns and villages where the people had voted against the APC was visited a more graphic revenge: in one village a pro-SLPP chief was stripped naked and paraded before his people, then set upon by thugs armed with night sticks; a man who had canvassed on behalf of the opposition was bound hand and foot and driven hundreds of miles from his home in the boot of a car. In Kambia SLPP voters were tied up and brought before a kangaroo court of APC youths. In Bo the paramount chief was beaten and dragged into a police station. In by-elections in Kono and Kenema the APC swung in easily after voters were frightened away from the polls by youths in red T-shirts armed with machetes and acid, who arrived and left in high-speed convoys. Bloody battles took place between the thugs and anyone who refused to be cowed. For a while in late 1968 the country teetered on the brink of anarchy.

Despite the growing outrage Stevens refused to condemn the violence. Moderate members of the government visited State House to demand the prime minister halt the country's drift into disorder. From his high-backed swivel chair in State House, covered in the finest Italian leather, Stevens offered them bland platitudes: he personally knew nothing of the origin of these attacks, he assured them. Below his window, in the forecourt of the presidential palace, lupine youths in red T-shirts and bandannas lounged, cruel and confident as predators. They jostled and spat at delegates who came to hand their petitions in to the premier, glared and hissed like cats at anyone who took issue with them, even members of their own party. The same young men lolled upon the veranda and in the front rooms of the home of S. I. Koroma, the representative for Port Loko just north of Freetown, from where some of the worst reports of violence were emerging.

Sorie Ibrahim Koroma was a dark-skinned African who favoured white suits in the style of Sékou Touré. He thought it amusing to keep a copy of Machiavelli's *The Prince* on the table in the room where visitors were asked to wait and he openly revelled in his nickname: *Agba Satani,* Satan's Chief Disciple. S. I., as he was also affectionlessly known, took a theatrical delight in cultivating dread and his name would become a byword for thuggery in Sierra Leone.

At the peak of the violence, a few months after the APC took office, the young minister of finance drove to Port Loko and confronted S. I. directly. The two men had a shared history. Both were Bo School boys; S. I. had been a prefect when our father arrived on a scholarship. Even then the older boy had never been more than a mediocre pupil whose career ended after the fifth form. What he lacked in intellect S. I. made up for in ambition. His ruthlessness and dogged devotion to Siaka Stevens had seen him climb through the ranks of the party and his power lay in his personal command of the youth wing. But S. I. bitterly resented being surpassed by young, western-educated men like Mohamed Forna, wooed by Stevens before the elections and then given positions of prominence. Our father was the senior minister of the two, and that night in S. I.'s Port Loko estate he ordered his cabinet colleague to call off his thugs, telling him he had no right to bring terror to the country.

Our father received his reply two months later. In the early hours of a warm January morning an unmarked Mercedes-Benz pulled up in front of the offices of *Freedom* newspaper. The lower windows of the offices were boarded up; the opposition newspaper had been attacked before. That morning armed men sprayed the front of the building with automatic gunfire, dust and masonry flew, windows exploded, some bullets ricocheted off the pipes on the outside of the building. Beyond one of the windows Francis Biareh, a twelve-year-old boy collecting newspapers to sell to drivers in the early-morning rush-hour traffic, was hit by bullets in the neck and chest. He fell to the floor. The car sped away.

Within the hour two hundred people had gathered on the pavement outside the *Freedom* building. Some of them gathered up the boy's bloody body and carried him through the city traffic to the prime minister's office. There they waited by the gates, and when the motorcade bringing the prime minister to his offices appeared the crowd began to press in upon the car. Someone hurled a stone at the windscreen. Others began to follow suit. The prime minister's driver slowed down for a moment, then he accelerated and swept on, past the crowd and down the hill.

The next day the prime minister did not attend the APC rally as scheduled. Our father and those moderate members of the government who supported him in his stand against the violence also stayed away. S. I. Koroma went, though, and addressed the gathering. He took to the stage and swore the killing of Francis Biareh was a blatant attempt by the opposition to turn people against the government. He vowed it would not succeed.

The playground for the junior school at Bertha Conton was a small triangle of bare earth at the back of the classrooms; it faced directly onto State House and boasted a solitary tree that barely ever saw the light. Sometimes, during break or lunch, when we heard the familiar sound of sirens starting up, we would stand and watch the prime minister's motorcade as it arrived and departed.

At school we did our sums on old-fashioned slates, because the school could not afford paper. Bertha Canton's teaching methods were Victorian: every day we stood behind our desks reciting passages from our shared primers, repeating the names of countries, capital cities, the names of the Apostles, or singing the national anthem for the pleasure of our teacher. Mistakes were not tolerated. You were caned if you arrived at school late, if you wet yourself, if you faltered on the capital of France, if you drew in your exercise books; you were caned for all infractions, however minor. And we were the lucky ones, privileged enough to attend one of the best schools in the country.

All the classes were held in the same massive hall, under a corrugated iron roof upon which the rain thundered so loudly the lessons sometimes had to be stopped. I was in a class with my cousin Fatmata—she and her brother lived with us at Minister's Quarters—and we shared our books and homework. Late one afternoon we sat round the dining-room table at home tackling our maths. We worked our way down to the last sum: four times six. No, said Fatmata, pointing at her own slate, it is six times four. We bickered lazily for a while. But it's all the same anyway, I shrugged, bored with the debate. I wrote the sum down as I pleased. The next day, as I waited at the front of the class to have the free will beaten out of me for getting my sums 'wrong', I realised Fatmata, who had been at school in Sierra Leone all her life, had known something I'd been slow to grasp.

In front of the porticos of State House sat a row of squat armoured cars, grey and sleek as blood-swollen ticks. When the last motorcycle passed through the gates, from outside they could be glimpsed for one fleeting moment.

In our father's first year as minister of finance the country had, for the first time ever, produced a surplus. The two most pressing needs in the country were healthcare and education. The money could either guarantee free primary education for children or it could go to the government hospitals, where even the most basic standards of healthcare were absent. Like a mother who has to choose which one of her children should receive the extra food, these are the judgements to be made in the poor countries like ours.

Although he was a doctor, our father argued strongly in cabinet for the money to go to education. Only a tiny percentage of people knew how to read and write, and if people could just understand the basic rules of hygiene, understand why they must take their children to be vaccinated, then more good would ultimately come of it than spending the same money on the hospitals.

Siaka Stevens spent the money on the fleet of armoured cars, for his own personal protection, bought from a British company who willingly advanced the extra money they would cost at an inflated rate. In time Stevens would eventually create his own personal army, adding two Internal Security Units and a Special Security Division, loyal only to him. He encouraged his minister of finance to give assurances to representatives of the world's banking community that in return for free development grants and soft loans Sierra Leone would sign no more credit agreements of the kind that had dragged us into debt once already. And while his minister was out of the country, Stevens took control of the finance ministry and signed the agreement for the cars himself.

In public Stevens lavished praise on his brilliant young minister, treated him as a protégé and honoured him as his right-hand man, leaving him acting prime minister when he visited Europe for medical treatment or went abroad on state visits. I stood in a crowd of cheering schoolchildren at the gates of Bertha Canton watching my father drive past. The car stopped; he climbed down to shake hands with the teachers and children close by. I was too short to see properly and struggled on tiptoe. 'That's my father,' I told the boy next to me as I used his shoulder for leverage.

He looked at me disbelievingly. 'No he isn't,' he had replied and elbowed me sharply in the ribs.

At the same time and in private the Pa undermined his finance minister constantly, allowed him to take decisions which he later overturned, skirted cabinet approval, sent over orders to make arbitrary payments: promotions for new Limba police officers, army commissions for Limba officers, a loan for the suddenly urgent construction of a rock-filled road less than two miles long, yet costing six million leones. The road would do nothing to ease congestion in the city. Both our father and M. O. Bash Taqi, the minister of works, defied Stevens, declining to rubber-stamp his demands and persuading cabinet to reject the project.

Our father took his complaints directly to Stevens himself. Pa Sheki, the 'father of the nation', as he liked to be called, hid his anger behind laughter. 'Why are you so worried?' he had joked. 'These debts won't be due until our grandchildren's day.' Stevens believed everyone had a price: so long as a leader shared the spoils everyone was happy. Within months of being in office the government was split and Stevens resorted to new tactics to outwit the defiant elements in his cabinet.

My father received a telephone call from Stevens summoning him to State House to attend a meeting at short notice. When he arrived he found several police officers, including the police commissioner, Jenkins Smith, as well as John Bangura, the force commander, accompanied by two of his officers. The story was told to me by Jenkins Smith; he had already been to my father for help when Stevens began to order a series of unauthorised promotions of police officers, hand-picked by the premier himself.

Stevens began: 'Ah, Dr Forna. I'm glad you're here. Sit down, won't you.' He indicated a chair in front of his desk, in a position where our father would be sitting with his back to the others in the room. The minister sat down. Stevens continued: 'I just want to let you know about a series of meetings we've been having. We have made a decision to synchronise the military and police communications systems.'

It was, quite simply, an outright lie. No such meetings had taken place and everyone in the room knew it. Neither the police nor the army had any wish to share a communications system—quite the contrary: they were keen to maintain their independence. The scheme Stevens was talking about was one proposed by a new contractor and cost three million leones, a vast sum of money. According to Jenkins Smith, Stevens was still speaking when the finance minister interrupted, slapping his hand palm down on the table for emphasis. He was angry and Jenkins Smith suspected he must have come to the meeting with the knowledge that something like this was likely to happen. In the plainest terms he told Stevens his ministry would not sanction such a deal; the plan proposed by the existing suppliers of communications equipment had come in at a tenth of the price.

Stevens had smiled and ignored the interruption, acting as though nothing had happened: 'I have called you here,' he repeated slowly, pulling his lips back and enunciating each word, 'because the three of us—' his wave encompassed Jenkins Smith and the brigadier—'have had a number of meetings.'

My father struck the desk, sharply this time, with his fist and he too repeated himself. Nobody else in the room uttered a word.

The police commissioner was the first to move. He stood up, put on his cap, saluted, clicked his heels and walked towards the door. The others followed suit, leaving the minister of finance and the prime minister alone in the room. In the hallway one of the men, a communications officer in the army, grasped Jenkins Smith by the hand: 'Thank you, sir,' he said. 'It does no good to be there when big men make palaver.' None of them could entirely believe the scene they had just witnessed.

Jenkins Smith told me what they all suspected: that Stevens must have stood to make money out of the deal. In the future, if it was ever investigated, it was almost certainly the minister of finance who would take the blame. But Stevens had been outmanoeuvred by our father's boldness.

Some time later, when our father was alone in the house, came the early-morning warning blast in the bathroom of Minister's Quarters 4.

I remember a man: dark and lean, he sometimes sat alone, waiting under the mango tree. He would talk with the servants who brought him his food, and as soon as our father came out of the house he jumped up to open the car door and rode along in the front seat of the official car next to the driver, with his elbow on the window frame. I don't remember his features especially, certainly not his name. Just the silhouetted matchstick figure, in a short-sleeved uniform, sitting on the roots of the tree behind our house, while I ran in and out playing with my brother and sister.

I remember Janet Thorpe, too. She was my father's confidential secretary at the ministry and she found an easy route to my affections by serving me cold bottles of Fanta and Vimto out of the fridge behind her desk whenever we visited the office. Sometimes she stopped by the house with a gift or a dish of something she had cooked herself. Janet was unmarried, attractive in an earnest way, with a bookish air about her and a way of folding her hands in her lap like an old-fashioned governess. She was fond of her boss, who had often confided in her about us, his plans to have his children live with him again. She didn't approve and she dared to tell him so; children were better off with their mother in her view, and his political life didn't leave him enough time for three young children. But she felt sorry for him all the same. When he came back from cabinet meetings it was Janet who listened while he gave vent to his growing frustrations.

So on the morning our father walked into the ministry building to find several of his staff huddled outside his door, it was Janet who was pushed forward in front of everyone else. She told him the rumour that was rife in the office: his own personal bodyguard was spying on him for Stevens. The man had been caught sending daily reports on all our father's conversations and meetings back to the prime minister's office.

Dusty files stacked in the converted school building that was once Bertha Conton School, papers containing names and addresses, salary scales, terms of pay and conditions: special information agents to the prime minister's office. Somehow a few

have survived the thirty years, even the day when most of the
government archives, including the cabinet papers and the records of the Ministry of Finance, were destroyed—that terrible
day in 1997 when the rebels of the Revolutionary United Front
left their bush hideouts and brought their ten-year war to the
capital. In seeking revenge on the elite they held responsible for
the misery, they wreaked vengeance on the ordinary people. As
they advanced through the country upon the capital they sliced
off the hands, lips, ears and genitals of men, women and children
and burned alive those who resisted them. In a display of disdain
for a corrupt and rotten system they torched government offices
and the law courts of the capital, sending a nation's history up
in smoke.

Among the yellowing, fly-spotted papers stored in the makeshift archive of our old classrooms are dozens of names, including
somewhere the forgotten name of my father's bodyguard. These
were the prime minister's web of spies, paid eight hundred and
forty leones a month—more than most Sierra Leoneans saw in the
year, certainly more than a teacher, a nurse or even a doctor in a
government hospital. A good price, then, in return for betraying
your neighbours, family, friends, or your boss—who you were
conveniently also paid to protect.

Our uncles—Bash and Ibrahim—visited us at home almost every
day, still ebullient. Bash lived only a few dozen yards away in another ministerial house. They came alongside others uncowed by
Stevens's bullying: men like Sarif Easmon, a medical doctor and a
writer who still dared to criticise the prime minister in the newspapers, and Cyrus Rogers Wright, another prominent Krio and a
lawyer. Lami Sidique, the civil servant who had helped bring the
APC back from exile in 1968, had been repaid by Stevens, who

had put out a warrant for his arrest. My father had once offered him a safe place in our house, knowing Stevens wouldn't dare send the police into the home of one of his own ministers. They would sit on the veranda facing the garden deep in discussion with our father.

Stevens had tried to fracture the so-called Tonkolili group. He had excluded Ibrahim Taqi, the man to whom he owed so much of his electoral victory, from the first government and left him on the backbenches. Ibrahim used his independence in parliament to tackle Stevens in public over the beatings and over the detention of opposition MPs. In due course Stevens gave him the post of minister of information, but if he hoped a government position would quell Ibrahim, he was wrong. After a year Stevens lost patience, reshuffled the cabinet and Ibrahim was on the backbenches once more.

Our father's massive election victory made him indispensable to Stevens. A rumour circulated that during the Privates' Coup the young soldiers had at first demanded Mohamed Forna as the country's leader. Our father had declined; it was Stevens whom the people had elected. But the soldiers had wanted the country led by a northerner, a Temne man after the Mende Margais.

Stevens owed his election to the northern vote and he knew it, for he possessed an instinctive understanding of tribal politics. He was a quisling, a man for all people. He variously claimed to be Vai—through his mother; or Limba—through his father, although he could not speak the language. He liked to tell Mendes how he was raised in Moyamba among their tribe and Krios how he was educated in Freetown. Once in power he set about strategically promoting many Limbas, especially within the police and army, in the knowledge that through this small and disenfranchised group he could gather a core of effective support. The one major group on whom he had no claim was the Temne, and in the early months while he still held on to power with a faltering grip, he relied on the support of the north.

Stevens was suspicious of northerners in his own government and sent spies to report the discussions between the Taqis and my father. Gradually the three men met more often in our house. In time the conversations shifted from the veranda to our father's ground-floor study.

It had become impossible to know who could be trusted, even in our own household. There were constant visitors: neighbours, young men in need of a job, constituents down from the provinces to discuss a local issue, former patients, people who claimed to be our supporters. But which of them had an ulterior motive, who was there to win false trust, report on the comings and goings, pose a sly question to the servants—it was impossible to tell.

In the spring of 1969, a year before we came home, our father had been made guest of honour at the annual Old Boys' Association convention at Bo School. He was the most prominent of the distinguished alumni, which included a number of ministers and members of the House of Representatives. Our father delivered the keynote address at the start of the weekend of celebrations. For an hour he spoke with emotion against the use of violence as a political weapon. He referred to many of the men sitting at tables around the room: the school had united them from every region of the country, he told them, yet politics was pitting one group against the other. He received a standing ovation.

S. I. Koroma did not attend the festivities at Bo School and so he didn't hear the minister of finance speak first hand, but news of the speech reached S. I. in a matter of hours. A day later he arrived unannounced at Spur Loop. He was a soft-spoken man, and he begged a little of the doctor's time. He thought that perhaps the doctor had made a mistake in saying some of the things he had. Dr Forna had spent a great deal of time in Britain—perhaps too much time, S. I. said. But this wasn't England. He laughed lightly as he continued smoothly: Politics in Africa were very different. Here politics and violence were inseparable. It was regrettable, but . . . He shrugged. He had a habit of picking imaginary pieces of lint from his spotless white suit. He smiled. Dr Forna didn't realise all of this, being an intellectual, he concluded—and he made the word 'intellectual' sound like an insult.

In March 1970 in Ginger Hall in the East End of Freetown youths in red shirts threw dynamite at Fulah shops and the homes of Fulah and Mende inhabitants. The attacks came in the early morning and dozens died in their beds in the flames. Those who could fled the city and their homes and did not dare return. In the Freetown City Council elections that followed days later so few SLPP voters attended the polls that the APC swept the board clean in an unprecedented victory.

❧ 23 ❧

We drove up to Magburaka to see Pa Roke. The trips up-country were an adventure: the journey took several hours on appalling roads and at times Sullay had to slow the car to a crawl and he and my father, who was in the passenger seat, pressed their fingertips against the windscreen to absorb the impact from the stones kicked up by passing *poda podas*. Villages lined the road like seeds springing up along the bank of a river after a drought.

At Mile 91 we stopped for refreshments and the roadside sellers homed in on the car, offering oranges skinned to the pith; sun-roasted peanuts with papery skin; mangoes, pawpaws and pineapples. We bought oranges and the vendor sliced off the top; we sucked the juice out, sieving the pips through our teeth. The empty baskets in the boot were filled with fruit to take to the family. All the time the crowd of people round us swelled. Some were there to sell, but most just came to stare. The car, our clothes, especially the fair complexions of my brother, sister and me, transfixed people. In the provinces, away from Freetown, children still shouted 'Oporto' after the seventeenth-century Portuguese traders or 'John Bull' whenever they saw a pale skin. They pressed their faces against the glass without shame, and behaved as though we too were impervious to their scrutiny.

I was uncomfortable. I hated being stared at, and on top of that I was sitting in the middle of the back seat, where the arm rest went. I leaned forward, gripping the two front seats, with my feet on the centre hump and my knees up by my middle. Inside I was experiencing a tumble of emotions: excitement about the trip and shyness because of the crowd; one of my legs was numb, too. But there was another feeling, a nagging in my brain that made me feel shivery and bad, restless and unhappy all at the same time. Yet I dreaded anyone asking me if I was all right. I had never had this feeling before: I felt as though I had been caught stealing. I felt guilty.

An afternoon, a week or two before, my father had come home carrying a young fawn. Her mother had been killed in a hunting accident, he explained. No one had seen the baby she was shielding with her body. The fawn was ours to raise. I was mesmerised. I knew immediately that I wanted to be the person who looked after the fawn. I reached out and touched her. The hair was slippery smooth and her skin shivered under my touch, but she had let me stroke her.

We had other animals—several dogs, which I regarded as mine; plus, until recently, a mongoose, a hooligan that chased the dogs, stole the sugar from the table and raced up the curtains until one of the dogs plucked up courage and dragged the mongoose round the yard by the tail and it ran away for good.

The mongoose had been followed by a parrot called Sheka, bought at market for my brother, who had shown no interest in the bird so I began to take care of him. Thinking to please my brother, I named the parrot after him. I fed Sheka peanuts and kept him in a cage with a broken lock, tied up with string. Each morning I found Sheka wandering about the floor, the knot carefully unpicked and the string lying on the floor next to his cage. In time the clipped red flight feathers on the underside of his wings grew back and the bird headed for the open window and the sky.

I didn't regret our animals leaving. I don't think it even occurred to me that they were supposed to be permanent fixtures. But there was something about the fawn's vulnerability that made her different. We kept her in my father's downstairs study and on that first evening I carefully carried a pan of milk which I set down beside her and watched as she lapped at the surface.

But we were young and we were excited. We wanted to be near the fawn and so we played in the same room, including her in our games: unwittingly terrorising and tending her by turns. By evening the fawn was showing signs of restlessness. I stood by the door holding the bowl of milk, watching her stumble around the room. She fell to her knees and couldn't seem to rise again. Every time she managed to straighten one leg another would crumple. I put down the basin and ran to fetch Auntie Yabome. My stepmother watched the fawn for a few minutes. 'She wants to die,' she said, with old village wisdom.

In the morning the fawn was lying on her side in the centre of the floor. I thought she was asleep and so I left the basin of milk next to her. When I went back and she still hadn't touched it I called Auntie Yabome again. Even then, it took me a while to understand the fawn was dead.

Somewhere in the left hemisphere of my brain I remembered what someone must once have told me, about the survival instinct of animals. Yet we had tormented the motherless fawn until she willed herself to death. I wondered about all the terrible things I had done, how I had tried to get rid of Auntie Yabome. I didn't really worry that my stepmother might lie down on her bed and decide to die, but I began to feel bad all the same.

We reached Magburaka at midday and stopped outside Pa Roke's house. It was painted red, with blue shutters and window frames. But there was no glass in the windows; they were just empty holes, like eye sockets. Everyone called the house 'Mohamed's house' because my father's brothers had set about building it for us to live in when he came home from Britain. After he was posted to Freetown the house lay empty until Pa Roke decided to move in. It was the only house in the street with a proper plaster facade; all the rest, including my aunts' and uncles' homes, were built of clay bricks with earthen floors that were swept clean morning and evening. None of them had electricity, running water or indoor plumbing. Out back, on the edge of the bush, was the latrine and as I sat, thigh muscles tensed, suspended over a stinking pit in the tiny thatched hut, it was the only part of our visits I regretted.

Pa Roke came out wearing his long gown. He rarely smiled.

'*Seke.*'

'*Seke, topia.*'

After several exchanges we went inside. There was a pause while we all sat down, then the greetings began again like a mantra. I hadn't learned to speak Temne. I sat there with my shoulders rounded, my chin sticking out, half listening, half dreaming.

People came over to greet my father, sat a while and moved on. Nobody ever seemed to be in a hurry. People say time moves slowly in remote places. In Magburaka time moved at pretty much the same pace as everywhere else, but it had a different texture. In Temne the days of the week have no names, the years have no numbers, there are no dates, no decades, centuries or millennia. There are three words to denote the passing of time: today, tomorrow and yesterday. Everything else is viewed in relation to those three positions and extends only a few days in either direction, perhaps because life in rural Africa is so full of hazards that people prefer to live in the here and now rather than speculate on an uncertain future.

This is a world without clocks. Hence, a day is divided into four parts: *prasok* or dawn, *beeth* is the rest of the morning before midday prayers, *dayan* meaning afternoon and *dafoi* refers to after dark. It was only after a long interval that one of Pa Roke's younger wives arrived with some food and we three children sat on the floor in the middle of the small room eating from a large plate of rice and *plassas*.

We dug into the mound, burrowing into the slopes in front of us, until gradually the pattern of roses on the tin plate began to appear. I remember I kept up a stream of chatter about it, and began to take food off the top of the pile and once I reached across and dipped my spoon into the rice on the other side of the mound, from where my brother was eating. We ate alone. I don't know where our stepmother was—perhaps she was out visiting our aunts. Pa Roke and my father did not join us. They stood over us, watching and talking in Temne. Pa Roke had a long, oval face like mine. He looked grave. He seemed to be gazing at the three of us intently. Every now and again he would ask something and once I saw him jerk his head in our direction.

In 1967 our father had travelled to Magburaka to tell Pa Roke he wanted to go into politics and to ask his advice. But our grandfather had told his son he was not qualified to tell him what he should do. Pa Roke belonged to a past world, one in which the elders chose the new chief, initiated him and guided him throughout his reign. They ruled following traditions that were hundreds of years old. The chief who refused to pay heed to their advice could be brought before the Poro society or a council of the elders. Pa Roke still sat and listened to cases in the *barrie* every day. When the British arrived they had ruled the people absolutely and by decree, yet it was they who bestowed a system on all the new nations in which people were supposed to elect their own leaders. No wonder a lot of people were confused.

Three years on, our father had come to ask Pa Roke's counsel again. He had been bitterly disappointed by his experience of government and had lost all faith in Siaka Stevens. The prime minister was an arch manipulator and tireless in his machinations; our father was dangerously isolated in cabinet. Pa Roke listened. What my father told him would not have been entirely new to the old man: the country rustled with rumours; some of the stories had appeared in the newspapers. Pa Roke warned his son that whatever he did he must be careful, and he should be wary of Stevens. The prime minister bore grudges, that much had been demonstrated by the fate of others; he would almost certainly take their fight to the finish.

When we were done eating another of Pa Roke's wives returned with a second dish. This time father and son sat down to eat together while we ran outside to find our cousins. Looking back I realise now the full weight of the discussion that took place between them that day. I imagine now it could only have been that day and no other because it was the last time I saw Pa Roke standing tall. He was already well into his eighties by then and not long afterwards he suffered a stroke. The next time we visited as a family he lay, partly paralysed, on the bed in the corner of the room. With each visit he grew thinner, but the fingers of his one good hand tapped and flew, as alive as ever.

In the afternoon we left Magburaka and Pa Roke and travelled north to visit the Bumbuna Falls, close to my stepmother's own village. The falls lie almost exactly in the centre of Sierra Leone, at the point where three rivers converge into one: the Tonkolili, the Seli and the Rokel. Down the water flows over one hundred miles to Freetown and the Atlantic Ocean. From the village we walked down winding bush paths to the river, just below the waterfall.

Over the edge of the rocks the violent rush of water pitched into a serene, drifting river, edged by boulders, skirted by kingfishers and herons. Here and there pale green weeds below the surface caught the sunlight and the water gleamed phosphorescent. Up close the roar of water was like pounding drums. Yet only a few yards' walk farther along the rocky edge of the water the silence of the lake completely overpowered the sound of the waterfall. It was as though the river were a lost child looking for its mother and as soon as the two found each other, the child grew quiet.

The villagers viewed the falls with awe and they claimed the waterside was enchanted. People avoided going there alone or at dusk. As we sat in the *barrie* afterwards someone told us a story about a woman who had been to fetch a last jar of water as night was falling. People had heard her screams as she ran back to the village, where she collapsed in the dust. At first she could barely speak but finally she told those gathered around her what had happened. She had seen a devil, they heard her say, a devil dancing on the water.

The woman was in the *barrie* with us and I glanced across at her. She was leaning against the wall with her *lappa* tied carelessly about her waist and a slightly sullen face; she was about twenty years old. She didn't react while the story was being told.

I, on the other hand, was spellbound. 'What did the devil look like?' I asked her.

'It had one big foot. Just one giant foot. It was too far out on the water.' She was loosening one of her tight braids. She let go of it briefly, waved her hand and shrugged.

'These devils—they have ears like an antelope and big teeth that stick out of their mouths, nostrils as wide as caves. Not-o-so?' The storyteller looked at her too, and put his fingers up on either side of his head like a pair of ears, then up to his mouth to make two fangs.

She glanced at him, neither answered nor contradicted. I pressed her: 'But what else? What was it doing? Did he see you?'

'I don't know. I didn't stay there. I saw it and I ran. That's all.'

'But did he say anything to you?'

She paused and she stopped fiddling with her plait for a moment. 'He was laughing,' she said at length. 'I could hear him laughing.'

I imagined the spirit as she had seen him: a solitary silhouette on the flat lake, turning, pirouetting, as graceful as could be on his one proud foot. He was enjoying himself in that beautiful place, laughing with the sheer pleasure of it all, of that I was certain. I thought that it was probably the woman who had frightened the devil, screaming and running away as she had, rather than the other way around. I wondered if he danced alone at dusk every day.

'I wish I'd seen him. I'd like to see a devil. I'd like to see a devil dancing on the water.' I privately made up my mind to try and catch a glimpse of him the very next time I could: the very next time we visited Bumbuna. I wondered about my chances of getting down to the water alone and unnoticed. Could I find my way back along the paths?

The man who had told the story in the first place chuckled. 'Oh no you wouldn't,' he said. 'You wouldn't want to see a devil.' He wagged his finger at me and shook his head. 'For then something bad will surely happen to you.'

In August our father gave us each money to buy Auntie Yabome a present for her birthday at the end of the month. We went along to Patterson Zochonis, or PZ, where we searched for a suitable gift among the merchandise. Our stepmother dressed with the greatest of care and in the height of fashion and after some searching we found our gift. In the shoe department: a pair of cream and lime-green platform shoes rotating on a dais. We hurried to count our money and left with the shoes hidden at the bottom of a bag.

Auntie Yabome and I were getting along a bit better, and I had managed to overcome my feelings of guilt sufficiently to continue to defy her when the occasion presented itself. Alone in the garden one afternoon, I heard a distinctive hiss from behind the bushes. I turned to see a figure beckoning me from behind the fence. I moved closer, peering through the foliage. It was Milik. I crept through the bushes until I reached him and we squatted down out of sight. Our fingers touched through the fence and he pushed some sweets to me as we whispered together for a while. After a few minutes Milik slipped away, back in the direction he had come.

Both Sheka's and Memuna's birthdays fell the following month, and in the house plans were underway for a big party on the same day to celebrate them both. My parents, worried I might feel left out, included me in the celebrations. For many years I believed it had been my birthday and I remembered that day as my birthday alone and no one else's.

The day began before anyone was awake. In the room I shared with Memuna it was scarcely light when my stepmother shook me awake. She told me to dress and come downstairs, and when I arrived there I found her already waiting in her car with the engine running. We were alone. I climbed into the front seat and we drove down Spur Loop and out onto the roundabout by Wilberforce barracks. I didn't know where we were headed and, because somehow I sensed the start of an adventure, I didn't ask.

The British high commissioner's house was built on the side of the hill above Hill Cot Road, and part of the house jutted out over one of the hairpin bends of the road. I passed it on my way to and from school every day and I liked it so much, surrounded by lawns and flamboyant trees, I dreamed about what it would be like to live there. I told everyone how one day I would buy the house. But I had never actually been inside. When my stepmother turned the nose of the car into the high commissioner's gate and we travelled up the long gravel drive to the porch, it took me a while to realise where we were.

Stephen Olver, the high commissioner, came to the door. He greeted Auntie Yabome first and then he turned to me: 'So, young lady, I'm told you would like to see my house.'

I nodded, transfixed and tongue-tied. The high commissioner called his son, a boy of about thirteen, and gave him instructions to show me around. For the next half hour I followed him from one splendid room to another, while he kept up an impressive commentary. We looked behind every door, upstairs and down, including the boy's own room, where a dozen model aircraft spun on wires suspended from the ceiling, like flies grown lazy in the heat. At the end of the tour I was brought back to the high commissioner's office, where my stepmother waited.

From the desk in the corner Mr Olver beckoned to me to sit in front of him and asked me if I would like a drink. A moment later a servant brought me the cold drink on a tray. The high commissioner asked me if I liked the house. I replied that I did, very much indeed. How much might I propose for it, then? He was offering to sell the house to me. I gave the question a moment's consideration. I had two leones in my dresser drawer at home and my pocket money was fifty cents a week. It took me a moment but I decided to offer him the entire sum of my savings. He laughed out loud. Up until then our conversation had been conducted in complete solemnity, and only at that moment did I realise that none of them had taken me seriously from the start.

At home I laid my indignation to rest. I shared many of the same presents as my sister, including matching doll's houses, made out of painted tin. We spent the hour before breakfast assembling them. In the late morning we gathered behind the railings of the veranda and watched an acrobat perform cartwheels holding first a glass of water and then a plate of rice. Although the man flipped over and over, ending up in the splits, not a drop or a grain fell to the ground. I recognised the tumbling man from the beach at Cape Club, where we spent Saturdays and where he often served drinks on his hands in exchange for pennies. People would throw coins on the ground and he bent over backwards like a crab to pick them up with his mouth. I did not see him as a busker, but as the most talented performer I had ever known. It was as though Nijinsky himself had put in an appearance and was leaping across the lawn.

At lunch time all the children sat in a circle and our stepmother brought out a record with a blonde woman on the cover and put it on: we sang along to 'Happy Birthday'. There were jellies, which collapsed in the heat, melting chocolates, pass the parcel and blind man's buff. We sat on balloons and tried to squash them and chased each other round the tree. My brother, whose birthday it really was of course, wore a smart white suit, a pale-blue shirt and a matching bow tie.

Late in the afternoon our father came home. He spoke briefly to my stepmother on the terrace, and then he came down to the garden. We persuaded him to join in our games on the lawn, he took off his jacket and shoes and humoured us for a long while.

The wonderful day seemed to belong to me, a miracle created with me in mind, still untainted by too much knowledge or by disappointment. But that was just an illusion.

It wasn't my birthday, of course, not even close. And on that day our lives changed for good. Our father had resigned in protest from the government. A resolution had been passed by the All People's Congress agreeing to turn us into a republic headed by an executive presidency, and many people—including our father—believed the country was now inescapably on the road to becoming a one-party state. Any minister who refused to agree to the new executive presidency would be refused the party symbol at the next election. Our father had left the house as Siaka Stevens's most senior minister; by the time he came home he was the government's leading adversary. And by bed time we couldn't even call the house home any more because it didn't belong to us—it belonged to the government.

In six years I had lived in eight homes: our first bungalow in Shettleston, which of course I could not remember; the apartment in Freetown rented to us by the Department of Health; a brief stay in the bungalow at Wilberforce barracks; and then, after my father resigned from the army, the tiny, airless flat opposite PZ. I couldn't remember them either. Then there was the house and clinic in Koidu, my mother's caravan, my stepfather's diplomatic residence in Lagos; and finally Minister's Quarters at Spur Loop, which we packed up and left within twenty-four hours: family, uncles and cousins, the servants including Amadu and Amara, the dogs, everyone.

My new and ninth home was a house in Tengbe Farkai. Situated on a plateau on one of the hills behind Freetown, where the old railway line passed on the way to Wilberforce, Tengbe Farkai was once a small village, now gradually being swallowed by the city. A bridge connected the village to the main road into town. Beneath the bridge, in a place they called Down Below, people lived in small, tumbledown shacks crowded around a trickling stream. From the steps of our new house I could almost jump and land on the steps of Uncle Bash and Auntie Amy's place. The two houses, reached via a short alleyway, stood side by side overlooking a shared compound of beaten earth. It was a far, far cry from the lush environs of Minister's Quarters.

Everywhere in the country, from Freetown to Koidu, from Pujehun to Kabala, people were absorbing the impact of the resignation of two of the country's leading ministers. In Tonkolili especially the local people were in shock. In August, after the APC convention had voted in favour of breaking away from Britain and turning Sierra Leone into a republic, our father, Ibrahim and Bash Taqi had held a series of emergency meetings in Magburaka. After they made the decision to resign they travelled up-country to inform the local chiefs and to hold talks with the elders of the Poro society, but the news had not been entirely well received. No one voluntarily departed politics in Africa. The elders felt they had worked hard to get their men into positions of power, and the same men owed it to them to stay. For many people in Sierra Leone democracy was just another system of patronage. You got your man into government and in exchange he looked after you. The very notion of resigning in protest, on a matter of principle, was not commonly understood.

In Freetown our father's resignation letter had been published in several of the newspapers. It appeared the morning of the day of the birthday party. When Auntie Yabome woke me up to go to the high commissioner's house it was already on the news stands. I had often wondered at the real purpose of our early-morning visit to the British high commissioner's residence and not long ago I asked my stepmother about it, but she couldn't seem to remember the visit at all. So I wrote to Stephen Olver, long retired by then, but he answered by return of mail—a short note scrawled on the bottom of my own letter to him—that these matters belonged to the past and he had no desire to discuss them.

While the Taqis' letters were short and gave little away, my father spelled out exactly why he would no longer serve Stevens. He laid the blame for the violence that had swept the country in the last two years at Stevens's feet: the death of the young boy at Freedom Press, the violence and intimidation at Ginger Hall, the beatings in Port Loko. The letter went on to detail their disagreements over the use and misuse of government funds, how Stevens had lied to the World Bank, and how the country's reserves were at risk from the prime minister's lavish spending. He accused Stevens of being behind the wave of diamond smuggling in Kono. But even that was not the worst of it.

Stevens thirsted for nothing less than absolute power. He was already in the habit of making decisions without recourse to his cabinet. Lately he had become obsessed with removing the queen as head of state in Sierra Leone. At certain official functions protocol dictated that a toast to the Queen of England was drunk, and Stevens had begun to grow increasingly impatient with the practice, which he took as a personal snub. He felt further upstaged by the governor-general, representative of the queen, whose arrival at the same public occasions was heralded by the Sierra Leonean national anthem. A few months before, at a banquet at State House, Stevens had ordered the national anthem to be played for his own entrance. The police bandleader obeyed and struck up with 'High we exalt thee, realm of the free'. Minutes later and in front of visibly baffled foreign dignitaries, the entire piece was played through for the second time when the governor-general arrived.

'This display of infantile vanity may appear trivial,' wrote our father, 'but to me with a trained medical mind, they are the manifestations of megalomaniac syndrome. It is the top of the iceberg submerged below a sea of personal shyness. This coupled with an insatiable thirst for power can only spell disaster for the country.'

Our father was among those who believed Stevens's plans to turn Sierra Leone into a republic masked darker ambitions. Given the opportunity to alter the constitution, the prime minister would use it to increase his own power beyond imagination. Our father wanted to warn the people of what was coming, what he saw in Stevens: the ruthlessness and a viciousness concealed beneath a mastery of charades. Pa Sheki fooled hundreds, if not thousands, with humour and charm. He enjoyed taking advantage of the gullible, and when someone he had duped left the room, be it a local chief or an international business consortium, he would turn to his aides and joke: 'Dem see soak leopard, dem call am puss.' Some people see a wet leopard and they mistake it for a pussy cat.

A few days before the resignations Stevens had left the country on a state visit to Zambia, appointing a relatively junior minister, S. B. Kawusu-Conteh, minister for the Southern Province, to act as prime minister instead of Mohamed Forna. Meanwhile rumours had already reached my father that Stevens planned to eject him from the government as soon as he left the country to attend the World Bank conferences. For some weeks Janet Thorpe had already been secretly typing drafts of his resignation letter. By September he felt there was nothing further that could be achieved by staying on.

Left alone to face the crisis, Kawusu-Conteh flustered and panicked. He called a series of hasty meetings with hard-core loyalists Joseph Barthes Wilson and Christian Kamara-Taylor, and they decided to save face by expelling the two ministers from the APC. A day later five thousand people converged on Freetown's Victoria Park for a public meeting at which the dissident ministers were to speak. Kawusu-Conteh attempted to stop the meeting going ahead, but Police Commissioner Jenkins Smith, summoned to Kawusu-Conteh's home late the previous evening, foiled his efforts by refusing to allow the police to be used for such a purpose.

That Sunday morning our father, the Taqis and Sarif Easmon were joined on the platform by Dr John Karefa-Smart, who had recently left his job as deputy director of the World Health Organisation and come home to Sierra Leone. John Karefa-Smart spoke first and the people listened patiently. But when Mohamed Forna took the stage the roar of applause stretched into minutes, rising high above the park until it reached the heavy, closed curtains of State House less than a hundred yards away. A group of forty red-shirted thugs appeared and began to shower the crowd with rocks from the other side of the wall. At the edges of the gathering people began to scatter as scuffles broke out; one man was struck by a rock in the eye. For a while it looked as though a full-scale riot could ensue. But a moment later, as quickly as they had come, the Red Shirts departed, climbed back into their vehicles and drove away.

The creation of the new party was announced a few days later. We called ourselves the United Democratic Party. The UDP was to be the third force to end bi-partisan tribal politics and our plan was to fight and defeat Stevens and the APC at the general elections, due within the next three months.

All this time Stevens himself had delayed his return to the country. As soon as the new party was announced he flew back from the safety of neighbouring Liberia. Hours after his plane touched down he made a broadcast to the nation: he declared a state of emergency and an immediate halt to all public meetings.

The UDP refused to be cowed. Our father responded, pointing out the state of emergency was illegal without a parliamentary mandate. In an act of defiance United Democratic Party vehicles toured the city streets with loudhailers calling supporters to another rally at Victoria Park. Once again thousands crowded through the gates, despite the blocks on all roads into Freetown. In the park the people found themselves surrounded by armed police, who stood guard and watched but did not move to break up the meeting. The party wasn't even officially registered and yet every day hundreds more people came to sign on as new members. The government newspaper the *Daily Mail* printed an article saying people were being paid to join, but the opposite was true. Folk from Freetown, from the provinces, Krios, Temnes, even Mendes, former members of the APC and people who had never belonged to a political party in their lives added their names to the growing list and paid their registration fee. Quite simply people were desperate to get rid of Siaka Stevens and the APC.

From the outset the real nerve centre of the UDP was our compound in Tengbe Farkai. Meetings were held there all day and into the night. There were endless comings and goings, familiar faces and new ones I had never seen. Many people just wanted to sign up and we directed them to the office in East Street. Our party symbol was the sun and the moon. At Tengbe Farkai I watched as cars drove in and out with the logo, sprayed in orange, on the side panels. It began to appear everywhere throughout Freetown, painted on walls, drawn in the dirt, emblazoned on shirts. The sun and the moon, source of light, symbol of unity. Wherever a person was in the country, or even in the world, at any time of the day or night, it didn't matter who you were, when you turned your gaze up to the sky there was the yellow sun or an amber moon, and they were exactly the same to everyone.

☙ 25 ❧

At six I wasn't scared of the dark, not at all, no. But gradually I
learned to be. The fear grew until, by the time I was an adult, I had
to switch on all the lights in the hall if I got up in the night and I
even started to leave the bedside light on when I stayed in a hotel
or a new place. At some point staying alone in a house at night
became simply out of the question. During the evening I would
sit still, pretending to be relaxed, trying to avoid any errand that
might take me upstairs or into the kitchen, or anywhere else at
all out of the safety zone of artificial noise and light thrown out
by the television. Later, instead of sleeping I would lie rigid and
cold with dread, falling in and out of consciousness, giving flesh
to the demons in my nightmares until the line between wakeful-
ness and sleep became indistinguishable and fear stalked either
side of the boundary. It isn't fear of the dark, per se, I suppose. It's
the fear of what the dark conceals. It's the horror that comes of
feeling hampered, disadvantaged by losing the use of one of your
senses. You can't see them, you have no idea where they are. Noises
are louder. One man can sound like ten. Ten men can sound like
one. Voices echo and multiply. Footsteps come out of nowhere
and suddenly fade away, as though they belong to spirits instead
of men. And they, whoever they are—they know where you are.

At Tengbe Farkai they started coming under cover of the night
to throw rocks through our windows. The first rock landed on
the roof, while we were at supper. The crash resounded on the
tin roof. We stopped eating and waited, startled into silence. A
second crash brought the household to life. Downstairs in the

yard Santigi, Amadu and Amara, who had been gathered around a shared plate of rice, were running to close the tall metal gates and bar the entrance to the compound. Rocks were falling all around. Outside in the lane shouts bounced between the high walls and disappeared into the black. There were scraping noises, the double tread of feet running in flip-flops; more stones hit the front of the house—one shattered an open window and the glass fell onto the ground below.

Our father left the room and reappeared holding his hunting rifle. He ducked out onto the balcony at the front of the house. One, two, three, we slipped out of our seats and followed him. He stood overlooking the alleyway in full view of anyone who might be below. He drew up a chair and sat down, the rifle across his lap. When he spotted us waiting there, he waved us behind him, and so we crowded in and wedged ourselves between the wall and his back to watch and wait. I did not feel afraid. I felt excited. And the tremors began in my knees and tickled my thighs and stomach as I stood squirming with my nose pressed into my father's shoulder. The alley was quiet. I didn't know whether they had gone for good, or if this was just the beginning. But I knew that if they came back we were waiting for them, and our father would deal with them in such a way they would really be sorry.

Ever since the announcement of the new party the leaders of the UDP had been receiving constant threats. Death threats were telephoned daily to the office in East Street. Red Shirts turned up at every meeting and rally. They heckled, jostled and spat and they set upon supporters of the UDP en route to the meeting place. The same youths drove past the offices at high speed, jeering at the people waiting outside to register. The day after our house was stoned our father, accompanied by John Karefa-Smart, whose family had also been badly frightened at his brother's house in Murraytown, requested a meeting with Banja Tejan-Sie, the governor-general.

Tejan-Sie murmured words of sympathy, for he had differences with Siaka Stevens himself. Stevens had never wanted Tejan-Sie, a northerner and a long-standing SLPP man, in his government. Since 1968 Tejan-Sie had been acting in the post and Stevens consistently refused to bestow upon him the full honour of his title, something known to chafe Tejan-Sie considerably. During his tenure as minister of finance our father had often brought his grievances to Tejan-Sie; now he asked the acting governor-general for help in arranging protection for the leaders of the UDP and their families. Tejan-Sie promised to see what he could do. Nothing could be done without the sanction of the prime minister, he warned, who now had a stronger grip on the police force than ever. He stood up and shook the hands of his former colleagues; the situation was clearly becoming dangerous and he promised them he would talk to the prime minister immediately.

Tejan-Sie was true to his word. He saw Siaka Stevens in a matter of a few hours. The meeting was followed by a swift announcement from State House: Banja Tejan-Sie, formerly acting governor-general of Sierra Leone, had been made the country's permanent governor-general. We were even more isolated than before. The next night, after the black descended, the thugs gathered round to stone our home, and they did the same every night after that.

Still the ranks of the United Democratic Party swelled. People were travelling down to Freetown from the provinces, using the back routes to circumvent the road blocks, turning up at the house and the office, offering their help. Some of the new arrivals volunteered to guard our compound from the Red Shirts and to keep watch at night. They moved in, sleeping on the hard veranda

and sitting around in groups of three or four during the day. They
were unfamiliar faces in my world. I steered round them, keeping
my focus on those adults I knew. Our stepmother and Auntie
Amy cooked around the clock, great vats of rice over open fires,
just to keep everyone fed.

While the protection the men offered was needed, the UDP
organisers decided they had to stop any more people coming
into Freetown. There was only a limited amount the people could
contribute and the situation risked getting out of hand. The only
way to stem the flow of people into the capital was for the leaders
of the party to take the message to the provinces themselves. Our
father elected to go and he travelled in a convoy to Port Loko,
S. I.'s constituency, and to Lunsar, a little distance farther north.
Despite the best efforts of the hired thugs thousands swarmed to
the rallies. Spurred on by this success the party organisers began
to lay plans to visit Makeni and Magburaka, home territory for
our father where we were guaranteed a triumphant reception.

We had stopped going to school, and neither did we go out to
the beach or to Cape Club or to the tennis club any more. Instead
we spent the days trying to amuse ourselves, endlessly repeating
our childish games. One afternoon Memuna stood in the centre
of the sitting room, counting aloud with her eyelids squeezed
shut; Sheka and I raced for the exits and while he disappeared
into the bedrooms I ran down the staircase to the ground floor,
heading for the kitchens and the storeroom. My plan was to hide
in a discarded rice sack, behind the stacks of empty baskets or
the giant vats of palm oil.

At the bottom of the stairs I saw a better opportunity: long coats
hanging from a peg on the wall. I pushed them aside so I could
slip behind, but as I did so I bumped up against something else
already there. I stepped backward, back into the light. A dozen
panga knives, the sort used for cutting wheat in the fields, were

propped against the wall, a sheaf of curved and polished blades. I stood still and stared at them. For a moment I stopped breathing. I must cover them up, and yet for a few seconds I could do nothing at all. I forced myself to open my fingers, let the coats fall and flutter back into place as though they had never been disturbed. I ran and hid in the storeroom and I stayed there for a long time before the others found me. I didn't tell my brother and sister what I had seen. I knew why the cutlasses were there and I worried about what trouble I might get into if anyone found out I had discovered them. Somehow, I knew instinctively this was knowledge to keep to myself.

We were playing on the red earth near the entrance to our compound a few days later. The sun was already low and within the hour the sky would switch from light to dark. There were voices in the lane and we looked up to see who was coming. We saw the alley full of people, crowding down the narrow path like a rush of flood water down an open storm drain. The three of us scattered in the direction of the house. We reached the bottom step, where Auntie Amy pushed us bodily up the stairs.

I climbed up to one of the windows overlooking the yard and watched as scores of Red Shirts invaded our compound. The men were armed with bottles, night sticks, machetes. They caught our volunteer guards unawares. Already two of the invaders had one of our men cornered against the wall. The man was trying to shield his face and head, half crouching, turned to the wall as the blows from the cudgels fell across his back. A man dressed in white raged through the crowd. Down the front of his shirt the splattered blood looked like red embroidery. Our compound was transformed into a battlefield as every man in the house had run out to grapple with the invaders. They were locked in each other's arms like couples on a dance floor. Above them a great cloud of dust billowed up over their heads and raised arms.

In the kitchens the women were boiling water with the idea of repelling anyone who tried to break into the house. A tall, thin, very black woman pushed past me and stared out at the fracas. Sucking air through her teeth contemptuously, she turned and ran down the stairs into the yard, where she deftly slipped off one of her stiletto shoes and struck a Red Shirt in the face. He screamed and clasped his cheek. The woman seemed emboldened and the last I saw of her she was wading deeper into the fray brandishing her shoe.

I left my place next to Memuna and Sheka and slipped away. I crept to the top of the stairs. No one noticed me leaving. Down the stairs I went, past the kitchens and the storeroom, until I reached the outside steps. I edged around the door and stood with my back pressed flat against the wall. I was only a few feet from the battle. I told myself I was really here to look for Apollo, to bring him in so he wasn't hurt, but I had no idea where he was. I considered jumping the short distance to Uncle Bash and Auntie Amy's house. I could see Amadu in the middle of it all. Amadu the cook, who would lose the hearing in one of his ears because of a blow to the head.

I craned my neck for a better view but it was all so disorderly it was hard to make out what was happening. Out of the clouds of dust two people lunged towards me. One was a Red Shirt. The other one—I don't know who he was—reached me first. He picked me up and rushed with me back into the house and up the stairs. Auntie Yabome hadn't even realised I was gone.

Our father wasn't there the day we were attacked. As my stepmother scolded me I saw her lips move, heard the words, but really I was transfixed by the look in her eyes: it was new, something I had never seen before and which I failed to understand. She could have punished me but she didn't. There seemed to be a hollowness at the centre of her anger.

The announcement banning the United Democratic Party came when the convoy carrying our father arrived in Makeni, the evening before a mass rally. Stevens had issued the order to arrest the leaders earlier in the day. But when the police commissioner refused to allow his force to be used to carry out a blatantly political act, Stevens turned to the army. Who knows how the prime minister persuaded the force commander to do his bidding? But he did. For the UDP and our family it proved to be the turning point. Our father had miscalculated, thinking John Bangura was a match for Stevens and would never send his men to arrest them. He had been betrayed twice in a few days: first by the governor-general and now by the head of the army.

As it turned out the officers sent to Makeni could not get near him to carry out their orders for most of the day—our father was surrounded by so many of his supporters. Later in the evening his young aide, on his way to visit a girlfriend, picked up the news broadcast on his car radio moments after he had left his boss at the home of the local doctor in Makeni, where they were to spend the night. The young activist turned the car and drove at speed down the unlit roads back to the house. If he was lucky they might both still have time to escape. The area was full of local supporters who would shield them for a few days; after that they could probably make it out of the country. He dashed up the steps of the house.

Although he listened, our father was opposed to the idea of going into hiding. Within minutes a contingent of Limba army officers arrived at the front door of the house and demanded entry. Our father nodded to the doctor, the owner of the house, to open the door.

The army had warrants for the arrest of two men—Dr Mohamed Forna and his aide—but they emerged from the house to find it surrounded by a crowd of defiant supporters barring the way. The soldiers and the people faced each other. Eventually the officer in charge gave orders to arrest each and every one of the protesters. So in all more than fifty men accompanied our father on his five-hour journey to Pademba Road Prison. The only person not among them was his young aide. He had not been recognised and in the confusion he slipped away and, a few days later, crossed the border into Liberia.

❦ 26 ❦

I saw a garden: waxy red and orange anthuriums displaying proud
yellow stamens; trails of lace-edged hibiscus; fragrant frangipani;
star apples and guava trees; scented lilies nodding their giant
freckled heads at me; spires of mighty amaryllis. The sun was
shining and the garden was empty. The three of us crept down
the dark, wooden staircase and out of the front door. In the heavy,
airless day the garden was suffused with perfume. I broke off a
piece of spiky Jerusalem thorn and watched the milk drip from the
broken end, felt it sticky on my fingers, beginning to bind them
together. We wandered towards the high wall of the boundary,
gazing at the fruit, considering whether to climb up and take
some down. The garden was alive. An iridescent blue humming-
bird, smaller than a baby's fist, flew from petal to petal ahead of
his plain, brown mate; a column of ants trooped into the earth;
a pair of tiny black beetles stood by and waited for them to pass.
Beyond the tall, wrought-iron gate someone was walking down
the road: a man carrying a basket on his head. He waved at us
and we called and waved back.

The man called Pa Cook appeared from the side of the house.
He was gesticulating at us. We couldn't tell what he was saying;
we thought he was waving at us too, and we waved at him. He
was old and quite bowed in the leg. It took him a long time to
reach us, even though he was trying to run. He looked peculiar,
all out of breath and worried as though it was his job to guard the
fruit. He pushed us, herded us back towards the house, and once
we were inside he shut the door and locked it from the outside.

We watched from the upstairs balcony as he made his way back round the side of the house to the kitchen.

Shortly before the arrests a convoy of United Democratic Party supporters on their way to the rally in Makeni had passed a vehicle carrying APC Red Shirts on their way to disrupt the same event. Lying on the front of the bonnet of the APC Land-Rover as it travelled through Hastings was a notorious Red Shirt who went by the alias of Omole. The two groups clashed and somehow in the ensuing fracas Omole had been knocked off the vehicle and run over by his own people. He was hurt; there were even reports that he had been killed. Stevens blamed the UDP for the incident and used it as an excuse to ban the new party and arrest the leaders, none of whom had been present when Omole was hurt.

In all over two hundred people were arrested; most were held at Pademba Road Prison. The army had been to Magburaka and to the Fornas' village of Rogbonko. They had searched all the houses and interrogated Pa Roke. They seized Uncle Momodu and Uncle Ismail, because they were brothers to Dr Forna, and they were held along with dozens of others at Mafanta Prison near Magburaka. Meanwhile in Freetown rumours abounded concerning the fate of the arrested leaders, including one that they were to be taken out of the country, possibly to Guinea to the notorious dissident detention centre, Camp Yaya.

Lawyers acting for the UDP leaders issued a writ of habeas corpus, demanding of the courts that the prisoners either be charged or released. At Tengbe Farkai, where we waited for our father to come home, men from the CID arrived to search our house. They slashed our mattresses and pulled the stuffing out of the chairs, while outside Red Shirts hovered in the street and chanted anti-UDP slogans.

We waited in the compound yard while men moved from room to room searching our belongings, even through our toys and clothes. At the end of the search the officers from the CID left, triumphantly bearing all our kitchen knives and a bottle of holy water, blessed by an Alpha, given to my father for protection by one of his supporters. The man in charge of the search carried it away, carefully holding the neck of the bottle between his finger and thumb, calling to the mob that it was acid. Auntie Yabome went down to the CID headquarters to reclaim our possessions some time later. In front of all the officers at the front desk she took the bottle, rolled up her sleeves and washed her hands in the holy water. But even that didn't stop the *Daily Mail* publishing a story later, saying a canister of acid had been found in our house.

The days passed. With nothing else to do one afternoon I decided to take Apollo for a walk. I found a lead and we set off down the lane away from the main road and towards Down Below. I longed to have a dog like the ones in my picture books—one who would chase sticks and sleep on my bed at night. I had never seen anyone in Sierra Leone walk a dog; at home none of the dogs was even allowed into the house. The area around Tengbe Farkai was new to me and I became lost. At some point I had passed a canal and then some houses, taken a few turns. When I tried to retrace my steps the passages and lanes seemed to have multiplied and shifted around. Some looked familiar and I started down one after another; a few minutes on I was suddenly unsure. I remembered I had read somewhere that dogs can always find their way home, so I slipped the lead from round Apollo's neck and as the dog trotted lazily on, I followed behind.

As I turned into the gates of the house I found the compound in chaos. It took me a while to realise they were all looking for me. I had surely been gone less than half an hour. Santigi saw me first and hurried off to be the first to tell my stepmother I had re-appeared. She didn't look at all pleased. Though I tried to describe how Apollo brought me home, she kept her hands on her hips, her mouth pursed, and drew air in through her nostrils. She warned me not to leave the compound again.

There were rumours of plans to kidnap Dr Forna's children. My stepmother heard them from one of our self-elected guards. She went directly to the police commissioner, Jenkins Smith, and asked for his help, explaining that we were all alone in the house. Behind his customary dignity and starched uniform, the police commissioner looked tired and resigned. He shook his head. The situation was now far beyond his control, he admitted, and there was nothing he could do to protect us. 'Leave the house, Mrs Forna, please,' he advised her. 'For both our sakes.'

A few nights later the Red Shirts gathered outside and began to throw rocks at our windows. Our stepmother carried us sleeping from our beds and put us into the back seat of the car. In the yard she started the car engine and the moment the gates were opened she turned the headlights up to full beam and drove at speed down the lane and out onto the street.

By the time we reached the home of Dr Olu-Williams and his wife the three of us had woken up and my stepmother had tried everyone she knew who might take us in, knocking on door after door in the dead of night. One by one they had all declined. People stood in their doorways, murmuring sympathetic noises, followed always by some excuse to send us on. The reluctance to get involved was so obvious that Auntie Yabome thanked them for nothing and climbed back into the car. With nowhere in particular in mind we were driving along Wilkinson Road, in the direction of Lumley, when we passed close by the turning to the Olu-Williamses' house. Auntie Yabome turned the car around and started up the steep, unlit road. Halfway up Lower Pipeline Lane she swung round to the right into their short driveway, coming to a stop under the covered porch of the big concrete house.

When Murietta Olu-Williams answered the knock on the door she had met Yabome Forna only once before. Under the light of the porch she recognised her vaguely. Murietta had been permanent secretary at the Ministry of Finance when our father joined the government; she was the first woman in Sierra Leone to hold the position. She was sociable and vivacious as well as politically astute. Our father held her in the highest esteem. Her husband, Sierra Leone's first surgeon specialist, worked at Connaught Hospital. Our stepmother stood on the doorstep; by now the tears were running down her face. She knew she was taking a risk; she was desperate: 'I have brought the children, Mrs Olu-Williams,' was all she said. 'Can you take them in?'

Mrs Olu-Williams ran upstairs to fetch her husband and together they tried to calm our stepmother and listen to her story.

'Where are the children now?' asked Murietta when our stepmother had finished.

'They're in the car.'

The older woman glanced at the vehicle. For the first time she saw the three of us, dressed only in our pyjamas, watching through the back window. Until then neither one of the elderly couple had realised we were waiting inside. At once the gravity of the situation was brought home to both of them and they urged us all into the house.

Auntie Yabome didn't stay with us. While we remained with the Olu-Williamses she moved from one house to another, returning to the house at Tengbe Farkai only by day. Every afternoon at the house on Lower Pipeline Lane we waited in the large sun room, which overlooked the garden at the top of the house. Late in the day our stepmother would arrive bringing with her clothes, comics and miniature boxes of our favourite Rice Krispies. Then one afternoon, a week after we had first arrived at the house, we waited and she did not come.

By day Murietta Olu-Williams went to her job in the government offices, leaving us under the supervision of Pa Cook, her
ageing retainer. In the evening she rushed home to check on us.
She confided in none of her friends. Nobody in Freetown knew
where we were. Yabome Forna was Murietta's only point of contact and the day she failed to appear, Murietta was alarmed. She
made enquiries, learned Yabome was being detained, held in a
cell at CID along with Amy Bash Taqi. A few hours later Mrs Olu-
Williams went to see the police commissioner herself. He plainly
knew nothing about the arrests but he promised to do what he
could. Before she left his office Murietta decided to confide in
him: she told him Dr Forna's three children were in her house.
'By God's grace,' she pleaded, 'please, you must do something to
help me. Get a message to her, ask her what I should do.' Jenkins
Smith tried to urge her to be brave, but both of them could read
the signs of what almost certainly lay ahead.

Our stepmother was released a day later. Santigi and the other
staff had also been arrested, and Santigi badly beaten in a cell at
the CID headquarters. Auntie Yabome stopped going back to
the house at Tengbe Farkai altogether. She moved even more frequently herself, never staying more than a night at any house. Our
former home stood empty: all our relatives, the servants, had fled;
Uncle Bash was in prison. Once she was released Auntie Amy
took her own children out of Freetown. The houses were raided
and much of what we owned stolen or vandalised. The vehicles
belonging to the UDP had been seized and the office at East Street
turned over; all the documents, including the membership list,
had been confiscated.

Within ten days the strain was showing on our stepmother's
face and, despite her customary flair, Murietta's brow was knitted,
her features drawn. The secrecy, the fear that one of them might

be followed, the dread of discovery even by an unexpected visitor to the house, brought them to the same conclusion. The charade could not go on. It was only a matter of time before Stevens or one of S. I. Koroma's men would search us out. In prison our father had heard the stories and the reports of the escalating violence and he smuggled a note out through a sympathetic guard: Take the children and leave the country. Now, he urged.

We had no passports, no visas and no money of our own. Yabome could not risk going into town to try to withdraw money from our account at Barclays. Murietta Olu-Williams was a resourceful woman, with a long list of contacts and, through her long involvement in the government and civil service, access to almost anyone in Freetown. She determined to help us escape. If money was what was needed, there was one place she knew where she could get it. She drove into town, headed for the offices of DiaCorp. Under Stevens diamond smuggling had brought chaos to the mining regions, and even though this meant lost revenue for government, the prime minister kept a blind eye turned. By 1970 it was an open secret that he himself controlled many of the illegal operations. The year before, millions of pounds' worth of diamonds had been stolen from the DiaCorp plane, and again it was widely believed that Stevens was behind the raid. The plotters had been overheard at the Brookfield Hotel the night before, and Ibrahim Taqi claimed to have documents to prove the prime minister's involvement in the heist and in racketeering. George Burne, the DiaCorp head, knew Murietta and was pleasantly surprised to see her. She closed the door behind her. 'I've got the children' were the first words he remembers her uttering.

We had travelled to Freetown from Lagos on our father's diplomatic passport, which had presumably now been confiscated—and anyway it was useless in our current predicament. Besides,

Yabome would need a visa to go to England. Murietta's next stop was the British high commission. At reception she asked to speak to the high commissioner as a matter of urgency.

Stephen Olver listened carefully as Murietta gave an account of her predicament: she told him about the rumours of kidnap, how she was hiding us for the moment, and said we needed his help to leave the country. The three children had a British mother, they were British subjects, she reminded him. Stephen Olver had been monitoring the situation closely and was well aware of the reputation of men like S. I. Koroma. The arrests had come as a shock to the diplomatic community. Within a matter of hours the high commission had issued us with emergency passports valid for six months and a visitor's visa for our stepmother.

It was a hazy early morning as we waited at the Kissy terminal to catch the ferry over to Lungi airport. The small dockyard was busy and smelt of fish and diesel; oily water lapped at the jetty. A pirogue of commuters docked and the people waded through the water with their shoes in one hand. Half a dozen cars for the airport waited in a queue to join the ferry when it docked. Mrs Olu-Williams walked into the ticket office while the three of us waited by the car. If anyone recognised us and started asking questions she planned to say our mother Maureen was in transit, en route to Europe, and we were all on our way to spend a few hours at the airport with her.

The ferry whistle sounded and the last foot passengers scrambled aboard. With one minute to go Yabome arrived, alone and on foot. She switched places with Murietta, who got out of the car. I was alarmed and sad to see her go: 'But aren't you coming with us, Auntie Murietta?' I pleaded noisily. She put her finger to her lips, thrust sixty pounds into our stepmother's purse and hugged us all goodbye.

Murietta had thought of everything. At the airport we were greeted by Mr Hancils, the airport manager. He greeted us, anxiety not quite masked by his formal manner; showed us into the VIP lounge on the upper floor of the airport building and left us there, closing the door behind him.

The room was large, decorated in plain, subdued colours with velvet chairs and a fawn carpet. Heavy beige velvet curtains hung in front of floor-to-ceiling windows. I pushed the folds aside and slipped behind them. There was the plane moving slowly across the tarmac: a huge beast, lumbering towards a man in white overalls waving orange batons, like an elephant performing tricks in a circus. From behind me I heard my stepmother's voice, calling to me to come back inside and close the curtain.

When the Air France flight was ready to board Mr Hancils came back into the room. He sat down opposite our stepmother and wiped his upper lip. 'Mrs Forna, please listen to me very carefully,' he said, slowly, deliberately. 'Once you are aboard the plane you are on international territory. What that means is that the government of Sierra Leone has no jurisdiction there, none at all.' He was watching her intently. She nodded. He continued: 'Once you are on board you are safe. Do you understand? If anyone tries to force you to leave the plane you must refuse, shout if need be. The captain and the crew know that you will be on board; they won't allow anyone to take you or your children off that flight. The plane won't leave without you, I promise.' Auntie Yabome nodded again and thanked him. 'Good luck.' Mr Hancils squeezed her hand as he stood up to go.

We were in the sunshine running out across the bubbling tarmac. We went ahead of the other passengers and the plane was empty when we took our seats. But the flight was fully booked and it was going to be at least another hour before we were ready to take off. I sat still while my stepmother fastened my seatbelt, then I began to search through the pocket on the back of the seat in front of me. Auntie Yabome covered me with one of the blankets and instructed us all to pretend we were asleep. And so I squeezed my eyes shut and turned my face into the headrest. I lay as still as I could and listened to the people as they shuffled down the aisle. I heard them talking to the air hostess, being shown into their seats. I heard the click of the lockers above me as they were opened, then slammed shut. I listened hard, waiting for the challenge, waiting for someone to shake me and accuse me of not really being asleep at all.

When I felt the plane begin to move I opened my eyes, carefully at first, and as we lifted into the air I looked out of my window. Down below, through the mangrove swamps, a river snaked towards the sea and I could see tiny flecks that were fishing boats. Gradually, as the plane climbed the clouds pasted white over the window and the view was gone.

At Charles de Gaulle Airport, where we were to switch planes for a flight to London, it was foggy. I was mesmerised by the airport building. I had never seen this Europe before. People moved along travelators, transparent plastic tubes criss-crossed the huge space bearing passengers to their flight gates. The place was bright and cold, and a woman's metallic voice gave instructions over the tannoy that the people understood and followed. In an overpriced duty-free boutique we bought sweaters from an assistant with dark red lipstick and nails. We had left Freetown with nothing, not a single suitcase or bag. I chose a bright, yellow scarf and matching sweater for myself and two hours later I stepped off the plane at Gatwick wearing them over my summer dress and sandals.

We spent our first night in the Angus Hotel overlooking Picca-
dilly Circus. Memuna shared with Auntie Yabome; Sheka and I
were put in the room next door. I pulled the cord by the window
and the chocolate-coloured curtains swished open. We looked
out onto the curved lights of the giant Coca-Cola sign and they
rippled on and off throughout the night, forming my first and
most abiding memory of London.

The next day the four of us went for a walk. The October day
was bright and bitter. On Waterloo Bridge I buried my chin into
the neck of my new blue anorak and pulled my fingers up into
the sleeves. I scarcely dared breathe. At home in the mornings
Amadu and Amara would put bottles of boiled drinking water
in the freezer. Sometimes they would forget to take them out in
time and the bottles would explode; afterwards we would help
pick out shards of glass and ice, one indistinguishable from the
other. There was a delicious excitement in licking the ice, which
stuck to our tongues, and in trying to avoid the vicious spears of
glass. That was what the air was like in England. It was cold and
sharp and made breathing fraught with danger.

My breath erupted in plumes of steam, like a pot on the boil.
What made it do that? I wondered. I looked up at my stepmother.
'Auntie Yabome,' I began.

She heard me and turned, but instead of answering my question
she stopped walking and addressed the three of us: 'From now
on I want you to call me Mummy. Do you understand? Mummy.
You're not to call me Auntie Yabome any more.'

Memuna and Sheka nodded; so did I. I waited. She didn't say anything else. I forgot what I had wanted to ask and then I remembered. 'Auntie Yabome, how come I can see my breath?' We had started walking back up along the Strand and I ran to catch up.

'*Mummy*,' she said slowly. '*Mummy*, how come I can see my breath?' But then she never gave me the answer.

Sheka and I had spent the night spinning on a revolving chair in our room. Next door our stepmother spent long hours on the telephone. Unattended through bath time, through bed time, we spun as fast as we could. No one came to interrupt our game. As the night progressed we took turns racing across the room and landing in the chair. Hit at just the right angle the chair shot across the room, twirling round and round as it did so. Eventually someone in an adjoining room, or possibly the unfortunate guests below us, must have complained, because some time past midnight the night porter opened the door to our room with his pass key. If he knocked, we didn't hear him—we were making much too much noise. And at the very moment the key turned in the lock, the hours of turbulence and motion had their inevitable effect on Sheka's stomach. Still reeling in the chair from his final effort to break the record, Sheka doubled over and moments later an untidy arc of vomit interrupted the precise geometric patterns of the carpet.

The night porter, who was a dark-haired young man wearing a grey morning coat, had been unexpectedly kind. He returned with a bottle of Milk of Magnesia, put us to bed between the fresh sheets, wiped the slime off the carpet and turned off the light with a stern warning not to move until the morning.

Now, as we entered the lobby of the hotel I saw the same porter behind the reception desk. He smiled and winked, then turned back to the couple in front of the desk. Both the man and the woman had pale, mauve hair and I gazed at it in wonder. Our stepmother had a sheaf of messages in her hand and was slowly turning them one at a time. As I waited next to her, I looked at the couple's silvery clouds of hair and I remembered my question. I decided to try it one last time.

'Auntie Yabome?' I began. She carried on reading. Louder this time: 'Auntie Yabome?' Still no answer. I felt a twitch of impatience, and the third time I positively boomed: 'Auntie Yabome!' Satisfied now because I knew I had her attention, I paused.

But instead of answering me she gripped me by the upper arm—I could feel her fingers digging into my flesh—and swung me round to the other side of the desk, away from the waiting people where, below the level of the desk, out of sight, she slapped me suddenly and sharply across the back of my legs. 'I told you to call me Mummy. Didn't I? Didn't I?'

'Yes,' I whispered.

'Yes, what?' she demanded, her face close to mine.

'Yes, Mummy,' I whispered. 'Yes, *Mummy.*'

Nothing made any sense. I thought my stepmother was *asking* us to call her Mummy—I hadn't realised she wasn't giving us the choice. Even so, my mistake had seemed so simple and I failed to see how it could really matter so much. I walked across the lobby: my face was hot and my calves were beginning to smart, I could feel the itch in my nostrils that meant I was about to cry. Through the descending blur I saw my friendly porter looking at me. For a moment he caught my eye, and then just as quickly he looked away.

After two days we moved into a service flat in Earls Court. Mrs Cobally, a fifty-year-old woman with unlikely honey-blonde hair, was the concierge at Grenbeck Court and for some reason, from the very first day when we stopped in at the office, she took a shine to our family and brought us all under her wing. In the evenings she left her husband in front of the television in their overheated apartment and slipped over to our flat bearing a bottle of Babycham or sherry. She would give the bottle a shake in front of Mum—'How's about a little of this, then?'—and wiggle past her into the sitting room.

We were now very careful to call our stepmother Mummy or Mum in front of anyone we didn't know, including Mrs Cobally. Mrs Cobally had given me a long, curious look when I once reverted to 'Auntie Yabome'. Thank goodness Mum hadn't heard. I didn't make the same mistake again. We dared not risk anybody discovering that Mum was not our real mother; we feared the attention of the authorities or anyone else who might begin to ask questions. While they sat together Mrs Cobally talked and puffed cigarettes, blowing the smoke through her nose like a dragon, topping up her glass all the time, while Mum took tiny sips from hers.

Our flat was on the ground floor at the back of the building. Below us was a paved expanse, unadorned by flower beds or potted plants, overlooking the tracks of the District Line. Twice every minute, day and night, the trains rumbled past. There was only one bedroom and we all shared it. At night I lay awake in the not-quite-dark of the city night, listening to the unfamiliar sounds of the tracks.

Earls Court struck me as a wonderful stately name. The first time we walked down to Earls Court Station to catch a train I imagined an old-fashioned steam engine with gleaming red flanks, puffing smoke like Mrs Cobally. I talked about our train ride all the way along the grimy pavement, spotted with blotches of ancient chewing gum and glistening stars of saliva; past Bestways late-night supermarket; past the uncollected sacks of black plastic; past the furtive, fumbling men who stepped out of neon-lit doorways; past the meths drinkers lying around the entrance to the tube station. My stepmother suggested the trains weren't really like that any more, but I ignored her. I didn't want anyone spoiling my fun. When the dull, sleek tube train arrived it bore no resemblance to the train of my fantasy, but I leapt through the sliding doors, determined that I was going to have my adventure whatever. I was disappointed, but I wasn't going to admit it to myself or anyone. The train was red—that at least fitted with the fantasy.

It started with the dog walk down the rutted lanes of Tengbe Farkai. I had an image of a world, one gleaned from pre-war readers and my own Janet and John books, full of clean, eternally smiling children and it seemed a better place to be. I was already nostalgic and I had barely begun to live my life yet. I was not unhappy really, but somewhere inside me I knew my childhood wasn't measuring up. I didn't make up an imaginary friend to comfort myself; I made up an imaginary world. I yearned for a past I had never even experienced. In November of 1970 I did not want to be alone and stranded in a dirty city while our father was in prison. I longed to live in a different world, a world just like the one inhabited by the boys and girls behind the covers of my books.

In my book of collected verse there was a poem entitled 'The Lamplighter' about the man whose job it was to walk the London streets every night lighting the gas lamps. As night fell I sat waiting by the main door of Grenbeck Court for him to come, just as the little boy in the poem had done. I knew about electricity and I could see the street lights all had bulbs, but that was the strangest thing: I just carried on pretending to myself that the lamplighter was on his way, until the lights began to flicker and then glow orange and my stepmother came to fetch me into the flat for supper. When she asked me what I was doing, I opened A Child's Garden of Verse and showed her the illustration of the lamplighter with his ladder and Victorian hobnail boots, lighting lamps in a London street just like Trebovir Road.

Mum told us she had engaged a tutor to teach us maths and English so we didn't fall behind with our lessons. Miss Bird did not let me down; she was exactly as she should have been. Her hair, the colour of silver and tea, was caught in a wispy bun at the back of her head and she wore good-quality—if somewhat elderly— cashmere in shades of green and brown. Miss Bird looked like an old-fashioned governess, who could have leapt from the pages of one of my old-fashioned books. She never raised her voice above a melodious whisper and she asked my opinion of the stories and poems we read. With Miss Bird we spent far more of our time reading poetry than tackling sums and that winter she gave me the keys to my escape, places to hide with a host of new friends: Scheherazade, Huckleberry Finn, Aslan and the inhabitants of Narnia, Guinevere and Lancelot, Don Quixote, Anne of Green Gables and Beowulf. I looked forward to our time together; I was pleased not to be in the crowded classrooms of Bertha Canton any longer.

Back in Sierra Leone Stephen Olver, George Burne and Murietta Olu-Williams caught each other's eye at public occasions and ex-changed a sly three-way wink. The driver who had taken us to the airport, on the other hand, had fled for his life. When he arrived back in Freetown without us, when Stevens and his henchmen realised we had escaped from under their noses, they issued an order for the man's arrest. He jumped right back into the car and drove out of town and didn't stop driving until he arrived in Mon-rovia, where he sold the car and lived for a while off the proceeds.

Most of the wave of support for the UDP had come from the western area; the Krios, many of whom opposed Stevens's anti-democratic behaviour; and the north, which followed our father and the Taqi brothers. In an effort to try to limit the damage to the APC in those areas Stevens had appointed another northerner to the finance post. Sembu Forna might have been our father's namesake, but our father had little respect for him. In the event he lasted only a few months before Stevens gave the job to one of his foremost allies, Christian Kamara-Taylor. S. I. Koroma was given Mohammed Bash Taqi's post as minister of development. The government was now in the hands of the extremists. Nancy Steele, head of the APC women's forum and one of Siaka Stevens's mistresses, advocated putting the leaders of the UDP against a wall and shooting them. The elections, due to be held in November, were postponed until February the following year.

Stevens condemned the UDP as a 'rebel group' funded by the CIA and he denied all our father's allegations. The state newspaper the *Daily Mail* printed a front-page story saying arms worth one hundred thousand leones were found at our house. The detentions were given two inches of coverage on the back page. In the House of Representatives the MPs voted to back the state of emergency and Stevens gave himself new powers of arrest and detention. Immediately afterwards there was a purge of Temnes in the army and six privates were accused of supporting the UDP and plotting to overthrow the government.

In November the courts dismissed the application for habeas corpus by the leaders of the UDP. The gutlessness of the judiciary caused many hearts to sink, but the few remaining members of the opposition SLPP stood up, one by one, in the House of Representatives to condemn Stevens for the illegal arrests of our father and the other men, and for spuriously declaring a state of emergency just to ban the new party.

Then in December Sarif Easmon was released from prison, the first of the detainees to be freed. He was unwell and released on health grounds, but it was a glimmer of good news all the same. It was rumoured in Freetown that all the detainees would be freed by Christmas.

In London we adjusted gradually to our new lives. We learned to help with the housework: in the mornings we pushed the carpet sweeper around the room and sprayed Mr Sheen on the coffee table; we laid the table for meals and afterwards we helped to wash and dry the dishes. Most of the chores fell to Memuna and me because we were girls. This was not a form of logic I had encountered before. I'd spent my entire life so far wishing I was a boy and now I was confronting the realisation that the advantages went further than wearing shorts to slide down the banister. After a few days the novelty of housework waned and I preferred to watch television. I had never had a TV set before and I was transfixed by everything from *Basil Brush* to *Hawaii Five-O*, but most of all I liked the advertisements: the super-hero toilet cleaner, the talking chimps, especially the housewife who was arrested for failing to use Paxo stuffing—'I promise I won't do it again,' she begged as the police led her away. This was my introduction to the consumer culture. At first I viewed the adverts as jokes or sketches in between the main programmes; it took me a while to realise they were supposed to be selling something. When I made the connection I suddenly became aware of how many things we needed, really needed: a mini carpet sweeper for the stairs, a cube to turn the water in the toilet blue, air freshener that smelled of spring flowers. Every day I made a new list and at the supermarket I begged Mum to buy them all.

In a short while my neglect of my share of the chores had me out searching for a switch again. Memuna was in trouble, too. Mum said she was responsible for me because she was the eldest sister. Memuna was cross about the unfairness of it all. I felt cross and guilty. We wandered up and down the road, listlessly at first and then with growing urgency, looking for a tree or a bush from which to cut a switch. In the end we went back to face our stepmother, each holding an inch of yellow privet. Mum thought we were trying to be funny. She marched outside to get a switch herself, but once in the street she made the same discovery: there were simply no trees, no green at all, in Trebovir Road.

On the last day of schoolwork before the Christmas break Miss Bird gave me a present. It was a tiny Wedgwood dish, with a sprig of wild flowers painted in the centre. In return I gave her a set of lace-edged handkerchiefs.

We woke up on Christmas morning to stuffed stockings and a massive tree, adorned with innumerable shining globes, threatening to overwhelm the tiny apartment. There were times when our stepmother was as kind as she knew how to be. I had never seen so many presents and for the first hour we lost ourselves in an orgy of opening. Among the pile of gifts was one marked: 'To Am, Love Daddy'. It was a teddy bear. I knew really that Mum had bought it and wrapped it herself, but I pretended for both our sakes that I believed it had really come from him. I played dumb and hugged the teddy bear, because dumb made me feel better. Mum had bought an Instamatic camera and we posed for pictures by the tree—to post to our father so he wouldn't feel like he had missed Christmas with us altogether.

Unbelievably, it snowed that Christmas: pathetic, spongy, soft flakes like polystyrene that fell out of a bruised sky to form a film over the yard. I ran out into it, yelling with phoney pleasure, and scraped up just enough to shape into a dirty mound into which I stuck two pebbles and a line of flinty stones giving the impression of a row of broken teeth. I acted as though it were the first time I had seen snow, partly to keep up the illusion, partly because I was genuinely confused about the exact circumstances under which I had last seen snow. That feeling again, of lives colliding, like flash frames from a long-ago dream that suddenly appear in your mind. Scotland and Nigeria, my life less than a year ago, were receding into a mass of blurred images.

When I had had enough and climbed the stairs to go back inside I passed Mrs Cobally's door, which was always slightly ajar.

'Come in here, pet,' she beckoned. The room was stifling hot and made breathing difficult. Mrs Cobally was smiling, wearing fluffy, high-heeled mules below black trousers and roll-neck sweater. There was a hole at the toe of her tights. She pressed a present into my hand. 'Happy Christmas, my darling. Fetch your mum—tell her to come round here and have a drink with us.' She gave me her powdery cheek to kiss. As I reached up I caught a whiff of the sweet diesel fumes of her breath.

I walked towards the door of our apartment and examined my present. She hadn't wrapped it up. It was a blue, plastic deer, with sharp little hooves and hard nubs of horns. I recognised it at once: it was the Babycham deer.

For years afterwards, whenever we remembered Mrs Cobally and how she liked a drink, and whenever one of the family reminded everyone, because it was funny, that she had given me the Babycham deer for Christmas, I would feel unaccountably annoyed. It wasn't so much that I was cross with Mrs Cobally; I wasn't. I even quite liked her. It was just that if I thought about that hideous little blue deer, I would have to admit to myself how wretched her gift made me feel. And if I did that, what else would I have to face about those first few months in London?

Ten months later, in the back of a drawer I found several packages, each wrapped in familiar paper: shiny blue and covered in silver stars. The parcels were wedged behind the rest of the clutter, the loose cutlery, Sellotape and paper napkins, in the sideboard drawer. The edge of one was slightly torn, giving a hint of the contents inside, though I knew at once exactly what it was: a red can of Old Spice shaving foam. I recognised my own careful block print and the childish kisses on the tag: 'To Daddy, Lots of Love Aminatta.'

⁂ 28 ⁂

One day, not long after we first arrived, a visitor came to Grenbeck Court. He was a large man, so tall he had to bend his head to pass comfortably under the lintel of the door. He arrived unannounced yet laden with gifts. I unwrapped my package: a fluffy pink duck with a yellow felt beak. I named it Ducky. The big man invited me to sit on his knee and, over the course of tea, he entertained me with tickles and pinches and even held me upside down by my feet, making me scream in terror and delight. Afterwards I put on his raincoat, which engulfed me like a flood and puddled onto the floor around my feet. He laughed and I showed off all the more. I liked the big man. His name was Tiny Rowland; he told me to call him Uncle Tiny.

In the previous year the Sierra Leone government had decided to renegotiate the Sierra Leone Selection Trust lease, with a view to nationalising the diamond mines in the near future, just as the governments of Ghana and Zambia had done. They put out the word that they would be looking for a partner in their new venture: SLST was unpopular inside Sierra Leone, regarded by many as a colonial dinosaur whose time was over. The promise of easy fortunes to be made brought a host of the world's wealthiest men over to our tiny country, scouting for ways to increase the sum of their riches. Among them was the chief of Lonrho, Tiny Rowland.

Rowland had met Mohamed Forna, the finance minister, on several occasions and signed a modest agreement to scout new mining opportunities in the interior. But Rowland was thought to have his eye on a bigger share of the pie, principally on the concessions owned by SLST and De Beers. Our father had been spoken of as a future contender to Siaka Stevens. Though he might be in prison right now and the UDP a banned organisation, businessmen like Rowland knew the landscape of African politics could shift overnight, as rapidly as the dunes in the desert. Wasn't 'no condition is permanent' our country's favourite maxim?

The mining companies shadowed every nuance and change in politics in Sierra Leone and all over Africa. These were the vested interests, although the term wasn't widely used in those days: they helped shape every political outcome in ways that could not be quantified and were not even understood. There were whispers, rumours that nothing ever changed in countries like Sierra Leone without the mineral concessions first being negotiated. As soon as the family of the man who was being spoken of as a challenger to Siaka Stevens was in trouble, they were there, more than happy to help. The nights in the Angus Hotel, the flat in Grenbeck Court, many of our expenses in London—these were all paid by De Beers. And here was a giant of a man called Tiny demonstrating his famous personal touch in business—swinging a child upside down by her ankles in the name of global capitalism.

Before long Uncle Tiny and the Lonrho empire would move on, lured by the challenge of greater conquests in the gold mines of Ghana. In the meantime he lent his car to take us to Sussex on Sheka's first day at school after the New Year. It was a white Mercedes, with a chauffeur: another kind young man in a grey uniform who held Sheka's head while my brother, overcome by nerves and nausea, threw up in the school car park.

The exiled family of a political prisoner and former minister, stranded in London, we attracted interest. There was a constant flow of visitors to the flat at Grenbeck Court. There were businessmen: British, Lebanese and Sierra Leonean; some had backed our father when he was in the APC, others were simply keen for an opportunity to curry favour for the future. There were student activists fresh from Freetown, former members of the APC who had defected to the UDP. Some had managed to evade the round-up and returned to London through Monrovia. They came back to their student digs, their law degrees and accountancy exams. They held meetings, and lobbied the British government as well as sympathetic British MPs about what was happening in Sierra Leone, and just as often they stopped by Grenbeck Court to exchange information gleaned from their network of contacts or to find out if we had heard anything new.

In prison for three months now, our father and the other UDP leaders had still not been charged with an offence, and were still denied access to their lawyers or to visitors. Clarkson, the detainees' wing of Pademba Road Prison, was filled to capacity. Shortly after reports of the arrests appeared in the international press the news came that the human rights organisation Amnesty International had declared our father one of their celebrated Prisoners of Conscience.

Our case was handled by the German and Luxembourgish branches of Amnesty and once, in the early days, one of the desk officers came on holiday to London and stopped by the flat to meet us. She was a young woman with golden hair, rosy cheeks and a wide, clear smile. Her name was Gita and she treated us all to supper. She ordered wine, which I had never had before, and let me try a little. She taught me how to hold the glass by the stem so my hand didn't warm the contents, swirl the liquid round and sniff the rising bouquet. Then she gently tipped the glass back and took a sip, urging me to copy her. I rolled the wine around in my mouth: the vapour tickled my nose; I swallowed. The wine was unexpectedly delicious. We never saw Gita again but from time to time we had letters from Amnesty telling us what they were doing to draw the world's attention to our father's plight.

And so we waited. The first months in London we behaved as though we were tourists: we visited Trafalgar Square and let the pigeons crawl over us; we marched the length of Oxford Street buying ourselves new clothes; we wandered awestruck through Harrods; we stood in Parliament Square and waited for Big Ben to strike the hour; Mum even bought us all tickets to Billy Smart's Circus when they performed at the Earls Court Arena. But as the weeks went by our enthusiasm for the sightseeing trips tailed off. We were ready to go home and yet we couldn't.

We couldn't continue to live as we had been, either: like guests in someone's house. Mum decided she needed a job. She enrolled in a secretarial course and signed up with the Brook Street Bureau. I imagined her going to work like the smart girl in the poster at Earls Court Station dressed in a tartan mini skirt, a pair of patent leather boots and tartan peaked cap. Memuna and I were sent away to boarding school—Sheka had begun at his new school already. We said farewell to Miss Bird and at the start of the Lent term, as I would one day learn to call it, we took the train to the town of Horley to High Trees School.

We arrived like snails carrying our homes on our backs: two grey trunks with our names stencilled on the sides, each containing several years' supply of clothes—six pairs of brown regulation knickers, two brown tunics, six pairs of fawn socks, sandals for indoors, lace-up walking shoes for out, Wellington boots, a brown mac, two brown-check summer dresses, and a copy of the Bible and the English Prayer Book.

That night, for the first time, I slept in a separate room from Memuna. She was put into the Blue Dorm with seven other girls; I slept in the Pink Room with the three youngest. We sat on the high iron beds in our flannel nightdresses, staring at each other mutely until Mrs Peebles, the Polish matron, came to turn out the lights. For a while I lay in between the cold sheets, under my candlewick counterpane, watching the patterns of moonlight on the wall. After a few minutes I heard sniffs and then a sob coming from the other beds. Within moments I began to cry as well. None of us said a word to each other and no one came to the door; we stifled our sobs into our pillows and eventually we cried ourselves to sleep.

In the morning we struggled into the new, unfamiliar clothes laid out on the chairs next to each of our beds, starting with two pairs of pants, one on top of the other, and ending with the cardboard-stiff blazer. When I had finished dressing I came across a narrow length of striped, silky fabric. I held it up. It was wider at one end than the other, tapering into a neat point. I had sort of an idea of what it was, but no earthly notion of how to wear it. So I draped it round my neck, where it hung limply. Moments later the bell sounded and I followed the rest of the girls down to breakfast—and for the whole of the first term until Easter that was how I continued to wear my tie.

'Student revolutionaries from the West African state of Sierra Leone were being hunted by police last night after a coup and counter-coup at the country's high commission in London . . .'

The announcement on the lunch-time news came while I was away at school. Ten of the young activists who used to come by our flat at Grenbeck Court, all members of the United Democratic Party, had taken over the Sierra Leone high commission in Portland Place to demand the resignation of Siaka Stevens and the release of all the political prisoners. Among them was Bianca Benjamin, our mother's old friend with whom we had stayed in Freetown during the election crisis in 1967, and Auntie Shineh, who was married to Ibrahim Taqi. The next morning their picture appeared in the *Times*. Away at boarding school without newspapers or television, we missed all the fun. It turned out Mum had known all about it, but she stayed at home because she worried that if she was arrested and ended up in prison, well—who would look after us when we came home?

The students were let into the building by an unsuspecting caretaker early in the morning. Flourishing a toy pistol, they rounded up the high commission's staff and locked them up in an empty office. Next door one of the protesters sat down at the high commissioner's desk and used his telephone to call State House in Freetown. He asked to speak to the prime minister and the operator, thinking this must be the high commissioner himself, put him straight through. The student leader informed Stevens that the Portland Place building had been occupied and the staff were being held hostage; he offered their release in exchange for the freedom of the political prisoners. Stevens hung up on him.

Upstairs the captive staff waved a handkerchief from the window and shouted to passers-by, one of whom eventually went to raise the alarm. Meanwhile downstairs the intruders called a press conference and in front of TV cameras and press men they announced themselves as the new government-in-exile of Sierra Leone. Half an hour later the police moved in to clear the building but they didn't manage to arrest the ringleaders who, in all the confusion, slipped away among the crowd of television crews and journalists.

Britain was beset by strikes: four thousand in that one year. The postal workers were on strike, the miners were unofficially out, and workers at Ford were threatening to picket. The escapade at the high commission contained an element of high farce which tickled journalists who had spent weeks writing about the threat of power cuts and rising inflation. The high commissioner had been in the news just weeks before, for taking a second wife while he was in Britain. The students were smart and audacious: they had outwitted the deputy high commissioner, who had been left in charge of the office while his boss was recalled to Freetown, as well as the British police.

In time their luck ran out. The students were caught and taken to Marylebone Magistrates' Court, where a judge set their bail at a hundred and fifty pounds. The case dragged on for almost a whole year. Stevens wanted the students deported back to Sierra Leone and he ordered their government grants be stopped. The students took their case to the Court of Appeal and then the House of Lords. The Law Lords gave everyone a full or a conditional discharge, and all the students were awarded political asylum in Britain.

Who can say for certain what impact the student demonstration had on Stevens back in Sierra Leone? But a week after the drama at the high commission the prime minister ordered the release of most of the political detainees from Pademba Road Prison, including the leaders of the UDP, John Karefa-Smart and Mohammed Bash Taqi among them. But for us the elation was short-lived. Our father's name wasn't on the list of the people who had been freed. He remained in prison.

A year later in Britain the miners were still out on strike and there were power cuts across the country. Over the Michaelmas term at school we ate our supper by candlelight and slept with socks on our feet and scarves round our necks. In Pademba Road our father slept and woke under the ceaseless burning of a single light bulb, day and night. Our stepmother gave up temping with Brook Street Bureau and accepted a permanent position as a secretary for a firm of Jewish architects in Soho Square. She moved us out of the flat at Grenbeck Court and into an attic apartment a few streets away in Philbeach Gardens. Mum, Memuna and I still shared a room but there was a tiny single room, a box room really, for Sheka. As the weeks trickled into months which widened into years, the visitors to our new place became fewer. We had come to Britain thinking that we would be there for a few weeks. We ended up staying three years.

❦ 29 ❦

The pale-blue aerogramme arrived on 6 July 1971. On the right-hand side, above the address, was a red eagle, with the words: 'Sierra Leone, Land of Iron & Diamonds, 9 Cents'. It was addressed to 'Sheka, Memuna and Aminatta Forna' and arrived at Grenbeck Court a few months before we moved to our new place. It was from our father. Inside, at the top of the page, was the oval stamp of the prison office in purple ink and our father's prisoner number: D 6/70. I looked at the address at the top of the letter, the signature of the prison censor, and I thought about my father being in prison and what that meant.

At Minister's Quarters a group of prisoners had come to clear the garden. We had watched them from the upstairs bedroom window as they scythed the overgrown grass. They wore ill-fitting, buttoned cotton jackets and trousers that had once been white. They were barefoot and worked silently, uncomplaining, before they were herded back into the unmarked prison Land-Rover. They did not look awesome or frightening as I thought criminals should, but rather small and skinny and old. Nonetheless we did not venture out to play until they were gone. We went to the garden where they had been working, looking for I don't know what—some evidence of their criminality left behind on the lawn, perhaps—then we saw the enormous pile of cuttings and we jumped into it, laughing, and rolled about there for the remainder of the day. Next morning we were back: we leapt straight in to begin again, only to find the cuttings were now alive with thousands of red and green caterpillars.

On our way to and from town I had seen gangs of prisoners by the side of the road. Their legs were chained and they worked clearing ditches and mending potholes. After my stepmother had finished reading the letter from our father I asked her: 'Does Daddy have to mend the roads and work in people's gardens now he's in prison?'

'What do you mean?' she asked. And I told her what I remembered seeing: men stripped to the waist; they had looked like moving shadows beneath the glare of the sun.

'No,' she said. 'Don't worry. He doesn't have to do that.'

'Why doesn't he?'

'Because he's not that kind of prisoner.'

'He's not *what* kind of prisoner?'

'The kind that has to mend roads.' She meant he wasn't a criminal, although the *Daily Mail* in Freetown did its best to portray him as one. All the same the idea of my father being forced to labour in front of crowds of onlookers chafed at my imagination. I could not let go of the terrible image.

At school on Sundays we wrote to our parents after we had been to church and eaten our lunch of grey meat and colourless vegetables. We filed into the unheated classrooms for letter-writing, sat at our desks and filled our fountain pens with ink, while a teacher handed out paper: plain white, ruled paper for everyone except the overseas pupils, who were issued with floating leaves of onion skin.

My father slept in a cell no more than six foot by eight foot. It had no natural light, except for a small opening protected by steel bars high up by the ceiling, but the electric bulb hanging in the middle of the room glowed day and night so that there was never a time when it was dark. After years under the bright light many detainees left prison with their eyesight permanently ruined. In the centre of the door was a peephole which allowed the guards to see in, but my father could not see out. The cell contained nothing except a blanket and a chamber pot, which was emptied once a day. On the first day he was stripped naked and issued with prison clothes. He was held in solitary confinement and fed a plate of rice and stew twice a day for two weeks, after which he was allowed out for a single hour of exercise in the evening. A whole month elapsed before he was taken to the shower block and given a bucket of water to wash. In time, through lawyers, he was able to request books, which he sometimes received: novels by Morris West, Edwin Fadiman and Solzhenitsyn's five-hundred-page volume *Cancer Ward,* which parallels a prisoner's life on a ward for the dying in a Soviet labour camp, and the cancer at the heart of the police state. After the first few months he was given writing paper.

In his letters my father urged me to work hard at school, praised me on my grades when they were good, and asked me if I had stopped sucking my thumb. I told everyone I had, but secretly I continued to suck it at night. He asked about the goldfish Goldie and Orangie, and remembered the names of the girls with whom I was currently friends at school. I wrote back in turn begging him to allow us home. I was allergic to England—my skin was dry and ashy, my lips were cracked and I couldn't help licking them, which only made the problem worse; my hair had turned frizzy and my fingers were tattered with bleeding rag nails. I hated being stuck at boarding school and I hated being in England, and in my mind one was synonymous with the other.

Our father placed an unshakeable faith in the British education system—as did many Africans in those days. They believed the key to success lay in a British education, of which by far the most superior was one acquired at boarding school. Going to Bo School had changed his life immeasurably. My father wanted me to become a lawyer (I got as far as completing my degree before

I gave up law for journalism) and Memuna, who was the bright-est of us, to become a doctor, as he had been. I can't remember what ambitions he had for my brother—something equally el-evated, certainly. As an adult, when I spoke to other friends of mine—other children of the empire growing up in Common-wealth countries after independence—I found we often shared similar experiences. Most of our parents did not own their own homes; foreign holidays were rare or unheard of; the bulk of our parents' income went on their children's schooling—this was the price of securing our future. Many years later I finally began to understand the sacrifices our parents had made to give us our education and why they cherished this particular dream. But at the time I felt as if I were being punished.

I must have gone on begging and pleading with him, and Mum must have described in her letters how I clung to her legs on the platform at Victoria Station at the start of every term and the end of each exeat, forcing her to prise me off and hand me over to the teacher escorting the Horley train. Three months into our second year apart, my father wrote to me at length: 'The Fornas, men as well as women, boys as well as girls, are brave people and they never cry. So you should not cry. Okay? The Fornas face everything bravely.' He promised, when the time was right, we would be a family again one day. But not just yet. Never just yet.

One Sunday at High Trees a new teacher came in to supervise our letter-writing session. His name was Mr Newman; he had a fat grey moustache and silver spectacles. At the end of the session we lined up as usual while Mr Newman wrote out our parents' addresses neatly on the front of our envelopes. When it was my turn I gave him our address in London. Mr Newman asked why, if I lived in London, my letter was written on airmail paper.

'My father lives in Sierra Leone.' I gave the most minimal and discouraging reply I could.

'And what's your father's address in Sierra Leone?'

'I don't know. My mum has it. We send our letters to her and she sends them to him. That's the way she likes to do it.'

'Well that's a bit of a silly waste of time, not to mention stamps. Why on earth don't you just post the letters from here, you daft girl?' I quite liked Mr Newman, really. He was very funny and when he called you daft he didn't really mean it. It was just his way. But I still couldn't tell him the reason my letters weren't posted directly to Freetown was because no one at school, neither teachers nor pupils, knew our father was in jail.

I left the old Nissen hut that served as a classroom with Caroline, one of my closest friends. I had spent a weekend at her home near Winchester and, in return, I asked her home to Philbeach Gardens. Caroline was clever, small and neatly turned out, with matching clothes and the kind of grown-up manners English children have.

'How do you do, Mrs Forna?' Caroline extended her hand confidently, formally. A beat passed before Mum took her hand. She greeted her pleasantly, but there was an expression upon Mum's face I couldn't quite read.

At Caroline's house I had slept in the spare bedroom, where everything matched the sprigged yellow paper on the walls: curtains, eiderdown, valance, dressing-table cloth, cushion covers. In the corner was a washbasin and a bowl of miniature scented soaps. When I invited Caroline to stay with us I imagined showing her to a room just like the one I had stayed in. But we didn't have a spare room and I shared the same bedroom under the eaves of the building with Mum and Memuna. At bed time it occurred to me for the first time there was nowhere for Caroline to sleep. I had spent the night on the divan in the sitting room, while Caroline took my bed. It made no difference to our friendship, but I hadn't invited anyone home since.

'Why is your dad in Africa when you're all here?' Caroline asked me. 'And how come you never go home to see him?'

It was the first time anyone had ever enquired directly. I suppose I could have made an excuse, but I didn't. A few minutes later, sitting on the damp grass of the lower playing fields, I asked Caroline if she could keep a secret. I told her my father was in prison and though I didn't understand all the details myself, I gave her the best account I could.

When I had finished speaking, Caroline regarded me gravely and at length. 'I've a secret about my father, too,' she said presently in a low tone which spoke of confidences about to be shared.

'What kind of secret?' I was a bit worried I had said too much and now I was eager to be reassured in any way.

'My father's a murderer.'

I looked her straight in the face. I certainly hadn't been expecting that. 'Who did he murder?'

This is the story Caroline told me that day on the playing fields, while we watched the rest of the boarders playing a game of Stuck in the Mud: Caroline and her family had lived in Cameroon, where her father was an executive with an oil company. They lived outside the capital, close to the rain forest in an area then being surveyed and scouted for drilling opportunities. In due course new reserves of oil were indeed discovered, the land was cleared and work began.

'One day,' Caroline recounted, 'some Africans came up to our house, lots, a whole crowd of them. They asked to speak to my father. They were villagers and they said they used to live on the land. Now the land was gone they had nowhere to go and nothing to eat. They were so poor. They begged my father to help them, to give them something to eat.'

'Why did they come to your house?'

'Because my father was head of the company. They thought he would be able to help them. They didn't know where else to go. They were just asking, begging.

'They stood there for ages. My mother didn't like it at all. She said they were treading on the flower beds and so in the end my father went out, but he wouldn't speak to them. He told them to go away. He said they must get off our land. So they all went away. There were old people and women and children.' Caroline stopped speaking.

When she began the story I had fancied maybe he'd pushed her mother down the stairs or put a poisonous snake into her bed. 'But that doesn't make your dad a murderer.'

The people went away and they never came back. I asked my father what would happen to them and he said he didn't know. But one of the Africans who worked for us told me they'd all died. They didn't have anything to eat and they died of hunger . . . all of them, even the children.' Caroline had tears in her eyes. 'So you see, your dad might be in prison. But mine's a murderer and that's worse. He killed all those people . . . he didn't care what happened to them.'

I wondered if Caroline was right. After all, nobody had sent her father to prison for what he had done. Caroline called him a murderer. We were children guarding our parents' shame, hiding from the world adult secrets we barely understood ourselves. Caroline never betrayed my confidence, nor I hers, although our friendship ebbed and flowed, as the affections of small girls are inclined to do. But even so, at some level we always remained close until the day we both left the school in 1975.

After the first letter, our father wrote to each of us separately and we came to expect his letters at the beginning of every month. Every now and again there would be an unexplained gap, and once for four consecutive months none of his letters reached us and none of ours reached him. When the airmails arrived at the flat in London Mum kept them until we came home at weekends and often I would ask her to read mine. I pretended I had difficulty with his doctor's script, but really it was an excuse for me to curl up and just listen.

Since the day we parted we had not heard once from my mother. After she married our stepfather and returned from Mexico our father had written to her to say the Mexican divorce was not recognised in Sierra Leone. He went to court in Freetown and obtained a divorce himself, and then applied through the Nigerian courts for custody. It was under this authority that he arrived in Lagos to claim us back; our mother saw no alternative but to hand us over. Since then, throughout all the upheavals, there had been no word from her.

Finally a letter did come: Christmas cards arrived at Grenbeck Court, posted from East Africa. There were three of them. The illustrations on the front cover were all by the same artist, coloured drawings of Masai people. Sheka's had a warrior carrying a spear, Memuna's showed a woman with a baby on her back. My own, the most striking in my opinion, was of a woman wearing dozens of coloured rings about her swan-like neck. Our stepmother had called us together one day and handed the cards to each of us. Afterwards she asked me: 'Do you remember your mother?'

'Sure,' I said, although I wasn't. I had stopped thinking of her so much lately. Sometimes, and for a few days after the cards arrived, the three of us talked about her together in secret. We called her 'Real Mum' now and if anyone had ever overheard us they would have been confused. Mum was what we called our stepmother, and then there was Real Mum or Other Mum. Sometimes we called them both Mum and Mummy interchangeably—we always knew who we meant. When we talked about Real Mum we talked about her hair, mostly her hair. Or we rehearsed certain memories over and over, like the time Memuna found cockroaches in her Wellington boots. Once at school we had sung 'Lord of the Dance' in assembly. It was the first time I had heard the song since our days in Koidu and I didn't understand why the words and the tune were so familiar, or why I knew them by heart. I suddenly felt overwhelmed by the memory of my mother and instead of singing along with the others I began to cry, cross-legged on the floor in the middle of two hundred other children. My form teacher picked her way across to me and led me out of the hall, assuming it was a case of homesickness. I asked Mum: 'Are we going to see Mummy again?'

Mum answered slowly: 'I don't think so, Am. I think she has a new family of her own now.'

'You mean she has other children?' This thought had simply never crossed my mind and it shocked me. 'How many other children does she have?'

'I don't know. One? Maybe two? I don't really know.'

Later I thought about what Mum had said and I wondered who they could be, these other children who had my mother now.

In my dormitory I had a friend called Helen, the only other person at the school, apart from Memuna, whose skin was the same shade as mine. Soon after I began at High Trees Helen had told me her mother was white and her parents were divorced. Helen lived with her mother, her new stepfather, who was white as well, and two half-sisters. But Helen and her brother were the only ones sent away to boarding school; she said it was because her parents didn't want them around.

'Is that why you're here, too?' she had asked. We'd been sitting on our beds in the Pink Room. Helen was picking at a scab on her arm—it made me wince to watch.

'No.' At the time I had explained how really I lived with my dad, although he was in Africa, so we couldn't actually be together. Helen looked at me and shrugged.

Poor Helen. I did not want to be like her. She had such an air of dejection about her that she attracted few friends. She spent most of her time alone, sitting on the swings or walking down to the main school. As the term strung out, long after the rest of us overcame our homesickness, I would hear Helen at night crying. I could see the outline of her body, her face turned to the wall, and though I leant out of my bed and whispered to her, she never answered me.

❧ 30 ❧

I was walking home with a paper bag of samosas from Bestways in my hand when the sound of car brakes snapped me out of my daydream. Up ahead a red car jolted to a stop.

'Here's an ugly one. Jesus look at that!' There were three men in the car, all in their twenties, all with short hair through which I could see the pink scalp. Their mouths contorted with hate: 'You're a fucking ugly fella, intchya? You're a right bloody ugly one.' Shouts of hard laughter crashed inside my ears.

I looked around. There was a man ahead of me: very tall, skinny, loping stride, shoulders hunched against the barrage of taunts. He had long ropes of black hair hanging down his back—I had never seen hair like that.

Next to him the red car revved, keeping pace with his walk. 'You're one fucking ugly nigger, intchya?' The man walked on, ignoring the car, behaving as though he hadn't heard. I followed on behind him. The engine roared and the car drove away.

Back when we lived at Grenbeck Court Mum and Mrs Cobally used to sit and watch *Love Thy Neighbour*, the tears coursing down their faces. Alongside *The Liver Birds* it was Mum's favourite TV programme. At school I had sometimes seen *The Black & White Minstrel Show*. It wasn't my all-time favourite programme, but I enjoyed the singing and dancing, the extravagant numbers and tap routines well enough. I was baffled, though, by the strange oily, black faces and white lips of the men and it took a while for me to realise they were supposed to be black men.

Once in a geography lesson I had told the class, at the urging of the teacher, that I came from Sierra Leone. I pointed it out in my Junior Atlas. It was one of the pink bits—the former colonies were always coloured pink. Afterwards the teacher talked to us about life in Africa, about how the natives lived and worked on cocoa plantations or grew coffee for the world market. At some point she segued into a description of rubber-tapping on a plantation, and showed us a picture of a brown man in a loincloth and turban cutting a V into the trunk of a tree. She asked me if I had ever been on a rubber plantation. I told her I hadn't. I couldn't seem to recognise any aspect of the Africa she described and I had begun to wonder if indeed I really came from there at all. I only realised after the umpteenth time it happened that people in England often talked about Sri Lanka thinking it was the same country as Sierra Leone.

A girl with dappled blonde hair two seats in front of me raised her hand. 'Is it true that when children in Africa are born their parents drop them on their heads. That's why they can carry baskets and things—on their heads—and we can't. Because their heads are flat?'

'Goodness, well . . . I really don't know,' said Miss Martin.

'Mummy says that's what they do,' replied the girl with absolute certainty.

'Well, I suppose it's possible . . . I really couldn't say. It sounds a dreadful thing to do,' murmured Miss Martin, putting her hand up to her breast.

'My mother says so,' repeated the girl, adding with finality, 'So does my father.'

I raised my hand. 'No they don't,' I said. 'Africans don't have flat heads. In Sierra Leone no one drops their babies on their heads, not on purpose.'

The girl swivelled round in her chair to look at me; the pageboy swung round and settled perfectly on either side of her cheeks; china-blue eyes regarded me disbelievingly. 'Well, how come they can carry so many baskets on their heads then?' She held up her book and pointed at the illustration of a woman with a baby on her back and a stack of six or seven baskets on her head.

I didn't know the answer. I wondered, too. 'I don't know,' I said.

'Well, then. I'm right, Miss Martin, aren't I?' The pageboy swung back the other way.

'Well, I suppose you could be,' concurred the geography teacher.

The next time we watched the minstrels dance down a staircase and drop to their knees, arms outstretched, grinning at the audience, the boy next to me asked: 'Is that what your father looks like then?'

I felt sad for the man walking in front of me down the London street, although I felt confused about what exactly had just happened. I gazed at the Rastafarian's receding back, his lanky legs. He did not know I was there. At that moment, while my eyes were still upon him, I saw him flinch: a shudder that ran through his body like a convulsion. The red car was back. The men had driven round the block and now they were circling us like wild dogs. The car horn bayed:

'Hey monkey!'

'Show us ya face, monkey man!'

It occurred to me that if they noticed me, which they hadn't so far, they might pick on me too. Our flat lay beyond the wasteland of the Earls Court Exhibition Centre car park on the other side of the Warwick Road. I still had quite a long way to go. I was wary of attracting attention by suddenly swinging back the way I had come. There was no side road I could turn down, no choice but to keep walking. My urge was to run up to the Rastafarian and walk with him, not because I wanted to show solidarity, although I felt deeply sorry for him, but because I was now genuinely scared and I thought he might be able to protect me when my turn came around. I was shaking, could hear myself breathing. I put my head down and walked on.

In the winter of 1972 on our portable TV set we watched men, women and children arriving at Heathrow Airport from Uganda. The pictures reminded me of our family, when we came to Britain dressed only in our cotton clothes. These people—'Amin's Asians' they were called by the newspapers—mostly wore billowing trousers and tunics. Their arrival, broadcast in black-and-white news images, looked chilly and bleak.

Sometime later I had managed to lock myself out of our flat during the holidays while Mum was at work. Memuna and Sheka were off somewhere else together, so I sat on the doorstep to wait. A Ghanaian woman who lived in the basement saw me there and called me in to wait in her living room. While I sat on the sill of the bay window and watched the street, she went about her business.

In the room a radio was playing very loudly. The show was some kind of discussion programme. A man was asking: 'Is it all right to call black people niggers, wogs and coons?' He was going up to people in the street and asking them the question. I thought it wasn't all right at all. I had never heard the words 'wog' or 'coon', but I knew what 'nigger' meant. I couldn't understand why the man was bothering to ask. But to my surprise there seemed to be lots of people who thought it was just fine.

'Is it acceptable to call black people niggers, wogs and coons, madam?'

'It don't matter. My dad always calls them wogs. That's what they are, in't they? Don't mean anything really.'

'Do you think it's all right to call black people niggers, wogs and coons, sir?'

'It's our country. If they don't like it they can go back to Paki Land.'

'. . . black people niggerswogsandcoons, sir?'

'. . . sticks and stones can break my bones. It's harmless, really.'

. . . niggerswogsandcoons . . . niggerswogsandcoons . . . niggerswogsandcoons . . .

I watched the woman. She seemed to be oblivious to the words coming from the radio; she was unpacking her shopping and storing things in the fridge. The room was cold and the air was heavy with stale cooking oil; the carpet was wrinkled and grey; the draylon curtains sagged unevenly on the rail. She was a large, slow-moving woman, with a wrap tied around her head, wearing an old cardigan and a pair of men's shoes. She acted as though she were deaf. As the radio blared she went about her business unceasingly: a poor African woman, away from her people, alone in a foreign country. Who was she to tell these people what she ought to be called?

At High Trees I suffered the early indignity of being forced to play Mowgli in a school production of *The Jungle Book*— wearing nothing but a pair of regulation knickers. We were all more appalled by the fact that my perfectly flat chest was on display to the class than anything else. In general we were of an age where children do not find differences of race or class remarkable. Gradually I moved on up the school, left the Cottage, where the junior girls slept, and moved into the main building with the senior girls.

In my first year in the upper school, when I was eight, nearly nine, a new girl arrived to join us. She was a weekly boarder and went home at weekends to ride her horses, and she left school two afternoons in the week to train and to compete at a place called Hickstead. Her name was Susan and she was worldly and self-confident in a way I had never encountered before. I had seen other new girls arrive: they sat in the empty seats at the front of the class and hung around together at break, shouting their presence silently, tongue-tied and trembling. It was ages before they made any friends with anyone. Susan was loud, with a habit of biting the split ends off her straight, sun-bleached hair and chewing her nails. On Mondays she came back to school with chocolates and sweets and shared them in the dorm after lights out. Susan and I instantly became friends.

We spent most of the term in each other's company. By then I had been at High Trees long enough to have earned a certain amount of respect and I taught Susan everything I knew: the dance routines to the tracks by the Bay City Rollers and Mud, the endless and minute modifications in games of Jacks, the complicated skipping routines we all practised for hours on the tarmac outside the kitchen annexe. Susan wasn't terribly interested, to be honest, but she went along with it up to a point, then she would cast me a look. At that moment we would break away from the game and wander off to sit and talk—well, mostly Susan talked about her life outside High Trees and I listened.

'Eeenie, meenie, macka, racka . . .'

We were in class waiting for the teacher to arrive when Susan told me it was her birthday soon. Two girls next to us were performing an impressive clapping routine and everyone was watching, except the swots who already had their books out.

'Rae, rye, dominacka.'

Susan whispered to me that she was planning a big party at her house in a few weeks' time, and everyone was invited. I was the first person she had told.

'Chicka pocka, lollipopa, om, pom, push!'

Susan's father was a wealthy businessman; they lived in a large house in Sussex with a swimming pool. He had given his permission for Susan's entire class to spend the day and she told us her father even planned to hire a projector and screen so we could all watch a film in the evening. After weeks cooped up at boarding school we were feverish with anticipation.

Monday morning, a fortnight before the party, Susan arrived at school with the invitations. She said she would give them out after lunch, and all through the morning the pile of envelopes sat at the front of her desk. I was sitting close enough to see the names in beautiful italic script, handwritten on the front of each envelope. I had never, ever received an invitation like that.

At lunch time we walked down to the main building and went to change out of our coats. At the beginning of each term the matron allocated the coat pegs in alphabetical order, and on the first day of term we swapped the name tags around to suit ourselves. Susan and I had pegs next to each other, even though our surnames began with completely different letters. We were busy preparing ourselves for lunch when Susan caught my arm, letting the others go ahead.

'What is it?' I asked. I was keen to get to the table. My stomach was rumbling.

'I'm sorry,' said Susan, looking me straight in the eye, 'but you can't come to the party.'

I stared at her. I thought I had misunderstood or misheard, but Susan's perfectly serious expression filled me with cold dread. 'But why not? Who else isn't going? Aren't you having a party any more?'

'It's my dad. He says you can't come.'

'Your *dad* says I can't come?'

'My dad doesn't like black people. He told me he won't have anybody black in his house. Sorry. Really.'

There were no other black kids in our class. Marius Georgiades, who was a Cypriot, was olive-skinned but unquestionably white. What Susan was saying, I realised, was that everyone was going to her birthday party except me. What took me aback was her utterly matter-of-fact tone.

'Have you told him—that I'm your friend, I mean, your best friend.' She nodded. 'Well, speak to him again. It's not fair. He doesn't even know me.' I was desperate to go to the party. I couldn't believe I was going to miss it and nor could I compute the explanation I had been given. I couldn't go to the party be-cause I was black. There seemed to me to be as much sense in it as asking someone the way to Brighton and being told that apples are green.

Susan handed round the invitations later the same day. I stood by and watched. In the excitement no one seemed to notice I hadn't been given one. After the weekend, when Susan came back to school I ran up to her: 'Did you ask him?'

'Yes.' Her father hadn't changed his mind.

'I don't understand—why not?'

'Dad says the reason is because once when I was a baby he left me outside in my pram in the garden and three big, black men came with broken bottles and smashed them over me. I was cut all over. I had to go to the hospital, he said, to have stitches. Of course I can't remember anything about it because I was just a baby, but he was there. So that's why, that's why he doesn't like black people. I mean, you can see that . . . can't you? If your baby was attacked.'

I didn't know what to say. There were a million things I could have said, but I didn't know where to begin. I nodded in silence.

After breakfast on Saturday all the children who were going to the party were called out of the dining room. As some of my friends passed me they whispered: 'Aren't you coming?' No, I mouthed and shrugged. There were quizzical looks as they hurried off. I spent the afternoon lying on my bed in the dorm, reading my book alone. After supper the girls and boys arrived back, high on sugar and sun, carrying paper bags full of Liquorice Allsorts, aniseed balls and coloured pencils; they were chattering like birds.

In my dorm the two girls who had been to the party smiled at me with sorry eyes: 'You didn't miss much really. It was just a party.'

'Yes, not even that good, actually,' said the other girl.

I knew that wasn't the point. I didn't know who they were trying to make feel better, themselves or me.

When Susan came back to school two days later she brought one of the goodie bags for me, and a piece of birthday cake wrapped in a blue paper napkin. I put it on the chair next to my bed, where I hung my clothes. And I left it there.

The Rastafarian kept walking as the taunts flew around us. We were quite alone—it was a one-way street between the busy Earls Court Road and Warwick Road, where few people passed, but now the silence was replaced by mocking laughter and the trumpeting horn.

Just when I was wondering how it would all end for us the hounded man did something that made me stand quite still. He turned round to face the car, threw his arms behind him as though he were baring his chest and lifted up his chin. He was showing them his face, the very features the louts demanded to see. His face was gaunt and hollow-cheeked; he had a thin beard and pro-truding teeth with wide gaps. It was an ugly face, but a nice ugly face. He bellowed: 'Leave me alone. Leave me a-lone! Why can't

you people just let . . . me . . . be?' Then he closed up again, turned
to the wall and covered his face with his hands.

The car sped away, engine roaring in triumph. I wanted to say
something to the man. I wanted to run up to him and say something kind. But I didn't know how. He still hadn't seen me and he
didn't look back now. He just carried on walking, still hunched
up; the loping stride had vanished. I sensed that if he knew that
I, a small girl, had been a witness to his humiliation it would
only be made worse, so I went on home, holding my oily bag of
crushed samosas.

31

I used to walk down a road, any road, and say to myself: If I can just hold my breath until I get to the end of this street Daddy will be released from prison. Or, if I was crossing a bridge and a train went underneath, I wished my father would be freed. Sometimes I'd stand there until train after train had gone by, eyes closed, amassing wishes. Three times over three years, as I cut the first slice of cake, I used my special birthday wish so that I could have him back. I wished on the full moon and the new moon, and then any moon at all. At Christmas, if I found the silver sixpence Mum hid in the pudding, I wished for my father's freedom. I wished for nothing else.

As time went on I increased my challenges: to reach the end of the road with my eyes closed without bumping into anyone or anything; to leap every other paving stone, dancing between them, promising myself that if I could make it ten yards, or twelve, or fifteen, I would somehow, miraculously, earn his freedom. Gradually I upped the ante: I'd work my bike up to speed then aim the front wheel at a pothole or a speed bump. If I don't fall off, if I can stay in the saddle, then they'll let him out of prison. Alone in the flat one afternoon I stood in the galley kitchen passing my hand as slowly as I dared across the ice-blue flame of the gas ring, once, twice, thrice, until the smell, like burnt bacon rinds, rose from the scorched ends of my fingernails.

I was walking down Philbeach Gardens when I swung out and stepped onto the zebra crossing without looking and without waiting. A taxi coming fast round the curve of the road braked forcefully; the driver leaned out of his cab and swore at me, shaking his head in exasperation. I kept my face turned away and walked on. When I reached the other side I exhaled: I felt as though I had passed a test or scored bonus points in some unknown contest.

There's a good reason exile was once used as a punishment. It is life apart, life on hold, life in waiting. You may begin full of strength and hope, or just ignorance, but it is time, nothing more than the unending passage of time that wears down your resilience, like the drip of a tap that carves a groove in the granite below. Exile is a war of attrition on the soul, it's a slow punishment, and it works.

A malaise seeped into our life at home, tainting our relationships with each other. My brother, my sister and I became incapable of being in a room together without a remark, or a look, or a gesture provoking a fight. Mum was out at work during the week, and while she was gone we turned on each other, honing young tongues on the bitter new pleasures of sarcasm and ridicule, turning the holidays into one long, exhausting trench war. Even the letters from our father telling us to take care of each other, telling my brother especially to look after his sisters, couldn't break the cycle of mutual destruction. Sometimes I think it had the opposite effect, making us all the more angry and resentful. Incapable of spending time together in the way we used to, our trio fractured: Memuna and Sheka, the two older ones, preferred each other's company while I spent much of my time alone.

My memories of those years, and the ones that followed, are mainly of being by myself, of feeling excluded by my immaturity. I was the only one who hadn't outgrown the Raleigh Chopper we were given our first Christmas in London, and I spent hours circling the streets or else parked outside W. H. Smith, where I whiled away afternoons at a time coveting shiny pencil cases and Caran d'Ache colours.

One afternoon during the holidays the flat was cold and shadowy, the heating was off, but the spring sun wasn't quite strong
enough to warm the air and a wan light filtered through the
streaked window panes. Memuna and Sheka were out together
and I was alone in the flat with Mum. Somewhere in the house
we had a key we used to let ourselves into the small park opposite,
where at one time we had all belonged to the playgroup (now I
was the only one who still went); we had been on trips to the adventure playground, and London Zoo, and on Saturdays we went
to the kids' cinema club. The heavy iron key to the park was not
in its usual place in the kitchen, so I went through to look for my
stepmother. I needed her permission to go to the park, in any case.

Mum was lying in the bedroom, on her side, facing away from
the door. She was wearing trousers and a sweater, her slippers were
kicked off and lay facing each other on the carpet, the curtains
were wide open. I couldn't tell if she was having a nap, though
usually she got under the covers.

'Mum?' I whispered. There was no answer. I turned and began
to withdraw, quietly as I could.

Just as I was closing the door I heard her: 'Am? Is that you?
What is it?' Mum's voice was muffled.

I crept forward a little and began to apologise. A few steps in, I
paused. There was something wrong with Mum: her face looked
smudged, and her eyes were shining. 'Mum, what's the matter?'
I had never seen her cry before; I couldn't remember ever seeing
an adult cry at all. I asked her again and as I did so the pitch of
my voice began to rise. I stood by her, hands by my sides, not
knowing what to do.

In the years we had been in London I had begun to think Mum
was beautiful. In my eyes she looked just like Diana Ross, with
her Afro hair, hooped earrings and high platform shoes. I used
to sit on her bed and watch her when she was getting dressed to

go somewhere. 'Mummy, can I have that when you die?' I asked the question about everything I liked. My favourite piece was an apricot velvet trouser suit she wore on special occasions. Memuna did the same—we raced each other around the room pointing at things. Mum, can I have that? A pretty silver bangle. Mum, can I have that? A bottle of scent. Mum, can I have that? When I was younger I used to make her handbags from scraps of cloth, sewn together with running stitch around three sides, with a handle of plaited wool. I genuinely didn't understand why she never seemed to use them.

'Don't worry, Am,' she said. 'It's nothing. It's just a headache, that's all.'

'Shall I get the aspirin?' I offered.

'I've taken some already. Perhaps a cup of tea, Am. I'll take a cup of tea.'

I went to the kitchen and lit the gas ring. A minute later the kettle began to rattle and huff, working up enough breath for a whistle. I found a cup and saucer and reached for a bag from the box of PG Tips. I carried the tea through carefully and slowly set it next to the bed. I looked at Mum: her face was still wet.

'Now what's that for?' she said. I didn't answer—I thought Mum was about to be gruff with me for crying, but she didn't say anything more. I curled up next to her on the bed and put my arms around her.

The doctor said what Mum needed was a holiday, but Mum loathed flying and so in July of 1973 we used up all her savings and set sail on the SS *France*, the second-largest ocean liner in the world, bound for New York. The crossing took five days: for me five mornings, afternoons and evenings of untrammelled independence. On the first morning, after a night of mild rolling, Mum couldn't rise from her bunk, and she pretty well stayed there for the entire journey, attended by a kind and solicitous deck steward.

Memuna and Sheka went down with seasickness too, and briefly
I was left to myself entirely.

The ship was a world which I could roam unchallenged, with
no one to tell me what to do. I swam up and down the salt-water
pool; ate four-course meals served by a uniformed waiter under
the swaying chandeliers of the dining room; went to the cinema
and sat entirely alone among the rows of seats; and lay on the deck
and watched the clouds, like Dr Seuss creatures, crossing the sky to
America. In New York we stayed just two days before we boarded
the Greyhound bus for Boston to stay with John Karefa-Smart,
who was now teaching at Harvard, and his family.

America was a glass of hot chocolate: six inches of steaming,
creamy chocolate, eight inches of vanilla-flavoured whipped
cream, sprinkled with hundreds and thousands, crowned by a
glorious, artificially gleaming cherry. America was Rosalie May,
eldest daughter of Uncle John, a beautiful former fashion model,
hopelessly extrovert and extravagant, who delighted in spoiling
me, thought her name was dull and told me she would change it to
mine. America was horror comics, which I read by the score until
I became too terrified to sleep; it was bread that tasted of sugar;
it was an endless succession of visits to Sears Roebuck, where
Mum kitted us out in a year's worth of new clothes. America did
not disappoint, and after five weeks we returned home the way
we had come. This time round Mum managed to acquire some
sea legs, and even joined us for the end-of-voyage gala dinner the
night before we docked at Portsmouth. We posed together at our
table, with happy smiles, and we sent the souvenir photograph
home to our father.

In September, a few days before I was due back at school, letters
arrived from my father. Mine began: 'My Dear Aminatta, Many
thanks for your sweet letters from America and the SS France.'
He told me I looked beautiful in my picture and then spoilt it

slightly by enquiring whether I was wearing my arch supports, and if I had been to the orthodontist yet. It was an ordinary letter in every way, and yet it was not. I can't remember if I noticed it at that time, or whether Mum gave the news to us herself. But when I look at the letter now, bundled among all his other letters to me written while we were in England, it stands starkly alone. The two pale-blue sheets are loosely covered in my father's familiar handwriting. He wrote using a Biro. It is not what is there, but what is missing that arrests my eye: there is no purple stamp at the top of the page, no censor's signature, no prisoner number D 6/70, no return address to Pademba Road Prison.

32

The humidity outside caused all the windows in the plane to fog over, obscuring what should have been my first sight of home. My smart white trousers were wrinkled and covered in crumbs, and my leather belt cut into my waist. My new blouse had come untucked and was riding up my back and I struggled with hand luggage as we eased our way down the aisle. Outside the temperature was in the mid thirties, and when the doors were opened steaming air, like hot breath, replaced the pressurised cool of the cabin. An English family behind me, arriving in Freetown for the first time, exhaled. Welcome to West Africa.

Our father and Ibrahim Taqi had been released together. A guard opened the door to their cells, led them to the entrance of Pademba Road and deposited them onto the busy street. They stopped the first taxi they saw. The driver recognised them, which was just as well because neither of them had any money, and he willingly drove them back to Tengbe Farkai. That night they borrowed a record player, sent Santigi out for beers and danced together to Johnny Nash singing, 'It's gonna be a bright, bright, bright sunshiny day'. They must have felt like kings, free at last. Siaka Stevens had sworn Mohamed Forna would be the last of the detainees to be released and he was, let out just a few days short of what would have been his third anniversary behind bars. Ibrahim Taqi aside, the others who had been part of the UDP had all left prison in the previous months and years.

In England Mum had written to our schools for permission to let us fly home early, before the end of term. We returned to

Philbeach Gardens for the last time, where we spent the whole night emptying drawers, cramming belongings into our suitcases, finding a space for items we didn't want to leave behind. We had gone to bed after midnight and risen in the early hours to dress in our best for the flight home.

We stepped into the sunlight and down the steps of the aircraft, behind the straggling herd of passengers making their way into the solitary terminal building. On the balcony a small crowd of people waved down at the new arrivals. I scanned the silhouetted figures. I didn't recognise anyone there. I imagined my father would be waiting beyond the immigration desks in the main hall. It would take us another forty minutes, at least, to pass through the anarchy of Lungi's airport bureaucracy. A few yards ahead of me one or two of the plane's passengers stepped around a man standing alone on the tarmac. I glanced at him, and away. And then I looked again. I dropped my bag and let it lie where it fell on the runway. I raced forward with the wind at my heels and I reached him first. First! I was for ever and perversely proud of that fact. Moments later we were all gathered around him, hugging and kissing.

My father was arrested when I was six years and four months old; now I was nine years and seven months. Yet even though I had not seen even a photograph of him all the time we were in London, for some reason I had never forgotten how the features of his face were composed. Indeed I remembered him well enough to see for myself how changed he was. The starchy prison diet, the lack of exercise had caused him to fill out; he wasn't fat, but he was bulkier. He had taken up a pipe and grown a dense beard, his hairline had receded slightly. Over the four weeks of the holiday I tried to persuade him to shave off his beard, so that he would look more as I remembered him. When eventually he acceded and returned home one evening with a clean chin, I was disappointed by the results. Certainly he looked more as I once knew him, yet somehow indefinably altered.

And I was different, too. I noticed the biggest change in myself when we arrived at the house in Kissy, where Santigi, and some of our cousins—Morlai, Esther and Musu—waited to greet us. When I opened my mouth to speak to them in Krio I found the years had robbed me of my childhood language. Everything people were saying around me was perfectly intelligible, I understood it all, but when I tried to answer it was as though I was on stage in a school play and had forgotten my lines. My mind was a blank. I tried a different approach, to take a thought and put it into words, remember each word, one by one, but that didn't work either.

Our new home was a modest, concrete-built house in Samuel's Lane, Kissy, in the industrial East End of the city, far, far from Spur Road and Wilberforce. We lived in the top apartment; the landlord and his wife lived below us. As part of the deal our father had spent several weeks refurbishing the upper floor: he had bought furniture and beds to make it ready for all of us. The house was set on the edge of a gully, with a stream running along the bottom leading up to a slaughterhouse. Vultures wheeled in the sky above; one of them had an old tin can tied to his leg with a piece of string and everywhere he flew he rattled through the air like a mechanical crane.

December had brought the harmattan and a ubiquitous layer of red dust coated the facades of buildings. On the days the wind really blew the dust erased the horizon and the view of the hills and even blurred the outline of houses.

Early on we went to visit Pa Roke and the family. In the north the dust of the city blew from the crevices of our clothing and the dirty buildings were replaced by infinite shades of green: the powdery velvet of the banana leaves, the lustrous wax of the mango trees, crinkly buds of golden lettuces planted in rows by the river next to mounds of deep, dark spinach and potato leaves. I felt my spirits soar, remembering how much I had—we all had—enjoyed these trips up-country.

Before he was imprisoned our father had begun to clear the bush and build a house next door to Pa Roke's. The house, a three-bedroomed bungalow, was built in the same simple style as the rest of the street with the difference that our house was made out of concrete blocks. There was a wasps' nest in one of the bedrooms, and some of the older boys among my cousins began to knock it down with a stick. As the honeycomb of earth crumbled, the wasps, with long swallowtails full of poison, flew furiously round the house. Someone was stung—a teenage boy, whose whole arm swelled up in minutes. Meanwhile the three of us ran around the house excitedly, choosing which bedroom we would sleep in, inspecting the kitchen and bathroom and trying the taps—it was the first house with running water in Magbesseh Street. There was still some work to be done, but it was almost finished.

Pa Roke lay paralysed by a stroke, on a low cot in the corner of the main room of his house. We filed in one by one and stood around him, murmuring greetings while he looked us over and whispered softly to our father. News of Pa Roke's condition had reached our father in prison; as soon as he was released more than a year later he travelled straight to Tonkolili to see him.

When our father defied the APC government in 1970 the whole family had become a target for the prime minister's fury. In Magburaka the Fornas had been threatened and had their homes searched by police claiming to be looking for arms; scores of people were arrested or detained. The government had determined to quell us all.

Our father must have felt responsible for Pa Roke. The house next door meant we could spend more time in Magburaka and

Pa Roke would have somewhere to lie in comfort. I smiled at Pa Roke. I thought he looked very long and flat lying there. I couldn't really hear or understand what he was saying—he murmured and gestured with his one good hand, while our father sat on the corner of the cot and held on to the limp fingers of the other one.

Our father had taken offices in Walpole Street, close to the Cotton Tree, just off the main road through the town, which had been renamed Siaka Stevens Street. The president's face appeared on all the country's new coins and banknotes, and on the stamps as well. There were photographs of him in the lobby of every building, though not our father's offices in Walpole Street. On a door on the second floor was a sign, 'International Commercial Enterprises', and behind it the offices, just a pair of rooms really, which smelled of new paint. We took turns sitting behind his desk and swinging in his chair. In a cardboard box on the floor I found a heavy wood and brass nameplate, left over from his days in government. I dusted it off and arranged it on his desk; it looked a little absurd, too grandiose for the modest office, but I was delighted and left it there while our father took us all out to lunch.

After a six-year absence our father had decided not to return to practising medicine. He worried he was out of touch with medical advances; perhaps he wondered, too, how many patients he would be able to attract as the foremost known opponent of the government. In prison he had decided there was money to be made trading rice and as soon as he was released he set to work on a business plan. A month or two later he was approached by a young man, another former political detainee, who had been turned away from his government job at the Electricity Corporation and was having trouble finding work. Abu Kanu was a trained accountant, and so our father agreed to take him on to do the company's books, warning that he would not be paid much at first.

Little by little they expanded; within a few months they opened a couple of stores in the provinces and began to buy and sell other commodities. They planned, one day in the near future, to start importing medical equipment and drugs from Europe, something our father knew about and which the country needed. Lying on his desk were brochures from drug companies alongside a number of syringes, still in their plastic wrapping, and our father's old metal stethoscope in its box. I asked if he would let me have one of the syringes—for the animal hospital I was creating—and when he agreed I chose a good-sized one from the selection and dropped it into my pocket.

But International Commercial Enterprises soon began to encounter obstacles. Abu Kanu had been to see a merchant about buying a consignment of tomato puree for one of their stores. Soon after he left the businessman received a visit from a pair of plainclothes officers. Within a short time it became a regular occurrence for people who had dealings with the company to be visited and questioned.

A lawyer who worked in the chambers on the opposite side of Walpole Street stopped our father on his way into the office, beckoning him over. He led our father upstairs to his chambers and stood him in front of the window. Before them was a clear view of the length of the whole street. The lawyer pointed to the red-brick church at the top, on the other side of the junction. The front of the church faced the side of my father's building. There was a small courtyard leading into the vestry, and just beyond the gates they could see two men sitting in the shade. The young lawyer, who had known my father slightly in times past, pointed to a building farther down the road, again on the same side of the street as the offices of International Commercial Enterprises. It was a low-rise building, painted yellow on the outside; inside it housed a doctor's office. The metal grid doors were open to the

streets, and just inside sat two more men. They were government
agents, who had been watching our father from the day of his release. Men from the security services even sat below the lawyer's
office, among the clients waiting in reception. From there they
watched our father, they watched our whole family: as we stopped
by the office to have lunch with our father, as we dropped in on
our way to Chellerams supermarket or passed by to collect him
on our way home from the beach. They watched us at home, too,
from the shadows of the veranda of the house opposite, the home
of Nancy Steele.

In August, just days after his release, our father had attended
the Medical Physicians Annual Ball at the Cape Sierra. The dance
was held around the open-air dance floor in the grounds of the
hotel, and was attended by over a hundred doctors as well as local
dignitaries and diplomats. The story was told to me by Karl and
Hildegard Münch, the former West German ambassador and his
wife, who had been good friends and admirers of Mohamed Forna
when he was a government minister, when Karl and he saw themselves as bright young men helping to shape a new country's future.
We were sitting in their parlour, in a modern suburb of Munich,
where I had flown from England to meet them in the year 2000,
some years after Karl had retired from the diplomatic service.

My father had arrived late and alone. He stood, dressed in
black tie, at the entrance to the ball. A hush passed from table to
table as the nearest guests recognised him. Though it was generally known that he had been released from prison, few people
expected him to appear in public so soon. My father smiled but
spoke to no one as he crossed the room to join a group of friends
at a table in the far corner. Excited whispers replaced the hush as
the news coursed from table to table, people craned their necks
to get a glimpse of him, but he sat with his back to them all and
did not turn once.

Late in the evening the bandleader announced the Ladies' Choice. Hildegard stood up. 'I am going to dance with Mohamed,' she declared. So far Karl Münch had managed to exchange a nod across the room with his old friend, but no more. He recalled how he had teased his wife, saying she would be the last nail in the coffin of his career. Germany was a significant donor of aid to Sierra Leone and for Hildegard, the wife of the German ambassador, to dance with the country's leading political dissident was an audacious statement—and she meant it to be: she wanted to demonstrate in public that Mohamed Forna still commanded the respect of a major European power like Germany. The dance was a slow waltz, and as the couple moved across the dance floor every eye in the room was upon them.

Afterwards my father escorted Hildegard back to her table. Karl stood up to greet him, grasping him by the arm as he did so. 'For God's sake, Mohamed,' he whispered. 'Leave the country. Get out as soon as possible. They will kill you.'

My father had brushed him off. 'Don't worry about me,' he replied. 'Things aren't so bad.' He joked about prison being the safest place to be at certain times, and with that the two men shook hands and parted.

The Münchs were not alone in trying to warn our father. His old friend Lami Sidique, who had left the civil service and was running a supermarket, said the same. Even Abu Kanu was beginning to wonder if they might both have more luck if they started somewhere new, for during the years our father had been imprisoned Siaka Stevens had systematically set about erecting the pillars of tyranny.

The country now had two separate paramilitary forces, loyal only to the president. Internal Security Units One and Two were staffed by troops brought in from Guinea; later they were brought together and renamed the SSD, the State Security Division—more popularly known on the streets as Siaka Stevens's Dogs. At the same time the army was slowly weakened, denied proper pay rises, ammunition and weapons. The moves served to emasculate John Bangura, the head of the army, whom Stevens both feared and hated and who had incurred the president's wrath by initially refusing to use his troops against the UDP.

In March of 1971 there had been an attack on the private home of the president. Stevens publicly claimed to have been in bed when his house was fired upon and to have been in fear of his life, describing how he dived for cover as bullets peppered his bedroom wall and tore up the mosquito net and bedding. Yet press photographs the following day showed no more than two panes of broken glass, and there was a more damaging rumour that circulated and refused to die. It was said that far from being in his house Stevens had in fact spent the night in the home of a professor at Fourah Bay College, a man who soon afterwards was awarded an ambassadorship and departed the country.

The next day Guinean MiG jets circled the air above the capital. John Bangura was arrested and charged with attempting to overthrow the government. Bangura, who had been drinking that night, had been persuaded by some of his men to make a broadcast to the nation, in which he announced the army was in control. He claimed he had only done so to prevent the spread of anarchy and because he had no idea of the whereabouts of the president. Nevertheless, he was found guilty by the court, condemned to death and later hanged.

In April 1971 Sierra Leone was declared a republic. The bill was rushed through parliament by Stevens, who used his massive majority to change the very safeguards designed to prevent a leader from flouting the constitution and seizing power. A judge, Okoro Cole, was named the country's first president; the following day

Okoro Cole resigned and Stevens assumed the presidency. Our father's political arch enemy S. I. Koroma was named vice-president and Christian Kamara-Taylor, another of his main opponents, became minister of finance. The governor-general, Sir Banja Tejan-Sie, fled to Britain, where he lived out the rest of his years in a suburb of London. Despite all of this, the facade of make-believe respectability satisfied the British government and they made no protest. Britain was pleased ultimately to be rid of Sierra Leone, the tarnished jewel of the empire.

The country's budget surpluses and foreign exchange reserves had been drained away. At the time of our father's resignation an astute desk clerk at the World Bank had sent a memorandum up to his superiors, asking whether the bank should continue with a loan to Sierra Leone in the light of the former minister's claims of corruption in the government. The bank had gone ahead anyway. Within a short time the treasury in Sierra Leone had begun to default on payments of overseas loans; by the time we came home the new banknotes, printed with Stevens's face, could not be exchanged in any bank outside Sierra Leone.

The country was crawling with spies, who reported every conversation, every whisper to the president. The newspapers had all been either brought under state control or closed down. Summary arrests, detentions and beatings had become commonplace. There was no opposition, no voice of criticism: people had learnt to fear for their lives if they spoke out against the government. And this was what, in the west, they called 'benign dictatorship'. Good enough for Africa, good enough for Africans.

Even in Britain the students had gone quiet since their media 'coup' at the high commission, though once during our father's imprisonment Mum, Memuna, Sheka and I had travelled along the length of the District Line to an anonymous suburban house where a photostat machine drummed away in a back room, and I grew bored playing with my dolls until eventually someone gave me dozens of sheets to staple and sort into piles.

In May of 1973, while the country remained under the state of emergency, Stevens called the general election, postponed for three years since the days of the UDP. In the bloodiest of campaigns ever the SLPP, fearful of violence, withdrew every one of its candidates. On polling day every APC candidate was returned unopposed. One thousand Red Shirts drove from Port Loko to Freetown in celebration of S. I. Koroma's re-election chanting: 'Unopposed! Unopposed!' The APC became the single party in parliament and in the country. Sierra Leone was a one-party state.

Only when his power was absolute did Stevens dare to free our father.

33

The Bottle-Top Devil whirled in the dust. We leaned from the top floor of the balcony to watch. From his shoulders and the crown of his head myriad bottle tops, strung together, fell in layers, covering his face and cascading to the ground around his dancing feet. As he turned and twisted the metal tops clashed against each other. Behind him, and all around, danced small children and youths bearing hurricane lamps. I stared down at him. The swirling bottle tops revealed glimpses of the man beneath: an arm, the sleeve of his shirt, a flash of a belt buckle, his naked feet. And even though I knew that beneath the terrifying creature was an ordinary man of flesh and blood just like me, I felt the unmistakable tingle of terror.

When the devil had finished dancing the small boys ran forward and collected the coins and notes we threw down. On Wilkinson Road, one of the main routes through the town, there was a place where cars veered off the road. The locals told of a she-devil who lived there, who lined her babies across the road, so the story went, and woe betide the speeding driver who hit one of them. We offered our coins in exchange for luck, to ward off misfortune and placate the mischievous devils. All through the holidays until New Year the devils of each secret society paraded the city and danced for the cheering crowds, who threw talismans and money at their feet.

At home we celebrated Christmas. Mum was Christian; so was Santigi, who had recently taken the name Simon Peter and sat on the back stairs reading from his Bible, one syllable at a time. Two days before Christmas vats of jollof rice and bahal simmered on the stove, peppered chicken and skewered meats roasted on wood fires in the yard. In town we went shopping for presents at Patterson Zochonis. I barely recognised the department store. There were hardly any shoppers to speak of, and little to choose from among the depleted merchandise. At the entrance sat the lepers and a man with both legs so hideously swollen with elephantiasis he could barely walk. On the way in I offered some money to an elderly man with leprosy, who was crouched on the floor. He put out his hand; the disease had left him with a palm and a thumb but no fingers. On the way out he thanked me again, smiled toothlessly and asked me my name. I told him. 'Which Forna?' he asked in return. 'From where?'

I wavered. I had worn my name with pride all my life, except sometimes at school when I was being teased about it. As I looked at the man sitting before me, for reasons I couldn't analyse I wondered if I should tell him or keep it a secret. Somewhere in my subconscious a memory rose like vapour of those last weeks we spent hidden behind walls in Freetown.

Out in the town, with my father, people still greeted him warmly everywhere we went—mostly the poor people, it has to be said. We had been waiting in the early evening for the car to be filled up at the petrol station when we heard a commotion on the other side of the street. A group of men had been pushing a lorry when one of them slipped and trapped his ankle under the wheels. My father went across to offer his help while we waited in the car. Long after the man had been freed, given first aid and dispatched, we were still there, as more and more people recognised our father and came up to shake his hand. When my father was with us I felt confident and utterly unafraid, but now I was alone, facing a beggar in rags and a dirty skull cap who wanted to know my name and I swam in uncertainty.

'Dr Mohamed Sorie Forna.' I barely moved my lips. It was the start, though I didn't know it, of never being able to utter my own name without watching the face of the listener, trying to guess what his or her response is likely to be.

The leper reached up to take my hands in his awkward stumps. 'God bless yousef, God bless you daddy, God bless oona all.'

On Christmas morning we exchanged presents. Among mine was an autograph book; it had a purple cover with three stars and smooth lilac pages. Also a small, plain bingo set with wooden numbers. I put this aside while I occupied myself with my other, more impressive gifts.

I can count off Christmases and birthdays on my fingers, working backwards remembering each one over the years: my sixth birthday, both the real and the mythical one, my seventh when Mum surprised me at High Trees, waiting in the chill of the front hall with a bag of presents and a cake, and all the other birthdays and Christmases after and before, starting right back to when I couldn't have been more than three or four and still lived with my mother. These are the building blocks of childhood memories— the reason, I suppose, parents try hard to make those days count, so that their children can store them up afterwards, carry them around in their minds as souvenirs of happy times.

How pathetically little I knew of what was really going on around me that Christmas. We had taken up where we had left off. My mother and father, even the three of us, smiled and pretended everything was normal, and to a large extent we succeeded. I was overjoyed to be home, to be with my father, to be a complete family. I still didn't understand exactly why my father had been imprisoned. I never asked anyone, including Mum, especially Mum, because I didn't seriously expect to receive an answer. I knew enough to understand that my father was not a criminal, yet the secrecy that surrounded all talk of him in London, our altered circumstances in Sierra Leone—I could not entirely interpret the meaning of these—and for the longest time I carried hidden within me a small, secret sense of shame.

That holiday I went around the house persuading everyone to write a message in my new autograph book. My stepmother tried to demur, saying I should be collecting the autographs of better-known people; finally she agreed and penned: 'If at first you don't succeed, try, try again.'

Next I presented my father with the book. He laid his pipe down on the coffee table. While he wrote I picked up the plastic pouch and sniffed the tobacco. I thought it smelled just like fruit cake, edible and delicious. Afterwards he handed the book back to me and I read what he had written there: 'Honour and shame from no condition rise; Act well your part: there all the honour lies.'

My father had signed 'M. S. Forna', and added the word 'Daddy' below. I read and reread his message and I was mystified. I couldn't guess at the meaning of the words, or why they had any significance for me. If the truth were told, I preferred Mum's easy adage. Some years later, when the binding of the book began to fall apart, I tore out the page my father had inscribed and held on to it, though even then I still hadn't managed to work out what exactly it was he had meant.

And yet now when I look back I remember. I remember how, when the two of us were alone together for a few brief minutes, I witnessed an incident as momentous as it was insignificant.

It was our regular outing, on Sunday, to go to Lumley Beach. Mum wasn't much of a beach-goer, but she came along all the same. Our father and the three of us loved the water. Lumley, lying just on the western edge of Freetown, was a spectacular beach which attracted hordes of people at the weekend. The beach was over two miles long. I knew that because we had once all had a discussion about how long a mile was, so our father had reset the milometer on the car and driven down the beach road. After we clocked the first mile we looked back along the beach, stretching out along the peninsula to the hotel at the end. One mile. By the time we had nearly reached the end of the road we had driven a whole mile more, two whole miles of beach.

It was late in the afternoon but the sun was still high; hawkers carried bottles of drinks in trays of melting ice; whole families basked like turtles in the water. I had left my sandals in the boot of the car and I walked back beside my father to collect them. Along the edge of the water the sand was cool, but farther up the beach it burned and I persuaded him to give me a piggyback over the dunes and across the bank of coarse grass with blades sharp enough to cut naked feet. As I searched for and found my shoes in the boot, wedged among the drinks coolers and towels, my father waited in the passenger seat, legs stretched out of the open door in front of him.

In the distance I heard the sing-song sound of sirens above the traffic on the beach road. A pair of motorcycles emerged out of the warped air rising up from the tar. They were followed by a black car, and then a white Mercedes; behind that was a third car and two more police outriders. It was the presidential motorcade. People sitting at the bar on the other side of the road stopped talking and looked up; children selling peanuts stood to attention by the roadside; vendors put down their loads and got to their feet; drivers pulled their cars in to the kerb and switched off their engines. The president was coming.

The motorcade progressed at an unhurried pace, the wail of the sirens reaching a gradual crescendo as it neared. For the first time I saw, ahead of the motorcycles, young boys running in formation. They were dressed in shorts and open shirts, and they carried long canes. *Raray* boys. They jogged down the middle of the road, forcing the oncoming traffic over to the side. Six-foot canes cut through the air, stinging the earth, flashing at the feet of nearby people. Get up, stand up for the president. I straightened up from buckling my sandals and turned towards the open-top car.

As the motorcade slid past I had my first and only real view of Siaka Stevens. He sat alone on the pale leather upholstery behind his liveried chauffeur. He was wearing a white suit and a cream straw Panama hat. There was the jaw, the pendulous lower lip and low brow that appeared on our stamps and on all the banknotes. The people around me clapped and waved. I waved along with them. The president waved back. We all waved again.

'Long live the Pa!'

'Pa Sheki, Pa Sheki!'

Stevens turned his head from side to side. I thought he was looking at me and I straightened my shoulders and stuck my chest out, but he did not seem to see me. His eyes shifted sideways and lingered there a moment. Then he turned away.

As the tail of the motorcade flicked past people breathed out, sat down, resumed their conversations where they had been interrupted. I turned towards my father. He was sitting exactly as he had been, in the front seat of the car, one arm draped across the headrest.

'That was the president,' I pointed out superfluously. 'Siaka Stevens.'

'Yes,' he replied. He moved to stand up.

'But you used to know him. I think he looked at you.'

'Yes,' my father agreed. I looked at him expectantly, waiting for an answer. When nothing more seemed to be forthcoming, I persisted: 'So why didn't you say hello? You should have said hello.' I would have liked to tell Memuna and Sheka I had met the president.

My father pushed down the lid of the boot and locked it with the key. Then he walked round and locked the car on the driver's side. We began back down the sand.

'Oh, I don't suppose he'd remember me, Am' was all he replied. And we made our way down the beach to join the others.

34

We flew back to England in January: alone this time, as unaccompanied minors. I cried at the airport, of course. I had allowed myself to imagine that once our father was free I wouldn't be going back to High Trees any more: I dreamed of going to school in Freetown, of wearing a blue check uniform and becoming an Annie Walsh girl. On the last night we all went out for a farewell family dinner at the Armenian restaurant on the bay next to Cape Club, where the wrecked fishing boat used to lie, and we sat eating our favourite *kebbe*. My father was relaxed, telling jokes—one about a man asked to recount the milestones in his life, who was pestered by his wife to include her name on the list. Eventually, when he had had enough, the husband turned to his wife with the words: 'I've been asked about the milestones in my life, not the millstones, my dear.' I tried to tell a joke of my own, about what I can no longer remember, but I stumbled at the punchline.

Our holiday ended on a high, and it was back to the routine of the Lent term. Memuna and I spent the exeat weekends and half term running along the empty school corridors, eating with the other overseas children among the empty trestle tables of the dining room. In a way I quite enjoyed staying at school when the other children were away: the teachers were more relaxed and we caught a glimpse of the personality beneath their brisk exteriors. As the weeks spun by we began rehearsals for the Passiontide Service at the end of term.

The next time I saw my father he was standing in the front hall of the school wearing a pair of white shoes. It was a Saturday morning at break. Memuna and I ran down to find him, dragging our friend Beverley, who giggled nervously when he shook her hand. We had no idea he was coming to visit; he travelled the short distance direct from Gatwick Airport to collect us from High Trees. He met the headmaster and some of our teachers and then took us for a day out in Brighton, collecting Sheka from his boarding school in Horsham along the way. All day long we teased him about his unfashionable shoes and we would not rest until he went into a shoe shop and bought a new pair in a more conservative shade. We had lunch in an empty hotel, and trudged alone along the pebble beach, head down to the wind, our school macs flapping behind us. Late in the afternoon we waited for him outside a small, terraced house while he consulted a fortune teller. The woman showed him to the door and greeted us; she was middle-aged with sparse, flame-coloured hair. As we walked away I pestered him to tell me what she had said. 'She told me I had three children,' he volunteered eventually, and I was impressed.

We went back with him to the airport, where he unearthed presents for us in his baggage in the left-luggage locker. In a passport photo booth he had his photograph taken and afterwards we all piled in on top of each other and posed, four times over, for each flash of the unseen camera.

Since his release our father had been denied permission to leave the country. Then, in mid March, he was re-arrested and accused of being in contact with a US embassy official, who was supposedly involved—according to the government—in dealing diamonds. Our father spent the night in custody at the CID headquarters, until it was proved the car seen parked outside the

American's house did not belong to him—he had part-exchanged it for another several months earlier. After his overnight detention, quite unexpectedly, his request to travel to Europe was granted. He stopped by Lami Sidique to say goodbye. 'Take my advice and don't come back,' his old friend told him.

When I came to the task of assembling the fragments of my father's life in the period after he was released from prison, I spent many hours reconstructing his trip in the spring of 1974 using old letters, tape-recording conversations with some of the people with whom he visited or stayed, retrieving my own memories of the weeks we spent together with family friends in Ireland.

That September of 1974 Sheka was due to leave his prep school, and my father was determined to secure him a place at an academically prestigious school in Elstree. My brother had recently sat his entrance exams and the headmaster of the school, who was minded to give him a place, had requested an interview with his father before they made their final decision. Among the many questions he was asked were several about the whereabouts of our mother—the school was nervous of being caught up in the middle of a custody fight, they were seeking reassurance. After the cards that arrived while my father was in detention we had not heard from our mother again. Of all the events that swirled around our lives, his life, the challenges he had seen and met, the one time my father confessed to feeling apprehensive was before that interview.

He stayed in St Albans with Brian Quinn and his wife Mary. Quinn now worked as an economist at the Bank of England and he had agreed to act as our guardian in Britain. A long-time confidant of our father, he warned him that letters from Freetown routinely arrived evidently opened and then clumsily resealed, and he added his voice to the many: he feared for his friend's safety if he continued to live in Sierra Leone under Siaka Stevens. But my father reassured him, as he reassured everyone, adding that he had spoken to Stevens to tell him he no longer harboured any political ambitions; he planned to devote himself instead to building up his new business. At that time, just free from prison, he was given to joking with people he knew well: it amused him to refer to himself as an 'unemployed, ex-detainee, ex-MP, ex-minister'. Quinn listened and nodded, but his disquiet remained all the same.

School broke up for the term and we all flew to Ireland, to family friends called the Rekabs in the Dublin suburbs. Our father left us there briefly while he visited the United States. In New York he saw the civil rights–era stage play *A Raisin in the Sun*.

Despite the play's renown and the fame of its author, Lorraine Hansberry—the first black woman to have a play staged on Broadway, who died when she was just thirty-four—I had never heard of *A Raisin in the Sun*. In June of 2001, for the first time in a decade and a half, the play was mounted at the Young Vic in London.

In the dark of the small auditorium I watched, mesmerised by the character of Asagai, a young African student dating Beneatha, the daughter of an African-American family. While Beneatha's family aspire to a life outside the ghetto, Asagai dreams of his country's independence. When the family's hopes of buying a new home—in a white neighbourhood—appear to be thwarted, Beneatha turns on Asagai:

> 'Independence!' But then what? What about all the crooks
> and thieves and just plain idiots who will come into power
> and steal and plunder the same as before—only now they
> will do it in the name of the new Independence—what about
> them?

To Beneatha, in her despair, progress has become an illusion and the human race is locked in an endless cycle of destruction. Asagai gives his reply:

> It isn't a circle—it is simply a long line—as in geometry, you know, one that reaches infinity. And because we cannot see the end—we also cannot see how it changes. And it is very odd but those who see the changes, who dream, are called 'idealists'—and those who see only the circle we call them 'realists'.

Walter, Beneatha's brother, is unimpressed and when Asagai is gone it is he who has the last word: 'You know what's going to happen to that boy someday—he'll find himself sitting in a dungeon, locked in for ever—and the takers will have the key!'

Did my father see himself in Asagai? Did the playwright's words strike him in the same way they struck me, straight to the core? Did he wonder then, after all the warnings, whether he should return to Sierra Leone? Or was there simply no question but that he would?

In America my father looked up a series of old friends from the weeks he had spent there while he was in office, and he paid a visit to John Karefa-Smart, who welcomed him warmly. In the three years since the arrests, contact between the former members of the UDP had eroded, the members were scattered or behind bars. There were a few meetings in the early days between those who had made it to the west, but by 1974 the party effectively no longer existed. Karefa-Smart had no intention of leaving his post as a professor of public health at Harvard to step back into the fray of African politics. He later remembered that their conversation had turned to business: my father asked his advice on contacting pharmaceutical and medical supply companies.

In Ireland I awaited my father's return with mixed feelings. I had pinched a packet of cigarettes from the lady whose house we were staying in, and lit them one by one in the garden, holding them between my fingers while they burned down to the filter, occasionally putting them to my lips and pretending to puff. One afternoon old Mrs Rekab looked out of the window and caught me, threatening to tell my father, though in the event she kept my misdemeanour between the two of us. I bought a book on the countryside and the four of us went walking in the hills, where I laid down bait to attract badgers in the bushes, planning to climb up there and wait for them after dark one night with a torch. With our father we planned a holiday in France at the end of the coming summer, so we could practise our French and our father could learn it. 'Seasons in the Sun' was top of the charts—it was our favourite song and we knew all the words by heart. At the end of April we flew back to London, where we went shopping for Sheka's school wardrobe for the coming year and bought new shoes for my ever-growing feet. We watched a movie, *Where Eagles Dare,* in a cinema where it played on a loop. Fleeing the rain we mis-timed our arrival so that we saw the ending first and then sat through the film again from the start. Our father gave us each a Timex, my very first wristwatch, and we finished the holiday eating together in a second-rate Chinese restaurant close to Victoria Station before we caught the train to Horley.

I later learned that in London our father also called on Sir Banja Tejan-Sie at the house in Cricklewood where the former governor-general lived exiled from his country. Sir Banja dreamed of his lost position and of being, once again, at the centre of politics in Sierra Leone. Years later I trod the path to the same house myself. By then Sir Banja was almost ninety. He sat in a high-backed chair at one end of the front room of a 1930s semi. The rest of the chairs in the room lined the walls in

a deferential semicircle. The former governor-general had telephoned my office after catching a political report I filed for the
BBC and asked me to visit him at his home. At the time I had no
idea who he was, but out of curiosity I accepted. I told Memuna
and Sheka about his call and suggested they come along too. Sir
Banja dominated the conversation, alternating between long-
winded speeches and bouts of flattery. He complimented me on
my abilities as a reporter and had even memorised sections of the
report's commentary; he seemed to be trying to discover whether
I had any political ambitions. But the moment he laid eyes on
Sheka, who arrived a few minutes late—the image of our father
and his eldest son—he appeared to lose interest in our conversation and turned his attention to my brother instead. A few weeks
later he sent me a set of gilded invitations to Westminster Abbey
to watch him receiving his latest set of honours from the queen.

Six years later I called on Sir Banja with the purpose of discovering what the two men had discussed during my father's visit long
ago. Sir Banja told me an extraordinary story. He claimed to have
had contact, back in the early 1970s, with Yasser Arafat, as well as
Mad Mike Hoare, the infamous South African mercenary whose
name has for ever been dishonourably linked with the Congo and
the war following the murder of Lumumba. Arafat, he said, had
offered to train forty fighters in Palestine to depose Stevens. Sir
Banja had been working on a plan during the time my father was
in prison. When the two men met he confided all to my father,
urging him—if he was interested in playing a role—to come back
and discuss the plan with him before he returned to Sierra Leone.

From London our father went on to visit pharmaceutical firms
in Frankfurt and outside Copenhagen. There he observed the
plight of the Greenlanders, and later commented to a friend
about Denmark's 'forgotten empire'; he was lonely, a loneliness

he described as clinging to him the whole time he was away from Sierra Leone, dispelled only by the presence of us, his children.

On his way back home he stopped over in London again, to wait for his flight to Freetown. News that the former finance minister and ex–UDP leader was in town had reached the student groups in London, and several of the young activists who had supported the UDP raced to meet his flight at the airport, but he avoided them, hurrying on past and out of the terminal building. In Cricklewood Sir Banja waited for him to return, but in the four days he was in London our father never went back to the former governor-general's house.

Sir Banja struck me as someone anxious to persuade other people of his own importance: after our first meeting he called me at home several times, sometimes late in the evening or very early in the morning, demanding to know why I hadn't been back to see him. I wasn't entirely sure who it was Sir Banja was more determined to persuade that he remained a player—himself or me. Sir Banja's story did not resonate with anything else I had so far learned, though by the time we spoke, after years of anarchy and banditry, the pale glow of Sierra Leone's diamonds had attracted foreign mercenaries to the country by the score. So I made call after call trying to find somebody who might verify what Sir Banja had told me, but not one other person, even those most closely connected with the events of the era, had ever heard rumours of a plot involving Yasser Arafat and Mad Mike Hoare in 1974.

As things turned out I never had the chance to question Sir Banja again. Just three days after our interview he collapsed and died on the pavement outside his home.

❧ 35 ❦

In another time, in another world, before he wrote a letter of resignation that was published in the newspapers, before he was arrested at the command of his one-time colleagues, before he was imprisoned for three years on the orders of his former friend, our father planned to build us a house. In his prison cell he spent hours drafting and redrafting his designs; in his letters to me he described the house in which we would all live before too long. We planned to start building and move out of our rented home in Kissy just as soon as the business was making some money, and in July of 1974 we sat around the dining-room table while he talked us all through the plans, infecting us with his enthusiasm for the project, and encouraging us all to add new features: a sewing room or a patio.

We were ten days into our school holidays, our summer holidays, although in Sierra Leone it was the rainy season. Just ten days. I didn't know the importance of those ten days then, of course, yet I remember them almost frame by frame. There was talk of the house, I remember that. And I remember swimming at Lumley, finding the water full of seaweed and thousands of tiny baby jellyfish, which stung us, sharp little pinpricks all over our bodies. I climbed up on my father's shoulders and refused to come down. 'Kung Fu Fighting' was the country's favourite song and it played constantly in bars, in the streets and from the drinking den on the opposite side of the gully. In the house we had our own craze for bingo and played boisterous games almost every evening. There was but one flaw marring the perfection, like a harelip on a newborn: Miss Dworzak.

At his offices in Walpole Street the Christmas before, our father had introduced the three of us to a young woman called
Adelaide Dworzak, a lawyer who was doing some work for him.
She was lively, effervescent and came from a well-known family.
Miss Dworzak, as we called her, joined us for lunch on that day
and from then on, whenever Mum wasn't around. She always
seemed to be there: dropping by the office to deliver some papers
or to ask him to sign a document, kissing us hello, and perching
on the edge of our father's desk while she talked—which she did
rather a lot, waving her hands about all the while.

Miss Dworzak was there again the next summer. We went for a
meal at the Cape Sierra, where Miss Dworzak laughingly encouraged me to order lobster, because I said I had never tasted it. The
waiter laid three lobsters at my feet. I chose one, glancing at my
father to check whether this was really all right. He was smiling.
I didn't fully grasp the purpose of the ritual with the lobsters, not
until I had finished eating. Only then did I realise the lobster on my
plate was the very one that had been alive at my feet half an hour
before. We swam afterwards, and then it rained. Goose bumps
covered my arms. I complained of the cold and Miss Dworzak
took off her white cardigan and placed it around my shoulders.

The sweater was still in my bag when I arrived home in the evening. I asked Mum's help in removing a tiny stain where I had spilt
something on the sleeve. Mum asked me to whom the cardigan
belonged. She said she wanted to talk to us. I fetched Memuna
and Sheka and we gathered in one of the bedrooms. There Mum
explained to us all about Miss Dworzak.

When Mum had finished she left the room, and we remained
alone still sitting on the bed. I turned towards the other two: 'Are
we not allowed to talk to Miss Dworzak any more? Not at all?'

'Mum doesn't want us to, but she says it's up to us,' Memuna
replied.

'But I like her, she's nice. Anyway, how is she going to break up our family? How can she do that?'

'Because she's Dad's mistress.' Sheka's voice was adult and deep. His tone made it sound as though the meaning were entirely obvious. He often acted that way, and it made me feel stupid, but truthfully I had no earthly idea what he was talking about. I sat there thinking about Miss Dworzak and what Mum had told us. True, I liked Miss Dworzak well enough, but I was afraid now, frightened that our family would be split up again, for the second time, for good even. The realisation travelled through me as a physical sensation: the saliva in my mouth dried up, my pulse drummed in my ears and my chest tightened against my lungs. The three of us agreed, there and then, that we would not utter another word to Miss Dworzak.

A day or two later we followed our father up to Miss Dworzak's office. Miss Dworzak greeted me, smiling her brilliant, orange-lipstick smile. 'Hello, my darling, what is it today? The beach again?'

I eyed Miss Dworzak for a moment. I pressed my lips together and remained silent. None of us uttered a word, not even to say hello.

At first Miss Dworzak didn't notice, she was too busy talking; it took a few more seconds for her to realise how rude we were being. But our father saw it immediately, he swung round looking at each of us in turn. He did not look pleased, but his expression was of bafflement rather than of anger. 'Say hello, kids.' His brow lowered, his gaze dropped on each of us, one after the other. 'What on earth is going on here? Say hello to Miss Dworzak!'

Nobody replied. We glanced at each other and looked down. I was nervous, I had never defied my father, but now I was angry with him. I gripped the floor with my toes to control myself, determined I would not be the first to break our pact.

Miss Dworzak must have sensed my wavering courage. Yes, she knew instinctively who was the weakest link. She was smart in that way. I felt her eyes rest on me; she beckoned me over. 'Come here, Am, come over here, darling. There, now you'll tell me what this is all about, won't you?'

I stood between the two of them, Miss Dworzak and my father. He towered behind me, while she bent down and took both my hands in her own, looking me straight in the eye. I couldn't meet her gaze. I bent my head.

'Come on, my darling. What's happened?'

'. . .'

'Am!' My father's voice was controlled and he spoke evenly. 'Will you please answer Miss Dworzak.' When I still didn't reply his frustration spilled over. 'What is wrong with you? What's wrong with the lot of you?' I didn't dare look at my father.

Miss Dworzak interrupted. She straightened up and put her hand on his arm: 'Leave them. It doesn't matter. You go on, I'll see you later.'

On the drive home our father was silent, his face clouded. I was worried he was about to demand an explanation from us, but as he drove, changing gear, the fingers of his other hand played upon the steering wheel, turning it in the direction of home; he didn't mention the matter again.

I was lying on my back on the edge of the surf with my eyes closed, watching the dark-orange glow of the sun behind my eyelids. With each wave the water rushed over my feet and ran up my calves. I creased my brow, concentrating, willing the motion of the waves to stop, just like King Canute, but they kept on rolling over me. When we were getting dressed to leave the beach I teased my father into trying to stop the tide. At first he demurred.

'Try, try, Daddy. Go on. Please, just try.' I urged him, giggling, pushing him from behind. I led him down to the water's edge.

He stood in front of the waves and put out his hand, palm flat to the Atlantic Ocean. 'Stop, waves. I command you,' he said in a reasonably theatrical voice. The next wave broke regardless: the water rushed over his sandals and soaked the hem of his trousers. I knew he couldn't stop the waves, but I had expected him to jump back, that was supposed to have been the fun of the game. I stared at his sodden trousers. 'You see, Am,' he said, 'I can't stop the tide.' That was Saturday.

Sunday. Mum and Daddy and Memuna and Sheka and I went to Auntie Nuhad's beach house at Juba. I don't remember too much about that day. Mandy, Nuhad's daughter who was our age, remembers playing with a blue, inflatable boat. Sarah Tejan, Nuhad's best friend, was there too, and she remembers it, an unremarkable day at the beach. Nuhad Courban was a striking, auburn-haired Lebanese woman, a wealthy socialite and hostess who moved in political circles. My father had known her for many years, and she was one of the remaining few with the courage to dare to be seen in his company. She was aware of his relationship with Miss Dworzak, and disapproved, not because she held any particular views on marital fidelity, but because she knew and liked Yabome. She had invited our family to spend the day with her and her daughter at the beach, to help heal the rift she could see opening up between the two of them. By the time we were ready for home it was already growing dark. As we packed up the picnic my father asked Nuhad if he could take the spare rounds of flat Lebanese bread—for Sheka, who was especially fond of it. She remembered that, an insignificant detail in an otherwise unremarkable day.

Monday. We seemed to have forgotten we had sent Miss Dworzak to Coventry, or we had failed to keep up our front, because there we were playing tennis at her parents' home, a pink, colonial-style house surrounded by high walls, with a tennis court that occupied most of the garden. I stood on the opposite side of the court from my father, playing against him with Sheka. Miss Dworzak stood next to a tray of cold drinks, watching from the sidelines. The ball sped past me, I moved towards it; my legs felt like concrete posts, I struggled to shift them. I felt as though I was locked into one of my dreams, trying to run: my limbs refused to engage or follow my brain's commands. I made an effort to lift up my arm to hit the ball, but I could barely hold the tennis racket. I missed. The ball hummed past me. Sheka glanced my way. Faintly, somewhere far away, I could hear my father calling to me to keep my eye on the ball. I heard the frustration in his voice and I wanted to please him, but I was tired and I couldn't play any more. I walked to the wooden bench at the side of the court and sat down upon it, my eyelids closing. Vaguely I saw Miss Dworzak come over; I heard her voice: 'Mohamed! For heaven's sake. This child is sick.' On the other side of the court my father tossed his racket aside and hurried over, frowning anxiously.

At home I slept for a while, and then I felt a bit better. I lay on my bed reading *My Family and Other Animals* until the early evening, when Sheka put his head round the door to tell me to come and look at the man whose arm had been blown apart.

The next day the rain comes down and the house is deserted. In the evening I stand in the sitting room making the preparations for a game: chairs drawn into a tight semicircle, fluttering squares of paper, unmarked cards, a bag of wooden numbers, matches in pink-tipped rows. Outside, under the flickering hum of the fluorescent light, two men stand with their backs against the night, watching everything I do. Two men with eyes like dank wells, wearing fake crocodile-skin shoes. I put down the cards and the matches and ask them what they want.

I leave the men where they are as I go to fetch my father from the master bedroom. I pass through the sitting room, down the hallway. I can see the closed door at the end of the corridor. It is painted brown, glossy brown. Down at my side I ball my hand up into a fist, ready to knock.

All my life I believed that it was I who went to fetch my father from his room the night Prince Ba and Newlove came to the house. But I was wrong. Outside, standing at the front of the house, Morlai had seen the CID car arrive and he had already spoken to the men. He directed them to the front of the house and watched as they began to make their way up the side stairs onto the veranda. Morlai did not follow them. He ran in the other direction, up the back staircase, through the kitchen and into the house, passing behind me as I counted out matches on the surface of the coffee table. Moments later I look up, notice the waiting men. Ask them what they want. Morlai hits his palm against the door of the master bedroom, a warning. He begs to be allowed to tell the officers from the CID that the doctor isn't home. But my father refuses. He comes out to face Prince Ba and Newlove, and meets me in the corridor just as I make my own way to the bedroom door.

Book Two

Book Three

36

Strange, how we managed to take up almost exactly where we left off twenty-five years before. I had not seen my cousin in all that time.

Morlai was dressed in green tweed trousers and lace-up shoes. The trousers looked as though they had been donated, sent out with the batches of second-hand clothes shipped to countries like ours, nobody worrying too much that they were inappropriate for the Tropics. Morlai's forehead was beaded with sweat and I handed him a tissue. He set his cup of tea down on the low wooden table and patted his brow.

'Do you remember how you were so sick, the day after Doctor was taken away? So sick! Because of what happened to your father.' He shook his head, sucked his teeth, flicked his fingers as though he'd touched something hot. Familiar gestures, every one. 'Ah, that day! That day. It was terrible.'

An image came to me of the way he used to amble along, shoulders thrown back as though he were gazing at the sky, trailing the back of his flip-flops along the ground and smiling. Now he was nearly fifty. In the last few years he had lost everything, seen two homes burned by rebel bands, hidden in the bush at the back of the houses with his wife and four small children, watching while his neighbours were lined up, pushed forward, one after another, to have their hands hacked off by narcotic-crazed child soldiers. Morlai's eyes were watery and clouded, but the smile, unbelievably, was there still.

'I had malaria,' I replied.

'The *very* next day!' Morlai ignored me and repeated himself with emphasis. 'The very next day! How could that be?' The story, I realised, had entered the family mythology, of how I took to my bed the morning after Prince Ba and Newlove came to our house. I was cold, shivering in the forty-degree heat, nauseous at the memory of the pappy, overly sweetened cereal I had eaten for breakfast. I lay in my bed and begged for a blanket. When Morlai brought it to me I threw up at his feet. My father had brought me home from the tennis game, intending to keep me under observation for a day or two. He thought I might have tropical flu, but he was more worried it looked like malaria. I realised now the only people who knew that were me—and my father.

In the panic that followed his arrest, I was forgotten. Eventually I went to see the doctor who ran the clinic at the end of the road. Memuna accompanied me, because Mum was spending most of her days at the CID headquarters. I remember sitting opposite the doctor, whose face was as lined as a walnut shell, watching as he filled out copious prescriptions. He gave them to me and ordered Memuna to take the same remedies. We were completely baffled by that: she wasn't even his patient.

By then the story was all over the papers. Our father had been arrested following an explosion at the house of Christian Kamara-Taylor, the minister of finance—at the very house where we had once lived at Spur Road. The authorities were calling it an attempted coup. The doctor, who must have had an unusually western mindset, had made up his mind my illness was psychosomatic and sent me home with bundles of chalky pills—placebos in all probability. A long time later I contracted malaria as an adult, following a filming trip to Mali—as soon as the symptoms appeared I recognised them.

'I really did have malaria,' I repeated. I told him how I knew—not that my father had already diagnosed it, but that I had had it again twenty years later. Morlai grinned at me. 'Anyway,' I added, 'you thought it was malaria at the time, too. I remember.' He had gone down with it himself a week or two later. He smeared mint toothpaste on his chest, a local remedy designed to bring the temperature down, devised by people who couldn't afford doctors' fees. He had put a little on my brow, too. But now he preferred the other version of the story. And so did I, except I knew it wasn't true.

We lapsed into silence. I took a sip of my tea. Morlai dropped several sugar cubes into his own cup, stirred the liquid and blew lightly across the top of it, wrinkling the surface. I looked out over the balcony of my stepmother's home. A few clouds were gathered on the horizon, the air was silted with the dust. A girl of about fourteen sat under the tree opposite, next to her a basket of smoked fish. She was idling the time away, singing to herself.

Automatically I scorned the idea that my illness was psychosomatic. Yet I could feel my response to being back in Sierra Leone and it was, in part, physical. Before I left London I woke up in the nights sweating with dread. Now I felt the apprehension: a shrivelling coldness. I shuddered involuntarily although it was late January, the harmattan was blowing itself out, within another month the temperature would reach its zenith.

The last time I was here, in 1991, there was no talk of war, just a few skirmishes up-country which Brigadier Joseph Saidu Momoh, Siaka Stevens's successor as president, played down to a public only too happy to ignore the inevitable for a little longer. Now I had returned to a scorched country, where anarchy and a civil war fuelled by diamonds and fought by children had been a way of life for nine years. The rebel army's hideous trademark mutilation of cutting off the hands from living victims had become the international emblem of this latest of African wars. I had seen the pictures and the footage sitting in my house in London: of farmers with stumps where there should have been hands holding hoes; mothers grasping babies in their truncated forearms; pretty girls with arms hacked off above the elbow.

The images played and replayed in my mind. I had arrived not knowing what I would find, in a country to which I felt deeply bound, whilst at the same time I feared it. For as long as I had lived my fate had been intertwined with this country. Yet Sierra Leone to me was both utterly familiar and ineffably alien: I knew it but I could not claim to understand it. But I was convinced of one thing. What happened to my family twenty-five years ago was just the beginning. The forces that set out to destroy us ended up destroying everything.

Santigi appeared to say hello. In all this time he had never left my stepmother's side. He must be over sixty but insists, to general amusement, he is no more than thirty. Mum pointed out that I, the youngest of the three children, am over thirty now, but that didn't deter him. Santigi clearly dyed his hair and was wearing dentures. In my presence he seemed overcome with shyness. He stood awkwardly, hands hanging by his side, while I kissed his cheek. I remembered them both as confident lads: the flares, the sunglasses, the illicit cigarettes, the slang phrases used to impress us. Morlai used to call me 'sister' and send me off into giggles every time. For a few minutes Santigi remained close by, leaning against the railing, watching us. Then he disappeared to start his chores, picking up the two chickens Morlai had brought for me to take to the kitchen.

A pair of live chickens: a precious gift for an honoured guest, all the more precious in the present climate when there was a shortage of chickens—of all food—in the city. By the end of the week we had received over a dozen birds from family and neighbours—mostly roosters, I noticed. They squawked and fought in a pen outside my bedroom window until one afternoon the cook went into the yard with a sharp knife. I had returned home bringing my husband Simon. People acknowledged both these facts with a symbolic offering. Home. But it hadn't felt like home for the longest time. It was lost to me many years ago, sometime in the mid 1970s.

I was still lying in bed, wrapped in blankets, when the CID men came to search our house. They rounded everybody up together in the sitting room, but they left me in my bed. From behind the veil of the mosquito net I watched the man searching my room. He pulled out each of the dressing-table drawers, rifled the contents and tipped them out. He opened the wardrobe. Printed summer dresses, cotton dungarees, bright shorts and beach shoes joined the heap on the floor. From the top of the cupboard he pulled down our empty suitcases, opened them up and tossed them aside. He wasn't one of the men who had arrested our father, though he had the same look about him: taut body, high forehead, sunken face with jutting cheekbones. He wore a large, cheap watch with a tarnished metal strap. His eyes and body roamed the room. I could hear the voices of other men as they moved through the house, shouting orders to Morlai to unlock doors. A second man put his head round the door and said something. The man searching my room grunted as he started flipping through my books, holding each one by the spine, shaking it, letting each one drop onto the floor face first, pages splayed open. He picked up my recorder from the music stand and put it back, carefully this time. Moments later he left the room, although I didn't register it at the time, without ever looking under my bed to where I kept my animal hospital.

Afterwards it was quiet. I waited a while. I opened the door of my room and crept out with bare feet. I stood at the door of my parents' bedroom. Empty drawers hung crookedly open; in the wardrobe a few items of clothing still clung to their hangers; the mattress was slumped between the bed and the floor; scattered at my feet were brown medicine bottles, wooden tongue depressors, gauze dressings—the contents of my father's upended medical bag. Mum was clearing up, and my cousins were helping her. I remember how none of us spoke; instead we worked in silence. Sheka was in his room, carefully replacing each item of his collection of objects back in the correct place on the shelf. Memuna and I tidied our room until everything was back where it had been, until we had made it perfect and obliterated all evidence of the CID's search. They came back time after time, but they never found anything. Once they confiscated a bottle of Mum's perfume, brandishing it as they left, claiming it was gun-cleaning fluid. We laughed at their stupidity—rather desperately, I recalled, because there was so little else to laugh at.

Morlai and I had not set eyes on each other since those days, but I had never forgotten him and always retained a special fondness for him above all my cousins. He wrote to me when the war was at its height, asking for help sending his children to school. Morlai's own education was interrupted, but he believed resolutely in the value of education. Throughout the worst of the fighting he kept on teaching his children, using a blackboard in the yard of the hut in which he now lives.

My stepmother appeared and joined us. She was sipping a cup of the decaffeinated tea I had brought for her from London. These days she worried about her blood pressure and her weight. She greeted Morlai warmly in Temne and asked after his family. There followed a rapid exchange and laughter. Morlai grinned, showing broad teeth, pulled his knees up and wrapped his arms around them, shook his head from side to side in a self-effacing manner. Morlai was protesting at something Mum had said, that much I could tell. He looked over at me and translated: 'Auntie Yabome is reminding me of the time I was a drunkard,' he said, laughing with embarrassment.

'A drunkard?' I smiled, a little uncertainly.

'Yes, a drunkard. For many years afterwards, I drank very heavily. I left Freetown, moved to Kamakwie. Auntie Yabome saw me around that time. This is what she is referring to. I was drunk for four years.' Mum interrupted again, saying something in Temne, but Morlai carried on until he had finished: 'For four years, just drinking. But I cannot tell you now how I felt, like we were going back into the darkness again.'

I had spent the final year of one millennium trawling through old newspaper reports, writing letters, rereading my father's letters to me, reading for the first time those he wrote to other people. I had traced minor and major players from the past, interviewed exiled politicians and his university friends. I had spent two weeks combing the British Foreign Office files released for public scrutiny under the thirty-year rule; I had even flown to Washington to visit the World Bank and to go through the files on Sierra Leone previously held by the State Department, which had been released several years earlier than their British counterparts. I slept in a borrowed apartment and made the two-hour journey every day out to the National Archives in Maryland. I had hundreds—maybe even thousands—of photocopies, dated and filed. I had dozens of tapes, catalogued and transcribed to fill several lever-arch files. I had a row of red A4 notebooks full of my own handwriting. In the end I could put it off no longer. In January of the new millennium I finally made good my resolution and travelled back to Sierra Leone.

It was impossible to fly direct to Sierra Leone any longer. No commercial airlines were willing to land at Lungi. I travelled to Freetown with Simon, through Banjul, where we spent two nights in a dreary beach hotel. The first evening we went out to get a couple of beers, walked down the dirty sand and past the rows of tourists on package holidays, lying in the sun while local men and children hovered a few feet away. Two plump young women stood up and strolled to the water; a couple of Gambian men fell quickly into step with them. They stood at the edge of the surf and watched while the women bathed and then followed them back up the beach, peeling away just before they reached the roped boundary of the hotel grounds.

The next day we left our hotel, sidestepped the beach bums loitering outside the entrance, and made our way through the dusty roads and walled compounds to a nearby suburb, to where Nuhad Courban lived. Many people had fled Sierra Leone for the relative safety of the Gambia, including Nuhad. She was beautiful still, her drop-dead elegance intact: copper hair, tanned skin, immaculately manicured fingers. We sat together, surrounded by orange hibiscus blossoms, in the garden of the bungalow where she lived. On the table between us lay a pack of cards arranged in an unfinished game of patience. On the telephone between London and Banjul Nuhad had told me a little of what she knew about the events of 1974, and in the couple of hours we talked she fleshed out her story.

On 30 July 1974, a few hours after the explosion in the early morning, people had thronged up to Spur Road to take a look at Kamara-Taylor's damaged house. Nuhad had accompanied her friend Sarah Tejan, who lived close by. Neither the house nor the garden was cordoned off; the place was empty save for the sightseers who wandered about at will. Nuhad walked up to the balcony to take a look at the shattered windows. From the outside of the house she peered through into the bedrooms. There was something not right. She noticed it immediately, even remarking on the fact to her companion.

'The beds were perfectly made. There were no indentations on the pillow, you know, where your head would lie. The top sheet was neatly pulled up. The broken glass was on top of the beds and hadn't been cleared off. You could see it plainly, the same in every room. Nobody slept in that house that night. I would swear an oath on it.'

She traced the layout of the house with her finger on the table, showing the position of the bedrooms and where the damage to the masonry, caused by the explosion, had been. I watched: I still remembered the layout of the house perfectly. The bedrooms upstairs all looked out onto a veranda, exactly the same as the one below, which curved around the back of the house. The dynamite had been thrown up onto the balcony.

'Later on everyone was remarking that no one slept there. Also, because no one was injured. No scratches . . . yet the glass splintered everywhere and the blast had gone off a foot or so away. By evening the whispers were all around town.'

Nuhad leaned back and took a breath. She offered me a cigarette and lit one for herself, apologising over the local brand. That evening when the family had re-emerged, she had even seen one of Kamara-Taylor's sons. He had recounted his story, insisting, she noticed, that he had been in bed asleep when it happened. In turn she congratulated him on his escape. She remembered she had added something about his hair—that he was lucky not to have any glass caught in his Afro; she'd felt a little silly as she said it.

Nuhad was arrested at her home later the same week and taken down to the CID offices. She was shown into a small room, full of shadows. There were several men in the room. None of them spoke. Nuhad was shown to a chair at the edge of the room, where she sat down. There was a name on the desk plate: Bambay Kamara, the deputy chief of the CID, a man she knew only by his reputation. The silence lengthened. A young woman was brought into the room and made to sit on a chair in front of the desk. One of the men began to question her. From the gist of the questions and the woman's frightened replies, Nuhad gathered that she was somehow related to Mohamed Forna, a cousin perhaps or a sister-in-law, and she was one of those who had been rounded up and was being held at Pademba Road. The woman pleaded. One of the men stepped forward and struck her sharply across the face. The woman screamed on and on: her cries served to incense her assailant all the more, and he struck her repeatedly until she slumped into silence. Nuhad watched in fear. The purpose of this awful display was not lost on her.

Bambay Kamara snapped his fingers and told one of the men to bring Nuhad a beer. She declined. He ignored her and repeated the order. The first woman was removed and a second brought into the room. She was cowering and Nuhad could see she was already badly bruised; a putrid odour arose from her. As the beating began again, Nuhad turned her face to the wall.

Later in the day Nuhad made a statement. She insisted upon writing it herself. She kept it brief, stating she was a friend of Mohamed Forna. The last time she had seen him was on Sunday when the family had been her guests at the beach. After she made her statement Nuhad was allowed home. By then, she guessed, members of her family must have begun to make calls to find out what had happened to her.

She was made to report to the CID every morning for a week, and on each visit she was made to wait, met with sly glances, calculated remarks, sexual innuendo, variations on an intimate intimidation. Finally a friend in the government recovered her passport and not long afterwards, at the urging of her mother to be gone as quickly as possible for her own safety, she flew out of the country, to Las Palmas, where she usually summered. She stayed away from Freetown for the next four months.

I left the Gambia the next day with Simon, catching an internal flight from Banjul's modern concrete-and-glass airport, built to impress the tourists on whom the country's economy depended entirely. We, who had not arrived as part of a package deal and were flying farther into Africa instead of out of it, received none of the honours reserved for holidaymakers. We arrived at six o'clock in the morning for the flight to Freetown and we waited there until midday. In between we stood in an interminable queue while our names were written by hand on the passenger list, queued again to have our bags searched, then sat on the concrete plinth around one of the pillars and played cards with a porter.

When at length the flight was called we crossed the tarmac to the plane and climbed the ladder. From the outside the West Coast Airlines aircraft looked respectable enough; inside was another matter entirely. The seats were tattered and stained, many of the seatbelts were broken, the overhead lockers were wooden and refused to open; instead our hand baggage was taken from us and thrown into a void in the tail of the aircraft.

As we waited in our seats before take-off I watched the two Russian pilots making their way to the cockpit. I wondered, briefly, what in the world could have brought these men to be here, commandeering an ageing aircraft in and out of unstable African states? Just as quickly, I put the thought out of my mind.

I spent the entire two-hour flight staring out of the filthy window at mangrove swamps, jungle and stretches of breathtaking coastline. My palms sweated. I was terrified we might crash. And then again, I was just as nervous of arriving, of being back in that country. As we circled in to land, where once there were fields of crops I saw precise rows of military tents, a helicopter landing pad, white tanks bearing the blue emblem of the United Nations. We taxied down the runway to a standstill, the only aircraft in the whole place.

Inside the old hall, which once thronged with people, three customs officials stood facing us. Between us on a bench lay our suitcases. They showed no signs of wanting them open, although I was already turning the combinations of the padlock. The officer nearest me, who had a peaked cap and tribal marks on his cheeks, waved for me to stop. He got straight to the point: 'What do you have for us?'

I wasn't sure I understood. 'There's nothing inside but clothes, personal stuff. I'm here to visit my family.'

'No.' He leered at my evident stupidity. 'What do you have for *we*?' He tapped his chest and then gestured along the line of customs officers.

'I don't have any leones,' I stalled. 'We've only just arrived. Maybe next time.'

He sniggered, 'Oh, we take all currencies,' sharing the joke with his friends. 'Sterling, dollars, ha, ha!'

I hesitated: I had been told to expect this. It was impossible to clear customs and immigration without bribing someone. I had a tape recorder and notepads in my bag, Simon had a set of professional cameras. They could make life very difficult and if I complained to their boss he would doubtless only demand an even larger sum from me, or worse, threaten to put me back on the plane. I dug into my bag and found a pound coin, reluctantly handed it to him. He inspected it and then passed it to one of his mates, who put it into his pocket. This is what we had come to. There was nothing particularly new in a customs officer looking for a tip. The change was in his attitude: corruption so shameless it didn't even attempt to hide. The man did not appear to know, much less to care, that there was a right way to behave.

The ferry was gone, sunk. So we completed the final leg of the journey to Freetown by helicopter, landing at the far end of Lumley Beach. The heliport was close to the army headquarters, and as our cumbersome passenger helicopter touched down I saw one of the sleek killing machines on loan to the Sierra Leone army take to the air. Manned by mercenaries, the attack helicopter flew low, almost skimming the surface of the water, guns prominent, elegant as a hovering mosquito.

My stepmother was waiting for us on the other side of the barrier. We hugged each other, loaded the car with our bags and the extra suitcase we had brought full of all the items that could not be easily bought in Freetown. As we turned out of the gate the driver began to turn to the right, the shortcut into Freetown. I sat forward: 'Do you mind if we take the beach road?' I asked. 'Would that be all right?'

'Of course not,' my stepmother replied. She passed the instructions on to the driver.

I turned to Simon. 'It's the most beautiful beach in the world,' I said. 'It's two miles long.'

37

I remember the first time I heard my father had been charged with treason—not who told me or how or when, I don't remember that at all. Instead I remember what I thought about it. The word spoke to me of olden times, of history lessons at school, of Lady Jane Grey, of the young Elizabeth I sitting outside Traitor's Gate, or Sir Walter Raleigh, Elizabeth's fallen favourite, of Joan of Arc engulfed in a halo of flames. I thought of Guy Fawkes surrounded by kegs of gunpowder below the Houses of Parliament. I didn't realise people could still stand trial for treason, and I couldn't see what it had to do with my father.

In London, in 1999, quite by chance I had been given the name of a lawyer from Sierra Leone. I didn't know what he might have to tell me, but I had learned that he worked in the attorney-general's office in Freetown at the time of my father's arrest. So I drove to Stratford in the East End of London, looking out for a pub called the Rising Sun—the landmark he had given me—which was on the corner of the road where he ran a legal advice centre. We met at the end of the day, when the dark was closing in. I parked the car and walked towards his office. The wind was bitter and it had started to rain. I rapped on the glass door and a genial-looking man approaching sixty emerged from behind a screen in the open-plan office, released the latch and let me in.

My conversation with Tejan Savage was a turning point for me, though he didn't know it and I was a stranger to him. In the last quarter-century a silence had descended over our family. We rarely spoke of the past. In our teens and twenties Memuna

and Sheka and I used to swap whatever information we had—
information gathered from our compulsive rifling and eavesdrop-
ping: fragments of the truth. Even then we talked in secret, always
in secret. I remember us in a smart wine bar in Covent Garden
sometime in the 1980s, muting our voices so no one would hear
us, unable to break the conditioning of our childhood.

When I made a new acquaintance I did not tell that person
my story. If the same person became my friend I might volunteer no more than the barest facts. People are bored or dismayed
by African politics, there is no glamour in the association, just
shame—a collection of failed states which have never learned to
govern themselves—the subject just made people uncomfortable.
But partly I did not volunteer any information because, well, I
didn't have much to give.

That day after my conversation with Tejan Savage I drove back
to my house through the dark and the rain, music playing on the
car radio. I didn't feel elated exactly; instead I felt gratified. I had
broken the years of self-imposed censorship: I had spent an hour
talking about events that had shaped my destiny. I had broken
the restraints for good.

Tejan Savage had been working as a state's counsel in the offices
of the attorney-general in August 1974 when the Criminal Investigation Department sent over several boxes of documents: the
results of their investigation into the explosion at Kamara-Taylor's
house. It was the job of the attorney-general's office to assess the
facts and the possible charges. In the morning all the state's coun-
sels were summoned to a conference. By the end of the morning
they had concluded there was no case to answer.

'We decided by a clear majority,' Tejan Savage explained,
slowly and with a lawyer's precision. 'The evidence conflicted
over whether Kamara-Taylor was at home or not. He said he
was, but then there were at least four witnesses who said he was

not. All the evidence was circumstantial. There were meetings at Murraytown. One witness said Mohamed Forna was present, at a time when he himself said he was up-country. There was nothing there that would amount to treason under the Treason and State Offences Act.'

The attorney-general was due to present his opinion to the president the next day. But there had been a leak from within the department to the offices of the vice-president, S. I. Koroma. Tejan Savage did not say how he knew this. But I already knew it was S. I. who had personally given the order to have my father arrested. That afternoon, at four o'clock, an unscheduled emergency cabinet meeting was called. An immediate reshuffle was announced. One member of the government was moved from his post: Luseni Brewa, the attorney-general. He was replaced by another man, N. A. P. Buck. Buck lost no time at all in publicly announcing charges of treason. And he eschewed the talents of his own department, bringing in instead an external lawyer of his own choosing.

The Monday after I arrived in Freetown we drove into the city centre, slowing every few hundred yards to pass between army checkpoints. Some were manned by UN soldiers, their blue helmets visible behind a wall of sandbanks, weapons aimed at the passing vehicles. Others were guarded by soldiers from the Sierra Leone army—the SLA—sullen-faced and sleepy. I felt unaccountably nervous, uncertain of whether to nod to the soldiers or feign indifference. As though my uncertainty was as visible as a flag, the very first time we passed through a checkpoint the soldier waved our car to a halt and insisted upon searching the boot before allowing us through.

The city was swamped with refugees living in makeshift camps. Around the Cotton Tree beggars reached into the windows of passing cars, imploring us for a few leones. Here and there among the crowds on the pavement I saw several of the amputees, bandages carefully wrapped and neatly folded, pinned around the stump of arm where their hands had once been. The roads around State House were surrounded by army cordons. The president and cabinet had decamped to a lodge up in the hills above Freetown. Many of the government buildings had been razed and they were operating out of temporary offices.

I had never read an account of my father's trial and I wanted a copy of the court transcripts, but from early on I realised even this simple task was not going to be straightforward.

Sierra Leone had not experienced proper, working government for decades and finally descended into anarchy by the close of the twentieth century. Joseph Momoh, who was handed the leadership by Siaka Stevens, ruled as a puppet of his own ministers for seven years. The people nicknamed him Josephine Momoh or Dandogo, meaning 'fool' in his own Limba language. During his years of rule he never devised a coherent policy on any single issue; instead he allowed his ministers to run their departments unchecked, typically as they had done in the past—for personal profit. Freetown gradually slid into deepening chaos. Civil servants, teachers, doctors and nurses went unpaid not for months, but for years. Blackouts became the norm rather than the exception; the water from the taps trickled, slowed and dried; petrol was in short supply; abandoned cars littered the streets; bands of stray dogs feasted on growing mountains of uncollected household waste. Government workers stopped going to the office or were forced to take additional jobs to feed their families; whole ministries were emptied as discontented employees pilfered and sold the office furniture.

On 29 April 1992 a band of young soldiers drove a truck down Tower Hill and along Independence Avenue, where they rammed

the main gates of State House. Momoh cowered inside his official residence before fleeing by helicopter to Guinea. Valentine
Strasser, a handsome, twenty-seven-year-old captain, took to the
public airwaves and declared himself Sierra Leone's new leader.
None of the members of the new National Provisional Ruling
Council was more than thirty years old, and none had any experience of government. Most had just been recruited into the army
to deal with increasing disturbances along the Liberian border.
For the first time in years the army had been issued with weapons,
and they used them to seize power. Strasser was chosen as leader
for the sole reason that he alone spoke English sufficiently well
to broadcast their communiqué to the world.

   Up-country the Liberian guerrillas who had been conducting
cross-border raids on villages in Sierra Leone were joined by a
new outfit calling themselves the Revolutionary United Front and
led by a Sierra Leonean former corporal called Foday Sankoh.
The RUF drove through the countryside, abducting children and
adolescents, forcing them to kill and dismember their own families, using drugs to urge them into battle, crudely amputating the
feet of any who tried to escape. Sankoh, who in his satellite telephone interviews with the BBC World Service swore revenge on
the corrupt politicians in Freetown, vented his hatred instead on
the country's poorest and most helpless, people living in villages
hundreds of miles from the capital. Meanwhile in Freetown the
NPRC elite were living up to the reputation of their APC predeces-
sors, driving smart cars, living in luxury homes, partying loudly
into the night and reportedly flying to Europe with pocketfuls of
diamonds to sell.

   In the countryside soldiers of the SLA went on the rampage,
looting, raping and killing, determined to enjoy the fruits of
power in the way their bosses in Freetown were doing. Some
of these bands of soldiers met up with RUF rebels to wage joint

campaigns—people called them 'sobels', soldier-rebels. At the end of 1995 Strasser was overthrown by his own vice-chairman, left the country and enrolled as a law student at a university in England. His only contribution to the country had been to introduce Cleaning Saturdays, when everybody, man, woman and child, was obliged to take part in a joint effort to clean the streets on the last weekend of every month. As it happened, Cleaning Saturdays had considerably outlasted the NPRC, and as I drove through the residential areas of Freetown I noticed the streets were undeniably tidier since the last time I had visited, just before Strasser's takeover.

The new NPRC chairman, Bio, determined to halt the elections scheduled for the spring of 1996 under pressure from the international community and banking organisations. At the polls the soldiers fired rocket grenades into voting lines, used their bayonets to tear the ink stamp from the hands of voters, careered through towns and cities firing into the air, seizing ballot boxes at gunpoint. The people refused to be deterred. Groups of women took to the streets and faced down the soldiers. My stepmother was among them. On the morning of the election, while armed soldiers roamed the streets firing at random to intimidate would-be voters and most people remained locked in their homes, she left the house on foot, joining her colleagues, collecting each woman, one by one, from her home on their way to man the polling booths.

But the newly elected president could not halt the turmoil outside the capital. Freetown had become a city under siege. Convoys of refugees arrived every day with tales of carnage, bearing the scars of horrible mutilation on their own bodies. New factions began to arise. The West Side Boys, who favoured Tupac Shakur T-shirts and mirror sunglasses, terrorised the outlying villages around Freetown. In the south a militia of traditional hunters arose to guard their own villages. The Kamajors decorated their costumes with charms and mirrors to deflect enemy bullets and they were victorious in their clashes with the RUF. Thousands flocked to join them. Sierra Leone had a second armed force and this one answered to the Mende defence minister alone, a certain Hinga Norman—the man who had stepped forward and stopped my father's swearing-in ceremony back in 1967. In Freetown the newly elected President Kabbah and his cabinet floundered. People who had risked their lives to vote were bitterly disappointed—'*Momoh way don go school*' was the comment on the street; a Momoh who just happened to have an education.

On 25 May 1997, a date etched on the memory of every person in Freetown, soldiers stormed Pademba Road Prison and freed some of their officers who were being held there. The soldiers invited the RUF to join them in a coalition government, and for one terrible week the two forces went on a looting spree across the capital. They were like deranged, murderous children let loose in a sweet shop: anything they wanted, they seized, anyone who stood in their way they slaughtered. When soldiers appeared for the third time at her home, threatening to kill everyone, demanding money and alcohol, my stepmother fled.

After enduring two days of shelling and gunfire at the Cape Sierra Hotel, my stepmother was airlifted out by American GIs who landed helicopters on Lumley Beach in defiance of the blustering rebel army. She arrived in Britain as a refugee, landing at Stansted in the middle of the night with nothing but a borrowed handbag. She lived in Britain for a year before we deemed it safe enough to return home. In Freetown Nigerian troops had been brought in as part of an international deal to retake the city by force and to halt the spread of anarchy which was beginning to threaten the whole region. The government in Sierra Leone issued assurances that they were back in charge, occupied only with wiping out a few pockets of resistance around the diamond fields. Early one dark October morning I drove Mum out to Terminal Three at Heathrow Airport, where I waved her goodbye. I watched her hurry through immigration, chatting to a friend she had met who was on the same flight. She forgot to look back at me; she was happy to be going home. Outside the rush-hour traffic was building: the drive home would take hours, so I walked up to the viewing gallery, where I searched for her plane among the flock of aircraft lifting into the sullen sky.

On 6 January 1999 the RUF invaded Freetown for the second time. They called their onslaught 'Operation No Living Thing': they sacked the city, killed and maimed hundreds, possibly thousands, of people, forced civilians to march ahead of the advancing troops as a human shield. Those who hesitated or refused were burned alive. The images—dogs feeding on piles of corpses in the streets, terrified civilians caught in sniper crossfire, child soldiers brandishing AK-47s—filled the television screens of viewers all around the world. Rebels and Nigerian-led peacekeepers alike were shown casually carrying out summary executions. Bizarrely, through most of it the international lines kept on working. I spoke to my stepmother from my own sofa, a soap opera flickering on the television in the corner, while over the lines came the sound of shelling and gunfire drawing closer to the house where she sat with the doors bolted and the lights switched off. I clung to the receiver, and it seemed to me so did she, touching fingertips across the thousands of miles, drawing out the conversation. I tried to think of something remotely useful to say. I felt hopelessly inadequate. In the end there was nothing left to do.

'Mum, I'd better go. Goodbye,' I said.

'Goodbye, Am,' quietly.

'I'll call again, I promise.' Another shell went off. Somebody in the room behind her shrieked. 'Goodbye,' I repeated. I didn't replace the receiver immediately; I waited to make sure she had gone. Sometime in the night a shell landed on the telephone exchange. I didn't get through again for another week.

Since that day the invaders had been repelled. And a year on hundreds of UN troops and several contingents of British troops patrolled the streets. But the city remained in a state of shock and nervous unease. Sierra Leone was a 'collapsed' state, the term western diplomats and agencies used to describe a nation effectively without a working administration. Left to its own devices the government was incapable of running the country.

I climbed the stairs of the Roxy building, where the Court of Appeal registrar was housed. The name I had been given was Thomas Gordon, the clerk in charge of the archives, whose office was on the first floor of the building. Morlai waited outside while Mum and I went in. The staircase was dark and littered; down the central well of the building water leaked continuously and green slime streaked the walls. At the bottom was a pile of debris thrown from the open windows, soaked and rotting. Along the corridor which led to the clerks' offices the smell from the latrines almost made me retch. I held my breath and hurried on.

Thomas Gordon, we were informed, was not in yet, but on his way from home. So we sat down on a wooden bench next to his desk. A man lay slumped across the desk on the opposite side of the room, fast asleep at eleven o'clock in the morning. Nobody in the office where we waited or in the adjoining offices, where we could hear the woman who a few seconds past had shown us in chatting to her colleagues, actually seemed to be engaged in doing any work. The desk in front of me was empty save for a large old-fashioned black telephone. Heaped on the floor were dozens of documents thrown in haphazard heaps. I could see they were trial transcripts, originals and probably irreplaceable. We waited there for an hour. I had already started to lose patience, but at Yabome's urging I managed to hold on.

Some time after midday the man at the desk opposite woke up. He wiped his face and gazed at us. 'Can I help you?' he said.

'We're waiting here for Mr Gordon.' My stepmother smiled urbanely, becoming newly occupied with the contents of her handbag. She didn't appear to want to venture much more.

'And what is the nature of your business?'

'We're here to collect some transcripts,' I butted in.

'What is the name of the case?' he asked. He opened an exercise book on his desk and picked up a stub of pencil. I thought we might be about to get somewhere.

'Mohamed Forna and Fourteen Others.'

'Oh.' He pondered a while. He didn't write anything down but continued to look at me. In turn I noticed he was quite young, younger than me by about ten years. 'What do you want with these papers?'

'I'm doing some research,' I answered.

'What kind of research?'

'Just some personal research. It's a family matter.'

The man looked at me, raised his hand and levelled his index finger. 'What's your name?'

'My name? Aminatta Forna.'

He peered at me more closely, inspecting my hair, my western clothes and manner; shades of disbelief crossed his face. 'Are you his wife?'

'Whose wife?' I asked. I was completely nonplussed.

'The man whose case you are interested in.'

'No, I am not,' I said flatly, rudely.

He seemed about to ask another question, then abandoned the idea. He folded his arms and laid his head down again. Just before he did so he remembered there had been a point to our conversation. 'You must see Thomas Gordon. He will be here shortly.' And he went back to sleep.

We left and came back half an hour later. By then Thomas Gordon had been in and gone again, this time over to the court building, they said. Someone offered to telephone him there. In time Thomas Gordon himself appeared. He looked like an archetypal Krio civil servant, lacking only his bowler hat and cane. He wrote down our request on a piece of torn paper, and then began to search through some of the piles of documents on the floor at his feet, apparently at random. After a few minutes he appeared to give up and made a couple of telephone calls. Finally he told us to return the next day at the same time, when a copy of the proceedings would be made available to me. He told us there would be a charge.

'How much?' I asked.

'Well, that's up to you,' he replied enigmatically, smiling, not moving to get up or to shake my hand. In the end we agreed a ten-thousand-leone 'research' fee. I counted the notes and remembered what the leone had been worth the day I offered to buy the British high commissioner's house, when I was six years old. It was then two leones to the pound. Now it was close to three thousand and the currency was recognised nowhere in the world except in Sierra Leone.

I went back the next day, and the day after that—in fact I went back every day for a month. Sometimes I succeeded in seeing Thomas Gordon, sometimes I didn't. I was sent to the high court registrar in another building, where I filled out a form and waited two days, only to be told that what I needed to do was submit a letter to the head of department stating which documents I required, and the reasons why I wanted them. No one seemed to know where the documents were actually held or if they existed at all. If they did, they didn't seem inclined to share the information.

There came a point when I realised the pursuit was futile, but by then I couldn't seem to extricate myself. I had become locked in a system where form existed without function: a labyrinthine procedure of no relevance to the final outcome which, anyway, seemed unimportant to everyone except me.

Each time I went up to the court registrar's office I passed the burned-out shell of the law courts. They had been built by the British in the nineteenth century and the grand white-and-blue colonial facades were surprisingly intact. Crows had built their nests on the window ledges, untidy heaps of sticks around which the large black birds hopped and squabbled. But through the gaping windows there was just a great void: floors, ceilings, walls, whatever had once been there was reduced to a pile of rubble.

❦ 38 ❦

On the way back to the house later in the day I noticed the ruins of the old CID headquarters. It had been one of the first buildings razed by the rebels on January Sixth. Foday Sankoh, the RUF's leader, had been held there once and imprisoned at Pademba Road during the 1970s; in fact he had been in detention during the same period as my father. He was held in Wilberforce, while my father was in Clarkson. After Sankoh was released he had sworn revenge on the APC government and retreated to the bush to raise his merciless ragtag army of bandits and children. I had been told that Sankoh, who came from the north of the country, had on more than one occasion maintained he was related to our family. It was more than a remote possibility, given the size of most polygamous African households. In Sierra Leone, with its then population of four million, there are fewer degrees of separation than in most places. It was even said by some that this terrible war was in some way a revenge for our father's fate. Sankoh was not the first to try to lay claim to my father's legacy, but he was perhaps the least likely.

As I watched a man stepped out from behind a ruined wall of the CID building, casually zipping his fly with one hand. I could see, through the empty doorway, other men facing the walls. It dawned on me that the place, so closely associated with the terrible events of the past, was now no more than a makeshift public toilet.

Morlai told me his story of what happened when he was arrested and taken to the CID. I found him the next morning, sitting on a low wooden stool at the back steps watching the cook fry plantains for breakfast. Another pair of chickens had been delivered for Simon and me, a white cockerel and a small brown hen. I sat down next to him, still in my dressing gown.

At daybreak on the morning after our father had been arrested Morlai returned to the CID carrying a tray of tea and bread for both our father and Ibrahim Taqi, who by then had also been arrested. He walked towards the main entrance, but there he was pushed back by the guard. Outside in the car park he protested. The guard struck him hard across the shoulders with the butt of his rifle, the tray toppled and the hot tea spilled on the earth. Morlai picked up the pieces and came home.

When the CID came to search our house a few days later Mum had been in town. She was on her way home, driving down Kissy Road, when a Fulah man, who owned a stall selling sweets and cigarettes in front of the flat and store where Abu Kanu lived, hurried over to her car where she stopped in the traffic. The Fulah trader hissed through the car window: 'Missus, den been cam na dis house, den been dae talk say den dae go na Doctor Forna een house.' The CID had visited and said they were on their way to our house next.

Mum drove home as fast as she dared. She pulled up outside the house and ran up the back stairs calling for Morlai. She and Morlai were standing in the master bedroom when the officers entered. They asked who he was and demanded to know what he was doing there. Morlai replied that he was a servant, changing the sheets on the bed. A woman officer walked up and stood directly in front of him. She asked his name.

'Morlai Sorie,' Morlai answered, unwilling to give his real surname.

Her eyes travelled to his breast pocket. She leaned forward and plucked out his college identity card. On the back it read: 'Morlai

Forna, c/o Mohamed Sorie Forna.' The woman slapped him hard across both cheeks. When the search of the house was complete they pushed Morlai down the stairs and bundled him into the back of the Land-Rover.

There Morlai paused in his story for a moment. Ola, my step-mother's young niece, appeared on her way to school. She bobbed a small curtsy towards each of us. Morlai and I nodded back and greeted her. She smiled shyly. Her hair was done up in tiny braids that reached from the edge of her scalp to the crown of her head, where the ends fanned out like pineapple leaves. Her oiled skin shone, dark and glossy as a tamarind seed. The evening before, Simon and I had driven down to the beach for a beer at sunset. We sat at a makeshift bar on the sand, watching a group of small boys playing in the sand. I had been charmed by their naked, abandoned play, until I realised what they were doing. They were belly-crawling across the sand, executing perfect mil-itary manoeuvres. The barman said they came from the rehabil-itation centre for child soldiers a few miles away, what was once a luxury beach hotel. I let my eyes follow Ola as she went to say good morning to the other members of the household; her genteel manners seemed to belong to another age entirely, not a world in which children of her age were turned into blank-eyed killers.

After she had gone Morlai resumed his story. He spoke, as ever, without a trace of self-pity. Once or twice he even laughed in a wry sort of way: 'People used to say there was a machine at CID,' he told me. 'That they used to flog the prisoners. It was supposed to be some sort of mechanical whipping machine. If they put you in that room, ah, you'd be calling on God to help you.'

The room was dark and smelled of chemicals. Morlai guessed it was used as a darkroom. He was left standing in the middle, turning his head this way and that, trying to make out shapes in the darkness. Then, without warning, came a whistling sound, and suddenly he was struck on the back of his legs, across his buttocks, across his chest. From all around him lashes cut through the air and into his body, striking him from every direction. He tried to jump, he held up his arms to protect his face. From the occasional shuffle and sound of breathing he guessed the blows were being dealt by men. Men who stood in each corner of the darkened room, armed with flexes. After a while he was dragged out.

Later he was taken to be interrogated. Morlai pleaded he was a student who lived in his uncle's house. He knew nothing. Someone behind him was smoking a cigarette and touched the glowing end to the skin of Morlai's back. Just when Morlai thought he might faint, his interrogators gave up. He was pushed into a holding pen where twenty or so men lay listlessly on the floor. There was no food, no toilet, only a small amount of water. Through the bars he could see the comings and goings as more suspects arrived. He didn't see anyone he recognised. After two days they let him go.

Two days, during which I was too ill to notice Morlai wasn't there. I remember how quiet the house was, though, as I drifted in and out of sleep. I thought little of it. I didn't realise we had become pariahs. No one came near us. The daily visitors, friends, the endless petitioners, the folk from up-country who came to pay their respects, the neighbours who stopped by and sat on the back veranda for hours playing draughts, slapping the wooden discs down on the outsize, handmade board—all had disappeared. The house had always rung with voices; now it was deserted. Mum, the most security conscious of individuals, even stopped bothering to lock the door when we all went out. If the CID turned up for an impromptu search at least they wouldn't break the locks. Even a thief wouldn't be caught dead near our house.

Around that time Mum too was detained. It was Prince Ba who came for her. By then our father and Ibrahim Taqi had been moved into cells at Pademba Road Prison, where they were being held in solitary confinement and refused all visitors. Miss Dworzak had tried to see my father, insisting she was his lawyer and should have the right. They arrested her, too. By then the round-up had begun in earnest: hundreds of people were being brought into the CID every day and crammed into the filthy holding pen until there was barely room to sit.

Women were brought in among the male suspects; many were wives of the men who had been arrested. One of the new intake was a heavily pregnant woman. Mum heard she later gave birth in Pademba Road. My stepmother was led to a narrow cell containing nothing but a chair. She could hear people protesting: someone's sister called out that she had only arrived in Freetown the day before for the Bundu initiation ceremony of her niece. The air was stifling. It stank of sweat and carried the sickly sweet odour of sewage. High up was a barred window, too high to see out. She sat on the chair and waited through the day. Nobody came.

In the early evening the door was unlocked. It was Prince Ba again. He told her she was being taken to Pademba Road. Mum's heart was beating fast, but she forced herself to walk slowly to the Black Maria and climbed into the back. Prince Ba locked the doors and walked round to the passenger seat. The vehicle turned out of the CID compound for the short drive to the prison gates. They pulled up and Prince Ba ordered her out. My stepmother gazed up at the tall, painted doors and waited for him to lead her inside, but Prince Ba was no longer there. She glanced round and saw him climb back into the front seat of the Black Maria and drive away. She was left to make her way home.

That autumn Memuna ran away from school. A neighbouring farmer brought her back, late one night. He had found her cornered by his dogs, hiding in a tree on the edge of his land. The next morning at breakfast the story was the talk among the pupils in the dining room. Before morning assembly I searched Memuna out, but my sister would not confide in me.

As for me, I just turned wild. I hid behind the library building and flung a stone at Marius Georgiades, who had looked up my skirt while I swung from a rope in the playground. I turned out to be a better shot than I had anticipated. In the headmaster's office I stared at the blue-and-yellow egg on Georgiades's right temple with awe. I was placed on Daily Report, a sort of suspended sentence, which required my teachers to enter a written assessment of my behaviour at the end of each class. I had to carry around a small blue notebook for the purpose and I could be stopped at random by teachers and prefects and obliged to produce it. If I failed, I could be punished.

At Halloween I sat outside the headmaster's study listening to the sounds of my friends as they bobbed for apples. I was not permitted to attend the party. There were only two pupils in the whole school who were on Daily Report. I was one, Robert Payne was the other. Robert Payne's reputation as a troublemaker was legendary and I was shocked to find myself in his company. We sat at opposite ends of the short corridor writing a composition on the story of the Willow Pattern. Robert Payne was taking the whole thing in his stride, urging me to join him and creep down the stairs to watch the party. But I felt desperately ashamed. I sat and wrote my essay out diligently, the blue-and-white patterns of the engraving in my textbook swimming through my tears.

A month later I was Robert Payne's equal. I swore at the matron and had my mouth washed out with soap; I fought in the playground; I gave up listening in class and stared out of the window; once I sat at the back of a French lesson firing missiles at the rest of the class until I was thrown into the corridor. The teachers were appalled by my behaviour. So were my friends, who one by one drifted away from me. I spent more of my time alone. I was incapable of analysing my behaviour or controlling it and I swung from one misdeed to another.

Towards the end of term an exhibition of antique Bibles was mounted in the school library. The headmaster made the announcement from the podium of the main hall. The books had been loaned by a private collector and the headmaster was evidently proud and pleased our school should be honoured and entrusted with the safe keeping of these priceless objects. A rota was to be drawn up so that over the weeks that followed everybody in the school would have the opportunity to see these rare and beautiful books.

In due course it was the turn of my class. We walked over to the wooden library building and for forty minutes we gazed in silence. There were at least a dozen different Bibles from earlier centuries: pages of tiny brown script on paper that was transparent with age; blue-black letters boldly printed on rough-textured leaves; columns of italic letters on wide, creamy pages. In the centre of the room was a Book of Hours, laid wide open on an empty table. I stared at the ornate lettering, the prayers, immaculately written by the hand of some long-dead monk, the gilded borders of the pages filled with the images of saints, their faces blank, their bodies intertwined with vines and flowers. On the next table was a tiny Bible, no more than an inch or two tall. Several of us gathered around it. Our teacher, glancing over our heads, told us it was almost certainly the smallest Bible in the world.

One evening not long afterwards I walked past the library. It was during prep and I was alone. It was almost dark. On a whim I decided to try the library door. It was open. I entered the darkened room, illuminated only by the light of the rising moon, which glimmered through the high windows. I stood there alone, surrounded by Bibles. I peered at the Book of Hours and again at the miniature Bible. Dark bookshelves crowded around me. Above me, among the rafters of the vaulted ceiling, some creature or bird scratched. Once we had found an owl sitting fast asleep on the cross beam in the library. Another time it was a bat, hiding in the folds of the curtains. I heard the sound of the supper bell and the faraway clamour of voices that rose in response. I worried suddenly about being locked in, or being found there at all. We were only allowed in the library during supervised periods. I moved back towards the door and opened it slightly. I hovered there for a second. Then, on an impulse that came out of nowhere, I turned back, reached out my hand, grasped the miniature Bible, put it in my pocket and slipped out, pulling the door shut behind me.

I joined the flow of pupils heading for supper. All through the meal I could feel the Bible lying in my pocket. At bed time I transferred it under my pillow and laid my head on top. I didn't think about what I was doing, I didn't pray or anything like that, although every now and again I slipped my hand underneath the pillow and held tightly on to the little book.

In the morning I woke to the memory of what I had done. I pulled up the covers of my bed and sat on top of it, lingering there until most of the girls had dressed and left the dorm. Beverley alone waited to walk down with me. I hesitated, not knowing what to do. I decided to try to secrete the Bible back into my pocket, but I was made clumsy by nerves and as I reached under the pillow my fingers fumbled and I dropped the book onto the floor.

Beverley's eyes went to it immediately. 'It's the little Bible!' she exclaimed. I could hear the surprise in her voice. I snatched it and shoved it into my pocket.

'No it isn't. It's mine. It's not the Bible, just a little book.'

Beverley didn't argue with me. She didn't even ask to inspect the book I was claiming was my own. Who knows why? She must have realised what she had seen. An hour later, after morning assembly, I ran out ahead of the other children as we made our way to the classrooms for early registration. The library door was still unlocked. I exhaled. I went into the empty library and I put the tiny book back on the table.

39

I trekked up the rutted track, abandoning the car with Dura the driver, to walk the last half mile or so to the houses. Along the way Morlai and I were joined by a young woman with a limp and a curled forearm. She spoke to me in English and told me her name was Aminata. I remarked we had the same name.

'I know,' she replied. 'I'm your cousin.'

Many of my aunts and uncles, along with my numerous cousins, now lived together in a large compound on the outskirts of Freetown. They had fled Magburaka in the last year, after the rebels captured the town. Magburaka and Makeni were now the twin capitals of the rebel stronghold in the north, under the control of the notorious RUF commander Colonel Issa and his men. No one had dared to return.

Adama, the most senior of my aunts, came out to greet me. Her eyes were as blue and hazy as an overcast sky. Cataracts, I realised. Her deep, matt complexion was lined by the sun and the wind; she looked as though she had been sketched in charcoal. Although she was over eighty, it seemed to me her beauty had barely diminished. Increasingly I found some faces were imprinted on my memory, while others faded. I remembered Adama well from our visits to Magburaka. She hugged me hard and looked into my face. '*Seke*,' she said. '*Seke*, Aminatta.' In the air between us hung twenty-five years, two continents and a war.

The compound teemed with children. There seemed to be hundreds of them, swooping like herons over a shoal of fish as they raced after a football. A woman washed clothes at a stand pipe in the corner; several children swirled sticks around the muddy puddle beneath. A small boy sashayed towards me, swinging his hips in a mock effeminate walk. On the bench next to Adama an older boy sat hunched, feet dangling loosely above the floor. His lids were half-closed, his head rocked back and his mouth hung open.

'He's backward.' A woman wiped a trail of saliva gently from the sides of the boy's mouth with a cloth. 'Mentally and physically.'

'Was it something that happened at the birth?' I asked her. She shrugged and smiled slightly. It wasn't that she didn't think it was important, I knew, just that his condition couldn't be changed. It was the way people thought: what you couldn't do anything about you learned to accept.

We sat together, the three of us, on the small porch in front of Adama's house: Adama on a low chair, I on the end of the bench, Morlai squatting on his haunches with his back to the wall. The woman I had spoken to carried through plates of rice and *plassas*, heavy with palm oil, and glasses of tepid water. While Adama spoke in Temne, Morlai translated into English, though Adama's eyes stayed on me throughout. As she talked the boy swayed, ever so slightly, to the cadence of her voice.

In Magburaka the rebels had ransacked the town and looted their homes. Terrified parents had hidden their children in the bush, in latrines, in the roof—anywhere they might be safe from capture by the invaders. Later the Fornas had fled, first to the old village of Rogbonko, where they hid concealed by the tall trees of the forest. Not daring to travel to nearby towns for food, they were forced to make do with whatever they could forage, fish or grow. During one of the short-lived ceasefires they decided to leave, carrying bundles of their remaining possessions, journeying by foot along the bush paths, hiding from rebel patrols and sleeping for only a few hours at a time. Memuna, my father's only full sister, had arrived in Freetown at my stepmother's door almost half her usual weight, exhausted, blighted by sickness. When I heard the news in England it was the first time in over a year that we knew she was alive.

I explained why I had come back to Freetown. Adama nodded. Ismail, my uncle, had left Sierra Leone after 1975 and had never returned. She thought he might be either in Liberia or in Guinea—so many people were displaced it was hard to know. Uncle Momodu was in Sierra Leone. He was the only member of the family still in Magburaka, where he lived in the house built by my father. How, I asked, had Momodu fared during the war? I waited as Morlai translated.

'Momodu has two sons in America,' Morlai said, holding up two of his fingers. I understood immediately. The more people I spoke to, the more I realised that this had become the new measure of wealth in Sierra Leone: not land, or goats, or wives, certainly not leones. No, a son or a daughter who had successfully emigrated to the west was all that mattered.

We went from house to house greeting the family: Salamatu, Dura, Sorie, Hassan, Osman, Abass—the list went on. I had never met most of my cousins, especially those who were younger than me. Everywhere I walked I was followed by an ever-growing band of people, children mostly, some related, others not. Two of my uncles, Aruna and Morlai, sons of one of Pa Roke's younger wives, led the way. Our shadows had shrunk to pools of black by the time they walked me back to the car. Someone helped me with my bag. We walked four abreast, taking slow steps, drawing out the time. At the car door we shook hands many times.

Just as I prepared to climb into the back seat I glanced back up at the sloping road, the way we had just come. Someone was coming after us. The man had his back to the sun. I couldn't make him out properly. A man wearing a skull cap and a traditional shirt. He was in a hurry but by the way he moved, rocking from side to side, treading cautiously on the uneven ground, I could tell he was not young. Uncle Alhaji. He was the most senior of my uncles, someone who had always been close to my father. He had lived for a while in Koidu when we owned the clinic. After the detention years he had helped out starting up the rice business.

Uncle Alhaji stopped in front of me, puffing hard, chest heaving, waving a piece of paper. Wordlessly he pushed it in front of my face. I reached up and took it from his hand. It was an old photograph. A photograph of my father. He was standing on a football pitch, dressed in shorts and an open-necked sports shirt. He looked impossibly young, younger than I did, almost—the thought occurred to me for the first time in my life. The picture had been taken in 1968 during an old boys' match at Bo School when he was a cabinet minister.

Fate. There it was, it hung in the air for a fraction of a second, before the diviner's stones scattered in the dust. My father lost his mother. Missionaries turned up at the village and the chiefs ordered each household to send one male child to their new school. My uncles stayed at home and were taught by the Imam. There was the fork in the road. There had been twists and turns along the way, but that was the deciding moment when their futures, and mine, divided. One to the west, the others into Africa.

The sun beat through the windscreen. I shifted on the plastic seat. I could feel the sweat sliding down the backs of my knees. The car did not have air-conditioning. I wound down the window but there was no breeze, the air was hot and coarse with fumes, the clamour from the street swept in. Horns sounded constantly, Lebanese pop music strayed from open shop fronts. Despite the shortages of almost everything there were still traffic jams and crowds in the East End and we were caught behind a long line of cars.

A small child crossed the road in front of me, leading another, even tinier child who kept hold of the other end of a stick as they wove their way through the cars. A man was standing at a pavement stall. Where both hands should have been, there were bandaged stumps. He clamped his purse to his chest with one arm and attempted to wrench it open with his teeth. I noticed nobody offered to help him. I looked at the stall keeper. I couldn't read her expression, whether it was patience or indifference. A moment later, when I looked back, the man was walking down the road away from me, holding a bag of tomatoes balanced between his chest and his forearms.

At Abu Kanu's building I climbed the unlit stairwell from the street up to the third floor, emerging into a corridor so dark I could hardly see where I was heading. I barely remembered my father's accountant, but I was apprehensive about our meeting. I had no idea what to expect. I knew only that many people had betrayed my father at his trial and Abu Kanu had been one of them.

I knocked on the nearest door and the man who answered said he would fetch Abu Kanu. So I stood and waited by the stairwell, hands gripped around my bag containing my tape recorder and notebooks.

Somewhere a door opened and closed. Footsteps sounded at the opposite end of the hallway. Abu Kanu appeared out of the gloom, a tall, well-built man with a round face and a receding hairline.

'Aminatta Forna?' I nodded and extended my hand towards him. Abu Kanu didn't appear to notice the gesture. Instead he embraced me and began to cry.

Minutes later we sat facing each other in a small room, equally poorly lit. A desk and a single chair faced the wall. Someone had brought an extra chair. The walls of the room were densely coated in glistening blue paint, unadorned save for a single calendar which was several years old. Beyond the orange check curtains a small veranda overlooked the street. Abu Kanu sat down, wiped his eyes and apologised.

Abu Kanu was the first person to be arrested. He was picked up the morning after the explosion at Kamara-Taylor's house, as he returned from collecting his car from the mechanic's shop. On the way back towards the city Abu Kanu had offered a lift to Sorie Dawo, a young man employed by one of their rice agents in Blama. Sorie Dawo was in town to help complete the purchase of a rice-threshing machine. He had spent most of the day before with my father at the factory showroom. Abu Kanu had just pulled up outside the store at 60 Kissy Road when the two CID men accosted him. He handed his watch and spare cash to Sorie Dawo, for safekeeping. Moments later Sorie was arrested, too. Abu was held alone in a cell for several days before he was taken to Bambay Kamara.

'I'd like you to help me' was what the deputy chief had said to Abu Kanu. *I'd like you to help me.*

Bambay Kamara told Abu Kanu that he was young, and he'd been used. If Abu agreed to tell them what he knew, he would be spared, perhaps even become a witness in the trial. In turn Abu Kanu insisted that he had only worked in Dr Forna's business. Bambay Kamara continued to speak softly to him for a while, persuasively. He asked him about a meeting at the store in Kissy Road. Abu Kanu agreed that he had seen two men come to visit the doctor, but he had not heard what was discussed: they had spoken for no more than a few minutes. Bambay Kamara nodded. He indicated that Abu Kanu should be taken back to the cell. This time he was put into the general holding cell, where he waited. A few minutes later he was fetched and brought back to the interrogation room.

'This time the room had completely changed around.' He looked at me. 'There was a chair and a rope hanging above it.' This he demonstrated with his hands. 'Bambay told me to sit down.' Two other men were in the room; one, he learned later, was Newlove. 'I'll see you, Abu,' said Bambay Kamara. He picked up some papers and left the room.

Someone placed a blindfold over Abu Kanu's eyes, his hands were tied behind his back with the rope suspended from the ceiling. The chair was taken away. Three hard slaps across the face— he sensed it was Newlove who had dealt these. He staggered, momentarily dazed. A kick landed at the base of his spine, then they started with the lash. After a few strokes Abu Kanu shouted: 'Before you kill me, just tell me what you want me to say.' He had an idea there might be a tape recorder in the room. A thought filtered through the pain—that perhaps later he might be able to retract. He shouted again, more loudly this time. He felt sure they backed off just a little then, unnerved by the amount of noise he was creating.

Bambay Kamara entered the room again and made a show of bringing the beating to a halt. The blindfold was removed. Bambay pulled up a chair and showed Abu Kanu a pile of statements, including those made by some of the key witnesses and a man called Bai Bai Kamara, whom Abu Kanu knew slightly. 'You see what people have told us about you,' Bambay Kamara said. He shook his head; he didn't want Abu to die for someone else's crime.

Abu Kanu was taken to Pademba Road Prison. A few days later they brought him back to the CID. As he passed one of the interrogation rooms the door was opened, deliberately, to reveal a tableau within. He saw his wife sitting on a chair; she was weeping. Their son, who was three months old, lay face down on the ground at her feet. He was motionless. The door was pushed shut.

Abu Kanu neither wrote his statement, nor was it given to him to read. He signed it, not knowing whom he had implicated. This was the way the CID worked: in the morning they would bring in a fresh round of suspects based on the 'confessions' of Abu Kanu and others.

Before I left Abu Kanu told me where I would find Sorie Dawo and hazarded a guess at the whereabouts of some of the other defendants. He didn't have any of their addresses, just an idea of where they might be. I might have to ask around a bit, he explained. None of them spoke to each other much any more, he told me. After twelve years together in prison there wasn't a great deal left to say.

I stepped out of Abu Kanu's building into the noise and heat of the street. I stood there for a moment feeling disorientated after the darkness and stillness of the interior room, where I had spent something over an hour. I looked up and down for Dura. There he was, standing by a stall on the other side of the road. He saw me and hurried across, searching for the car keys in his pocket.

Out of the recess of a nearby building a man approached me. His hair was matted into short, thick dreadlocks, his clothes were wretched. He was saying something I couldn't make out, and as I climbed into the car he leant in after me. I glanced up at him and noticed how young he was, in his teens, no more. I tried to hear what he was saying. Dura rushed around and shooed him away before climbing in himself and slamming the door. I stared at Dura: he was normally the gentlest of souls. He almost always found a few coins for a beggar.

'One of these rebel boys,' he muttered angrily.

'He's a rebel?' I glanced at the beggar and back at Dura.

'After January Sixth,' said Dura, 'some of these boys just lost their minds.' He tapped his skull with his forefinger. 'Because of all the evil things that they did. Their families don't want them back any more. So they come and beg on the street.' Dura's mouth was turned down. He looked in the rear-view mirror and changed gears as though he didn't plan to waste another breath on the subject. His house, his two wives and his children were in eastern Freetown, which had taken the brunt of the invasion on that day. As we eased out into the traffic I let the matter drop.

Freetown was full of living ghosts: amputees, deranged rebels. And then there was me: I was beginning to feel like a revenant. A day before I had been downtown by the old City Hotel taking photographs for my journal. Yabome was chatting to some of the sellers in their booths. One of them, a woman in her fifties, advanced upon me. She was tall, well dressed, with carefully coiffed hair. She embraced me with tears in her eyes, just as Abu Kanu had done, only she clung to me for so long people around us had to persuade her to release me. I was used to the effect my name could have; the recognition that so often accompanied it. But such displays of emotion, after so long? I put it down to the war. People looking back, remembering how things once were, imagining how they might have been different.

40

A few mornings later Morlai turned up at the house sweating, his breathing laboured. He was limping badly, swinging his leg out awkwardly as he walked. It had taken him nigh on half an hour to walk up Lower Pipeline Lane to the house, he told us. Yabome rang the doctor and Simon and I drove him there, waiting two hours outside the reception room until the doctor had a chance to see him.

The receptionist was curious about us. 'Who are those people to you?' she asked Morlai, every time Simon or I stepped back inside and asked how much longer it would be.

'This is my cousin and her husband,' answered Morlai. The woman looked him over with a dubious eye. By the time we reached Sorie Dawo's house we were two hours late for our meeting. I expected him to be long gone, but he was still waiting for us.

Sorie Dawo sat on the plastic-covered sofa, cupped his hands over his face and wept. At first we let him. There was no shame in it. But Sorie Dawo cried on and on. He turned to Simon to explain, and despite Simon's murmured protests Sorie Dawo persisted.

'He used to call me "namesake", you see. Namesake. Because I was Sorie. He was Sorie.' Abu Kanu had said my father used to call him 'little brother'. Santigi too described how he called him 'kinsman' because Santigi was a Loko and Pa Roke had been born a Loko.

Sorie Dawo told his story at great length. He spoke loudly and slowly, in heavily accented though otherwise good English. 'My name is Sorie Dawo,' he began, as though he was giving evidence.

'I lived in Blama District. I worked for International Commercial Enterprises.' He determined I should write down every sentence, and if I paused at all he would jab his forefinger at my notepad. Try as I might it was impossible to hurry him on, although I assured him the tape recorder was running, recording his every word. And so I gave up. Sorie Dawo explained how he was related to our family on his mother's side; how he worked for Manu Dawo, his uncle, who was the Commercial Enterprise agent in Blama; how he was trusted to carry the profits from the rice sales back to the head office in Freetown; how he secured deals for hundreds of bushels of rice in various parts of the country; and how he had helped in the purchase of the company's first rice-threshing machine in Bo.

It took us two hours to reach the relevant part of his story, by which time Simon had gone, Morlai had fallen asleep, twisted uncomfortably in his chair, and my wrist and fingers ached from writing. On Monday, 29 July, he had met my father at the Walpole Street offices and they had gone together to College Road to view a German-built rice-threshing machine—he called it a *'wallah'* machine. This one was to be based at Blama, at the Old French Company stores, where the rice would be husked and boiled on site. The negotiations took the better part of the day, and it was early evening when they parted.

The next morning Sorie returned to the office to collect a cheque for the machine and to organise its transport up to Blama. My father gave him a couple of leones to catch a *poda poda* to our house in Samuel's Lane and get something to eat. On his way back to town he encountered Abu Kanu at Blackhall Road. Abu Kanu was on his way to collect his car from the mechanic and then he was going to Walpole Street: if Sorie didn't mind accompanying him to the mechanic's shop he would give him a ride. They were driving down Kissy Road in Abu's car when they were pulled over by two men who had been travelling in the vehicle behind.

Sorie was questioned by Bambay Kamara and by the two men who had arrested him, Francis Ngobeh and Seth Amadefu. He protested he was merely an agent for the company and was in Freetown for the purchase of a rice-threshing machine. After six days he was taken to Pademba Road. On 27 September his detention order was signed by the president. He was taken from the cell he shared with two other men and placed in solitary confinement. The prison officer in charge even took away his blankets, and he lay shivering on the floor. They seemed to delight in tormenting him, cutting his rations, soaking the floor of his cell with water so that he was forced to stand up or huddle in the corner. He remained in jail for five months; when he was released the trial had just ended.

Later I pored over my notes, trying to fit the pieces together. Sorie Dawo spent the whole of the day with my father. That put our tennis game with Miss Dworzak later in the evening, when he had finished work. That would figure. My father had stopped briefly on the way home and bought a bottle of brandy at Lami Sidique's supermarket—Lami Sidique himself had told me so, although I didn't remember. Of course, I had been unwell.

It was later the same evening that the injured man had been brought to our house in Kissy. This had occurred around seven o'clock. I had been lying on my bed reading after supper. Morlai, Santigi and Yabome had all confirmed what I remembered. They were certain of it. Yet the attack on Kamara-Taylor's house had not come until four o'clock in the morning, according to all the people who had heard the sound of the explosion itself, and even the police. That part alone made no sense. Although Morlai, Mum and I talked around and around it in the days that followed, we could not account for the discrepancy.

*　*　*

The afternoon found us at Victoria Park market, where I trawled through second-hand school books. I wanted a map of Sierra Leone, but all that was available was an old Shell map, the kind that used to be issued free of charge from petrol stations twenty years ago. It was the best I could do. The huge undercover market was half empty. Beside the piles of western-style training shoes and T-shirts was the occasional stall selling tourist carvings. I wondered how on earth the stallholder could possibly make a living.

I had the map in my hand and I was in the act of agreeing a price for it, haggling in a mixture of Krio and English, when I heard a series of sharp cracks, like the sound of burning bamboo splitting in the heat of the fire. The stallholder heard it too. He looked from left to right and without a word he disappeared, ducking out of sight behind his stall. The crackling sounded a second time. Somewhere in the back of my brain I dimly recognised the sound. I had heard it before somewhere. Behind a voice, distantly over a telephone wire. Gunfire!

The strange thing was how silently we all ran. No one screamed. People rushed up the hill towards State House, young men, women carrying babies; vendors left their display boxes by the kerb, children scattered. A *poda poda* had lurched to a stop and the passengers burst out of the back doors. One man dived through the passenger-seat window, was momentarily stuck half in, half out, and then scrambled to freedom. I ran a few yards and then veered sharply to my right, down the side of the booths. I saw a hairdresser's shop and headed for the door. I turned to look for Morlai. I caught sight of him running up the street, hemmed in by the crowd, his head turning frantically from side to side as he sought me.

'Morlai!' Morlai saw me and struggled to break free of the mass. I reached out my hand, searching for his. I grasped his hand and pulled him bodily out of the crowd.

'It's all right! It's all right!' said Morlai—he was grinning suddenly. The stampede had stopped, people were standing around.
I heard laughter. 'It's the electricity,' explained Morlai, panting,
pointing at the overhead wires. We walked back a few paces and
looked down the street. A broken electric cable danced on the
road, crackling and sending up showers of sparks like a firework.

The man who had leapt from the window of the minibus stood
nearby. He was young, lanky and dressed in jeans and gold chains;
now he looked sheepish. My heart was still beating fast. People
began to tease each other, falling about, laughing hard, too hard.
A woman next to me in a tight *tamula* and *lappa* shrieked at the
sight of the map seller as he re-emerged from beneath his stall.
Her neck was taut and knotted with veins as she pushed her face
forward. Her laugh was shrill and unending, a cascade of discordant notes.

Two days later the city was in uproar over the semi-finals of the
African Nations Cup, Nigeria versus Cameroon. Many people
supported Nigeria, the leaders of the West African peacekeeping
force who brought an end to the rebel invasion in January one
year ago. By inference anybody who supported Cameroon must
therefore be a rebel. The match was shown all over town: anyone with a television put out a few chairs, posted a hand-drawn
flyer and charged a few thousand leones admission to an open-air
viewing. The match had ended in controversy when a ball kicked
by a Nigerian forward hit the crossbar of the Cameroonian goal
before bouncing down onto the ground. The umpire disallowed
the goal, but the action replay showed the ball had bounced just
inside the goal line.

Outside the *New Citizen* newspaper building a gang of open-
shirted young men were locked into a shouting match, arguing
and gesticulating in the middle of the street. I had witnessed the

same scene replayed all over town: in the streets, down at Government Wharf market, outside the law courts, where I made my daily pilgrimage to Thomas Gordon's office. Dura sounded the horn to pass by, and though they acknowledged the car, and began to drift to the side of the street, the argument raged on.

We made our way to the Commercial Bank building, located within the two streets that passed as the business district of Freetown, to meet Bai Bai Kamara. I had been told he was now a director of the bank, but when I telephoned they had been unable to contact him for me. So instead Simon, accompanied by Morlai, went out to the last address we had for him, the place where Bai Bai Kamara was living at the time of his arrest: 70 Kissy Bypass Road.

The address turned out to be a three-storey block on a busy road. The flat on the second floor was Bai Bai's, but at a glance it was evident no one lived there any longer. Fingers of black soot stretched upwards from charred window frames; the apartment inside was a hollow ruin. Strangely neither the flat above nor the one below had apparently been touched by the flames. Whole families had made their homes in the stairwell. Bai Bai Kamara had indeed lived there, until January Sixth. Someone supplied the name of another street where Bai Bai might be found and there Simon and Morlai asked again at a local shop. The shopkeeper nodded and pointed to an elderly man sitting on the kerb, wearing a grubby woollen hat and a dusty jellaba. Simon approached him, presuming this must be someone who could point out the house where Bai Bai lived. The man turned out to be Bai Bai himself. In the poorest country in the world, being on the board of a bank didn't necessarily amount to much.

I turned up at the bank building to meet him two days later. The security guard was clearly expecting me. He chatted while we waited, asking after my family and even my husband. He seemed to know a lot about me. Bai Bai Kamara appeared, a slim, dark-skinned man, dressed this time in a faded green safari suit, wearing an embroidered skull cap and carrying a briefcase, badly worn around the edges. We travelled to a nearby restaurant, where I had arranged a private room for our talk.

We faced each other on opposite sides of a desk. Bai Bai waited with his hands folded on the table in front of him, while I produced my notebook, pens and tape recorder. I unwrapped a fresh cassette and loaded it carefully. I checked the recording levels. At length I was ready to start. My intention was to conduct this interview just as I would have any other in my years as a professional journalist. It was an obligation I held myself to. I never talked about 'my father', only ever 'Dr Forna'; I did it to encourage people to respond to me as a more or less impartial enquirer. It seemed to work. It never failed to surprise me how easily people appeared to forget who they were talking with. Even in my personal notes and transcripts I eschewed the familiar and used my father's full name instead. There were reasons I needed to impose this facade of control. It unnerved me to delve into the past, to ask questions without knowing whether I might hear something in reply I would find hard to accept. It would have been easier to stay in London, never to have come here at all, to leave matters undisturbed as they had lain for decades. I had found a way to live with the past, and I was aware I was now jeopardising that.

Bai Bai Kamara had been politically active for most of his career, he told me. First through the SLPP, then in 1970 he had joined a new party called the National Democratic Party, which soon merged with the UDP. He had been thrown into prison under the emergency laws and held, without charge, in the detainees' wing, Clarkson, at the same time as my father.

On his release Bai Bai had failed to keep a low profile, continuing to campaign, to hold political meetings and to tour the provinces, in defiance of the state of emergency that persisted. In due course, at the end of 1973, he moved back to Freetown, where he was in touch with a man called Habib Lansana Kamara. Habib was an ex-soldier who had been in prison at the same time as the rest of the men, though he had never been connected with the UDP. He had been accused of being part of a military plot. Stevens's paranoia was increasing and he was especially nervous of rebellion from within the ranks of the army. After the killing of John Bangura he made liberal use of his increased powers to carry out frequent purges. The prison was crammed with three times the number of prisoners it had been built to hold. Habib was an outspoken type of character, and when he was sacked from his army post as a store-keeper, to anyone who cared to listen he would denounce Stevens and the APC government who had robbed him of his freedom and lost him his army career. No one took him particularly seriously but, said Bai Bai, he had heard my father once warn Habib to take care, everyone was being watched. Habib came from a rice-rich region called Wallah, and after the prisoners were released my father offered to buy rice supplied by Habib for his business. Habib lived most of the time in Wallah, travelling to Freetown from time to time, to deliver rice to the Kissy store managed by Abu Kanu.

At the time of the explosion at Kamara-Taylor's house Habib had been in Freetown with one of his wives, at a house he kept in Murraytown. When the arrests started in earnest he fled across to Lungi, where he hid in a village until his capture two weeks later. He was brought across the water in a boat one morning in August, handcuffed, beaten and bowed. The CID accused him of being at the centre of the alleged plot to overthrow the regime, and Habib's subsequent statements had implicated everybody, including Abu Kanu, Bai Bai himself and my father.

Bai Bai in turn was arrested and subjected to the CID's interrogation technique. He leaned across and showed me the inside of his forearm: on the skin was a constellation of precise, round, hard scars. Half a dozen officers questioned him, throwing questions at him from all sides. After several hours Bai Bai was worn down; he started to talk, agreeing with whatever they put to him. In the time I had spent with Abu Kanu, a few days before, I had sensed Abu still resented Bai Bai for this betrayal. Abu Kanu had held out longer than anyone. Bai Bai caved in quickly. In the end, though, Habib, Bai Bai and Abu Kanu had all implicated each other. Their statements, read to the court, described a trip to buy dynamite in Lunsar and test it on the Mange river, dynamite supposedly paid for by my father and delivered in crates to his office afterwards.

The man opposite me told his story deliberately, precisely, with neither apology nor shame. At the trial he recognised only one of the four witnesses who gave evidence for the state against the fifteen men: a former private in the army by the name of Morlai Salieu, who had been in Wilberforce block at Pademba Road. Habib Lansana Kamara had also been in Wilberforce. In 1974 Bai Bai had met Morlai Salieu, quite by chance, it seemed, waiting for a bus into town. Bai Bai explained:

'I met him one morning at Kissy Bypass. He was stranded and wanted to come to town, so I offered to pay his fare. He wanted to see Dr Forna, that's what he told me. I asked him why. He said he wanted help with a job. He had been forced to leave the army and had no work. Then there was some trouble about a court case. I directed him to Walpole Street.'

Bai Bai and Morlai rode the *poda poda* together into town. Morlai Salieu got off first. When he was out of sight a passenger behind Bai Bai leaned forward and whispered a warning in his ear, that the man he had been sitting next to was an informant to S. I. Koroma. Bai Bai listened, but in the days that followed he put the matter out of his mind. He did not see Morlai Salieu again until the first day of the trial.

* * *

It was the end of February and hot as hell. I was sweating, streaked with dust and tired when I stepped back into the same restaurant to meet my stepmother. It had been a long, long day. Everything in Freetown took three times, four times as long as it should. I had commandeered the whole family—Simon, Morlai and Yabome—into helping me in different ways every day. I found my step-mother waiting at a table with three men. I recognised one as Bai Bai Kamara, but the faces of the other two men were new to me. Empty soft-drinks bottles and glasses were stacked on the table and the restaurant was completely empty.

The men at the table gave their names: Albert Tot Thomas and Unfa Mansaray, both former defendants from the treason trial. Bai Bai had brought them to meet me. Not having a telephone himself and not knowing how to contact me otherwise, he had come back to the restaurant where we met. The restaurant owner, a good friend of the family, allowed them to wait. That had been at lunch time, almost five hours ago.

I ordered a bitter lemon from a waitress, tried to gather my wits and listen to each of their stories. I searched for paper and a pen. Albert Tot Thomas was the first to speak. He was a small man, with a domed forehead. His face was a pattern of vertical and horizontal lines: a straight, unsmiling mouth, deep grooves that ran from his nose to his mouth, his forehead cross-hatched with lines. His manner was earnest and sincere.

Back in 1973 Albert Tot Thomas had been a small-time busi-nessman, buying and selling on commission. He had also been acting editor of the SLPP paper *Unity*, which was being targeted and threatened with closure by the APC government. Albert had written and published an article asserting that the APC were plan-ning to rule Sierra Leone through a military commission, and as a result he too found himself detained without charge at Clarkson wing, along with a fellow journalist, Dwight Neale, who worked as a stringer for the BBC World Service. He was freed shortly after the elections the same year.

Before then Albert had known my father only by reputation. 'I only met him one time. That was when some of the police had arrested one of our people in Kambia. They were holding him, refusing to charge or release the man. Some of us went to see Dr Forna at his office, to petition his help.' Stevens was out of the country and my father was acting prime minister for a few days. He secured the man's release from the police cells. A year later Albert Tot Thomas and Mohamed Forna found themselves in prison together.

In 1974 Albert was occupied with setting up a fishing business and went to Murraytown, a part of Freetown, once a fishing village, where most of the fishermen who launched their boats at Lumley lived in a grid of narrow, quiet streets. He was looking to buy lead weights for his nets. Knowing Habib Lansana Kamara he briefly stopped by his house in Milton Street to ask where he might locate some weights to buy. On the first visit Habib was not at home, so Albert went back on another day. He told me he reckoned that Habib's house must have been under observation, because after Albert was arrested in early August Bambay Kamara questioned him about the purpose of his two visits.

The CID chief had ordered Albert's arrest, and he wanted to know if Albert had seen Mohamed Forna at Habib's house. Albert said no. Bambay asserted that Albert had been seen there with Mohamed Forna on the night of 29 July. Albert wasn't sure if that was even the night he had been to Habib's house in Milton Street, but he was confused and Bambay Kamara was insistent on the date. Albert said he thought there might have been some people standing at the back of the house, but he hadn't been able to see

who they were. It was Mohamed Forna, said Bambay, leaning back
confidently and slapping the table. Someone else had seen him
there along with Ibrahim Taqi, holding a conversation beneath
the banana tree.

The conversation took place in a room where three other men
were under 'interrogation'. Albert recognised Unfa Mansaray from
party meetings of the SLPP. Unfa was lying handcuffed on the
floor; a CID officer was standing using his full weight on Unfa's
chest. Another officer dropped onto his knees on Unfa's chest.
Unfa was winded and gasping, unable to shout or breathe. Moments later Albert was presented with a short statement. It said
he had seen Mohamed Forna and Ibrahim Taqi at Habib Lansana
Kamara's house in Milton Street, talking beneath a banana tree
on the night of the coup attempt. He signed it readily, thinking
he might be able to hire a lawyer in town and refute the statement later.

Instead of being released, as he had imagined, Albert found
himself lying alone in a cell in Pademba Road. The door was
locked and never opened, not even to allow him to wash or exercise. Once a day food was pushed through a hatch at the bottom.
He lay in his own squalor, without access to a lawyer or his family,
until he heard he had been charged with treason.

The next time Albert saw daylight the defendants were handcuffed, chained together and herded out of the prison on a series
of site visits, to locations where meetings were said to have taken
place and the plot hatched. He saw Mohamed Forna for the first
time since they were in Clarkson together.

One of the addresses they visited was the house in Milton
Street. The men shuffled into a small room and listened while
the officer in charge read a series of statements by witnesses who
claimed to have attended meetings where the overthrow of the
government was plotted. Albert presumed the purpose of this

was to encourage people to confess, and many did: some of the soldiers who had been arrested began to babble, calling names, pointing fingers, contradicting each other, saying anything at all which might save their own skins. It was obvious whose names they wanted to hear. Forna. Taqi. A CID officer noted down each fresh allegation.

Albert was more or less forgotten. He said nothing. Instead he gazed out of the window at the yard at the back of the house, an ordinary patch of bare earth separated from the next house by a low wall. There was a small hut where the women washed and cooked. Not a soul was in evidence; Habib's family had either been arrested or fled. He noticed something about the yard, something significant.

'There was no banana tree there.' He spread his hands palm up on the table. 'Not a single tree. I tried to use that fact later, so as to prove my statement was falsely given.'

Albert Tot Thomas, Bai Bai Kamara, Abu Kanu: they had the same air about them. At first I mistook it for a curious indifference, but it was—I came to understand much later—simply a lack of expectation. They weren't looking for sympathy or understanding. They told their stories, while I prodded them onwards, checked for inconsistencies, interrupted with questions. In return they asked me nothing. They had waited for me for half a day for the opportunity to be heard, it seemed, and no more. I pondered how peculiarly western was my search for the truth, as though it were there to be found at all. Would I have that confidence if this had really been my country, where arrests, detentions and beatings had become as common as ant tracks in the dust? Perhaps if it had been I might feel their loneliness in the face of fate. Perhaps, if I were Unfa Mansaray.

Unfa Mansaray was a cook who worked in the Patterson Zochonis employees' compound next to the Wilberforce barracks.

He knew a few of the soldiers, who from time to time would come over to his kitchens to gossip, and perhaps be given something to eat. There was a lot of rebellious talk at that time, he said, especially among the Mende officers who were his friends: they wanted something to be done about the APC; they wanted David Lansana brought back as head of the army. From his house next to the barracks Unfa heard the explosion at Kamara-Taylor's house on the night of the 29th. The next day Unfa went to a funeral and then worked until late in the evening. He arrived home to discover men from the CID were looking for him. He left straight away and caught a *poda poda* down to the CID headquarters, where he presented himself to the officer in charge. The desk officer asked if he was Baba Mansaray from Kambia and showed him a photograph of the wanted man. Unfa said no, he thought it was a simple case of mistaken identity. They kept him a week in the public pen. Soon afterwards they took him into a room to begin his 'interrogation'.

It wasn't until Unfa Mansaray appeared in court and heard his statement read aloud that he discovered he had 'confessed' to holding meetings in the PZ compound, to being present at a meeting of the plotters at the house in Milton Street and reporting on the progress of the scheme to my father at his office in Walpole Street—this last in the company of Saidu Brima, a steward at the PZ compound and one of the chief witnesses for the prosecution.

'You didn't write your statement, then?' I confirmed, glancing up as I jotted down his words.

'No, madam,' he replied, meeting my gaze.

'Didn't you read it?' I asked.

He shrugged and gave me a look which seemed to suggest the question was not worth asking. 'Well, I can't read, madam,' he replied quietly. Unfa Mansaray held himself as straight as a palm, his expression was as serene as a drifting river. There was an air of dignity about him that made this fact somehow surprising—that and his flawless English. Of course I knew barely a tenth of the population in Sierra Leone could read and write. If Unfa had been literate he certainly wouldn't have spent his life as a servant. No one had read his statement back to him. When they had finished, they dragged him to a table and pushed his thumb into an ink pad and then onto the bottom of the piece of paper.

❧ 41 ❧

I saw a photograph of my father. It was printed on the cover of a newspaper pull-out section headlined 'Treason Trial Special' published by the Government Information Services. I found it on a chair on the back veranda of our house. I stopped what I was doing, sat down and stared at it.

The picture was taken from above and showed my father on his way into the high court building at the start of his trial. He was striding purposefully, alone. I peered closer and studied his features. His beard had grown back unevenly, his hair looked knotted and uncombed, he was dressed in the same short-sleeved suit he had been wearing the day he was taken away.

My stepmother's cousin Auntie Binty, who we had known in London, had come to stay with us for a while from Nigeria, bringing her children Edward and Elizabeth. She walked onto the veranda. Too late, I looked up. 'What's so interesting?' she asked, smiling forcefully.

I didn't reply; instead I tried to push the newspaper back where I had found it, tucked into the back of the old, broken armchair.

Auntie Binty leaned across, pulled it deftly out from underneath me and gazed at the cover. 'You don't want to be reading that,' she announced, still smiling, holding on to the newspaper. 'Why don't you go outside, find the others? Go on.' She tucked the newspaper firmly under her arm.

The trial of Mohamed Forna and Fourteen Others had opened at a special session of the high court on 10 September, two days short of Sheka's thirteenth birthday. Sheka had already flown back to England to begin at his new school. Mum had decided Memuna and I should go back to school late. We were staying on a little longer in the hope we might be able to win a little public sympathy for our father. I felt proud and unkindly I boasted to Sheka, one day when he had upset me, that I was staying to help our father and he was not.

Our father stood accused of attempting to overthrow the government of Sierra Leone, of conspiring to kill the minister of finance, Christian Kamara-Taylor, the vice-president, S. I. Koroma, and the force commander, Joseph Momoh. Stevens himself had been on a state visit to Rome at the time. Our father was also accused of planning to attack, seize and take over the magazine at Tower Hill and the telecommunications exchange at Wilberforce. Standing alongside him in the dock was Ibrahim Taqi and his former adversary and army boss David Lansana. The fifteen comprised a diverse range of men: a former paramount chief, two ex-ministers, a former brigadier, a tanker driver, a shopkeeper and a cook; Temnes, Mendes and Krios; SLPP, UDP.

I was sitting at the dining table in my stepmother's house when I came across that image of my father again. The picture was not exactly as I had remembered it. When I looked at it again two and a half decades later I saw he was not by himself. There were other people in the picture, surrounding him: armed men in helmets and battledress. I counted eleven of them. Eleven soldiers. Yet they seemed to be keeping a slight distance between themselves and their prisoner. The overall impression, despite all the people around him, was that my father was alone.

Behind me a fan pushed humid air around the room; assorted documents in front of me stirred, as though rifled by unseen fingers. Besides the newspaper cuttings, there were also seven thick bound volumes of typed manuscript on the table. The covers were dusty and brown with age, the staples that held the pages together rusted. These were the transcripts of the trial, obtained, finally, from one of the lawyers who had defended several of the other men.

Mum's search to find somebody to represent our father had taken weeks and ended the night before the trial opened. Old lawyer Yilla, whose main qualification was his willingness to accept the brief, had demanded cash up front. Shineh Taqi, only just qualified as a lawyer herself, was part of the team representing her husband and some of the other defendants, and she alone among the lawyers had managed, just once, to see the men in prison. Using her every resource she had wrung a court order out of a judge to grant her access. Even then the director of prisons refused to allow her inside the gates until he had direct authorisation from the president himself. He had even threatened to have her arrested. That's how the law worked in Sierra Leone. Stevens controlled everything; nothing happened without his sanction.

In the days that followed the announcement of the charges Mum and Auntie Shineh went from one set of chambers to another trying to find someone to represent their husbands. Suddenly every lawyer in the city was unavailable—too busy, they said, or else about to take a last-minute vacation in Europe. One evening the two women drove together to the Sierra Leone Telecommunications Office, behind the bus depot in downtown Freetown, where they placed a long-distance call to a senior Sierra Leonean lawyer, the former attorney-general under Albert Margai, now living in the West Indies. Berthan Macaulay had even successfully defended himself against charges of treason arising out of the fiasco of the 1967 election, at a time when there was still some semblance of judicial independence. He remained unafraid of the APC. He agreed to fly to Freetown and take the case.

My stepmother and Auntie Shineh left the SLET offices relieved, jubilant almost, unaware that an operator had eavesdropped on their call and the information was already on its way to powerful men in the government.

Berthan Macaulay arrived in Freetown a few days later and checked into the Paramount Hotel in the centre of town. Shortly after his arrival he was visited in his room by S. I. Koroma. S. I. knew that Berthan Macaulay was related by marriage to Adelaide Dworzak, who was still detained at Pademba Road. He proposed a deal: Adelaide's freedom in exchange for the lawyer's promise to drop the case and leave the country.

Macaulay telephoned Shineh Taqi in her office. She listened to what he had to say; she could not advise him. Her disappointment was acute, but she would understand, she told him, if Adelaide was more important than the case.

By then Adelaide had been in the women's block of the prison for six weeks. In all that time she had neither washed nor bathed, except with an occasional bucket of water. With no idea what was happening beyond the door of her cell, she received the news of her release without warning. This is what she told me. She was led to the prison gates; her blouse was filthy and torn under one arm, her hair was matted. Her bra had been taken away and not returned. For most of the time she was held in a cell too dark to even see the plates of food pushed through the door. Blinking in the sunlight, she found herself being driven by Berthan Macaulay directly from Pademba Road Prison to S. I. Koroma's Freetown residence at Hill Station. S. I. himself greeted her, offered her a seat and opened a bottle of XO Cognac. He held the bottle up to her; she accepted and he poured her a triple, murmuring words of consolation. They sat together while he appraised her and made meaningless small talk. Only then did he permit her to go home. Less than a week later Berthan flew with Adelaide out of the country.

At some point, not all that long ago, I learned to be careful of people who said they had been great friends with my father: people whose faces I didn't recognise, whose names I had barely ever heard. It took me a while to analyse the suspicion that flared with the sound of those words. In time I put my finger on it. There was a difference between the way those who claimed friendship spoke about my father, and the way his true friends talked about him. Or, to be more precise, it was the fact that his real friends, in conversation with me, spoke of him. The others talked about themselves.

'I was great friends with your father,' declared Berthan Macaulay the day I telephoned him at his offices in Kingston from my home in London in 2000.

The lawyer, who still practised despite his advanced years, denied the rumours that had persisted through the years: that Adelaide Dworzak's freedom had been traded in exchange for an assurance to the vice-president. S. I. had released Adelaide quite by chance, he said. The visit to his hotel room, the curious audience with Adelaide, none of these things had any bearing on why he had suddenly lost interest in the case. We spoke for a few minutes and I kept him on the line with questions. He sounded as though he was in a hurry. Gradually, the irritation in his voice became plain. He thought I was impertinent, that much I could tell. I asked him straight: 'So why did you pull out then. If it wasn't because of Adelaide?'

Way down the line from Jamaica the pitch of his voice rose suddenly. 'I didn't defend your father because he had no money. They hadn't paid me a single penny. I even paid my own hotel bills. I had taken time away from my work, flown all the way from Jamaica. I'd been in the hotel three nights and then I discovered nobody had any money to pay me!' It was all delivered in one indignant rant. I waited. Then he said: 'Your father was an old, old friend of mine.'

'Then why wouldn't you help him out?' I asked. 'I mean, if he was such a good friend you'd want to help, surely?'

He didn't reply. Instead he moved on: 'S. I. was surprised I wasn't taking the case, especially as Adelaide was a girlfriend of your father's.' I wondered if this was calculated to throw me off, if he thought perhaps I didn't know. 'And I was a good friend of your father.' He was beginning to repeat it like a mantra.

I'd had enough. 'Please would you stop saying that. Just stop saying that,' I said. I didn't wait for a reply. I said goodbye and put the receiver back on the hook.

When I called Berthan Macaulay I believed some kind of deal had been done to win Adelaide's freedom—even Adelaide herself had said so. As I sat at my desk afterwards I pondered our conversation, wondering what on earth had motivated Berthan Macaulay to change the story, if that was indeed what he had done. What would make a man think it was better to say he had failed to defend a friend because that friend couldn't afford to pay him than to admit he had been placed in an impossible situation? Yet there had been in his voice no hint of sorrow or of regret, no evidence of a sense of duty, professional or personal. It was as though our whole conversation had taken place in a moral vacuum.

A moral vacuum. That's what it was like, back then. The day the case opened in Court Number One Red Shirts heckled and spat upon members of the defendants' families as they made their way into court. The defendants were brought in a prison truck, handcuffed and chained. The stench arising from them was so terrible the courtroom had to be sprayed with disinfectant twice every day, before they arrived and after they departed. Ali Badara Janneh, the social welfare minister, had ordered the removal of all toiletries, combs and toothbrushes from the prisoners' cells and denied them washing facilities. Back in 1971, Janneh had stood on the platform before the crowd at an APC party convention and said the UDP leaders, then in detention, ought to be shot.

None of the defence team, who were each representing several different people, such was the dearth of lawyers willing to take the case, had managed to meet their clients. Yet the judge refused their request to do so. When the lawyers threatened to withdraw he tried to forbid it. He granted them an hour. When, at the end of the recess, the lawyers insisted on being given more time the judge accused them of being obstructive. One lawyer walked out. The judge conceded a day. A single day to prepare the defence of fifteen men in a capital case.

The jury was packed with APC supporters; my stepmother even recognised two of S. I.'s first cousins. The defence used the right of each of the fifteen defendants to challenge a juror, but it was like fighting a Hydra. One government stooge was removed and another rose instantly to take his place.

One thousand and seven pages, typed on an old typewriter with slightly irregular keys. The trial lasted sixty-seven days. The documents are a crude facsimile of justice. On and on it goes: numbered paragraphs, applications, replies, rulings, submissions and objections litter the pages. The text is interspersed with lengthy legal arguments. The verbosity of the judge is offset by the frequent errors of spelling and phonetic renditions of the court stenographer. There are pages and pages of evidence, descriptions of alleged meetings, volumes of names, some of which I recognised, others which meant nothing to me at all. At first I found myself

forced to refer often to the list contained at the front of the first
volume to remind myself who was meant by the references to the
Second or Fourth or Seventh Accused, the names of PW_3, PW_5
or PW_{12}. By the end of a whole day I had begun to memorise the
names of the fifteen accused, the eighteen prosecution witnesses,
the fourteen defence witnesses, the four defence lawyers and the
seven lawyers representing the state.

Outside the window came a rhythmic knocking, of wood
against wet cloth and stone. The women next door were making *gara*, tie-dyeing sheets of cloth to create elaborate patterns,
pummelling the finished product with wooden bats to raise a
shine before they took it to the market. The women sang as they
worked. The occasional horn sounded from the road beyond, as
vehicles approached the sharp bend outside our house. The cook
laid and cleared the table around me. Ola curtsied on her way to
school in the morning, and found me there when she came home
in the middle of the afternoon and bobbed again. By then I hardly
noticed her. Everything around me receded from my conscious
thoughts as I read on, plunging deeper into the trial.

Day one opened with the testimony of Christian Kamara-
Taylor, the acting vice-president. He swore he was at home, woken
by an explosion in the early hours of the morning. He described
how he had collected his children from their beds and fled the
house, encountering two of his ministerial colleagues who were
on their own way over to investigate the blast.

Then the prosecution produced four witnesses, one after the
other; each gave evidence against my father. They placed him at
the centre of the supposed plot to overthrow the government,
claimed to have seen him at dozens of meetings inciting soldiers,
proposing the assassination of the president, producing wads of
cash to buy ammunition and uniforms. Between them they spun
a story of a plot, masterminded by my father and Ibrahim Taqi,

costing thousands of leones, involving dozens of soldiers and huge caches of arms.

The lead witness was the former soldier, Morlai Salieu. He swore before the court that he had visited my father's offices and there been given money to plan a coup. On 29 July he had gone to a house in Murraytown belonging to Habib Lansana Kamara. They waited there until the dead of night, when they had travelled to a nearby cemetery and met up with a large group of soldiers in combat clothes. The men were split into groups and issued with sticks of dynamite. The first group, said Morlai Salieu, set off to attack the home of Christian Kamara-Taylor with orders to seize the minister and hold him. The second group of men was to do the same at the house of the head of the army, Brigadier Momoh, and the third group of soldiers were given orders to kill the guards at the army magazine and seize the ammunition supplies. Morlai Salieu himself was part of the fourth band, which was dispatched to attack the house of the vice-president, S. I. Koroma. As they departed to carry out their missions, he told the court, Mohamed Forna wished them all luck.

And so on it went. The second, then the third, and the fourth witness swore they had seen him at Murraytown cemetery issuing orders to soldiers the same night. Bassie Kargbo, an army orderly, insisted that Dr Forna had once proposed a plan to assassinate the president as he left a reception at the Cape Sierra. Saidu Brima, the houseboy at the PZ compound, claimed he had seen Dr Forna at Habib's house in Milton Street in a meeting during which the government's downfall was plotted.

That the witnesses were planted and coached I had already been advised. Two lawyers—Eke Halloway, who had defended several of the accused, and Serry Kamal, who represented a number of the soldiers during the court martial which followed (Serry Kamal was the same man who had taken my father aside a few months before to warn him he was being watched)—told me a child could have spotted it: the repetition of key phrases, the absence of detail; under pressure the witnesses buckled and declared they could not remember. When that happened the judge would accuse the defence lawyers of harassment and order them to desist. At the end of the day the witnesses were herded into a separate vehicle back to the CID headquarters. After several hours they were transported again to Pademba Road, where they slept together in the same cell. The judge himself was seen going to visit S. I. Koroma each and every evening of the trial.

One by one the statements of accused men were read aloud by officers of the CID. The statements dramatically compounded the damage done by the witnesses. Habib Lansana Kamara claimed my father and he had met and finalised details of the coup on the day before—the Sunday, the very day we had spent with our father and Nuhad Courban at her beach house. My father was put in two different places at the same time on that day, one clear across town from the other, and neither anywhere near the beach where we had swum and played. On the night of the 29th he was reported in four separate locations. The prosecution lawyers were so confident they couldn't be bothered to take care of the details.

After the reading of the second statement the defence lawyers asked for permission to see the documents for themselves. Judge Marcus Cole denied the request, described the application as irresponsible and accused the defence, not for the first time, of attempting to obstruct proceedings. That was the way it went. Whenever the defence made an application, no matter how reasonable, it would always be dismissed and the objections overruled. At the end of the prosecution's case lawyer Yilla stepped forward and spoke on behalf of all the defendants and their lawyers. He submitted a plea of 'no case'. The judge dismissed it out of hand.

At home we waited in the abandoned house for Mum to come back. She left every morning by eight. Often she was not back until nine in the evening. Though sometimes she went alone, most days Sullay drove her to the court building. She came to rely on his silent support when she faced the crowds outside. Sullay was related to our father on his mother's side, and he stayed by us through the trial despite the warnings of his relatives. At the lunch-time recess a woman judge would sometimes provide Mum with an hour of sanctuary, allowing her to wait in her own office, away from the jeering Red Shirts, until the afternoon session opened. The only people who kept company with us still were Mum's trio of girlfriends. There was Auntie Fatu: four foot nought and plump, she giggled compulsively even during the worst of times; Auntie Marian, stately and cerebral; pretty little Auntie Posseh. I would jump up from whatever I was doing to run outside every time I heard the sound of an engine. Almost always it was one of the aunties, delivering a covered dish of *plassas*, fried plantains, or a basin of pap, coming to check on Mum to see how she was coping.

One afternoon Mum came to us. She said she was going into the prison to see our father.

'Can we come?' we asked.

'No. Only one person can go in. But you can write letters, I'll take them with me and make sure he gets them.'

'Can you take a present? Wouldn't Daddy like a present?'

'Yes, but just one each. And it will have to be something small.'

It was agreed. The next day was Saturday and we would go into town, for the first time in weeks, to choose our gifts. I remember how I sat in my room that afternoon, chewing the end of

my pencil, trying to work out what to say in my letter. I decided
to begin by decorating the piece of paper. I drew flowers on the
border with a red pencil. Red petals and a yellow centre. Yellow
petals and a red centre. I added more, bluebell-shaped flower and
then a huge sunflower in the bottom corner. Gradually I began
to fill up the paper entirely, leaving virtually no room to write. I
stopped. I crumpled the piece of paper up and threw it into the
bin. I took another of the sheets Mum had given me and I wrote,
'Dear Daddy.' I paused. What should I say? What I wanted to do
was to ask the horde of unanswered questions that played in my
mind, which I hadn't even managed to formulate into thoughts,
never mind words, or even sentences. I wrote: 'I hope you are
well.' I stared at the sentence. I started all my letters the same
way, but now I was struck by how silly it sounded. I went back to
Mum to fetch another sheet of paper and began again. This time
I stuck to facts. I began to describe how I had trodden on a snake
one day, and how the local people burned the scrub until they
flushed it out. Actually, I had been horrified at the time. A snake
was seen as a bad omen. The mob caught the snake and skinned
it alive as I watched from the balcony; all the while I held myself
responsible for the creature's agony. An afternoon or two before,
I had felt the movement underfoot, glimpsed the flash of scales
through the bushes as I wandered back from the slaughterhouse
stream. I went there all the time, now there was no one to stop
me. Later, I had told Morlai about the snake. For the rest of the
afternoon after the killing the snake's corpse lay on the side of
the road, glistening pinkish in the sun, next to the smouldering
scrub. Even the vultures wouldn't touch it.

I didn't tell him any of that. Or how we thought we'd lost Pusu,
the kitten we had named after Musu, and how Memuna went out
into the rain crying and didn't reappear for hours, by which time
everyone was searching for her. Instead I wrote about our visit

to the Van der Weydens, schoolfriends of ours whose parents were newly posted through the British high commission. Mum dropped us off in the morning and I'd been really looking forward to it. With the trial on it had taken a long time to find a day when we could go. But the visit hadn't gone well. Exactly how or why I can't recall now—just a memory of blonde Mrs Van der Weyden and how she seemed to stare at us. At the end of the day Mum turned up, late, looking tired, and Mrs Van der Weyden called us down from Jeannie and Diane's room and said goodbye as if she was in a hurry. We weren't invited back. I told my father about how much fun we'd had. I kept my letter deliberately bland, filling up the rest with an imaginary trip to the beach and a catalogue of which tunes I had mastered on my recorder.

The next morning we went to town. I took fifty cents from my dressing table. The money had stayed there through the constant raids and searches by the CID. I kept the five ten-cent coins deliberately within view, just waiting for one of the invaders to steal it, then I would have something else to hate them for. We didn't go to PZ this time; instead we browsed among the smaller Lebanese stores. What would be right? Not socks or a tie or anything like that. Over on a shelf, behind the imported refrig-erators wrapped in plastic, I found a miniature yellow and red fan. The shopkeeper found some batteries and showed me how it worked: he placed it on the counter, tilted it upwards, so that the air blew into my face. Memuna and Sheka were equally en-tranced. We checked with Mum whether the prison cells were hot. Very hot, she said. So in the end we bought three, one from each of us, imagining he could place them all around his cell for maximum efficiency. I discovered later, much later, that the cells at Pademba Road are cold.

Mum wasn't allowed to carry anything into the prison, as it turned out. She spent twenty minutes waiting in the visitors' reception. When our father was brought in they were forbidden from touching. They sat opposite each other at a table. Two guards remained close by for the duration of the thirty-minute visit. Our father had lost weight, and he was unwashed and unkempt, but his spirits were good. Mostly they talked about us, not the trial. Mum needed money for our school fees and the trial was costing everything we had. When they parted he told Mum to cheer up. Things may not be as bad as they looked, he had said. He had not entirely lost faith in the judiciary, who still had time to demonstrate their independence from the government. It might yet all come right.

My father was on the witness stand for three days. It was the talk of the town. Three whole days, and Tom Johnson, special prosecutor for the state, never succeeded in making him contradict himself once. He even resorted to using my father's old resignation letter to try to prove he had a grudge against the government. My father described how Morlai Salieu had visited him in his office several times, starting in March, each time begging for money or for help. He said he'd been to Milton Street twice, once to check on a rice consignment and another time to drop off malaria pills for Habib Lansana Kamara. The second time he had been accosted by a man called Kemoko Suma, who claimed to have known him during the APC's period of exile in Guinea. Kemoko had a sick child. My father gave him fifteen leones for medicine. Kemoko was one of the people whose statements were read to the court: he claimed the money was given to buy arms. Kemoko Suma was with Bassie Kargbo when they approached my father at his office in July. Bassie was a Temne and, assuming him to be on a visit from up-country, my father had asked them all to wait for him at Abu Kanu's flat above the store in Kissy Road. Bassie and his colleagues, three young privates, had indeed spoken of a coup and tried to canvass his support. My father warned them off and sent them away. They had not returned. All the other accusations he refuted, and he flatly denied being anywhere near Murraytown graveyard on the night of the 29th.

Tom Johnson asked whether he trusted Habib Lansana Kamara.

'Habib has always been honest with me,' my father replied. Tom Johnson read out the section of Habib's statement which implicated him, and asked if it were true.

'No,' replied my father.

'Have you no conscience to say that your loyal and trusted business agent is telling a lie against you?'

'I have a heart and a conscience, my lord,' replied my father. In the same way he refused to condemn Abu Kanu or the other men whose words were used against him.

Lawyer Yilla called no witnesses in his client's defence. Nuhad was gone. Adelaide, who might have been able to provide who knew how many alibis, was far away in the West Indies. Sorie Dawo, who was with him all day on Monday at a time when the prosecution claimed my father was in various parts of town finalising details of the night's coup, was lying in a cell in jail.

Then came the turn of the fourteen other defendants. Abu Kanu had protested bitterly as his statement was read to the court. Judge Marcus Cole ordered a trial within a trial. Francis Ngobeh, the officer from the CID who had written Abu's statement, was called up to the witness stand. Abu Kanu, he insisted, had co-operated of his own free will. Next Abu Kanu took the stand and graphically described his suffering at the hands of the CID officers. His evidence runs to five pages. At the end of it, on the bottom of page four hundred and sixty, are the judge's findings: 'In all circumstances I am absolutely justified beyond reasonable doubt that the said statement Exhibit L of the Sixth Accused was made voluntarily. Objection overruled.'

Every single defendant attempted to withdraw his statement. Habib Lansana Kamara, upon whose statement the prosecution had relied heavily to build their case against my father, declared he too had been tortured. Of all the men, he appeared to have suffered the most. His hands, feet and waist were bound with rope and he was pistol-whipped shortly after his capture at Lungi. When the vehicle that brought him from the docks arrived at the headquarters, officers of the CID fired jubilant shots in the air and taunted him, calling him 'brigadier' and 'colonel'. One of them tripped him up at the entrance to the building and they thrashed him where he lay on the ground. On four different occasions he was tortured, until he begged Bambay Kamara to let them kill him. The judge ordered the jury out of the room while he listened to an account of the interrogation from the officer in charge, who swore the prisoner had been cooperative. In the case of every defendant Marcus Cole overruled the objections of the defence. The statements stood. The accusations against my father were reported every day in the 'Treason Trial Special', naturally, but not the protests of the men who had made them.

The defence switched tactics. Under cross-examination Albert Tot Thomas told the court Bambay Kamara had offered him freedom in exchange for implicating Mohamed Forna and Ibrahim Taqi. There was no banana tree at Milton Street, he insisted. Unfa Mansaray, the last defendant, closed the case for the defence. His statement from the dock was short and simple. He maintained that he had never met Mohamed Forna, and knew him only by reputation as a government minister; nor had he ever attended a meeting at a house in Milton Street. On the day of the supposed coup attempt he had even been at a funeral with Bassie Kargbo, one of the main witnesses for the prosecution. I read through his account twice. It was, in every way, exactly the same as the story he had told me, more than twenty-five years later.

The account I read was not the way I had imagined my father's trial at all. I imagined—well, what exactly? That the prosecution's case would have been much more ingenious, more inventive, I suppose. Instead there it was: seven volumes in which the end was written before the start, in which every word demonstrated a contempt for the truth that was brutal, undisguised and arrogant. My father had not been facing one man or even a government, but a system, an entire order, in which everyone from judge to juror knew their role. I understood now why my father only ever cooperated in his trial, no more. Ibrahim Taqi produced several alibis to prove he was somewhere else, drinking with friends in a bar, at the time. And he gave a passionate speech from the dock. But it was useless. There was no law, no justice, just the legal trappings of a corrupt colossus that moved unhaltingly forward, engulfing everybody in its wake.

One evening I stood, dressed in my shorts and my sandals, on the open road at the front of the house watching for the car bringing Mum and Sullay home. The light was fading fast, turning from yellow to amber. I squinted to see if I could spot the telltale swirl of dust, away down the road beyond the houses. In the distance I could see bats leaving the hills, flying silently, sometimes alone, sometimes in pairs, towards the city and the sea. Way off I heard the sound of an engine and I listened as it drew closer. I began to walk down the lane towards it. A car came round the corner. Not ours. I stepped back to the side of the road to let it pass. The car slowed and a woman leaned out of the open window. She looked as though she were about to ask me something and so I turned towards her. She drew back her head. I thought she had changed her mind. Her neck snapped forward and a great glob of spittle flew through the air and landed at my feet. The car swept on past me, following the track round to the right, towards Nancy Steele's house, while I stared down at her spit, writhing and shrivelling in the dust like a jellyfish on the beach, changing shape and drawing in at the edges almost as though it were alive.

42

I should have guessed, back then, how badly things were going when Mum turned to *sara*.

Mum, Santigi, Morlai, Musu and Esther knelt in a semicircle around an Alpha. The Alpha sat with his eyes closed and his palms turned upwards. In the centre of the gathering stood a basket of eggs and a cockerel with its feet bound. The bird's eye, as bright and hard as a marble, darted this way and that. The Alpha's monotonous chants, like the humming of a trapped bee, rolled around the walls of the room, gathering momentum, dropping to a quiet murmur a moment later. I stood still, caught on my way from the yard to my room, not certain of whether to go forward or back. Only Morlai opened his eyes and glanced at me. The Alpha kept his eyes shut, his lips barely moving as he prayed. I dropped to my knees and crept forward. I knew instinctively this ceremony was being performed for my father.

When the prayers were over the Alpha took the eggs and the cockerel and put them into his bag. Then he took three scraps of paper, prayers written in Arabic script, and bound them in string and cloth. The first of the *shebe* he tied to the branches of the mango tree at the back of the house, the second he concealed beneath the foundations. The third he said should be buried outside Pademba Road. Morlai agreed to accompany the Alpha to the prison gates. He kept his distance, he told me, as the Alpha, dressed in his long blue gown, approached the tall metal gates. He watched while the man tried to kick a hole into the earth with his heel and drop the *shebe* into it. But he failed and attracted the attention of the guards. In an instant they seized him and set upon him, then and there, in the middle of the busy street. Morlai slipped away.

A few days later I found another Alpha in the house. This one was sprinkling holy water in the corners of the sitting room.

Now we were in a new millennium. Even in Freetown people had mobile phones and e-mail; an Internet café had opened in the centre of town. Yet Yabome had still not relinquished her respect for the traditional beliefs. Earlier in the afternoon I had returned to the house to find a sheep chewing the small patch of lawn at the front of the house. A white sheep with a single black ear. A ewe.

Sorie Dawo had a dream, you see. He had seen me dressed in white, at the top of a Christmas tree, he said, like a fairy. I was talking. There were hundreds of white people gathered around the base of the tree listening to what I had to say. Sorie Dawo went to his Alpha, who divined the dream. The woman at the top of the tree will one day be very successful, said the Alpha, and many people will listen to what she has to say. But in order to ensure my luck I had to make an offering: 'A male sheep. White. Seven white cola nuts. One piece of white shirting,' Sorie Dawo repeated.

Mum had determined to perform my *sara*, even before Auntie Memuna, on a visit to the house, told us my father had received the same *sara*. He hadn't carried out the ceremony for good fortune by the time he was arrested. After that I found Sorie Dawo's warning hard to ignore. What harm could it do, I told myself, to go along with it all?

Later, in the evening, we sat on the balcony, the sound of the crickets overtaken by the hum of the generator. On the days when there was mains electricity the evenings were noticeably more peaceful. The streets had begun to empty as the curfew approached; most people had already arrived back home.

The *sara* sheep was gone. Yabome told me her sister had promised to go to the market on Saturday and look for a white ram.
Presently she spoke: 'You know what happened to them all, don't
you?'

'Who?' I said, knowing full well.

'These people. All of them. Every single one.' I knew what was
coming next. For a lot of people here it was enough, but not for
me. Yet who could fail to be impressed by the dramatic irony in
Bambay Kamara's final moments, summarily executed without
trial by the NPRC in 1992, accused of plotting against the new
military government—from his cell in Pademba Road Prison.
The soldiers took them all down to the beach early one morning,
tied them, blindfolded them and shot them. The charges were
trumped up, of course. Even those who hated Bambay believed
he was murdered. But, live by the sword . . .

'S. I. paralysed.'

'Paranoid, do you mean?' I asked.

She caught my drift. 'Paralysed and paranoid, both. Away in his
house, for a long time he was like that. He wouldn't let anybody
see him.' S. I. Koroma died convinced Siaka Stevens was trying
to kill him. He had suffered a gruesome car accident in a Mercedes loaned to him by Stevens. The accident had happened at a
village on the way to Magburaka, where S. I.'s convoy was headed
during the violent election campaign of 1977. Makari was the seat
of one of the men who had stood trial alongside my father, Chief
Bai Makari N'Silk. Months later, following medical treatment in
Germany which was only partially successful, he struggled back to
work, desperate to hold on to his position. Stevens liked to make
jokes at his vice-president's expense. *All man de fom sick for no
dae cam wok, S. I. dae fom well for cam wok.* Most people pretend
to be sick to get out of work; S. I. is the only person who pretends
to be well so he can come to work. Stevens snubbed S. I.'s years of

faithful devotion, electing the dull-witted Joseph Saidu Momoh as his successor instead. S. I. suffered a stroke and retreated behind the walls of his home. Mum had seen him just once, sitting in the back seat of his parked car outside Choithrams supermarket, drooling from the corner of his mouth while people gazed in at him through the window.

And Christian Kamara-Taylor? He died in the provinces after a long illness, a public death painfully lacking in dignity.

'Can you imagine lying like that, in the back of a truck, without even enough money to get a car to take you to a hospital? People coming to stare at the corpse in the rain. Look at Kamara-Taylor!' Yabome snorted and sat back with a look of grim satisfaction.

'I don't suppose he knew much about it,' I commented. Although perhaps, I thought, if Sierra Leone had even the most basic medical care he might have made it. Those who could afford it flew out of the country to hospitals in Europe. Kamara-Taylor was evidently down on his luck. He had gone to a traditional healer, too late. The truck hired to carry his body to Freetown had broken down.

'People here believe nothing happens for nothing,' concluded Yabome emphatically.

It didn't end there. N. A. P. Buck, the government prosecutor, lost his mind a few years later and was seen wandering the streets. Marcus Cole's son died in a car accident. The judge himself was killed ten years on, when the car in which he was travelling collided with a stolen vehicle and overturned on the road from Gatwick Airport into central London. The whispers reached me then and had never stopped. You see, you see, the believers murmured quietly. *Hakeh.* Divine justice: it catches up with everyone in the end.

I didn't argue with Yabome. The truth was I didn't care what happened to those people. It wasn't enough for me. It would never be enough for me. My preferred justice was of a different kind, a more worldly justice altogether. What about all those ordinary people in this country who lived and died in prosaic and yet unimaginable poverty? They had done nothing to deserve their fate except to be born in the wrong country in the wrong class.

And what of Siaka Stevens, the master of it all, who died in his bed and whose obituaries, full of praise, were published in the British newspapers?

43

There are those times when people hide something, or put some precious object away for safe keeping or perhaps for discretion's sake, and then forget where they have hidden it. Sometimes people forget about whatever it was entirely; then you hear how their children or grandchildren unearth the same item years on: a note folded into the pages of a book, a photograph tucked behind a mirror, a heart-shaped stone in a jar full of odds and ends. Memory, I discovered, works the same way. For years Yabome had hidden her thoughts from the world, at a time when talk was perilous. She had taught herself to forget. Now she was being forced, by me, to remember. I was her listener, hungry for every detail, but the hardest challenge for us both was to brush away the layers of secretiveness and unlock her memory.

One morning Yabome came through and took a chair next to mine on the veranda. She offered me a cup of tea, pouring water into a china cup from the red flask the cook filled with hot water and put out in the mornings, alongside the Lipton teabags and the powdered milk. She sat down. After a few moments she began, as though apropos of nothing in particular: 'There was this one time.'

I put down the book I had been reading. This was how the memories came, one by one.

More than a year after the trial ended Yabome had paid a visit to the offices of a family friend, a man by the name of Mohammed Swartaka Turay, recently appointed solicitor-general. He was someone who had stood by us, one of the few of her former acquaintances who didn't cross the road when he saw her coming.

Yabome and he were talking, small talk, nothing more, when his secretary put her head around the door. 'She said she had three boys outside, who were asking to see him. He asked who. She came back with the names, saying they were witnesses at the treason trial. Mr Turay made like this—' Yabome put her hand down to her side and made a motion, as if to say 'stay back'. 'He told her she should let them enter.'

If we talk fine, when de trial don, dem say dem go send we all overseas. This was what the boys had come to say. They did not recognise Yabome; she sat on the opposite side of the room and kept her eyes fixed on the view from the window. They had come to ask Mr Turay to prevail upon the authorities. No one else would see them, neither the attorney-general, nor Bambay Kamara, nor the vice-president. *If we talk fine, when de trial don, dem say dem go send we all overseas.* When the trial is over, if we performed well, they said they would send us all abroad.

Morlai Salieu, the chief witness, had been among them, Yabome recalled. Some years on she was working in the personnel department of Sierra Fisheries. A new secretary arrived. One of her staff there whispered to Yabome that this woman was married to a man who had given evidence against her husband during the trial. Time had passed, and the girl was young. She would only have been a child at the time of the trial. Yabome left her alone. Just once the young woman, Isatu, had remarked cryptically, 'My husband knows you,' but then volunteered nothing more. Morlai Salieu, though, never once showed his face at the office. Yabome thought she knew where Isatu was working now. If we could trace her, she might lead us to Morlai Salieu.

A few afternoons later we met Isatu in the underground car park of an office block in Gloucester Street. Dura had been sent there with a letter and instructions to wait for a reply. Yabome's note had not indicated what it was we wanted, and the girl who faced us was clearly apprehensive. She was about the same age as me, neatly dressed in a fawn skirt and a blouse with a bow at the neck.

While Yabome spoke, her voice soothing, quiet, I remained silent. I had made a decision to let my stepmother handle the conversation. I could hear a little of what she was saying: she was reassuring the young woman, telling her it was all history now, we were just family who wanted the facts, nothing more. By the time her lunch break ended Isatu had been persuaded to ask her husband to come to our house the following Saturday between nine and ten o'clock to meet me. That was all she could promise to do, but it was something.

At seven thirty on Saturday morning I left my bed. It was just becoming light. The generator, and consequently the air-conditioning, had been turned off at midnight. And though the room usually stayed cool for a few more hours, gradually the temperature climbed. Fear of crime was now so acute in Freetown that every household slept with the windows locked. Nobody dared sleep, as we used to, with the windows flung wide open to the skies, nothing more than a mosquito net draped over the bed. As the sun rose, the room became unbearably hot. I gave up trying to sleep.

At breakfast the cook laid an omelette in front of me, but I found I had little appetite. It was eight fifteen. Morlai Salieu might arrive within the hour. I had no idea whether he would show up, or what I was going to do if he didn't. He presented my most solid lead so far. He was the first witness the prosecution produced and he had provided the key testimony at the trial. Was he prepared to be honest with me? I had spent the evening before at home: I declined an invitation to go out. Instead I trawled again through the pages of my father's testimony, in which he disputed Morlai

Salieu's claims. I returned to my room, showered and reviewed my notes for the third time.

It was nine thirty. There was no sign of him still. I took a cup of coffee and stood on the balcony and looked out over the street. All was quiet. The houseboy in the house opposite was sweeping the step with an old-fashioned switch broom, flicking water from a bucket across the tiles to dampen the dust. The rhythmic whisper of the broom above the background of the low rumble of traffic on Wilkinson Road was the only sound to reach my ears.

At nine forty I spotted a lone pedestrian walking up the empty street in the direction of the house. Was this him? Part of me prayed it was not—I dreaded meeting him. I had begun to tell myself he wasn't coming. This man was slim, grey-haired and in his fifties—about the age I reckoned Morlai Salieu to be—dressed in a short-sleeved grey suit and ankle boots and carrying a man's leather bag, the strap around his wrist. He stopped at the gate. The dog shoved its snout under the gate and barked. I called to the watchman to let the visitor in.

Morlai Salieu showed no sign of nerves or reticence. Amie, the housekeeper, offered him tea or coffee. 'I never drink tea,' he replied shortly, 'so bring me coffee.' When she returned he took the cup from her without thanks and loaded it with sugar from the bowl. We had not shaken hands, but I had nodded to him, introduced myself and also Yabome, who by now had joined us on the veranda. Up close I observed how shabby his attire was: the bag was battered, the boots badly trodden down at the heel; the pinstripe print on his suit had begun to wear away in patches. I began to explain why I wanted to talk to him but he cut across my words:

'None of it was true,' he began. 'Nothing in that statement was true.' He had clearly arrived in confessional mode. Within moments he was talking of torture, how he was forced into his role, his unwillingness to become a witness. I hadn't meant us to start immediately, but I wasn't going to stop him. I rushed to fetch my tape recorder and notebook. I wanted this for posterity.

When I returned he continued, but his tone had altered. His voice was strident, indignant. He complained that the politicians had reneged on the deal they had made with him. So much had been promised and he hadn't seen a cent of it. 'Not one penny,' he insisted. He slapped his hand flat down on the bench. They were rogues who had used him and his colleagues only to discard them later. I made no move to take my tape recorder from the case, I dared not interrupt. Morlai Salieu cast around, sipped noisily from his tea cup, holding the saucer up under his chin. He glanced from Yabome to me and back again, waiting for us to say something. He seemed genuinely to expect our sympathy.

Morlai Salieu talked for an hour and a half. On the tape recording his voice is slow, pedantic, unusually deep, monotonous; it sounds almost as though the batteries are running low. He ignored my first question and started by giving me an account of his life instead. 'My name is in the history of Sierra Leone,' he declared, jabbing the desk with his finger. 'I overthrew Juxon-Smith on the seventeenth of April. I was the particular private.' He was referring to the Privates' Revolt of 1968. It was true he had been one of the rebellious juniors who locked up their officers in Daru demanding more money. I would later come across his photograph in one of the files I had copied from the US State Department, a young man with a hat pulled down over his eyes, holding a machine-gun across his chest in a pose of pure bravado—an unexpected forerunner of the current images printed in the foreign press of the young boys who fought on both sides of the war, posturing for the camera with their weapons. As he recounted events Morlai Salieu rewrote the history of the country with himself at the apex. He claimed to have gone to Guinea to meet the APC politicians in exile there, including Mohamed Forna and Ibrahim Taqi. Ibrahim Taqi, I knew, had never gone to Guinea. 'Ibrahim Taqi? Are you sure?' I checked.

'All these politicians. These ones who were arrested for this coup later. Maybe not Ibrahim Taqi.' He continued undeterred, speaking with assurance. From time to time he threw out dates. Quite a few were incorrect. It became evident he thought I knew nothing at all. I knew how he must see me: a young western woman busy noting down his words. I wondered if he had taken in exactly who I was.

Once the APC were in power he was offered a diplomatic posting in Canada, but turned it down when Siaka Stevens made it clear he was needed in Freetown. Somehow, though, Morlai Salieu never succeeded in rising above the rank of private. Then, in 1971, he was accused of being part of a military plot, by rivals who wanted him out of the army.

That was how he ended up in Pademba Road, occupying one of the cells in the block opposite the imprisoned leaders of the UDP, who had resigned because Siaka Stevens wanted a one-party state and for everyone to drive on the right-hand side of the road. I snorted at this, unthinkingly. He stared at me, then stretched his lips into a sort of grimace, as though he had taken a bite out of a dry lime. 'After we were all released we started visiting ourselves. I was going to Dr Forna, Ibrahim Taqi—'

'Where?' I interrupted. So far I had mostly let him talk at his own pace.

He hesitated: 'Samuel's . . . Kissy.' A pause. 'His office at that time was down in . . . in Walpole Street. I used to visit him there. At one time when I went there he told me that they are planning to overthrow Stevens because all what he is doing is not in favour in the nation.'

'Who? Who was planning to overthrow Stevens?'

'Some of the soldiers and some of the politicians. I supported him, but I wanted to know how. How are we overthrowing, what weapons are available? I said I would find out.'

'Was Dr Forna planning it, or had he heard a rumour?'

'A rumour. A rumour.'

So Morlai Salieu sought out his army contacts, naming two of the men who were later court-martialled. I noted down their names: Regimental Sergeant-Major Kalogoh and Sergeant Davies. They confirmed a coup was being planned. But Morlai Salieu wasn't satisfied that they had sufficient by way of weapons, so he went back to Dr Forna, who assured him Abu Kanu had just purchased a quantity of dynamite. Morlai Salieu remained unconvinced and offered his counsel. 'What I would advise you is to leave everything. Hands off! Stay away from that. Well, in my presence, he accepted.' Morlai Salieu couldn't remember the date of this or any of the meetings. I pressed. He insisted he didn't know. 'It was all around that time.'

'What kind of weapons did you want, then?' I asked.

'This AK-47, GPNG, grenades, mortar bombs . . .' Morlai Salieu told me how he had refused to be part of the plot. Later he found out the plan was going ahead: a band of street boys had been brought in to supplement the soldiers. He warned Dr Forna again that the whole thing was ill-advised.

I watched him as he spoke, fiddling with his fingernails, picking at the soft flesh under the rim, digging out particles of dirt. His nails were rather long.

'Did you find it strange that men like Mohamed Forna and Ibrahim Taqi would organise a coup with some sticks of dynamite and untrained boys?' Or take advice from someone like you, I thought. He didn't answer or even acknowledge my question. Now we were onto the night of the attack. A friend appeared at his house with the information that everything was on. They travelled to Dr Forna's house, our home, at Samuel's Lane. I would have been there at the time he described; so would my father.

'Dr Forna was not there. We came to his office and he was not there.' The two travelled to Milton Street. The only person there was Sergeant Davies. They waited two hours. At about eleven thirty Ibrahim Taqi and Mohamed Forna appeared with a third man, a soldier with a badly wounded hand. Morlai Salieu wanted to know what had happened. He was told a grenade had exploded in the man's hand. He gave his advice again: call the whole thing off, he had said. He took a decision to leave there and then. Passing through the East End on his way home he heard the dynamite explosion.

'All the way from Wilberforce to Kissy?' I glanced up in surprise.

'From the magazine,' he said. 'The road to parliament.'

His story didn't add up. It had been claimed at the trial that there had been a second explosion at the army magazine at Tower Hill. There were no photographs. No evidence was produced. The defence had disputed the claim. In London I had interviewed the second-in-command of the army at that time; he had been adamant that no army installations were attacked that night. One stick of low-grade dynamite, of a type generally used by fishermen, had been thrown at Kamara-Taylor's house. He had inspected the damage for himself.

All of this had taken more than forty minutes. The recorder clicked off. I turned the tape over. So far nothing Morlai Salieu had said differed dramatically from the testimony he had supplied to the court. Apart from his own role, that was. He kept distancing himself from the plot, then describing himself as part of it. He couldn't seem to make his mind up. I let him continue. I noticed his cup was empty—he picked it up and stared into it ostentatiously. Then he replaced it on the saucer.

Bassie Kargbo had given Morlai Salieu's name to the CID. He was handcuffed and suspended from the ceiling: 'Oh, it was unbearable. They started to take cigarettes. They tortured me—most of the others—you heard shouting, crying, this, that. Blood all over the place. Up to now the mark of the handcuffs is there.' He stretched forward and displayed his wrists, turning them over. I inspected them. There were no marks there. I frowned. I added the observation in the margin of my notes: 'NB: I couldn't see anything.' I wondered what this man's game was. Some details of the story were credible enough, other parts were not. He wavered whenever I asked a question, there were inconsistencies, leaps of logic and downright lies. Later, when I was going over our conversation, plucking out the names of people he had mentioned, I came to the realisation that the only names he had supplied were of people who were no longer around to verify his story. At the time, though, I let him go on.

Following his interrogation Newlove gave him a prepared statement to sign and he was taken to Pademba Road. Two days before the start of the trial two CID officers came with a list of names. The men were called and led up to reception. He said there were eight of them. I asked for their names. He listed five and no more. 'Go on,' I said. He changed his mind and told me there were only five men. The prison chief announced they had been selected to escape punishment, provided they were willing to cooperate.

Presently they were taken before Bambay Kamara in his office at the CID. Bambay pressed an intercom and suddenly the voice of the president filled the room. Siaka Stevens told the men they had been selected to help the prosecution in the case. If they did their job well and testified in court according to the statements they had already given, they would be well compensated.

'How did you know it was the president?' I asked. I wondered what technology had existed then. Was it speakerphone, a tape recording?

The man in front of me insisted it had not been a tape recording. 'I know his voice very well. I've been with him so many years.'
And there it was again. The claim to be a key player, always at the
centre of events, so close to the president he knew his voice. How
many Sierra Leoneans could claim that twenty-five years ago?
The broadcasting service was rudimentary and Stevens hadn't
been much given to making speeches except occasionally at APC
rallies. I noticed, too, that when Morlai Salieu referred to Stevens
he spoke in the present tense.

The witnesses were coached by Newlove and Amadefu for
seven days until, on the eighth day, Morlai Salieu was able to
recite his own statement by heart. Soon after that he testified in
court. When he talked about his day in court he spoke with pride.
I asked him about one of the other witnesses, Saidu Brima, whose
name he hadn't mentioned so far. He seemed never to have heard
of him, dismissing my question with a wave of his hand. 'It was
only two of us, Bassie Kargbo and me. We were the two witnesses.
I was the main one. Along with Kamara-Taylor, we were the ones
who gave evidence.'

I remember how I watched him, trying to summon up a suitable degree of loathing. Instead I felt nothing—a vague dislike,
contempt. Every now and again I was jolted into an acute awareness of where I was and what I was doing. This is what I had been
waiting for. But mostly I just felt tired—exhausted—and strangely
emotionally detached, as though I were watching a show of this
man and me.

After his release, Morlai Salieu and Bassie went to State House
to try and see Stevens as well as to Bambay Kamara, asking for
jobs, but they found themselves shunned. He denied visiting anybody else. They were all hypocrites, he went on, who had wanted
his help, but then they turned their backs on him. Now he sold
Lotto tickets for a living over at Wellington. He railed for a while

against the way he had been treated, the *hypocrisy*—he tapped the table with a matchbox he held in his hand to emphasise the word—and against the one-party state. That's what had brought all the fighting, he sighed elaborately. He himself, for one, had always been pro-democracy. Always. He believed the multi-party system was the only way forward.

I ignored him. 'So how much of your statement was true?' I asked.

'None of it.'

'Well,' I said, 'what you've told me is broadly the same as you told the court. So what was different?'

He looked confused. 'Well, they said Mohamed Forna was the person responsible. He gave so much money. I can't remember it all now.'

'But from your account you are saying he was involved.'

'He wasn't involved.'

'But you told me you saw him at Milton Street on the night of the attack. Did you see him there?'

'I saw him. He came in with a soldier with his hand damaged. I don't know whether they met on the way . . .'

'Was the soldier's hand bandaged?'

'Not bandaged! Very badly damaged. I saw the blood myself.'

'And this was late in the night?'

'Yes. Eleven o'clock. Just before the blast. I was on my way home when I heard it.'

I knew my father had not left the house that night. I also knew the soldier was brought to us in the early evening, no later than seven o'clock. My father had cleaned and dressed his hand; I sewed the bandages myself. I also knew the explosion at Kamara-Taylor's house was around four o'clock in the morning. The magazine, if it was attacked at all, was certainly not dyna-mited before then. So it would have been impossible for him to still be on his way home from the house at Milton Street more than four hours later.

'There's something you told me that I don't understand,' I began carefully.

'What is it?' He sounded helpful.

'You said you saw Dr Forna with the wounded soldier at Milton Street on the night of the blast?'

'Yes,' he said. I explained why I believed that to have been impossible. He listened, uttered a sound, somewhere between a laugh and a cough. 'Well ...' He dragged the word out. 'Well, I don't know how you get that.'

I repeated myself. Several people were in the house that night. I had interviewed them all. When he answered, Morlai Salieu began somewhere else, talking about the period two or three days before. He hadn't seen Dr Forna, he insisted. 'I didn't even go to Milton Street with the purpose of making a coup.' This time I didn't interrupt him. I noticed he was slowing down. 'But I saw that man, perhaps if it wasn't the doctor it was Ibrahim Taqi, or somebody else ... Three of them came in.' Ibrahim Taqi had a cast-iron alibi for that night and that time. Several alibis, in fact. He had been in a bar called the Yellow Submarine. Morlai Salieu was beginning to ramble now, talking about Habib Lansana Kamara and the role he had played in the operation, blaming him for the fiasco; he, Morlai Salieu, had taken the decision to pull out.

After a long while I interrupted: 'Are you saying you saw Dr Forna there or not?'

He stumbled: 'Well ... I ... from my own memory ... maybe it was a vision ...' He kneaded his forehead. His words came out in staccato, partial sentences. 'After this rebel intervention ... my whole mind is gone. I was completely sick. I did not think I would survive. My statement ... I memorised it. But everything that was in my brain. I don't know ...'

And that was where we left it. We spoke for another five or ten minutes, but he had stopped making sense. The conversation went round in circles, with me asking what was true and what was false; him contradicting himself from one moment to the next, shaking his head, saying he couldn't remember. He blamed the war. His English began to falter. Before the second side of tape ran out I turned the tape recorder off and stood up. I thanked him formally. I even shook his hand. As he picked up his bag and prepared to go, he seemed to linger. I waited. He said something in a low voice and I bent forward to hear him. He was asking me for money.

I listened to the tape a few weeks later, and again many months afterwards. Only when enough time had passed, when I was in a completely different environment, away from Sierra Leone, did some clarity emerge. Up close I had found Morlai Salieu unfathomable; the interview baffled me. I was being lied to, but I could not understand why. Later, a new perspective emerged. I realised I had been so fixated on what *I* wanted out of the interview, what it meant to *me,* that I had overlooked Morlai Salieu's motivation in agreeing to talk. His sole purpose had been to exculpate himself. It became evident as I listened to the whole interview through from the start. He had devised a version of events that left him blameless. The only problem was he had miscalculated how much I already knew.

Morlai Salieu had been informing for S. I. Koroma. He admitted as much during the trial, under cross-examination. In the pages and pages of text I had somehow missed the reference the first time I read through the transcripts. When I met him a second time, by his booth in Wellington, where I had searched him out, I challenged him. I wanted to know what his role had been: had he actually operated as an *agent provocateur,* as some of the other defendants believed? He denied it absolutely, shaking his head vigorously. Though he admitted he had been to see

the vice-president to ask for a job afterwards, in the same breath
he declared he never worked for him. It occurred to me how the
mention of S. I.'s name had this effect: people were wary, still, of
talking about him. Throughout my search he alone remained a
shadowy figure, the unseen puppet master, like a character in a
second-rate thriller. I confronted Morlai Salieu again over the lie
he had told me about the night of the 29th. He was angry and in
turn he challenged me.

'How do you know?' he demanded. 'How do you know? You
were not there.'

'Oh, but I was,' I told him. 'But I was.'

❧ 44 ❧

The sun rose ahead of us, up over a wandering horizon, to emerge through cloud-streaked skies as we drove due east out of Freetown. The procession of eight United Nations Land Cruisers and almost as many aid agency vehicles thundered through the narrow roads, leaving pedestrians consumed by the great cloud of dust kicked up from our tyres. Through Kissy we joined Bai Bureh Road, where we passed schoolchildren and villagers awaiting transport into the city centre. A dozen children in pristine green and white uniforms scrambled aboard a truck going in the opposite direction. For the first time since I had arrived in Freetown we passed through road blocks without so much as slowing. A *poda poda* pulled out of the kerb and then lurched to a stop to allow the convoy past.

Gradually the houses gave way to green. We crossed a bridge over a flat, wide ribbon of river. Below us a woman with a baby bound tightly to her back gathered crops from mounds of earth, wading ankle deep through the edge of the water. In the distance the mist rose in ethereal curls from the smoky mangrove swamps, leading down to the sea. Some minutes later we arrived at Hastings, the modest landing strip that served as the country's second airport, now a base for United Nations troops. Rows of military tents occupied the ground to one side of the road. On the tarmac stood a helicopter and in front of that a row of white tanks: strangely pristine, virginal beasts.

At a social gathering on Sunday a few days earlier I had struck lucky. I had been offered a place on a UN convoy heading north by a friendly logistics expert for the World Food Programme. The road to Magburaka was in rebel hands and littered with hazards, the journey would be dangerous and difficult, impossible even to contemplate in a private vehicle. Yabome herself had not dared to leave Freetown for seven years. Without a doubt the offer to travel under the auspices of the UN presented our best chance of reaching the town. I accepted without hesitation and Simon elected to accompany me. When the trip was confirmed on Monday we hastily assembled everything we had been told we would need: bedding, canned food, torches. I dithered over my tape recorder, then packed it in with my other belongings. Simon selected a couple of lenses for his camera. Early on Wednesday morning, thirty minutes before the allotted departure time, we gathered in the parking lot outside the large private house which the World Food Programme had converted into its headquarters in Freetown. It was still dark when the watchmen opened the gates and signalled the first of the vehicles out onto the road.

The dawn departure had been precipitated by the need to pass through the Occra Hills before the West Side Boys, or any of the other rogue contingents of rebels and sobels who operated from bush hideouts in the forest, were awake and in a mood to waylay us. The hills were no man's land, disputed territory fought over by the rival guerrilla gangs. The area on the other side, stretching north to Makeni and Magburaka and beyond, was under the control of the RUF. At Hastings we checked in briefly with the regional commander. The air was tepid as we stood at the roadside, ate buttered rolls and drank a little of the coffee we had brought with us out of polystyrene cups. At the sound of a horn the assembled company of aid workers and UN staff climbed back into the vehicles and started the ascent into the Occra Hills.

The first town we passed through was Waterloo, much of which had been destroyed in the war. Clay bricks dried in the sun by the side of the road. People were occupied rebuilding their lives: binding poles, spreading wet earth across wooden frames to create walls, thatching roofs with palm fronds. They paused in their work, glanced up only briefly as we passed. Young men watched with unsmiling eyes. Children waved. There was a time in these parts, not so long ago, when the sight of several dozen westerners would have been regarded as extraordinary. Now the aid agencies were a new, though different, occupying force.

Outside Waterloo the road gently sloped into the first of the three hills. The vegetation along the roadside closed in, so that the view from either window was reduced to a dense wall of impenetrable green. Mostly the road was good, although in one or two places the tarmac had been dynamited and we were forced to slow down and ease our way into the hollow, climbing steeply up the other side, engines roaring, tyres gripping the crumbling earth. Shortly afterwards we drove over a short series of log bridges across deep gullies. These were the most dangerous moments, when it was possible we might be fired upon by snipers in the trees. As it was, we passed without incident. For a moment at the crest of the hill I had a rare and brief view of the vast acres of forest. They were lit by the morning sun: undulating, steaming, seductive. The only sign of life was the smoke drifting here and there across the tops of the trees. In that instant I saw this country of mine through the eyes of the stranger I had become, glimpsed the exotic Africa the first Portuguese and British traders must have seen. Ours was a country of immeasurable beauty, at once full of promise yet riven with unknowable perils.

We left the Occra Hills, crossed the dark and languorous waters of the Rokel, and at Massiaka we turned left and followed the road to Makeni. This was not the route I knew from old, when I used to drive to Magburaka with my family. In those days we took the low road, through Yonibana and Mile 91: a more direct route to Magburaka. The northerly road passed through Makeni and then curved south again to Magburaka. At Massiaka it became evident we were in rebel territory when we passed through the first checkpoint: a wooden pole, lowered and raised by means of a length of rope. To the side of the road stood the operator: a boy of ten or eleven, bandy legged and barefoot, wearing a pair of ragged shorts and nothing else, save a large sub-machine gun strapped to his back.

The roads were deserted. We had scarcely seen a soul. Once we passed a boy carrying a dozen great, green gourds, another time a single woman carrying water, and another with firewood: one long branch balanced carefully on her crown. The pedestrians disappeared down the bush paths at the side of the road, to villages hidden from view behind the screen of trees. The whole way, for four hours, we did not pass a single other vehicle although there were plenty of burned-out, rusting hulks at the roadside. My eye was caught by a kingfisher darting across the telephone wires in front of us; by the scarlet fruit and silver bark of a particular tree; a red-headed lizard disappearing into the undergrowth. Here and there I glimpsed sight of bound bundles of straw, placed high among the branches of some of the trees. I recognised the symbols of the Poro society. The trees marked the boundaries of the sacred Poro bush: to walk there or to eat the fruit of the tree was forbidden. Otherwise there was little to break the monotony of the road.

I stared silently at the speeding landscape, allowing myself to be mesmerised by the blur of green. I began to dwell on what I had achieved so far and what I hoped to gain by making this journey back to Magburaka.

In Freetown I had spent the last ten days searching for the former military orderly and trial witness Bassie Kargbo. The last anyone had heard of him he was living in Wellington. This

information had been given to me by Unfa Mansaray. But since
the January Sixth invasion no one had had any news of his whereabouts. Morlai volunteered to go to Wellington and ask around,
accompanied by one of our cousins—a young man called Obai
who worked in his father's rice store on nearby Bai Bureh Road.
Obai thought he knew of a Kargbo family living in the locality,
but since Kargbo was by no means an unusual name, I did not
allow my hopes to rise. Sure enough, they turned out to be a different family. But they directed Morlai and Obai to another house,
and then another. Slowly, painstakingly, they had returned over
a period of several days, following every lead until, remarkably,
they succeeded in locating Bassie Kargbo: a fifty-year-old man,
living one hour's walk away off the main track, in a small house
high on the hillside.

The interview had proved long, tough and frustrating. The four
of us sat on a hard bench in the shade at the side of the house.
Morlai acted as interpreter. Bassie barely spoke Krio, let alone
English, so most of the conversation was conducted in Temne.
Bassie opened by repeating sections of his original testimony.
This time I interrupted and stopped him. I told him how many
people we had already spoken to. I begged him to be truthful. He
paused, made a show of trying to remember and then changed
his account.

Bassie Kargbo confirmed what I now knew, that the witnesses
had lied in return for promises of money and army jobs. Without
a trace of shame, although at least without any of the indignation Morlai Salieu had displayed, Bassie Kargbo described how,
after the trial, Bambay Kamara had taken Morlai Salieu, Kemoko
Suma and Bassie to State House to see Stevens himself. The office
was on the top floor, he remembered. Stevens had told them to
see Joseph Momoh, the army chief, assuring them he would find
them each a place in the military. They had gone along to see the

force commander but were turned away time and time again. They tried to go back to see Stevens, and also called on S. I. Koroma, but they were sent on their way.

Bassie mixed paint for a living. I looked around me. He seemed pretty destitute, sitting shirtless and slack bellied. The house was no more than a hut. A few chickens scratched around an ants' nest. On the wall before me was a rainbow of paint smears. Against the sordid background the colours appeared unexpectedly vibrant and momentarily they distracted me from the conversation. There was no sign of any children or relatives, which was unusual. Just Bassie and his young wife, a girl in her teens, who sat on the ground and listened as we spoke.

In court my father had openly admitted he had been approached with talk of a coup by Bassie and another soldier, but that he had refused to entertain their talk. When the purpose of their visit to the rice store at 60 Kissy Road became clear, he had terminated the discussion and urged them to go home. Abu Kanu's statement from the dock corroborated every detail of his account. I was certain this must be the truth. My father knew he was being watched day and night. He would have been careful with whom he spoke and wary of being entrapped. Under a dictatorship, in a world where political talk of any kind could result in arrest and detention, who would take the chance and discuss the overthrow of the government with strangers? That had been his reply to Tom Johnson during the trial. To do so would have been foolhardy to the point of madness.

'He was more interested in his business, some business he had. I remember. He told us he did not want to be involved,' Bassie conceded to me.

In court Bassie had claimed the small sum of money my father had given him for his bus fare was to buy arms. He had also placed him at Habib Lansana Kamara's house and at Murraytown

cemetery on the evening of 29 July. I wanted to hear him withdraw the allegations now, but he was disinclined to discuss it. He
insisted that anything he had said in court was drawn from his
statement, written for him by a CID officer, and subsequently
committed to memory. He could not now remember it all. Later
on, when I tried to press him on details of his own actions, he
began to obfuscate in much the same way as Morlai Salieu had
done. It was impossible to know whether his refusal to be drawn
further was an attempt to pull a veil over his guilt or conceal an
altogether more sinister role.

I trudged the long path back down the hill feeling dissatisfied,
trying to make sense of it all. Several questions remained unanswered, not least the precise part played by Bassie Kargbo and
Morlai Salieu. Linked to this was the question of what exactly had
taken place that night. Bassie insisted that a group of soldiers and
civilians had met at Murraytown graveyard, but that he himself
had decided to leave and hadn't taken part in any attack. This
was exactly what Morlai Salieu had claimed. Was it possible they
slipped away just in time to report back to the authorities? The
only thing the two of them had told me that I accepted was that
they had lied in court. That much I had proved. None of the rest
of the information they had given me could I treat as reliable.

Unfa Mansaray told me he had seen the soldier accused of
leading the attack, Regimental Sergeant-Major Kalogoh, in the
barracks that very night. Every one of the defendants to whom I
had spoken denied being anywhere near Murraytown cemetery.
All were convinced there had never been a real plot, that Morlai
Salieu and Bassie Kargbo had fabricated the entire story.

But something had taken place that night. I had one memory.
Just one. It was my single solid item of information and I clung
to it: the soldier who was brought to our house early that same
evening. I needed to find out about him. From the newspaper

reports and the transcripts of the trial I had his name: Kendekah Sesay. His fate, I had also learned, was linked with my uncle, Momodu Forna.

The RUF headquarters in Makeni were based in what had formerly been a World Food Programme regional administration building. Most of the windows were broken, the offices long emptied of anything of value. In the courtyard in front of the building, in the shade of the cutlass trees, groups of soldiers gathered, sitting along the walls or splayed in a couple of rotten armchairs. They were boys and young teenagers mostly, dressed in the haphazard uniform of African rebel armies: flip-flops and shorts. The lucky ones among them had combat jackets. Some sported T-shirts bearing the logos of western manufacturers of sporting goods; some were bare-chested. Gold chains and home-made charms adorned their necks and wrists. The older boys wore sunglasses. All of them carried weapons: the ubiquitous AK-47 plus an assortment of pistols, rifles and machetes. A small boy crossed our path, weighed down by a pair of bullet belts slung, bandolero-style, across his body.

Before we could proceed farther and on to Magburaka we needed to gain clearance from Colonel Issa, the RUF commander for the district. Our large delegation now included several official observers from the United Nations mission in Sierra Leone, UN-AMSIL, whom we had picked up at their base on the outskirts of town. Accompanied by twelve of the RUF leaders we entered a large meeting room on the ground floor. There was broken glass on the floor, a table, a few overturned chairs and benches along the wall. The wooden floor and the wall panels had swelled and splintered with damp. The air carried the odour of decay. Aware that we were not directly involved in the proceedings, Simon and I chose a discreet position on one of the uneven benches. Behind us and at every other window, dozens of rebels argued and jostled, trying to get a view into the room from the outside.

Colonel Issa, it turned out, was not there even though the meeting had been scheduled for some weeks. General Kallon, a small man wearing an outsized ceremonial jacket, complete with gold epaulettes, a red beret and a pair of empty spectacle frames, announced he was in charge. Ian, the logistics officer in whose vehicle we had travelled, was unhappy and he let it be known. He was intent on waiting for Colonel Issa himself. There was a heated discussion. General Kallon appeared offended and declared with bombast that he had the authority to deal with all matters in the colonel's absence. In the turbulent discussion that followed every member of the RUF command in the room interjected loudly, gesticulating as they gave voice to their individual opinion. To my eye several of the men appeared to be high on drugs, or drunk at the very least. People were interrupting each other, constantly talking at cross purposes. There was no humour on any of their faces and little attempt at civility. All the while Ian and a UN colleague tried to hold the discussion at bay until Colonel Issa arrived. Twenty minutes passed, and there was still no sign of him.

I gazed at the faces of the men in the room and the boys hanging through the open windows. I found I could not prevent the thoughts that streamed through my mind, the continual flash of the images I had seen, of the terrible atrocities each and every one of them must have committed and witnessed. I wondered how many of them were local boys. Many of the rebels came from Liberia. There were also known to be contingents of mercenaries from Burkina Faso who fought alongside them. More than a decade ago, when the civil war raged across the border in Liberia, Sierra Leoneans consoled themselves, saying such barbarism could never occur among our people. I had been among those who believed that anarchy and evil had no place in the society I knew, where respect for elders was profound, the authority of the family entrenched. Liberia was a place where people spoke with Americanised accents, used dollars; it was more American than African. We thought what happened there could never happen here—until, that is to say, it did. The RUF kidnapped children and compelled them to slit the throats of their own parents. The act was more than just symbolic. The killing of a mother and father represented the killing of authority. The newly orphaned recruits belonged, body and soul, to their captors.

I switched my attention back to the conversation at the other end of the room. The temperature had risen a notch. Colonel Issa had been radioed, and although his men claimed he was on his way, he had yet to appear. General Kallon stood with his arms across his chest; anger danced across his features.

Ian was speaking in precise, clipped sentences. 'This meeting was arranged many days ago. We have travelled here all the way from Freetown. A lot of us have made the journey. We have work to do and we need to speak to the colonel before we begin. Now you tell us he is not here. This is no good.' He made a crossing motion with his hands in the air in front of him. Then he turned and indicated Simon and me with a sweep of his hand. 'I have even brought two journalists here from England with me. What sort of report will they make about the way the RUF do business?'

This was not only a grave error, it was not strictly true. Ian knew and accepted that I was making the journey not with the intention of filing a report, but to reach Magburaka and find my family. His irritation had got the better of him and he had tried to humiliate General Kallon in front of the gathering. Now, in the silence that followed his words, every pair of eyes was fixed upon us.

The meeting broke up shortly after that, brought to a temporary halt until Colonel Issa arrived. For the time being, though, there was no way of reaching Magburaka. The town was at least forty minutes' drive away and we were all under orders to travel any distance only in convoys of at least two vehicles in case of either breakdown or ambush. We stood in the car park and waited, trying not to think about what might happen to us. I had a sense of impending disaster and there was nothing I could do about it. Most African countries did not have the same tradition of free speech as Europe and America. Journalists were often regarded as spies. When Patrick, a colleague of Ian's, offered us a sightseeing trip around the locality we readily agreed. We were keen to put some distance between ourselves and the rebel base and I had the feeling, though it remained unspoken between us, that Patrick shared our opinion.

Less than a mile down the road Ian's voice crackled across the broadband radio in the Land Cruiser. 'You must return to base immediately!' He meant the UNAMSIL headquarters. 'I'll meet you there. Don't go anywhere else.' Ian's voice was taut and edged with panic.

Ian hurried out to meet the car as we drew up outside the building. He looked pale and serious. A problem had arisen. Colonel Issa had arrived back at base to learn from General Kallon that there were two journalists at large in the area. The colonel was red-eyed and drunk. Words had been exchanged. Ian, who had dealt with the colonel before, had never seen him so enraged. Colonel Issa had sent out radioed instructions to every one of the rebel checkpoints with orders to stop our vehicle, and to arrest us if we were caught taking photographs. Ian feared for our safety: he wanted us to return to Freetown immediately.

We sat on the steps of the building, Simon and I, while Ian and Patrick determined what should be done with us. I had my head in my hands. I couldn't believe I had come this far only to turn back now. To tell the truth I was pretty irritated with Ian for the blunder he had made. He was now deep in conversation with

Patrick, leaning against the bonnet of the Land Cruiser. I tried to read their gestures, work out which way the discussion was going. Finally Ian walked over to us. Our fate, it seemed, had been determined by logistics: there were no available vehicles to take us back to Freetown. We would stay in Makeni until the morning and leave at first light. In the meantime he agreed to take me to my family in Magburaka; he had a meeting in the town. He could leave me with them for forty-five minutes.

The Hotel Adams was a moss-covered ruin, abandoned ever since I was a child. In its heyday, when Magburaka was the centre of the colonial administration, the hotel provided accommodation for railway passengers travelling between Bauya and Freetown. The Hotel Adams aside, the centre of Magburaka was surprisingly intact. I tried hard to remember the layout of the town. The wide, straight avenues were lined with palm trees and identical low bungalows, built of clay bricks with dark-red corrugated-iron roofs, each equidistantly spaced, sitting in its own small plot of land with a water pot by the front door. They all looked the same.

We stopped at the main square in the centre of town to ask for directions to Magbesseh Street. The driver and I climbed out and we approached a woman selling cola nuts. She was curious and asked what business we had in Magburaka. The driver, who was a Temne, told her my name. Within a few minutes I was surrounded by well-wishers. People put down their wares and shook my hand; a man selling shirts called across the square to his friends to hurry over: 'Aminatta Forna! Dr Forna's daughter.'

'Mohamed Sorie een pickin.'

'Welcome, welcome!'

'Are you going to see your family?'

Someone squeezed my arm. People massed around me. I felt disoriented, bewildered; at the same time I was nodding and

smiling, comforted by the warmth of the welcome. I had not expected it at all. I didn't know any of these people nor did I recognise their faces, but they all knew me, every one of them. Someone
pointed the way to Magbesseh Street. At Ian's request we made a
short detour along the way. Less than half an hour later the two
Land Cruisers drew up in a cloud of dust and exhaust fumes and
dropped us in front of the house my father had built in Magbesseh
Street. News had travelled fast. Uncle Momodu, who had heard
the news that I was in the vicinity clear across the other side of
town, had hurried back, and was standing on the porch to meet
us wearing a fresh navy-blue gown, leather sandals and a fez.

Uncle Momodu barely seemed to have aged: he looked just the
same to me. His sons—Abdul, Hamdeen and Abdulai, all young
boys in their teens—came out of the house and greeted Simon and
me in perfect English. We retired to the front porch. Immediately
we were surrounded by a small crowd of children and neighbours.
The local Imam arrived, resplendent in purple, and took a seat
alongside us. I greeted him with a few words of Temne and shook
hands. Simon extended his hand, holding the elbow of his right
arm in the customary Muslim style. We sat down.

I didn't know where to begin. I was desperately conscious of
how little time I had and yet I was wary of plunging straight
in without warning, of asking sensitive questions relating to the
past without an appropriate prelude. The minutes passed. We exchanged civilities for the second time, then the third time. Someone brought two glasses of water. I took a couple of sips. It was
lukewarm. We continued to sit. I hoped people would soon lose
interest and leave us alone, but the crowd around us, rather than
diminishing, seemed to swell. After a few more minutes I asked
Uncle Momodu if perhaps we could take a short walk.

Pa Roke's house was still standing, painted red with blue
shutters. I noticed for the first time how beautifully carved the

latticework was. It had been sold, Abdul informed me; someone who was not a relation lived there now. Auntie Memuna's house opposite stood empty. As we walked down the road we were followed by the throng of people, who by now must have numbered upwards of twenty or thirty: the whole street had turned out to see us. I followed the path around the back of the houses with Uncle Momodu, his sons and the crowd of villagers in my wake. Twenty yards on I came to a halt when I realised I was standing in front of the latrines. I started to retrace my steps. I turned to Uncle Momodu, who was at my elbow: 'Can we talk, please?' I asked in desperation. 'I have to leave soon and I can't come back. I have to return to Freetown in the morning. I must talk to you.'

The house was completely empty of furniture. Uncle Momodu led us into the master bedroom. The mattress on the bed and the wall behind were scorched—by the rebels, explained Uncle Momodu. They had tried to set fire to the place when the RUF had first overrun Magburaka four years before. The bathroom had been destroyed: basin, toilet, tub all smashed. This house had been the realisation of a dream for my father, but we had never stayed so much as a night in it.

We spent the remainder of my visit sitting on the bed, deep in conversation. All except for the last five minutes. For that brief time we gathered in front of the house taking photographs: Momodu with his sons, Momodu alone, regarding the camera with an unsmiling face, striking a rigid pose with his hands by his side, like the old-fashioned photos of the Fornas taken at great expense and ceremony by the photographer in Magburaka's high street. Momodu and me. Behind us the Imam and a scattering of children gaze upon the proceedings. In the final image of the series, at Simon's urging, Uncle Momodu, alone again, manages a small, slight smile. And then we were gone. Ian reappeared and we were sucked back into the air-conditioned interior of the Land Cruiser.

'*Owa!*' I called. I waved. A dozen voices chorused in reply. This was not how I had imagined it at all, my return to Magburaka. There had been no choice, but still it felt wrong. I remembered how our visits to Magburaka used to be. We would spend languid hours with Pa Roke, just keeping company. We paid our respects to the family elders one by one, never hurrying for fear of causing offence. I used to be bored by it when I was a child. Yet now I had never felt more alien, more like a foreigner. I had arrived in a white four-wheel drive covered in official insignia, spent less than an hour and disappeared again.

As darkness fell at the Sisters of Mercy mission in Makeni the metal gates of the compound were closed and several of the vehicles backed against it. About twenty aid workers, all male, were spending the night here. There had been a few other women among us, but they had been found separate quarters. I had elected to stay where I was since Simon and I would be leaving at dawn. Once the elaborate security precautions started Ali, a young deaf boy whom we had spent the last half hour teaching an improvised game of blackjack, had departed. The Sisters of Mercy was close to the RUF base and had on several occasions in the past been attacked by drunken fighters who took potshots at Father Victor, the old Catholic priest who ran the mission, as well as several of the western aid workers. Over the years everything had been looted, including the mattresses on the beds, removed from beneath the patients who had been lying upon them. Later we gathered around the fading beam of an upended torch, smoking furious quantities of cigarettes, playing cards. There were a couple of jokes, in a spirit of bravado, about the chances of an attack that night—particularly in light of the day's events.

I lay on the metal frame of my cot, listening to the sounds emerging out of the darkness, to the snoring from the other beds, the occasional animal cry from behind the walls of the compound.

I asked myself, for perhaps the fiftieth time that day, what I would have done if Colonel Issa or any of his men had tried to hold us. Would I have revealed my identity? Certainly that was the advice before I left Freetown: tell them who you are, they will never harm you. Yabome had believed that, reassuring herself that we would come home unscathed. Yet if I had suddenly decided to declare myself, would they even have believed me: travelling under the auspices of the UN, accompanied by a British husband, posing as a journalist? I wondered about that. On hearing my name, even our Temne driver had at first regarded me with incredulity. In Britain, living in a large, industrial city with home, career and friends, in a life I had created for myself, I rarely paused to question my identity any more. Out here, caught on a high wire between my past and my present, I had never felt less certain of who I had become. I slept fitfully, dreamt of being shot at, and woke before it was light.

By midday we were back in Freetown. Among my many regrets was the fact that I had not been able to see the Bumbuna Falls again. I wasn't even sure if they were still there. They had once been threatened by a planned hydro-electric project, but I presumed the war had put paid to that. I had asked our driver, but he did not know the way to the falls, and besides, we were under instructions to go straight back to the city. On the way into town we were caught behind a procession. People on their way to a wedding, I thought at first. They were mostly middle-aged women resplendent in silks and embroidered gowns sporting elaborate hairstyles. Six male drummers followed behind, toting enormous goatskin-covered drums. People leaned from the balconies above. The traffic inched by up the long, steep hill. A diminutive figure led the parade, wearing a wooden mask that fitted entirely over her head, carved braids of hair around a finely featured face; cascades of black-dyed raffia fell around her shoulders. It was the Bundu Devil, mascot of the women's secret society.

Six weeks after our encounter in Makeni, following an altercation with a UN peacekeeper, General Kallon shot one of the Kenyan soldiers in the face at point-blank range. Under the orders of General Issa the RUF took five hundred peacekeeping troops hostage, including three British soldiers. The killing sparked an international incident involving the government of Sierra Leone; Kofi Annan, the UN secretary-general; and Tony Blair, the prime minister of Great Britain. The British men later escaped through the bush to a hero's welcome in the British newspapers. By the time I heard the news I was far away, back in my study at home in London.

Momodu was born the second son of Pa Roke Forna's fourth wife Marie. He was the old man's sixth son. Mohamed, my father, was the second male child born to the ill-fated Ya Ndora, Pa Roke's sixth wife. But the untimely death of two brothers in between them placed Mohamed directly behind Momodu in the family ranking. This is the way it was, and would have remained, except for a slip of fate that sent Mohamed away to school and eventually to Britain to become a doctor. When the letter arrived to say he was on his way home with a British wife and three children Pa Roke prepared to welcome home his son. Momodu alone stood apart from the family's celebrations. 'I hope that Mohamed does not think that by marrying a white woman his children will be treated as superior to ours,' he was heard to comment.

Their relationship was characterised by fraternal love and sibling rivalry. Momodu was a frequent guest in his brother's house in Freetown, where he went on business, and he grew close to his fun-loving Scottish sister-in-law. In the beginning Mohamed often sought the counsel of his brother and never made a decision on a serious matter without first calling together all his elder brothers. In his years as minister of finance he shared with Momodu his frustrations, his growing distrust of Siaka Stevens and his fears for the country. Momodu opposed Mohamed's decision to resign from the government, believing his brother stood a better chance of challenging the government's excesses from the inside. During the brief glory days of the UDP, as the stakes grew higher, Mohamed confided in his brother less. As the UDP began the tour of the provinces, Momodu confronted his younger brother in Magburaka, and demanded he accompany him to consult with the brothers who were waiting for him at home. Mohamed declined. That very evening Mohamed was arrested in Makeni and placed in detention at Pademba Road Prison. Momodu too, who had never been part of the UDP, was imprisoned at Mafanta and released after three years, just one month before his brother.

When his sons were freed from detention Pa Roke warned Mohamed: 'Your enemies will only miss you once.' Intrigue and manipulation had become the currency of Sierra Leone under Stevens. Within six months rumours were rife that Mohamed's life was in danger from his enemies within the APC. Momodu took a warning to his brother and soon after Mohamed left for Europe. Momodu thought he might stay away, but in Mohamed's absence a whispering campaign began that he was plotting against the government. Mohamed cut short his trip and flew back in an attempt to put pay to the rumours.

Though they were engaged in the rice business together, in all that time Momodu saw his brother on fewer than a handful of occasions. When Mohamed was arrested on 30 July Momodu was in Magburaka. The news took several days to reach him. As soon as he heard it he made his way directly to Freetown. On his way to Samuel's Lane he was intercepted by a soldier by the name of Steven. Momodu did not recognise this man, but listened when he told him of the whereabouts of a wounded soldier who had been treated by Dr Forna and subsequently taken to a hospital in Magburaka. The soldier mentioned Abu Kanu's name: it was he who had driven the man up-country and delivered him to a certain Dr Osayo at Magburaka.

Momodu hastened back to Magburaka. Late one night, together with his brother Ismail and with the connivance of a male nurse on the ward, Momodu crept into the hospital. They took Kendekah Sesay from his bed, dressed him in the long, blue gown of an Alpha, the trailing sleeves of which concealed his injured hand, and drove him with haste to the family village of Rogbonko. There he was hidden in a little used hut, under the care of one of their sisters, who was sworn to secrecy.

The Russian pathologist at Magburaka Hospital said that by the time Kendekah Sesay was admitted to the hospital's care he was already a dead man. The extensive injuries to his hand had turned septic, the poison had entered his bloodstream, his skin was clammy, a rash covered his body. He was past the critical stage for treatment and his internal organs, already invaded by the bacteria, were beginning to fail one by one. The doctors recommended the hand be amputated. Kendekah Sesay refused. They did not seek to persuade him: in truth he would die either way. A second doctor I interviewed, one who had jointly conducted the post-mortem on his body after it had been fished out of the river behind the houses in Rogbonko, said there was no evidence of foul play. Kendekah Sesay had not drowned—his lungs were clear of water. Nor was there evidence of any toxic chemicals in his blood. Although the pathologists came under great pressure from the government to produce findings to the effect that the man had been murdered by someone, a doctor possibly, their investigations showed nothing. Kendekah Sesay had almost certainly died of his wounds.

Momodu disposed of the body. He placed the corpse in a rice sack with four nine-inch blocks and he carried it beyond the boundaries of the village, where he heaved it into the river Rosana. It was the rainy season and the water flowed swiftly through the narrow channel. The sack disappeared from view. Later, back in Freetown, Momodu confided all this to just one person: Ibrahim Ortole, a former member of the UDP from Port Loko, an erstwhile confidant and a business associate of his brother. Unknown to Momodu, Ibrahim was tainted. The information was passed to S. I. Koroma. Momodu fled to Kono. The CID arrested his wife and forced her to lead them to where her husband was hiding. They used her head wrap as a banner tied to the antennae of the Land-Rover as they entered Kono in triumph to bring Momodu back to Rogbonko. Police divers retrieved the sack containing the soldier's remains from the water. Momodu, chained and shackled, was forced to carry the dripping bundle back from the river and through the streets of the village.

In Freetown Momodu stood by the side of the mortuary table, on which lay Kendekah Sesay's body. The cool water had preserved the corpse remarkably well. On the opposite side of the table was Mohamed, along with the other men who had been arrested. In front of Mohamed Momodu was forced to formally identify the corpse and confess to his role in disposing of it. He could see the shock and disbelief on his younger brother's face. When it was over he watched as Mohamed was led away to make his first formal statement in front of Bambay Kamara.

This was the fate, as recounted by my uncle Momodu, of the man I had helped my father tend when I was ten years old. I had given my little bottle of Dettol and sewn bandages. My father had cleaned and dressed the wound, but Kendekah Sesay was already in shock, beyond the care of an ordinary physician. He needed to be taken straight to a hospital, my father had instructed. I remembered the colour of his face, the terrible ashen pallor, a ghostliness emerging from under his skin: the colour of death.

Uncle Momodu had finished his story. He was silent for a moment.

'In the end this was one of the reasons for the verdict,' he said, finally. I was quiet. It must have cost him a great deal to admit. He had thought he was helping his brother and he only ended up making matters worse. I knew that Momodu had long laboured under the responsibility for what he had done within our family. And yet, to a certain extent he was right, but not entirely. During the trial the prosecution had maintained that Kendekah Sesay was the soldier who had thrown the dynamite at Kamara-Taylor's house, but beyond that he had been relegated to a curiously minor role in the whole affair. When he cross-examined my father Tom Johnson had barely asked about Kendekah Sesay. He had posed one or two questions about Momodu's involvement, which my father had not been able to answer. That was it.

Uncle Momodu spoke for a few minutes more. He was back in 1964.

'Mohamed took the train to see us in Magburaka. He had met a friend on the train, but he wanted to talk to me alone, as his brother. He told me he wanted to join politics. I told him, "You are a small boy, yet. You are not ready." In turn he told me there was too much need, not enough time. By thirty he wanted to be in a responsible position.' Uncle Momodu paused, shifted his position. He was leaning forward with his elbows on his knees, opening and closing his hands as he spoke. 'He was brave. Not afraid at all. When he was a small boy he was just like any other. He was docile, polite. I warned him, in 1974, that there was a danger to his life. He did not seem to care.'

'How could he not be concerned?' I asked.

Momodu shrugged and gave his explanation: 'It seems he did not believe me. I thought perhaps he had spent too much time in Britain. He did not know this country and its ways any more.'

I pondered the mystery of Kendekah Sesay for a long time. The soldier had been the one real tragedy in the prelude to the entire affair. Who was the mystery Steven who told Momodu that Abu Kanu had taken Kendekah Sesay to Magburaka? That simply could not have been the case. Abu Kanu was arrested early the next day—he could not have made it to Magburaka and been back in Freetown by then. It would be difficult enough to make the round trip in that time today, twenty-five years later, when the tarmac road stretched the entire distance—impossible back then. Kendekah Sesay's state when he arrived at Magburaka Hospital suggested he may have been hidden somewhere else first; by the time he was taken to a hospital he was dying from septicaemia.

Kendekah was the only link between my father and any of the events on that night. My father was followed wherever he went, his every activity filed and reported. Our house was watched around the clock from Nancy Steele's windows. It was simply inconceivable that the authorities did not know my father had treated the wounded soldier.

It seems so apparent now. Obvious, in fact, from the moment it dawned on me. I guess at the time I was deluged with information, trying to sort the material facts from the irrelevant, make sense of the conflicts and contradictions, desperate to work out whose account I could trust and who was a liar. It took me for ever to grasp what later seemed so glaringly self-evident. The prosecution's case against my father had rested almost entirely on the evidence of the four witnesses who each swore they had seen him at the Murraytown cemetery in the dead of night, issuing orders to men gathered there, sending them out to attack the homes of government ministers. To admit they knew my father had given treatment to the wounded Kendekah Sesay meant placing him somewhere else on that night. It was not a treasonable offence to attend an injured man. In order to obtain the verdict and the sentence they wanted, they needed to place him at the centre, at the very heart of the alleged crime.

❧ 46 ❧

We were back at Hastings Airport among the huddle of passengers waiting for the airport gates to open. In my hand I held my passport, ticket and the police clearance all travellers required to leave the country. We would be shuttled from Hastings to Lungi in a small eight-seater plane. In Lungi we would catch the West Coast Airlines flight to Banjul. There was an overnight wait in Banjul and then on to London.

The last forty-eight hours had passed in a blur. Morlai had failed to appear at the house on two consecutive mornings. At first I had put his absence down to a mix-up over the dates I would be away in Magburaka. Morlai would not have known the trip would be cut short as it had been. I imagined he would be there on Monday.

On Sunday morning, as I carried a cup of tea out onto the veranda, the house vibrated with the rhythms of the church next door. The people locked themselves into the empty courtyard at evening curfew and began praying as Sunday dawned. The city was in the grip of a religious revival. I found Sarah, Morlai's wife, sitting on the balcony alone. I was surprised: on the occasions when she visited she always brought the four children along with her. Morlai, I assumed, must be out back keeping company with the household. I greeted her with enthusiasm, but Sarah's expression remained strangely blank, as though she were undertaking an enormous effort of self-control. No sooner had she returned my greeting, in a voice that contained no tremor, than she made an announcement: 'Aminatta. Morlai has asked me to come here and to tell you that he is dying.' Then she began to cry silently. From her bag she took a wadded handkerchief and pressed it to her cheek. I was silent. I asked her what on earth she could possibly mean.

During our absence in Magburaka Morlai's leg, which had continued to trouble him, had grown worse. When the painkillers and the anti-inflammatories supplied by the doctor did not appear to work Morlai had placed his faith in traditional medicine. The healer had given him a poultice of herbs to apply to the afflicted area, but it did no good. In a short time Morlai could neither walk, nor sit in comfort, nor lie. The pain took away his appetite and at night Sarah heard her husband's groans of anguish. That Sunday morning Morlai had awoken feverish; his breathing was shallow, he was unable to move and barely even capable of speaking. Sarah was frightened. Though she did not want to leave him, Morlai begged her to make the two-and-a-half-hour journey across town to me to ask for our help.

How fragile is life in a country like this. Morlai had endured and survived so much. In the end he was almost felled by an ordinary infection. Early on Monday Simon and Dura had fetched him from his house and driven him to the doctor. The doctor took one look at him and called the hospital. The joint of his hip was badly inflamed, the poison had collected and was spreading to the rest of his body.

I had sat next to Morlai's bed in the long ward at Connaught Hospital. He was lying awkwardly on his side, his leg bent under him. He opened his eyes. His first words to me were words of apology: 'I am so sorry, Aminatta. I am sorry for this trouble.' He looked exhausted, his eyes were tinged with yellow, sunken, ringed by great dark circles. When Sarah had told me Morlai was dying I thought she just meant he *felt as if* he were dying. Who, after all, could die of an aching hip? I realised in those moments how close Morlai had come. I held on to his hand. I had an eerie sense of history repeating itself. I considered the fate of the unlucky Kendekah Sesay, who had died of blood-poisoning. His injuries had been far worse. There had been maggots feasting in the wounds of his hands towards the end, I was told. Nevertheless, in a western country or with proper and immediate treatment, Kendekah Sesay need not have died.

Connaught Hospital was once a good place for the sick to be healed. Two blue pillars mark the entrance on the corner of Percival and Wallace Johnson Street. Visitors and patients pass through an iron gateway beneath a golden crest of the lion and the unicorn. The pillared two-storey buildings housing the wards are built around a central courtyard. Covered concrete walkways lead from one building to the next. In the shade of the trees families can sit during visiting hours. Neat black-and-white painted signs point the way to the dispensary, the operating theatres and the different wards. Connaught used to be a model colonial hospital. But for most patients Connaught has become a place to die.

A tide mark of dirt circled the cream-painted walls of the ward. It was possible to make out, from the stains on the wall, where a bed had been moved or taken away. The blanket on which Morlai lay looked discoloured, whether through age or lack of washing I could not tell. I had felt the grit on the floor underfoot as I walked the length of the ward to his bed. Above our heads flies spun around each other in lazy figures of eight. There was one nurse, no sign yet of a doctor.

Later, as Yabome, Simon and I stood outside the doctor's surgery waiting to talk to her about Morlai's treatment, I stared at the floor by my feet and watched an army of ants swarm over the corpse of a gecko lizard and start to devour the eyes. There were no seats. I stood away from the wall, but as the hour passed

I found myself reluctantly leaning against it. A family appeared at the top of the stairs and slowly made their way towards us. At the head came two young men, propping up an elderly man. The old man was dressed in a trailing, white gown and could barely support himself on his own legs. Agonisingly, inch by inch, they progressed towards us down the corridor. When they drew abreast one of the young men switched places with his sister at his grandfather's elbow and knocked on the door of the doctor opposite.

After a few moments the door opened and the doctor surveyed the family. 'Wait downstairs,' he said and turned to go back inside. The young man explained they had been sent upstairs by the receptionist. The doctor shook his head firmly. 'No. He should not have sent you up here. Wait downstairs.' The door closed. I watched as the family retraced their steps.

The row of wooden shelves at the hospital pharmacy was empty. There were no customers. A crowd of people begged at the door, not for money but for medicine. The pharmacist stared at the list of drugs and equipment the doctor had given us and snorted. He suggested we try the privately owned Lebanese chemist nearby.

By the time we returned to the hospital the day was almost at an end. Sarah had arrived after work, still wearing her police officer's uniform. Her sons and her small daughter were with her. She would sleep the night on the floor by Morlai's bed. We handed her the gauze, needles, intravenous tubes and bandages. The drugs had been left with the doctor, who warned us to lock the rest of the things away, for there were a great many thefts among the patients at night. Sarah's monthly salary came to a fraction of the money we had just spent on antibiotics and medical equipment. The cost to us had been thirty pounds.

We had spoken to Morlai to say goodbye. We were due to leave in the morning. Morlai apologised over and over, but I felt like the guilty one. I berated myself for not noticing how much pain he had been in during the past few weeks. I had acquired a tunnel vision, nothing else mattered, I was fixated only upon my own purpose. Every day I pressed on, thinking only of what new information I had acquired, where my next goal lay. When Morlai tried to tell me he was unwell I had failed to listen to him properly. Finally he had ceased to make the effort. While we spoke I saw the nurse at the end of the ward rise and begin to usher the visitors outside. I kissed Morlai on the forehead and Simon shook his hand. I could see the effort had exhausted Morlai. We walked slowly away from the bed.

At Hastings there was still no sign of the airport staff. Beyond the gates the hall stood empty. The number of people around us had grown and a young street entertainer had begun to work the crowd. The man was a natural comic. He had drawn everyone's attention by addressing a weeping woman, one of the passengers, in a loud voice. Pretending to be her lover or her husband, he strutted and shouted, swore he would not leave her—she had but to say the word. At first, believing this to be a lovers' quarrel, we had all rather uncharacteristically looked away, though I had found myself unable to resist surreptitiously watching him. When I caught his eye and saw the smile he gave me I realised this was an act. He passed his hat around, pronouncing to the crowd, who by now were laughing out loud—all except the tearful girl, that is: though he was but a beggar he had made it his ambition to be the prince of beggars. He deftly retrieved his hat and at the approach of a security guard he slipped through the crowd and was gone.

A second performer stepped forward. He was a man of about sixty dressed in a pair of outsized canvas trousers cut off at the knee and tied at the waist with a piece of string. He had a small moustache and a streak of almost white hair across the top of his crown. On the ground he spread out a blue plastic sheet containing his props: a small pile of rice, a bottle of water, a glass, a tin plate. He straightened up and a moment later he went down on his hands, flipped his legs up and over him until he was upright again. Then he collapsed into the splits. I caught my breath. I watched him tumble, first holding a plate of rice in one of his hands, next holding a glass of water, tumbling so fast that the glass performed an entire revolution and yet he never lost a drop. It was an act I had once known almost by heart.

Musa. That was the name of the man who had entertained a small girl at a party she believed was her sixth birthday. Through all this time he remained a performer. I tried to make him remember the day. Perhaps it was the emotion of all that had occurred in the last few weeks, in the last two days especially: it suddenly became overwhelmingly important to me that Musa remember. I felt as though I had stumbled upon a vital witness to the past. The old entertainer smiled and nodded at me. I tried to describe the day at Minister's Quarters thirty years ago. He was still smiling, looking through me, evidently humouring me. After a while I let him go. It was enough to have seen him there.

The gates opened and we were pushed through with the swell of bodies. Suddenly there was barely time to say goodbye to Yabome. At passport control we stood in front of a young woman and her two male colleagues seated at a rough wooden desk. We handed our documents over. The young woman stared at the inside page of my passport, her expression sullen. 'Forna?' Her tone was brusque.

'Yes,' I replied. I waited.

'What kind of business has brought you to Sierra Leone?' I told her I was visiting family. The woman arched her eyebrows.

The man next to her, who was in his fifties, looked at the passport. 'Which Forna?' he asked. The familiar pattern: I had become used to it again.

'Mohamed Sorie,' I stated boldly. 'Dr Mohamed Sorie Forna.' The expression on the face of the woman officer remained unchanged. Obviously the name meant nothing to her. She opened her mouth to ask me another question and snapped it shut as her colleague elbowed her.

'Nineteen seventy-five?' He looked at me and I nodded, yes. He took Simon's passport and lifted my own from the hands of his colleague. 'Please go through,' he said. 'Someone will bring your papers.' We stepped past the desk, past the scramble of passengers, and into the waiting area.

I took a seat. I sat and stared out of the open-sided building at the runway, watching the steam begin to rise as the sun heated the damp tarmac. I remembered how, once, my brother and sister and I had hired a taxi to bring us home from Lumley Beach; Mum was at work, there was no one to collect us. The taxi-driver had chatted on the way home and asked us the same question. I remember the astonishment on his face as he swivelled around in his seat, taking his eyes dangerously off the road. He had a good look at us. When he dropped us outside the gates of the house, holding on to our wet towels and snorkels, he had waived the fare.

An hour later a small aircraft landed and taxied to a stop. By now the last of the passengers had made their way through the check-in, through health and immigration. The woman from the immigration desk approached and sat next to me on the moulded plastic seats. She handed me our passports, freshly stamped with exit permits, and then lingered as we both watched the Russian pilot step down from the cockpit of the plane and walk towards the building. As I struggled with my hand luggage she offered to carry one of the bags and walked with us to the end of the queue to board the plane. Then she shook my hand and disappeared.

47

Progress had stalled. I had flown back to Sierra Leone in December of 2000 on a Ghana Airways flight loaded with people returning home for Christmas. At the check-in desk Simon and I had waited more than two hours while passengers ahead of us, overburdened with two, three times the baggage allocation, tried to persuade the airline staff to allow them to board. When our turn came the baggage clerk gratefully waved through our two small holdalls and we watched them trundle out of sight on the conveyor belt, in between the boxed microwave cookers and the folded pushchairs. After an overnight journey we were delayed for twelve hours in Accra, where we waited for our connecting flight. It turned out the plane that should have carried us to Freetown had belly-flopped onto the runway in the previous week. Air Ghana was down to a single plane: the aircraft on which we had arrived. In the meantime the plane had been sent to collect passengers who had been stranded in Abidjan for the last four days. When it returned to Accra it would take us to Freetown.

We boarded at six in the evening, just as the darkness was beginning to close in. The air was surprisingly cool, the sky overcast as we waited on the tarmac, holding boarding passes that bore no seat numbers. An hour later the plane stopped over at Abidjan, where we sat on the runway for nearly three hours more while the ground staff tried to open the hold and retrieve the suitcases belonging to the disembarking passengers. The mood among those still on board was growing tense: with the curfew hour rapidly approaching in Freetown we were in danger of having to turn back. After eleven o'clock air traffic control at Lungi would not be able to give us clearance to land.

I called to the flight attendant nearest me and explained the problem: 'Umm,' he agreed urbanely. 'We are doing the best we can. I'm sure we will be taking off soon.' He smiled pleasantly and returned to his position by the cabin door. I walked up to him and repeated myself. I asked him to take my message to the captain. I had the impression he did not understand me. His manner remained pleasant, but he did not move. I sat back down. A few minutes later, unable to contain my frustration, I walked up the gangway and through the First Class cabin to look for the captain myself. I found him, standing with his back to the cockpit door, surrounded by angry passengers already engaged in trying to persuade him to fly straight to Freetown instead of Monrovia, which should have been our next scheduled stop. Eventually, and to my surprise, the captain concurred and made an announcement over the tannoy. We relaxed. Then he flew to Monrovia anyway.

We landed at Lungi two hours after I had resigned myself to returning to Accra. A senior airport official on board had used the plane's radio to alert the airport authorities, bypass the regulations and keep the runway lights burning. At one in the morning, after a thirty-hour journey, we passed through immigration. That night we slept at the airport, on an old sofa in the VIP lounge. People lay with their heads on their hand luggage, on the seats and floor around us. The toilets were blocked; there was no running water. I looked around, taking in the heavy velvet drapes hanging from the floor to the ceiling across a tall window that looked out onto a view of the runway; the shag carpet, matted and stained; the semi-defunct air-conditioner rattling and wheezing on the wall opposite. The decor hadn't changed at all, not since I hid in the same room when I was just six years old, waiting to fly out of Sierra Leone and into three years of exile.

Since the day of our inauspicious arrival I had directed my efforts at tracing every one of the Mende soldiers court-martialled for their part in the alleged coup attempt. There had been nine. Five of them were dead. Upon their release from prison three had taken work in Kenema in the south. They had become security officers: two at the Sierra Rutile mine and the third at the Tongo Fields diamond mine. I went to the Ministry of Mines to check their records of employment and the feasibility of travelling to Kenema. I discovered the mines had been overrun by the rebels in 1992. Many of the staff were taken hostage; others had fled or been killed. The diamond mine was now controlled by the RUF, who used the income from the sale of so-called blood diamonds to buy arms. Of the whereabouts of the last remaining soldier there was no word. It was just as likely he was dead, sucked into the void of the war and the fighting between the RUF and the Kamajors. The life expectancy in Sierra Leone of a soldier, even a former soldier, was short.

My search for the mysterious Steven reached the same conclusion. I hadn't even managed to discover his surname. There was something odd, bizarre even, about his anonymity, in a country such as this, where blood ties counted for so much. It made him seem like an imaginary character and I began to wonder if he existed at all. Uncle Momodu had no idea—he hazarded a guess that Steven might have gone back north and probably joined the rebels.

Morlai had been discharged from Connaught Hospital in June after almost three months. All the time he was there I kept in contact through Yabome and worried he might die of something else, a secondary infection picked up from the unhygienic surroundings. His joint had been drained and a small piece of shrapnel removed, the cause, apparently, of the infection. He still walked with the slightest of limps, but in almost every other way he was back to his former self.

Together Morlai and I pursued a further lead, this time to find an ex-fisherman and street boy by the name of Alimamy Bakarr. He had featured at the trial, though his evidence had not mentioned my father. He was rumoured to have been the person who threw the dynamite at Kamara-Taylor's house—this last piece of information came from the defendants. This was the talk, apparently, among the soldiers during the time they were all in Pademba Road together. Alimamy Bakarr, Morlai Salieu and Bassie Kargbo all came from the same area of Port Loko: S. I. Koroma's constituency.

Bassie Kargbo, for a sum of money, promised to locate Alimamy Bakarr who, he said, had moved from Waterloo, where he had lived for many years, to a Freetown slum near the harbour known as Saw Pit. We had twice arranged a rendezvous and each time Bassie Kargbo showed up alone at our agreed location—the rice shop on Bai Bureh Road. On both occasions he had demanded more money from me before he would promise to try to set up another meeting. I had begun to doubt whether Bassie Kargbo was telling the truth, so Morlai offered to go to Saw Pit himself, accompanied by Bassie Kargbo, to find Alimamy. I wanted to go with them, but Morlai was adamant: it was far too dangerous a place and I would only attract attention. He would be better off alone.

Alimamy Bakarr's digs turned out to be a drug den. Morlai described it to me later: people lying together on the floor of an upstairs room, openly injecting drugs, smoking cannabis and heroin. Morlai could not disguise his revulsion. Alimamy Bakarr appeared swathed in heavy gold chains. At first he had agreed to speak to Morlai. But each time Morlai went back Alimamy made a different excuse and once slipped out at the back while Morlai sat on the wall at the front with his notebook and the list of questions I had given him. Finally Alimamy stopped answering the door altogether, leaving Morlai waiting, watching the addicts arrive edgy and nervous and leave, sated, a long time later: slow moving and glassy eyed as chameleons.

One afternoon I lay on my bed, inert with mental fatigue, enumerating my many frustrations with the country and with the task I had set myself. It had taken me months of work to get this far, and every step of the way I felt I was pushing against some mighty, unspoken resistance. Time and time again I had felt that hardly a fact or a single item of information had been volunteered; every day I made half a dozen telephone calls; I trekked out to interview anyone who would talk to me, then found myself returning to the same place to ask for more information—questions I had omitted to ask—and to chase details they did not think, or perhaps wish, to supply. This was as true of people who had no reason to dissemble as of those who did. As I lay there, in the hot room, staring at the ceiling, I did something I had never done before: I allowed the dark thoughts to crowd in one by one and my anger turned towards my father. How could he have been so trusting of his so-called friends, even of his sworn enemies? This was the question I asked myself over and over. How could he have flouted the warnings, allowed the danger to come so close?

'Leave them in their ruined country,' I wrote in red ink in the pages of my notebook, 'surrounded by ruins, ghosts, flies, motherless children. Fly back to Britain—comfort. How could he have trusted them? Ever? Ever?' I made a list of everything that infuriated me. 'Fatalism. Disloyalty.' I wrote leaning heavily on the nib of the pen so that now the words appear strident: 'No conscience. No personal responsibility. Who cares about accountability?' On the opposite page I wrote: 'They say God has punished them all. But look around you! Look around! It's not over yet.'

Yabome must have realised my frustration, for I made no attempt to hide it. The next afternoon, on our way back to the house from running an errand in town, she directed Dura off the main road and up a short street just off Main Motor Road at Congo Cross. We climbed down from the car in a compound containing two houses and a round open-air seating area, just like a village *barrie*. Something about it felt familiar. I had been here once before, long ago.

The house belonged to Frank Jalloh, head of the CID in 1974 at the time of the arrests. We sat on an old velour sofa in a spacious and somewhat underfurnished reception room while someone went to fetch Frank Jalloh. In due course he appeared: a short, fleshy man with dark skin and a thick neck, dressed in cotton pyjamas. The three of us—Yabome, Simon and I—sat on the sofa, while Frank Jalloh took a large chair opposite us.

Somewhere along the line on her mother's side Yabome and Frank Jalloh were related, it turned out. This was so often the way in Sierra Leone. Yabome opened with the traditional greetings, declined the offer to send out for cold drinks. After a few minutes she turned to the reason for our visit. She explained what I was doing, appealed to him to speak to me.

Frank Jalloh regarded her, neither agreeing nor demurring. He was silent, impassive. Whatever he was thinking, his face betrayed no sign of it. Presently he began to describe the evening my father was arrested and taken to the CID: 'I found them there. Sitting in my office. Forna and Taqi. Sitting in my office. When I came in. They had been arrested.'

I wasn't sure if he wanted to begin straight away. I asked a question—what, exactly, I cannot now recall.

'They were in my office. The two of them. I allowed them to wait there while this thing was going on.' He didn't move on. Instead he repeated himself two or three times more.

Yabome was sitting on the edge of the sofa, waiting politely. After a few more minutes she eased herself slowly up: 'Yes. Well, see what you can remember. It's a long time ago, but you can think about it in the meantime. She'll ask you what she wants to know. Let's say tomorrow? By ten o'clock?' I scrabbled in my bag for my notebook, hastened to write down the appointment.

'They were sitting in my office when this thing started. I found them there. The two of them. Forna and Taqi.' He was still using exactly the same phrases. We shook hands and left.

The next morning I faced Frank Jalloh. This time we were sitting outside on the porch. He was dressed in a long, pale-blue gown, embroidered at the neck. He was fiddling with a short-wave radio. He didn't offer me anything to drink. I sat down and took out my notebook. I had not brought my tape recorder this time, feeling instinctively it would be an error. I didn't want to do anything that might put him off.

'So what do you want to know?' He placed the radio on the battered metal table at his side.

'I need to know about the events of the twenty-ninth of July. The night of the dynamite attack on Kamara-Taylor's house.' It had come down to this. I knew what had not happened on that night. I did not know what, if anything, had really taken place.

A silence followed. Frank Jalloh picked up the radio, adjusted the tuning knob, set it down again without turning it on. 'I found them already there when I got to the CID. Taqi and Forna. I knew them. I asked them, "What are you doing here?" They said, "They have brought us here." They had been arrested.' As he spoke I wrote down his words. 'I went to my office and sent for them. They said, "We don't know what we are doing here."'

Frank Jalloh's feet, crossed at the ankle, barely reached the floor. He was sitting in front of a grubby, cream-painted wall. Behind him was a window to the room where we had met the day before.

I sat with my back to the compound. There was nothing on the veranda save our two chairs and the metal table with the radio on it. When I arrived a boy had been sweeping the beaten earth of the yard and I could hear the incessant sound of the broom, to and fro, to and fro. Sweeping the same place he would sweep again tomorrow. I waited for Frank Jalloh to continue.

'I found them already there, in the CID.' He was repeating what he had told me yesterday. I assumed he would continue the story and I listened in silence, letting him take it at his own pace, not wishing to rush him. But after twenty minutes I found I had scarcely added another word to my notes. He had checked the station diary, he told me, but there was no mention of the arrests there. He had called the commissioner of police, a man called Kaetu Smith, who would not tell him anything. I jotted that down, beginning to feel my patience ebb away with the minutes. Beyond that sliver of detail we had not progressed. He continued to cover the same ground while I tried to hold on to my residual calm. He picked up the radio again. I allowed the silence to lengthen.

'What happened next?' I asked eventually.

'I don't know. I found them there already. After that I was removed and posted to Kono.' I could scarcely believe what I was hearing. Was that it? Was that what I had come here for?

'But you must know something—about the facts of the case.'

'Why would I know?' He was being deliberately obtuse. He held the radio in his hands; his fingers were short and thick, the palms and the backs of his hands smooth and plump.

'You were the head of the CID. You must have discovered something before you went to Kono. Tell me whatever you do know.'

'Why are you asking me?'

I frowned. I was temporarily silenced. What on earth was he talking about? Was this some sort of joke?

A young woman had appeared at the doorway behind him. She adjusted her *lappa*, folded her arms across her chest, and was listening as we parried. I pressed on. He blocked me. I noticed the glimmer of a smile on her face. A few minutes later, when I glanced at her again, she was smirking openly. I was completely baffled. I had no understanding at all of why I was being treated in this way. Already it had taken a full forty minutes to get to this point.

'Why did you tell me to come here, then? Why did you agree to see me?' I demanded. Anger coloured my voice and there was nothing, but nothing I could do to disguise it. I knew I was breaking with every convention, challenging an older man who was my social senior in this society. I was risking everything but I was unable to contain myself. In that instant came the release, like falling, I felt the last vestiges of my self-control slipping away.

'It was *you* who wanted to come here,' he replied, unruffled. The woman sniggered audibly.

With that sound I jumped to my feet. 'Is it funny? Is this so funny?' I demanded of her. She didn't reply. 'Maybe you find it amusing but I do not. Not at all. This is my father, my family we are talking about. And you think it's funny to see me sitting here wasting my time.' I directed all my rage at her until, with satisfaction, I saw the smile slide from her face. She stared at me, shock mingled with uncertainty across her features. Frank Jalloh sat silent and unmoving. I groped behind me for my chair and sat back down. The woman disappeared into the house. That's it, I thought, certain he would ask me to leave. I gave it one last shot. I decided to reveal my only card: 'Did you know that Kendekah Sesay was brought to our house that night?'

Frank Jalloh looked up, his eyes, small and dark, curtained by folds of flesh, were directed at me. I had him. I had his attention. Silence while he regarded me, properly and for the first time. He nodded, slowly, still watching me. The game was over. Yes. Yes the CID had known. 'Yes,' he said.

I drew a dividing line in my notebook, across the page at the point where the interview changed course.

On the night of 29 July or, to be precise, the early hours of the morning of the 30th, Frank Jalloh was woken at home by the commissioner of police, who informed him there had been an attempted coup, and that the matter was already being investigated by Jalloh's deputy Bambay Kamara. In turn Frank Jalloh telephoned Bambay Kamara at his home, asking why he had not been informed of the matter straight away. He was, after all, the CID boss. Bambay merely apologised for the omission. On his way into the offices the next morning Frank Jalloh encountered his deputy again. This time he learned that Bambay had already visited the crime scene and collected the evidence.

'Kamara-Taylor had called him first. Instead of me, he called my deputy. Bambay was hand in glove with the politicians. It was even Bambay who gave instructions to the chief of police. Without consulting me!' On the last three words of the sentence Frank Jalloh's voice, which had barely broken above a sort of thrumming monotone, soared momentarily with indignation. He went on to describe his relationship with his second-in-command. Bambay visited State House regularly; he was known to be a favourite of Stevens and S. I., he said. Often the president or the vice-president would call the CID on some matter, talk to Bambay first, and only then ask to be put through to Frank Jalloh. It had got to the point where orders were being issued over Frank Jalloh's head straight to Bambay. By 1974 the whole situation was beginning to vex Frank Jalloh considerably.

In the afternoon of the same day, the 30th, Frank Jalloh decided to visit Kamara-Taylor's house himself anyway. He collected a sample of the dynamite, observing, he told me, that the explosion was so near the master bedroom it would have been impossible for anyone sleeping there to have escaped unhurt. Later, much later, when he heard Kamara-Taylor insist he had been at home, he came to his own conclusion. Kamara-Taylor and the family must have been appraised of the attack before it happened.

The sample of dynamite he collected that day matched a type sold exclusively by one manufacturer: Delco, who were based in Lunsar. Frank Jalloh visited their factory himself and spoke to the manager. He learned the dynamite had been sold to several soldiers. The manager identified Kendekah Sesay, who by now had been reported absent without leave, as being among them. Frank Jalloh interviewed some of the soldiers who had been in the Murraytown barracks on the night of the 29th. He learned that Kendekah Sesay had been injured early in the evening when a stick of dynamite detonated in his hand during a clandestine demonstration. Kendekah was hidden somewhere in Freetown before being sent to Magburaka Hospital in a taxi. The driver of the taxi was a man by the name of Yamba Kamara. The vehicle had been chartered by an unconfirmed person. At Magburaka the trail went cold. Frank Jalloh discovered Kendekah had mysteriously disappeared from his bed on the ward one night a few days after he arrived.

A trawl of the army followed. There were numerous arrests and interrogations. Frank Jalloh had conducted most of these himself with the permission of the commander-in-chief. Some of the meetings the soldiers confessed to had indeed taken place at Habib Lansana Kamara's house, close to the barracks in Murraytown. But not one of the soldiers named Mohamed Forna in connection with a conspiracy or placed him at any of the meetings, nor did they name Ibrahim Taqi. Habib Lansana Kamara, in Frank Jalloh's opinion, would have been happy to see the army mutiny. He hated the army authorities for the way he had been treated. If there was talk of a rebellion he would have been only too pleased to support it. But Frank Jalloh believed Habib Lansana Kamara was probably only remotely connected with whatever occurred that night. It was Habib's link to Mohamed Forna that drew the interest of the authorities.

S. I. Koroma himself telephoned Frank Jalloh and told him where to find Kendekah Sesay's body. The first time he called and instructed him to send his men to arrest Momodu Forna. In a second telephone call he told him to prepare a team of divers. I asked Jalloh about the man, Ibrahim Ortole, in whom Momodu had confided about Kendekah Sesay.

'Ortole was an informant. I saw him with Stevens, sitting in Stevens's office. Stevens trusted him. He had been informing ever since the days of the UDP. He would tell them where the party was holding meetings. They would go and send in their boys.' Although Frank Jalloh claimed he had known and respected my father—'a great friend', no less—he had never passed on the information that Ibrahim Ortole was operating as an informant.

As the investigation progressed Frank Jalloh was summoned to State House to see the president. He used the opportunity to complain that Bambay Kamara was undermining his authority. 'We have respected you all along,' Stevens had told him, 'but if you don't want to do your job, then perhaps you should leave.' He recognised he was being given an ultimatum: cooperate or go. As it was, they took the decision for him. He was sent on assignment and then transferred to the far north-east of the country well before the trial opened. His job as head of the CID was handed to his rival Bambay Kamara.

Frank Jalloh spoke for a while longer about Siaka Stevens: his fear of Mohamed Forna and his hatred of Ibrahim Taqi. 'Stevens knew Forna had been a competent minister. But by that time they were persecuting everyone from the north. He hated Taqi.

Stevens thought he could fool everyone about the money he was taking, but he knew Taqi was out to get him. Forna and Taqi were together so much of the time.' There he stopped talking.

We sat in silence. It was half past twelve. We had spoken for two and a half hours. I had covered thirteen pages of my notebook with writing. My fingers were stiff and my wrist ached, but I made no move to go. Dura had already arrived to collect me and I had waved him away. I would have to walk home now. Frank Jalloh sighed heavily. He looked away, reached for the radio and turned it on. His attention was no longer with me. He fiddled with the tuning dial and held it up to his ear. The hiss and high-pitched whine from the instrument filled the air. It was as though I was no longer there. The interview was at an end.

48

I had spent twenty-five years in ignorance and one year gradually uncovering some of the truth, and yet now I could barely recall what it felt like not to know. It was as though this terrible knowledge: of the lies and the manipulation, the greed and the corruption, the fear and violence had been with me for ever. So this is innocence lost, what it feels like. The country had changed, I had changed. Lumley Beach, where I sat with Simon watching a sulphurous sun disappear behind the bank of clouds stretched across the horizon, was no longer the same. As for the past, it was irrevocably altered.

On this beach I had learned to swim, during long, hazy afternoons, where my greatest regret was that the sunflower on my red-and-blue swimsuit was not in the same place Busy Lizzie had hers. Now, at regular intervals the attack helicopter from the air base behind us took off and landed, skimming the water as it descended, causing us to break and stare up at the sky, partly because the noise drowned out everything else, but also because of the sheer awe the sight inspired. At every table around us UN soldiers sat and drank beer. A raucous game of beach volleyball was still in play behind us. On the road soldiers manning the road block sat behind razor wire and a sandbank. Children hawked groundnuts to the soldiers, tradesmen brought garish sarongs to display before our table. A seller placed Nomoli figures on the sand in front of me—miniature soapstone icons to the god of fertility buried by the farmers in the fields before the harvest. I spoke to him in Krio: gradually I had recaptured a little of the lost language of my childhood. Other vendors thronged around us, attracted by the possibility of a sale, but then stayed on, preferring conversation to the rigours of the hustle, enjoying the novelty of listening to me speak. 'You are a daughter of Sierra Leone,' smiled the man with the Nomoli, whose face was as deep and broad as one of his own carvings.

Some questions remained to be answered and probably never would be. The identity of the person who had thrown the dynamite at Kamara-Taylor's house remained a mystery as did the identity of whoever brought Kendekah Sesay to our home in Kissy that night. No one in the house at that time was certain. It seemed likely he was brought by his fellow soldiers from the barracks, possibly Habib Lansana Kamara, their ex-colleague who lived close to Murraytown barracks. Where else would Habib have taken him but to our father: a dissident and a doctor? That there were rumblings of discontent and open talk of a rebellion in the army seemed certain. I also believed that Morlai Salieu and Bassie Kargbo had infiltrated the ringleaders and been sent to my father and Ibrahim Taqi's office to try to draw them into a conspiracy, real or illusory.

There was one more conversation still to be had. Saidu Brima, the steward at the PZ compound and the last of the main witnesses, was brought to me, unexpectedly, by Unfa Mansaray. Yabome had pulled off this particular coup, and she delivered the news with a small smile of triumph. I was astonished to discover the two men were still in touch. It had never even occurred to me to ask Unfa Mansaray about Saidu Brima's whereabouts.

'Ah, but I have forgiven him,' Unfa told me when I expressed my surprise. 'I saw how they were beating him that time in CID.' The reconciliation had taken place soon after Unfa's release from prison. To this day they lived close to each other up at Wilberforce.

Saidu Brima was a tiny man whose movements were stiff and uncertain with arthritis. He had worked for a long time as a steward in the houses up at Wilberforce, and still lived there in his own little hut. He sat opposite me across the dining table at Yabome's house, scarcely able to look up, speaking in an almost inaudible whisper, hands clasped on the table in front of him. Yabome sat next to him, encouraging him to talk. He was not one of the men who had visited the solicitor-general's office asking for money and favours the day she had been there. That was Morlai Salieu and Bassie Kargbo. The third man, Kemoko Suma, I had tried to locate. He was last heard to be somewhere in Guinea.

Back in 1974, Saidu Brima confirmed, there had been talk all over the barracks of an uprising. The soldiers were in and out of the PZ compound all the time, and this was how he got to hear about things. They were not discreet. One of the Mende soldiers, Regimental Sergeant-Major Kalogoh, who was among those later arrested and charged with masterminding the plot within the army, was the most vociferous and would boast openly about ejecting the present commander-in-chief in favour of their former boss, David Lansana. Bassie Kargbo worked at the time as Kalogoh's orderly. But Saidu Brima did not take Kalogoh's bravado seriously; he thought few people did. None of the soldiers had any weapons. Stevens didn't trust the army, and only the Internal Security Units were properly equipped. Someone talked about going to Lunsar to buy some dynamite and, just once, Saidu Brima was given a tiny box of ammunition to hide under his bed. As the night of 29 July approached the rumours were thick that a military rebellion was about to take place. When he heard the explosion Saidu Brima was in his own quarters, only half a mile away from the minister of finance's house.

Saidu Brima did not recognise Mohamed Forna or Ibrahim Taqi. A CID officer pointed both men out to him during one of the site visits from Pademba Road, telling him to remember just what they looked like. By that time Saidu Brima had already been burned with lighted cigarettes and whipped with a belt. He did not elaborate on the torture; I saw how his hands plucked at the crocheted tablecloth as he spoke. The knuckles were swollen. His fingernails were ridged: the sign of some deficiency or another, or was it a heart condition, blood pressure? I couldn't remember exactly. He had agreed to tell Newlove, his interrogator, what he knew—the rumours that had been circulating around the barracks. He mentioned a meeting at Milton Street. The beating and interrogation went on for the whole morning. Newlove asked him about Mohamed Forna and Ibrahim Taqi. Saidu Brima replied he did not know them; at least, if he did it was only by reputation because they had once been well-known politicians. They had never been mentioned by any of the soldiers. In the afternoon Newlove read his statement back to him. Then Saidu Brima was taken to the cells.

In solitary confinement in his cell at Pademba Road, Saidu Brima could hear prisoners being brought in, the comings and goings of the guards. After a few days he was moved from Wilberforce block to Clarkson. Two weeks later he was brought back to the CID headquarters, along with Bassie Kargbo, Morlai Salieu and other men selected to become potential witnesses. Bambay Kamara called them into his office one by one. When Saidu Brima's turn came the new boss of the CID set down in front of him a statement. It looked exactly like the one he had made when he was first brought in. Bambay called for rice and *plassas* to be brought for the men. It was the first decent meal Saidu Brima had eaten since his arrest. Bambay watched while they ate their fill, calling for more rice to be heaped upon empty plates. Then he told them why they had been brought to the CID building.

'What did he offer you in return?' I asked.

For the first time since he had started talking Brima looked up at me. 'Nothing, madam. I promise you. Only that if I did not cooperate I would be charged. And if I made any mistake. They said if I even spoke to anyone about it when I was released, anyone at all, they would arrest me again. Bambay said they would be watching me.' I could see he wanted to be believed, and I did believe him.

It was not Newlove but a different officer, someone he did not recognise, who took him into a separate cell to coach him. The statement he memorised was not the same as the one he had originally made. It contained one difference. The names of Mohamed Forna and Ibrahim Taqi had been inserted, alongside a description of a meeting at which they were all supposedly present at Milton Street. The statement also said he had seen both men at Murraytown cemetery late on the night of 29 July, when he was among the group of men assembled ready to go out and kill two government ministers and the commander-in-chief of the army. Brima learned his new statement by heart. He followed Bassie Kargbo into the witness box. His initial testimony, given at eleven o'clock one morning over a week into the trial, lasted one hour. He did not make a single mistake. He went back to prison. A few months later, in January, he delivered the same false testimony at the court martial of the soldiers.

It was strange how every new piece of knowledge served to wipe my mind and leave me devoid of feeling. I had wanted to know and yet the knowledge seemed to defeat me. It was like a virus running through my body: it left me weak and helpless. I had wanted to know, but I had never paused to consider what effect knowing might have upon me. To know now, twenty-five years too late, left a feeling of overwhelming powerlessness, of a kind I had never experienced before. I had the knowledge I had desired for so long—and what good did it do?

For a moment I was frozen, sitting where I was, my eyes fixed on the delicate patterns of the tablecloth while I pulled my mind back from the past. Saidu Brima excused himself to go. I looked up to find him standing there, waiting.

'May I go now, madam?'

'Yes, yes. Of course.' I could barely summon a response. I retreated into a display of manners. I stood up. 'Thank you very much for coming here. You've been most helpful,' I mouthed automatically.

He pushed his chair back into the table, still hovering. He spoke again: 'I am sorry for all of this, madam. For all of you. I am sorry.'

There it was. I had wondered if it would ever come. Finally I had stopped waiting for it. The first and only time anyone had ever expressed regret for all that had occurred. In my search I had come face to face with just a fraction of what my father had endured: the moral absence and dissociation of people like Morlai Salieu, still full of rancour that he had never been paid for his services. Morlai Salieu had done it all so easily and for the promise of so little. Lawyers and judges had willingly completed the work of corrupt men, men who used the law but had no respect for it. I didn't blame the man in front of me. Saidu Brima was just about the only person I didn't hold responsible. He was a poor, uneducated man in a barren country. His destiny did not belong to him.

The strangest thing of all was that Unfa Mansaray came to Yabome and pleaded for her to help Saidu Brima, who was out of work. And so she did. She hired him for the duration of my stay to cook and carry out some of the extra chores around the house. Some mornings I would sit and watch him from the veranda as he laid the breakfast table. He worked his way round from setting to setting, silently, unaware of my eyes upon him, moving as fast as his arthritis allowed. I gazed at this man and reflected on how we came to be together under the same roof—and I wondered at the unreality of it all.

*   *   *

I had planned to stay in Sierra Leone a little over two weeks. There was talk of elections in February and once the campaigning started emotions in the country would begin to run high. I needed my work done before that happened. Simon and I were staying on over Christmas, but the only reservations we could get were on a flight leaving three days later. We would not be able to see in the New Year in Freetown. As it was the Christmas break coincided with the end of Ramadan. The government had declared a three-day holiday and relaxed the curfew; the people were in high spirits. It was almost possible to forget we were a country at war.

The day after Boxing Day we left the picnic at a beach known as Number Two River, where the river meets the sea, ahead of the other guests, in order to return to the house. Lami Sidique had traced Ibrahim Ortole and sent a message more or less ordering him to come to the house and meet me. It seemed a long shot, and Yabome was doubtful he would show, but I was determined that I would be there if and when he turned up.

The car park at the beach had been full of UN and NGO vehicles when we arrived and the beach was crowded. We sat in the shade of a small, privately hired rondavel, and ordered fresh grilled fish, salad and beers. As we ate a beggar worked the rounds, swinging himself on his crutches across the rough grass and sand, going from one party of westerners to the next. His face bore an elaborate expression of appeal, of studied tragedy, as he stretched out his hand for money. One of our companions, a man I had met on our previous trip who worked for a European government, objected to the beggar's presence. The waiter shooed the man away. There had been a brief discussion, I remember, about professional beggars and bogus operators who pretended to be war amputees.

It was a shame, it was generally agreed, because people were losing sympathy with all the amputees as a result.

An hour later, as I made my way back to the car to fetch my swimming costume, I passed the same man, who was now sitting in a wheelchair under a tree. His crutches leaned against the tree behind him. Despite the conversation I had just listened to, I felt badly for him. His feet, swaddled in thick socks, did look strangely truncated, as though his toes were missing. I walked over and promised I would give him something before we left.

As we loaded our belongings into the back of the borrowed jeep I looked around for the beggar, but he was nowhere to be seen. We had been persuaded to give a lift to a local woman, a sister to one of the waiters, and she asked her brother what had happened to the beggar. We learnt he had already gone, about half an hour earlier. The waiter assured us the man was there every day, but I knew we would not be coming back.

The drive back to Freetown was about fourteen miles and took at least an hour. Parts of the road were in an appalling condition where the rocks and earth had erupted through the ancient tarmac. As we approached one of the worst stretches, where the road climbed sharply and the foundations had been destroyed, leaving nothing but fifty yards of exposed, ragged rocks, I saw ahead of us the beggar in his wheelchair pushing himself along the empty road. Simon pulled over next to him as I dug in my purse for a few notes. I climbed down and handed them to him. I wondered where he could possibly be headed along this deserted highway. 'Where do you live?' I asked.

He supplied the name of a village I did not recognise. I turned to the woman sitting in the back of the Jeep with her basket on her lap. She raised her eyebrow and grimaced before she replied. 'It's very far.'

Once the wheelchair was loaded into the back, its owner climbed up and sat behind me. As we set off I turned and asked his name: 'My name is Mohammed,' he replied, smiling at me. 'And I am very grateful.' He was a young man, I observed, and when he smiled it was remarkable how the cowl of the beggar slipped from around him, revealing a good-looking youth with a cheerful, handsome countenance. Mohammed liked to talk. With a little prompting he told us how he made the ten-mile journey to Number Two River every day to beg. Sometimes he was lucky and had a lift, but not often. Where the road was at its worst he would wait by the side until someone offered to help him across. The wheelchair was his pride and joy. He had won it in a wheelchair race organised by a western charity and held in the stadium in Freetown. Many of those wounded in the war had competed, but it was Mohammed who had won and gone off with the coveted prize. Simon and I exchanged a glance at the gladiatorial image his description conveyed.

The rest of Mohammed's story emerged as we covered the miles towards Freetown. This is what he told us:

He was born and raised in the south, in Kenema. He was a panel beater by trade. When the mechanic's shop where he worked closed down he travelled north to Makeni, where he found work making machetes and *panga* knives. When the rebels invaded Makeni they had sliced off the ends of his feet. Salamatu, his young wife, to whom he had been married for only a few months, was seized and carried off. She did not return home for more than a year. When she did come back both her feet had been hacked off above the ankle as punishment for trying to escape. They had a small hut in a village just outside Freetown, one of the many small settlements lining the road along the coast. But Salamatu was too ashamed to be seen in public—she even refused to use her crutches—and so it was up to him to beg for them both. He was still smiling as he told us all this. I had the impression he was grateful to have some listeners. His smile widened when he described the change to his life. Things were getting better: Salamatu had just given birth to their first child, a daughter.

The three of us listened in silence. The waiter's sister, who must have heard similar stories many times in the last few years, had not uttered a word for a long time. She looked profoundly saddened. Simon was staring at the road ahead. I was gazing at Mohammed.

Just past the checkpoint into the next village Mohammed directed us off the road to the left, where he asked Simon to stop. We were in front of a small, traditionally built house. Like everything else in the village it was covered in a heavy layer of the dust from the road, which settled in the grooves, outlining the shape of each brick as though they had been painted to look that way. As we brought the wheelchair down from the back, Simon whispered to me to give him a few thousand extra leones. I called to Mohammed, but instead of taking the money he reached for my other hand, and with this disarmingly carefree gesture he pulled me along behind him: 'Give it to Salamatu, give it to her. Wait until you see how pleased she will be.'

We made our way down the side passage. Mohammed and Salamatu lived in a tiny clay-brick hut in the back yard of the house. He introduced me to his landlady, telling me how kind she had been in allowing them to live there. In front of a hut a woman sat on the ground by a smouldering cooking fire. She was nursing a baby. As I approached she covered her breasts, then reached up and shook my hand. She was not more than about twenty: skin unblemished, hair woven into neat braids. Salamatu and Mohammed must have made a striking pair on their wedding day, it occurred to me. She sat with her legs stretched out in front of her and inadvertently I glanced down. As I did so I saw she made a move to pull her *lappa* across her legs, but not before I had seen the horror that contrasted with the serenity of her face. These were not neat amputations performed by a surgeon's knife. One foot had been sheared off below the shin, the other sliced diagonally across the ankle bone. The skin around the wounds was rough, the flesh chapped and grey—the appearance was more of hide than human skin. Above the missing feet the flesh was thick, dense and splayed as though she had, at some point, tried to walk and the body had compensated by building up layers of tissue. They looked like the feet of an elephant.

Mohammed retrieved the baby and handed her to me. She was a few weeks old, with the skin only the newest babies have: shiny and wrinkled like a fresh leaf unfurling in the early morning.

'Guess what she is called?' said Mohammed loudly and exuberantly. I looked at Salamatu for an answer.

'She's called Aminata,' she replied with the gentlest of smiles. Mohammed, the father of Aminata. It wasn't a truly remarkable coincidence—they were probably two of the most popular names in the country—but I was pleased with it, pleased it should occur to me on my last day in Sierra Leone.

After we left Mohammed and Salamatu I began to wonder all over again whether I was right to come here, seeking salve for old wounds among people whose own suffering was so raw. And yet Salamatu, Mohammed and Aminata's fate was linked with my own. My childhood had borne witness to the trickle that would one day break the dam. This was what my father had foreseen with the first, early manifestations of tyranny: the end of the rule of law and the descent into anarchy. 'Let history be my judge,' he wrote at the end of his letter to Stevens on the day he resigned from the government. *Let history be my judge.* Salamatu and Mohammed represented to me the anguish of this nation, as well as its hope.

Needless to say Ibrahim Ortole did not turn up to face me.
I waited on the veranda, watching the road, for two hours, just
in case. I did not know what he looked like, but all the same I
searched for his face among the people returning home from the
mosque at the end of Ramadan, on the eve of Holy Day. The people were swathed in robes; those who had been to Mecca wore a
white head-dress loosely draped over their heads. They were has-
tening home before dusk, to prepare tonight's feast. In the house
Saidu Brima had taken delivery of a dozen dishes sent to us by
our neighbours. He laid each bowl or plate out on the table and
covered them in cloths. We were alone in the house. Yabome had
already begun the long round of evening visits. Ola and the rest
of her cousins were out.

We were leaving at midday the following day. There might just
be time, before the flight, to go and find Ibrahim Ortole on the
other side of town. Simon was ready to give it a try. I walked slowly
across the floor to the telephone to call Lami Sidique. I sat on the
edge of the sofa for a long time, listening to the ringing tones at
the other end. Nobody was home. I replaced the receiver. As I
did so I had already made up my mind I would not try again. It
was over. I was finished here, really finished. Someone who knew
once warned me that this time would come, and that it was really
a moment to welcome and not to regret. If only I were writing a
novel, I would contrive a neat ending with the strands of the plot
all tied up into a bow. But if I was looking for the ultimate proof
of guilt of the people who had been our enemies, then wasn't it
all around me: in the rebel war, in the fate of people like Salamatu
and Mohammed, in the wanton destruction of a country's future?

I knew it would take me many months to absorb all that I had
learned. To begin to live with my new past. I had shed my old
past, the one filled with unanswered questions, secrets and ghosts.
From now on, when I met people who belonged to the past I

would not ask myself: Who are you? What did you know? What did you do? One day doubtless I would come back to this country of mine without the sense of apprehension, without the feelings of incalculable despair the very thought used to promote. For the moment all I wanted to do was sit on the veranda in the evening air and watch the people on their way to celebrate Holy Day.

A man was walking up the hill. He was wearing a striped green gown and hat, making his way purposefully towards the house. In the contrast of sun and shadows I did not see his face. I stood up and leaned over the railings to try to get a view of him but he stood out of sight behind the metal gates, while he waited to be let in. I had been told Ibrahim Ortole was plump, while this man was tall and straight. I felt a conflict of emotions; my sense of duty struggled against the new inertia. The watchman bent down and opened the gate to allow the stranger inside and I watched as he walked up the drive. He looked up at me and waved. For a moment I failed to place this man, dressed in flowing gowns. He was carrying something in his hands. Then I recognised him. It was Unfa Mansaray with a cake he had baked himself: a gift on Holy Day.

49

Running. Running. Feet down steps. Quickly, quickly. One, two, three. Memuna, Sheka and me.

We ran down the back stairway of our house in Kissy, skirted the edge of the crevasse and went inside through the door into the kitchen of the family below. The front room was crowded, everyone from both families: Mum, Morlai, Santigi, Musu, Esther, Sullay and all the people who lived there. There were upwards of fifteen of us. We sat quietly and listened to the sounds of the ISU soldiers as they arrived at our house: shouts, slamming tail gates, boot soles hitting the dust, the dull clank of heavy metal, ammunition belts rattling like chains, and the dog Apollo barking impotently, on and on, as the men raced in every direction until they had us surrounded. No one spoke, nobody breathed. We sat around on the chairs in the middle of the room, staring at the floors and the walls and the windows, like people on a bus, avoiding each other's gaze and the temptation to utter a sound.

Upstairs now. I could hear them there. Muffled thuds and footsteps on our floors. Voices and words. What were they saying? Someone in command. Where were they now? In our sitting room. Along the passage. Quiet. Strange sounds, shuffling. Hovering feet maybe. The pistol-sharp crack as the lock on a door gave way to a shoulder or a boot. Not my room then—I had left our door unlocked in the scramble. The scrape of furniture along the stone floor. I turned my ear upwards to the sounds. Doors slammed. The thud of our books and belongings as they fell to the floor. Papers fluttering. The distinctive tinkle of a mirror breaking. Seven years' bad luck. The sounds merged and unfolded, repeated in waves over and over, all except the barking dog, who was silent now.

I looked at the faces around me: glistening foreheads, darting eyes, a head cocked, eyes watching the ceiling as though they might penetrate the layers of plaster and polystyrene tiles. There were not enough chairs for us all. Santigi stood with his back to the wall, feet apart, shirtless in shorts. He had been doing the washing when the soldiers came. Musu pressed her nails into her palm, again and again; her chest heaved with the effort to control her breathing. Chief Sumano's wife, the owner of the house, got up and moved quietly about the room. Preparing herself. In case they knocked on the door.

Time passed. Slowly we crept to the window. A whisper marred the silence. Someone moved the curtain aside and we looked out. Two trucks were parked at the front of the building, alongside a white CID Volkswagen. A man stood with his back to us. He wore a red beret and had a rifle slung over his shoulder. Another figure, identically dressed, was away to the right. The stone-breaker and his family were outside their *panbody*: hands over their heads, eyes on the dirt in front of their feet. By the door was an untidy pile of their pathetic horde of belongings: enamel bowls, aluminium pots, a gas canister, a few limp clothes. A third soldier ducked out through the opening and passed them by. He did not so much as glance at them, and the stone-breaker and his wife did not look up at him. We hovered behind the glass, in the discreet silence of the room. God, please let them not come over here. Someone touched my shoulder, edged me back from the window sill. It was open, but we dared not risk closing it.

A movement over to the left. I turned my head. Someone on the stairs at the side of the house. Coming down. On the landing now. Three pairs of legs. Two in khaki, one in brown slacks. A pair of familiar shoes. Brown suede shoes. I held my breath. One step, two—they were almost in view. I pushed my face up to the window. The whisper floated on the stillness of the room: 'It's Daddy.' I turned to Memuna and Sheka. My scream tore through the silence: 'Daddy!'

A hand over my mouth. Pushed it away. I struggled against the other hand on my shoulder, the same someone pressing me hard against them. Across my chest, holding me. Slip down and slide. Onto the floor. I crawled away past their knees. Towards the door. Hands reaching, too slow. Nobody fast enough for me: Sheka, Memuna, we three. He was going, walking in the direction of the trucks. We reached the door: 'Daddy!'

My father stopped in his tracks and slowly turned. Time hovered like a dragonfly above the water. None of us moved.

'Let them go,' I heard somebody in the room behind me say. 'Let them go.' Who was it, a man or a woman? I remember the words, but not the voice. *Let them go.* Somebody who saw that it was impossible to hold us. Or perhaps there was some other reason, known to them but not to me. Perhaps it was Morlai. Years later he looked me in the eye, smiled at me and said: 'Remember how you ran? How you ran?' I felt the hands begin to relax their grip, one by one, releasing me.

Somewhere in those infinite seconds, as I shook off the last of my restraints, I saw my father turn to his guard. I saw the man shake his head. I was out of the door. I was running away down the length of the house. I called again. He must see me. Memuna and Sheka ran at my side. The guard hesitated, then he took the key and released the handcuffs. My father turned round and stretched out both his arms to receive us.

I cannot remember what we said to each other. I cannot remember him being led away again. I remember nothing really, except having my arms around his waist, only the railings of the veranda separating us. I ran so fast I felt as though I would run through them. Instead I hit them hard, almost bruising my ribs. I didn't care at all. He held us all close, the four of us together. He spoke some words, reassured us, promised he would see us soon. I remember that. I believed him utterly. Perhaps that was why I let him go? I don't know. But somehow he was gone, taken away from us.

The next I recall I was upstairs in my room waiting behind the closed door while the soldiers went on searching our house. Memuna sat on her bed and I sat on mine, as we had been ordered to do. I had my feet on the floor and my hands in my lap. We were facing each other.

'Are you scared?' she asked.

'Yes,' said I.

'Don't be frightened. Come on.' She stood up and put her arm around me. 'Let's look out of the window and see if we can find the little brown dog you saw this morning.' We colluded, the older and younger sister: we both wanted a reason to look out of the window again.

There was no brown dog to be seen. Instead I could hear Apollo barking at a soldier, one of those still surrounding the house. The dog was being persistent, inching forward, jumping back at the slightest movement. The soldier swatted at him like a fly. The dog backed off and came at him again with bared teeth. A few moments later the soldier had had enough; he stepped forward and kicked Apollo in the ribs. His companions laughed at that. The soldier took his rifle off his shoulder and mockingly took aim. Others paused to watch the fun. They were loading the truck, herding the people in: the family from downstairs, the

stone-breaker. I saw them climb up one after the other, in front
of a soldier who pointed his gun at them. They stood together in
the back like cattle, while another soldier fastened the tail gates.

Memuna was pointing away in the distance, keeping up our
pretence that we were really looking for a stray dog. I looked over
in the same direction. Neither of us saw the soldier approaching until he appeared below our window. He shouted at us and
gestured with his arm to come down. We ducked away from the
glass, ran back and sat on our beds the way we had been before,
the way we were supposed to be doing. I prayed the soldier would
go away. But he didn't. I could hear him yelling at the open window. I ran across and sat with Memuna. Now, I really was afraid.
I didn't want to be arrested and taken away to prison.

We waited. The soldier was still shouting. His voice was harsh
with anger and authority. *Bo you there! Commot.* Memuna and I
looked at each other: 'We'll have to go down.' She said it first. We
walked to the door and opened it. Morlai was in the hallway. We
babbled at him in our fear.

Morlai walked to the window and looked out. The soldier
shouted to him to send us down. 'Please, they're only children,'
Morlai called back. Yes, I thought. That's what I am. I am just a
child.

The soldier took Morlai instead, ordering him to come down
and get into the back of the truck.

'It'll be all right,' said Morlai as he went. 'I'm coming back later.'

I nodded, grateful, allowing myself to fall backwards into the
synthetic comfort of his lie. My brain was empty of everything,
even guilt, washed with relief that it wasn't me they were taking
away.

After Morlai had gone, and the soldiers too, I went in search
of the others. I couldn't find Mum. Sullay was wandering around
the house. Tears leaked from his eyes and down his face. He

didn't wipe them away. His nose was streaming too. Why doesn't he care? I thought. Sullay opened his mouth and uttered a cry, a huge frightening noise, as deep as a cavern. I stared at him. I had never seen a man cry before. I had never seen anyone cry like that.

I built myself a hut in the bush in front of the house where the builders had left a tall stack of concrete blocks. I couldn't shift them—they were too heavy for me—so I used one of the recesses and built a roof over myself with old cardboard boxes I had salvaged from the storeroom. This was the place where they found the snake, but I didn't care. The snake couldn't harm me. I built a hut and I stayed inside it for the longest time. Nobody knew where my hut was, with the exception of Edward, who had helped me build it. I went back inside the house for my meals and to sleep. The rest of the time I wandered around by the slaughterhouse stream.

It was Christmas time. Auntie Binty was staying and so were Elizabeth and Edward. This Christmas we did not go to the beach. In the middle of the afternoon on an ordinary day I put the book I was reading down on the floor of my hut and I walked into the house. Memuna was sitting on the settee in the middle of the room. Auntie Binty was next to her, her arm clasped around my sister. Everybody in the house was there, too. Edward was standing a little distance away, hands by his sides. Elizabeth, I discovered later, had been sent to her room. Auntie Binty, sitting on the arm of the chair, was hugging Memuna, clasping her to her side, making crooning sounds of comfort. 'She should never have said that. She didn't mean it.'

I walked up behind them. They didn't see me. Memuna didn't cry very often and so I was curious, just curious mostly. Not exactly concerned. 'What's the matter?' I asked loudly.

Auntie Binty turned and looked at me. 'Nothing—Mem's just a little bit upset, that's all. But she's going to be all right.' She gave Memuna a squeeze and looked at the top of her head. 'Aren't you?' Back to me she smiled: 'You don't have to worry.'

Memuna still had her hands covering her face. I could barely see her in there, so many people were crowded around her. 'Is it true?' I heard her voice. 'I want to know if it's true.'

'Of course not. Elizabeth doesn't know what she's saying,' replied Auntie Binty.

'What did Elizabeth say?'

Auntie Binty looked at me. That smile she gave me, it was too wide and too—what exactly? It was too still. It didn't turn into a laugh, get any bigger, or drop by so much as a millimetre. It was one of those grown-up smiles designed to deceive. Her eyes gave it away; they were fixed upon me. And her body too was rigid. She didn't want me there, I could tell, and so I determined to stay.

'Elizabeth and Mem had an argument, that's all. It's over now. Elizabeth ended up saying something that upset Mem. She's sorry and she's gone to her room. She won't have any supper. So you might as well run along. Go on. You too, Edward.'

'What was it she said?' I asked the question again. Santigi, Esther, Musu—none of my cousins were looking at me. They began to move, as though waking from a sleep or a stupor, suddenly deciding they had chores to do, a pretence of being busy created with the purpose of discouraging me. They did not want to answer. One by one they left the room, off to the kitchen, where I knew they would sit around on the rice sacks and talk about whatever it was that had happened. Whatever they were trying to keep from me.

I moved closer and tried to peer at Memuna. All I could see was the top of her head; her hair was untidy where Auntie Binty had ruffled it.

'I want to know what Elizabeth said,' one more time, louder.

Memuna looked up at me, past Auntie Binty. Her face was blotchy, eyes red; she had been crying for some time. She took a breath and her chest heaved and subsided. Then she spoke:

'Elizabeth said Daddy was in prison and that he was going to die.'

50

On Tuesday eight coffins, built of unfinished, bleached timber, were delivered to the gates of Pademba Road Prison. There were several witnesses to their arrival and the word soon spread around the city.

On Wednesday Mum was in downtown Freetown, at the travel agent booking her ticket to come to England and meet us at the end of term. Auntie Fatu had accompanied her. Mohammed Swartaka Turay was scouring the city. He had been to her small apartment above a garage in Wilkinson Road and found it empty. Mum had moved there after our landlord, Chief Sumano, was arrested. The chief's mother had been to plead with S. I. Koroma for her son's release. She told Mum what he had ordered her to do: 'Get rid of Forna's filth.' The two Armenian brothers who owned the garage were the only people who would take her on as a tenant, and they even waived the rent.

Mohammed Swartaka drove around town until he saw her car parked outside the travel agency. He stepped through the glass door just as she paid for her ticket. *Leave the country, Yabome*, he told her. My stepmother replied she was leaving anyway. *Look.* She waved the ticket. *No*, he was insistent, *you have to leave now*. Somehow he made her understand: he persuaded the clerk to book her on the next available flight, departing at ten o'clock on Friday night.

Exactly eight months previously, on 16 November 1974, the jury at the trial in Court Number One of the high court retired for just one hour before returning a unanimous verdict. Guilty. All defendants on all counts. Judge Marcus Cole placed the black cap on his head and pronounced the sentence in a voice devoid of emotion. In the gallery the families of the defendants wept. Mum left the court, walked past the crowds, with Auntie Binty at her side, holding on to her own tears until she reached the sealed anonymity of the car.

The appeal, twenty-one days later, was turned down instantly. The matter was passed to the Mercy Committee. The Chief Imam led a delegation to see S. I. Koroma at his offices, as did some in the legal profession, belatedly stricken by their consciences. The protests were muted. Stevens had cut the tongue out of the populace. Instead people began to wear their hair in a new style: Mohamed Forna and the fourteen others. Seven braids descending on either side of the crown and a single braid in the centre, running from the peak of the forehead to the nape of the neck. Nancy Steele gathered her APC women's group together and marched through the streets demanding the executions be carried out in public.

At Christmas Mum drove with the three of us to State House and left us waiting in the car outside while she went to the gates and asked to see the president. 'Will you get his autograph for me?' I had asked stupidly. I continued to let the small pieces of knowledge I had acquired float on the surface of my awareness, refusing to draw them under for fear of drowning. 'Don't you know who he is?' Memuna asked me angrily as we watched Mum walking away from us towards the gate house. But I did and I didn't. I could not absorb the idea of a country in which the president was a man of hate. Mum waited for an hour at the gate house while we bickered and sweated on the plastic seats. Finally the president's office telephoned down: the president would not see her today.

Or any day thereafter, as it turned out. Mum went back time and time again, always to be given the same message.

Outside Kamara-Taylor's house we sat on the back steps and stared at our old mango tree. Memories flew up from the silt at the bottom of my consciousness: of how we used to pick the green fruit and sprinkle them with salt; of Milik telling his stories in the shade cast by the branches; of the solitary figure of the body-guard sitting apart and alone. Mum left us there, warning us not to mention to a soul we used to live here. I looked around me, at the Ministers' Quarters, the gardens, our life as it once was. It created an uncanny feeling, of real and unimagined *déjà vu,* of lives already lived, lives past and forgotten. I didn't know, then, everything that had taken place at that house on Spur Loop. I just wanted to tell someone that this was once my home.

Day after day we did the rounds with Mum while she pleaded for our father's life. Kamara-Taylor would not see her; nobody would. We didn't go with her to S. I. Koroma's house, although Mum went to his office once with some of the wives of the other condemned men. It did no good, no good at all.

At Easter we spent our holidays in cheerless, chill Hackney with Mum's younger brother, a law student in London, in his student digs. In June, when we were all back at school, the Mercy Committee turned down the plea for clemency. All hope now rested with the president.

At Pademba Road eight of the prisoners were taken up to the cells closest to the gallows. The others were moved to cells below. Those on the lower floor began to be given exercise privileges. One day, when the guards were busy, Abu Kanu climbed up to one of the windows on the upper storey of the block. Knowing what was to come, he and my father said goodbye. In all the time they had been in prison together, throughout the trial and the sentencing, Abu had never seen his friend shed a tear. My father had told him, 'When I cry I will cry only for my children.' The remainder of the time my father lay there alone, wearing a dark-blue sweater with the letter C crudely cut out of white canvas and stitched onto the front, rising to eat the single plate of rice pushed under the door every day.

What must it be like, I have often wondered, to find yourself at the mercy of your enemy? One after the other, he watched the hopes retreat into the darkness. Was there ever a moment when he did not think of it? Did he ever manage to forget, to dwell on happier thoughts? What were his regrets, if there were any at all. And what did he say in his prayers? Who among us can imagine what it feels like to lie alone at night while the thoughts chase sleep away, to escape into dreams for a few hours, and to awaken into those elusive moments of peace, grasp them briefly in your fingers—before they are plucked away? Even though, far away, the palest light of dawn brightens the sky, the blackness descends once more to shroud the vivid colours of the dreams. No one ever asks a condemned man these questions—or perhaps they do but receive no reply. For what words could describe the wait until the end?

In the afternoon of 18 July the condemned men were taken out of their cells into a separate room and weighed. Each of the weights was recorded in a large ledger. That afternoon my father and Ibrahim Taqi stood at the small square of window in their cell doors and sang to one another—an old tune, one that my mother taught herself to play on the guitar and the five of us liked to sing together in Koidu:

> Hang down your head, Tom Dooley,
> Hang down your head and cry,
> Hang down your head, Tom Dooley,
> Poor boy, you're bound to die.

It was Bai Bai Kamara who whistled the tune for me the day
we sat in the restaurant together in Freetown, three verses the
whole way through and the refrain. In 1975 he cried: 'Stop singing, Doctor,' from his cell below them. 'This is a bad night. Pray!
Pray instead of singing.' He was suffering from malaria; he let go
of the bars of his window and fell back to the floor. Sometime
in the early evening Bai Bai Kamara, Unfa Mansaray, Albert Tot
Thomas and Abu Kanu were moved out of the block and taken
to cells in Wilberforce.

As darkness fell the sounds of merrymaking began to rise from
the prison courtyard to the ears of the men in Wilberforce, Clarkson, Howard, Blyden, in the female block and in the condemned
cells. Music played from a transistor radio as the executioners
and guards swallowed liquor and palm wine delivered in quantities to the prison. In the hours leading up to midnight they grew
drunker and drunker.

Sometime that evening our father sat down and wrote a letter
to his wife. He asked her to trace our natural mother and thanked
her for her efforts to save his life. From memory he itemised everything he owned: some proceeds from the rice business and
shares in two or three local companies, a bank account in England
containing a few thousand pounds set aside for our schooling.
He left it all to us, his three children. Ibrahim Ortole, I noticed
when I read the will again much later, owed him a considerable
sum of money.

A little after ten o'clock Mum boarded her flight at Lungi. The
British Caledonian plane taxied down the runway and lifted off
into the gathering clouds of the rainy season. She stayed in her
seat throughout the flight, neither read nor ate, refusing the solicitations of the air hostesses.

The last person to speak to our father, with the exception of
his fellow prisoners and his executioners, was Dwight Neale, the

journalist who had once been in prison with him. While we accompanied Mum on her visits to State House, our father refused to beg Stevens for his life. Instead he used the paper and pen supplied to him for his mercy plea to compose an account of his life from boyhood to his death, relating his hopes for the country, his experiences in politics and the guiding principles that caused him to relinquish his position. He carefully created a factual account of the part he had played in the country's recent history, a testimony that would outlive him. To the case against him he devoted no more than a page, pinpointing the lies of Morlai Salieu and Bassie Kargbo.

The executions began at midnight of 19 July. I was asleep in my dormitory at school. The aeroplane carrying Mum was crossing the Sahara, thirty thousand feet up in the sky.

The first two men to die were soldiers. The civilians were executed in the order in which they were indicted by the court. Mohamed Forna, First Accused, my father, walked the length of the block, past the cells of his companions, towards the noose waiting for him behind the door at the end of the building. I close my eyes and imagine his final walk: his stride, just like my own; broad, flat African feet inherited by me; his handcuffed hands: long, strong fingers, slightly flared at the tip and reborn in my brother; the broad, intelligent forehead, the same brow I see in my sister every time we meet. The men were hanged every half an hour, the men in the other blocks told me. They could tell, you see, because the music and the sounds of the guards' bacchanal died for a few seconds, then rose up again more clamorous than before. If you listened very carefully in the moments in between, you could hear the sound of the trapdoor.

Dwight Neale, who stayed with the men until the last, left the prison after the final execution. The nightly tempests of the rainy season had started. He walked through the darkness, through the pouring rains of the storm, impervious to the wet, to the lightning that lit the streets and the answering bellow of thunder. Reaching the East End, he found a shebeen and sat there drinking until dawn, when he stumbled, soaking wet and cloudy with alcohol, into his office. Inside his jacket pocket was the letter my father had given him, which would not come to light until the twentieth anniversary of his death, when Siaka Stevens was dead, the APC had been overthrown and the country was on the brink of war.

The next day my father's body, and those of the seven other men who had been hanged, were displayed in open coffins before the crowds outside Pademba Road Prison. Stevens had promised a public execution; in the end he had slaughtered them in secret and displayed his trophies afterwards. Under cover of darkness the bodies were removed, loaded into military trucks and driven out to Rokupa cemetery on the road to Hastings, where they were doused with acid and dumped in a mass grave. Amnesty International alone protested the killings.

At school in Surrey I woke up and gazed at a cloudless sky from my bed in the alcove. Mum was waiting for us downstairs. She had come straight to the school from Gatwick. I was surprised and pleased to see her there.

The next I remember is sitting in a chair in the corner of Brian and Mary Quinn's sitting room in St Albans and listening to Brian as he talked about my father. He spoke as though he were delivering a speech. The room was spacious and formal, with sliding doors onto the gardens, a pale carpet, embroidered cushions and polished claw-foot tables loaded with photographs contained in silver frames. The last time I had been in this house was with my father. I stared out of the window at the sloping lawn, while Quinn's voice rumbled through me. He was describing my father's qualities. I began to cry, knowing what must surely be coming. I wanted him to stop his speech and tell me if something terrible had happened to our father, yet at the same time I could not bear to hear it and I wished, more than anything else, for him to carry on talking for ever.

I knew it and I still would not believe it. When Quinn had reached the end I asked: 'How did he die?'

I can see Quinn's expression now. A Scot, he was always a controlled man. I witnessed the momentary blankness, the recovery that preceded the answer: 'Stomach ulcers. He contracted stomach ulcers. In the end it became very serious.' It was all he could come up with in the moment and it wasn't a very convincing answer, but it was enough for me.

For a year thereafter, whenever I had to tell someone that my father was dead I gave the same explanation, forcing myself to ignore the baffled, sometimes incredulous expression of my listener. I buried the knowledge as deep as I could and it struggled to emerge. I developed nervous tics: a sound halfway between a cough and a hiccup that I could not control, a compulsive twitch in my forehead that gradually spread to the whole of my face. I fought the knowledge and it fought me.

That summer Mum rented a one-bedroom apartment in London, in Manor House. At the back was a small garden. We had no friends, there were no parks or places to go nearby and so for several weeks Sheka, Memuna and I spent the days digging the flower beds and clearing weeds. Mum's friend Auntie Joy, who lived in Kent, came to visit us. I was very fond of her and we sometimes spent exeats from school in her lovely house with its garden full of roses and rhododendrons. I grasped her hand and pulled her outside to show off our handiwork. I remember her stricken face as she stood at the kitchen door, and now I am able to see the garden through her eyes: devoid of sunlight, earth exposed and dark, barren flower beds in which the local cats defecated; no birds, not a single flower, tree or shrub. We had sweated and laboured hard to create a garden in which nothing grew at all.

Once I went to Rokupa. The cemetery had long disappeared, cleared to make way for government-promised new low-cost housing units that in the end were never completed. I bought some oranges from a woman sitting with her companion at the side of the path in the shade of one of the few trees, skinned oranges stacked on a tin tray before her. She told me her name was Agnes. In turn I gave her mine. 'So, Aminatta, you have come to see our place,' she replied.

The place they call Rokupa is a flat expanse of cracked, red earth scattered with the husks of unfinished houses. Rows of clay bricks, carved from the soil, were baking under the sun. People had long given up on the government and were building their own homes. I followed the path away from the orange seller to where I had been told the cemetery once was. I passed a pair of men digging a hole with long-handled spades and arrived at a vast area of open, litter-strewn scrub. Ahead of me were the hills of Freetown; behind me a steeply sloping path to a small fishing bay and the sea. In the centre stood a small green monument, a pavilion with arched latticed windows and a white domed roof, rather like the minaret of a mosque. The grass rustled in the wind blowing off the sea. I could hear children shrieking and the sounds of the people meeting the fishing canoes as they arrived. The sun was high and burned down on me; the air was dry, acrid underneath. Rokupa lay on the edge of Freetown's industrial zone and the harsh vapours of chemicals mixed with the scent of the earth.

I stood still. I was alone. The dust dried my cheeks and bit into the back of my throat. I had always imagined my father was buried in a grave with a headstone, somewhere in Magburaka, perhaps. The silence over where my father's body lay I had long equated with the greater silence that smothered everything about the past. It had taken me until I was in my twenties to ask my stepmother the question and to discover that the authorities had claimed the bodies of the executed men, saying they belonged to the state, denying the families even the dignity of burying their dead—and the people the possibility of a shrine.

From somewhere behind me came the sudden, shrill cry of an animal in pain. I turned round. A gang of children were gathered, heads together, kicking something on the ground—it sounded like a small dog or a puppy. I walked towards them, planning to intervene. A woman sitting on the steps of her house saw me, called me over, asked in a challenging voice what my business was in Rokupa. I told her I was looking for the place where my father was buried. Oh, she grunted and looked abashed. When I turned round both the children and the dog, if that is what it was, had gone. There was nobody there except a little girl sitting alone in the dirt.

I needed to discover where in this huge expanse the bodies were buried. Was I walking above the bones of my father? A woman carrying a load of wood on the top of her head passed me by. I thought for an instant of asking her if she knew anything about what had happened here, but she was too young. Most of the people who lived here now were Temnes. Dura began to ask on my behalf. People gathered around us. An elderly man carrying a bundle of plastic bowls remembered the night the army sealed off the graveyard and arrived in trucks, working by torchlight in the darkness. There were fewer houses there then; most of the place was bush. The people were warned not to leave their homes. In the morning the locals came out here to look. He pointed to the place where they noticed the earth had been disturbed: for a long time a giant breadfruit tree had grown there.

After I had spoken to the old man I walked on. Once I had visited a clairvoyant, who described my father's death: 'Suddenly falling through the air, so light-headed. Thank God it's all over.' We had both stared at each other in shock. I prayed she was right. What did I want to mark my father's memory now: a headstone? A plaque? A monument? Blocks of stone or concrete that would crumble away in this lonely place.

Honour and shame from no condition rise; Act well your part: there all the honour lies. 'Give my love to the children,' he had written in his last letter, 'and tell them that short though my life has been, they will be proud of me when the truth of the last ten years will be known to all.' Stevens had him convicted of treason, killed him, poured acid over his bones, tried to erase every trace of him; he wanted to destroy everything my father had represented, the ideals of men like Mohamed Forna and Ibrahim Taqi. Well, now I had the knowledge. Four months later I sat down in my London study and I began to write. His story. My story. Our story. The first ten years of my life and the last ten years of his.

I realised I had been standing in Rokupa for over an hour. I turned to go. As I made my way back to the car I caught sight of the little girl I had seen sitting on the ground. She was swaying under the huge weight of a plastic container of water balanced on her head. Her cotton dress had slipped off one shoulder, her feet were bare and I could hear the soft patter as the soles of her feet touched the earth. Fine red dust covered her skin, glistening like dark gold. Every few steps a dozen or so drops of water splashed out of the open neck of the container, showered around her, miniature rainbows fell onto the sand. She looked at me and smiled.

I remember her now, as I write, the little girl who once was me. If I concentrate my will I can still summon her, sometimes. She is there, the girl who believed there was a place somewhere on this earth, a place where a devil came down at dusk to dance alone on the water.

Acknowledgements

This book is dedicated to the memory of my father.

From the outset Yabome Kanu, my stepmother, has given me her absolute trust. I would like to thank her for this and for many things, not least the great help she has been in my endeavour. Above all I am grateful to her for the courage she has displayed and has inspired in me.

My cousin Morlai Forna acted as my researcher in Sierra Leone. I am especially indebted to him for his tireless efforts. The extraordinary story of my family's past came to me through the collective memory of my uncles and aunts. I am grateful to them and the whole Forna family for this and other kindnesses.

My very belated thanks to Dr Alfred and Murietta Olu-Williams for helping my family when it was dangerous and difficult to do so, also to Brian and Mary Quinn who were good friends to us during those years. Santigi Kamara has never wavered even through the worst of times.

Any opinions expressed in this book are entirely my own. I would, however, like to thank the following people for agreeing to be interviewed and for sharing with me their recollections of that period of Sierra Leone's history, details of the era and in some instances vital eyewitness accounts and personal testimonies: Shineh Bash Taqi, Professor Hamid Bash Taqi, Amy Bash Taqi, George Burne, Bianca Benjamin, Nuhad Courban, Mohammed Deen, Professor Cyril Foray, Dr Bernard Frazer, Professor John and Sheila Hargreaves, Frank Jalloh, Dr Ulrich Jones, Dauoda Kamara, Dr John and Rena Karefa-Smart, Berthan Macaulay, Karl and Hildegard Münch, Alhaji Lami Sidique, Jenkins Smith, Alfred Brima Sesay, Tejan Savage, Abdul R. Turay, Dr Mohammed Turay, Major General Tarawali, the late Sir Banja Tejan-Sie, Janet Thorpe, Susan Toft, Adelaide Whest. A great many other people took my telephone calls, answered my letters and requests for information. I am grateful to them all. My thanks also to Brian Forsyth, Marion Hall, Ken Hepburn, Jean l'Anson, Annette Main for sharing their memories of the time my family spent in Scotland.

I owe a debt of gratitude to the late Dr Jim Funna of the World Bank, also to Dr Günter Conrad, Dr Evangelos Calamitis, formerly of the IMF, and Elkaneh Coker for their invaluable contribution to my understanding of the country's economic history.

For documents and details relating to my father's trial in 1975 I am obliged to Eke Halloway and Serry Kamal. Abu Kanu, Bai Bai Kamara, Unfa Mansaray, Albert Tot Thomas, Sorie Dawo and Pa Issa Jalloh shared with me their own experiences of that episode. I am grateful to them for their willingness to revisit the past on my behalf, also to Saidu Brima.

In Freetown I was the grateful recipient of much moral support and practical assistance from Sayo Kanu, Joy Samake and Alex Kamara. David Jordan at the BBC helped me towards becoming an author in the early days. During the long months of writing my dear friend Michael May sustained me with daily calls to buoy the spirits, and the occasional evening of jazz. Gillian Slovo and Ken Wiwa kindly read early chapters and provided me with comments and their encouragement. My thanks go to all of them.

David Godwin is a remarkable agent whose energy and enthusiasm made everything happen. At HarperCollins my very special thanks go to Michael Fishwick for his spirited support of the project, and to Lucinda McNeile for her confidence and keen judgement.

My mother Maureen Campbell White spent many hours with me to share her own compelling story. I am immensely grateful to her and to my late grandfather Robert Christison, who will always be in my thoughts.

There have been times when writing this book has been more than usually difficult. My sister Memuna Forna has provided a bedrock of loyalty and support as well as the benefit of an acute mind. She has my heartfelt thanks. And finally, thank you to my husband Simon Westcott—as always.